Zero Mostel

A Biography

Jared Brown

ATHENEUM

New York   1989

Excerpts from *The Making of a Musical* by Richard Altman and Mervyn Kaufman, Crown Publishers, 1971, reprinted with permission of the authors.

Excerpts from *World of Our Fathers*, copyright © 1976 by Irving Howe, reprinted by permission of Harcourt Brace Jovanovich, Inc.

Excerpts from *170 Years of Show Business* by Kate Mostel and Madeline Gilford, with Jack Gilford and Zero Mostel, copyright © 1978 by Madeline Lee Gilford, Kazmos Productions Inc. and Lucy Prinz, reprinted by permission of Random House, Inc.

Excerpts from *James Joyce's Ulysses in Nighttown*, adapted and transposed by Marjorie Barkentin and Padraic Colum, copyright 1914, 1918 by Margaret Carolyn Anderson and renewed 1942 and 1946 by Nora Joseph Joyce, reprinted by permission of Random House, Inc.

Excerpts from reviews and articles by Jack Kroll that appeared in *Newsweek* magazine October 19, 1964, April 1, 1968, and September 19, 1977, are reprinted with permission.

Letters from Sam Jaffe and Joshua Logan and material from The Toby Cole Archive at the Universtiy of California at Davis are quoted with permission. The correspondence and Harvard University speech of Zero Mostel are quoted with the permission of Josh Mostel.

Atheneum
Macmillan Publishing Company
866 Third Avenue, New York, N.Y. 10022
Collier Macmillan Canada, Inc.

Library of Congress Cataloging-in-Publication Data
Brown, Jared.
  Zero Mostel : a biography / Jared Brown.
    p.   cm.
  Bibliography: p.
  Includes index.
  ISBN 0-689-11955-0
  1. Mostel, Zero, 1915–1977.   2. Actors—United States—Biography.
I. Title.
PN2287.M77B76   1989
792'.028'0924—dc19
[B]   88-32163   CIP

Macmillan books are available at special discounts for bulk purchases for sales promotions, premiums, fund-raising, or educational use. For details, contact:
Special Sales Director
Macmillan Publishing Company
866 Third Avenue
New York, N.Y. 10022

10 9 8 7 6 5 4 3 2 1

Printed in the United States of America

Designed by Nancy Sugihara

Acknowledgments

I would like to express my appreciation to the following individuals: Judy Brown, Janet Gottschalk, and Josh Mostel for reading and commenting upon the manuscript of this biography before publication; Betty L. Corwin, Elizabeth L. Dribben, Dean Howd, Raphael Mostel, Pennell C. Peck, Cynthia Schroeder, Steven W. Siegel, and Alan R. Starsky for providing information of various kinds; Gary Cadwallader for his research assistance; the Hatch-Billops Collection of New York City for allowing me to quote from their tape of Lou Gilbert; David Patrick, acting chairman of the Department of Theatre at Western Illinois University 1986–87, and Gene Kozlowski, chairman 1987–88, for assigning me a teaching schedule that permitted me to write this book without more strain than would otherwise have been involved; and the following sources for providing financial support for this biography: the National Endowment for the Humanities, the Illinois Arts Council, and the following offices at Western Illinois University: the University Research Council, the College of Fine Arts, the Department of Theatre, and the Office of Public Affairs and Development. Judy Brown's editorial assistance was as helpful as always, and—as always—is particularly appreciated.

Contents

Illustrations

With Bea Lillie, testing the authenticity of his Tony award for *Rhinoceros*
(UPI/Bettmann Newsphotos)

In a scene from *A Funny Thing Happened on the Way to the Forum*.
Should Zero be looking so unhappy?
(Bettmann/Springer Film Archive)

Rehearsing for *The Merchant* with Sam Levene
(UPI/Bettmann Newsphotos)

and for *Fiddler on the Roof*
(UPI/Bettmann Newsphotos)

Zero shortly before his death
(Courtesy of Howard Rodney)

Introduction

Zero Mostel's career as a performer, which had started so promisingly in 1942, seemed to be on the rebound early in 1960. After ten years of relative inactivity, during which time Mostel had fallen victim to McCarthyism, he had good reason to believe that the difficult and often humiliating downward spiral of his career was about to be reversed.

Allegations that Mostel had been a subversive began to surface in right-wing circles in 1950, followed two years later by direct testimony before the House Committee on Un-American Activities (often called HUAC) that Mostel was a Communist. Called before HUAC in 1955, Mostel invoked the Fifth Amendment to the Constitution, claiming the right against self-incrimination. Even prior to his appearance before the committee, the mass media—in which Mostel had had several notable successes—had begun to boycott him; after his appearance, the boycott was total: he was blacklisted, unable to find employment on radio or television or in the movies. In the Broadway theatre and in nightclubs, where he had achieved his greatest fame, offers of work became rare; and those offers that were made called for him to accept a much lower salary than he had received in the past.

Denied the opportunity to work regularly, Mostel and his family adapted to the blacklist as well as they could, scraping out a meager existence as Zero retreated to his artist's studio on Twenty-eighth Street in New York. Not having anticipated the blacklist, Mostel had saved very little of the fortune he had once earned. He took the few opportunities that presented themselves to perform on the stage and in nightclubs, but the money he received paid for little more than bus fare. His wife attempted to supplement the family's income, but her efforts had little effect.

Things began to look brighter in 1958. Zero's performance as Leopold Bloom in an off-Broadway production of *Ulysses in Nighttown* was hailed by New York critics as a brilliant piece of work. The production was later moved to London and from there to the International Festival of the Théâtre des Nations in Paris, where Mostel was voted "best actor." His dormant film career resumed in 1959, when, for the first time in years, he was offered a movie role. Later that same year, Zero appeared on American television in *The World of Sholem Aleichem*, a production that defied the blacklist not only by employing Mostel but also by using several other actors who had previously been classified as "unemployable" because of their political activities.

But despite the revival of his performing career, Zero's economic plight was little better than before. His salary for *Ulysses in Nighttown* never exceeded $350 per week in New York or in Europe; the film (a short subject entitled *Zero*) paid only $500; and Mostel was given $750 for *Sholem Aleichem*. And, of course, there were periods between engagements when Zero brought home no money at all, so that his *average* earnings were pitifully small, although to the public it must have seemed that his successive appearances on the stage, in a film, and on television would have been highly profitable.

At last, however, it seemed that the slow accumulation of credits was about to pay off. In December 1959, Zero was signed to appear and receive star billing in a Broadway production of *The Good Soup* at the gratifying salary of $600 per week.

Then: disaster. Mostel's return to Broadway was aborted on the afternoon of January 13, 1960, when he was run over by a bus, which ran directly—and sickeningly—over his left leg. He was rushed to Knickerbocker Hospital, where the doctors agreed that amputation would be necessary. Zero, fully conscious, shouted that he would not permit them to amputate his leg.

He was transferred to the Hospital for Joint Diseases, where Dr. Joseph Wilder agreed to attempt to save the crushed limb. Mostel remained in the hospital for five months, during which he underwent four operations; still, there was no guarantee that the leg would not eventually have to be amputated.

Less than five years later, Zero Mostel was—astonishingly—at the very top of his profession. Having won three Tony awards in five years, he had become one of the few performers on Broadway whose name alone was enough to attract a large and loyal audience. He had reestablished his television career and was about to become a major film actor. He was invited to visit the president in the White House; the government of Israel asked him to vacation in their country—at their expense; schools and universities prepared to give him honorary degrees. He had become more than a popular entertainer; in an incredibly short time, he had become a treasured national institution.

How was it possible for any individual to turn the circumstances of his life around so quickly and so thoroughly, to go from catastrophe to triumph in so brief a time? For most human beings, such a recovery would have been unthinkable; but Zero Mostel was not an ordinary human being. If his comeback bordered on the miraculous, it can be attributed to one of many qualities: a spirit that *refused* to be broken, an ego so massive that Mostel could not conceive of failure, or a will to succeed so strong that no force on earth could defeat it. Undoubtedly, all three factors were involved. Perhaps, too, one should add the following into the equation: the unceasing desire of his wife to see Zero become a world-famous star; the support of his friends, to whom he had once shown intense loyalty and who now returned the favor; and, of course, a talent of remarkable proportions.

Even if Zero Mostel had not been run over by a bus, his comeback in show business would have been unlikely. The blacklist was a devastating experience to all who endured it, destroying many careers and shortening some lives. Performers who overcame the blacklist to return to their former positions in show business were rare; performers who achieved greater success after the blacklist than they had known earlier were extraordinary; performers who endured the emotional trauma of blacklisting *and* suffered crippling physical injuries—but rose above them to greater career heights than before—were unique. There is, in fact, only one example: Zero Mostel.

*   *   *

As everyone who saw him perform can attest, Zero Mostel's style was to enlarge upon reality, often to such a massive degree that his manner bordered upon the monstrous. Only Zero could dominate a stage or a movie screen (for better or worse) in his unique way. And this larger-than-life quality characterized not only Mostel's performances but his personality as well. If the totality and rapidity of his recovery were so remarkable that they border on the mythic, so does the nature of the man seem gargantuan. His appetite for life was prodigious, his talent monumental, his story the stuff of fable. By accident of birth and environment or by conscious design, Zero Mostel was an *individual*, unlike anyone else on earth.

One aspect of his character—or, more accurately, perhaps, of the way his character was perceived—helps to illustrate the difference between Mostel and other, more conventional, persons. Among his relatives, friends, and co-workers, no two people seem to have formed the same impression of the man. One individual characterized him as an alcoholic, for example; others said he drank in moderation; one told me he never drank *at all*. Some actors found him wonderful to work with: unfailingly creative, always generous; others dreaded being on stage with him, fearing that he would behave in unpredictable ways that could embarrass—even humiliate—everyone else in the production.

Even the facts about his life are in dispute. Did he study to be a rabbi at the Jewish Theological Seminary, as one of his surviving brothers recalls with certainty? If so, the seminary has no record of it and his other surviving brother cannot remember it. Or was he indifferent to religion, as another member of his family has suggested? Was he a man of integrity whose decency was beyond question? Most of those I interviewed saw him in precisely those terms. Or was he selfish and unprincipled, a man who willingly and willfully harmed other people to satisfy his lust for money and fame? That is how he was described by two particularly bitter colleagues. Friends spoke of his unflinching loyalty; others said that he dropped certain of his acquaintances capriciously and inexplicably after he achieved stardom. Was he a generous man who gave freely of his time and energies to others? Anecdotes will be found in this book to show that that was the case. Conversely, however, other stories tell of a man whose ego was so inflated by self-importance that he had no time for anything or anyone unless he could see a direct benefit to himself. Was he a quiet, contemplative man with a serious interest in art? Yes. Was he possessed of so much charm that many people found it impossible to dislike him or to object to his most outrageous behavior? Yes. Or was he a man so driven by his compulsion to perform (and to outperform others) that his mere presence embarrassed those who could not abide his constant shouting and exhibitionism? Yes. He was simultaneously a man of enormous virtues and equally prodigious character flaws.

Such inconsistency is frustrating to a biographer. But the frustration, resulting from an inability to fit every piece of the puzzle of Mostel's life and character neatly into place, lessens when one realizes that Zero Mostel was perceived differently by different people, perhaps because each person with whom he came in contact tried to characterize him in the way ordinary human beings are conventionally characterized. But he was *not* ordinary in any sense. Except for the one generalization agreed upon by all who knew him or saw him perform—that he was wildly, extravagantly, formidably bigger than reality, onstage and off, and in every respect: his physical bulk, his attitudes, and his appetites —his life resists neat definition. A biographer can, however, present a chronicle of Mostel's activities, informing the reader when there are conflicting reports of those activities, detailing Mostel's often contradictory behavior and attitudes, and attempt to assemble a coherent— if not a consistent—picture. It would be pointless to try to reconcile the contradictions that surround Zero, for they, more than any unity a biographer might try to impose, defined the man. Perhaps, too, those very contradictions were what made him an extraordinary performer as well as a unique individual.

1

Foundations

Israel Mostel, whose son would become known as Zero, came from Eastern Europe, where he was born in 1873 and raised in an Orthodox Jewish family. Israel's parents, the owners of a vineyard, taught their son the intricate discipline of wine-making, after which he took his part in the family occupation. His lifelong devotion to the Jewish faith was another legacy from his family, as was his erudition. He read avidly, and in several languages; he was fluent in German, Italian, Aramaic, Hebrew, Yiddish, Polish, and English. His knowledge and wisdom won him admiration from all who knew him. Eventually, he came to be looked upon as a sort of lay rabbi: a teacher, a man with intimate knowledge of Jewish tradition and customs. Zero would later tell friends that his father was an ordained rabbi, but that does not seem to have been the case.

Cina Druchs, who was to become Israel's second wife, was born in Poland in 1877, the youngest of eleven children. Orphaned at six, she was raised in Vienna by her oldest sister, whose husband was a man of some wealth. The wealth made it possible to send Cina to college, where she was able to exercise her considerable intellect. Like her future husband, Cina was an ardent reader who knew several languages.

Israel Mostel and Cina Druchs both emigrated to the United States and settled in New York (Israel in 1898, Cina—or Celia, as she became known in America—in 1908), each unaware of the other's existence. But soon after Celia's arrival she met Israel, who was by then a widower. Within a few years they were married. Israel already had four children by his first wife; Celia gave him four more, including Samuel Joel, who would call himself Zero when he entered show business. Sammy was born in the Brownsville section of Brooklyn—"a poor, crime-ridden neighborhood," as he later described it—on February 28, 1915, the seventh of Israel's children; in all, there were six boys and two girls. The family lived in a house that "you might even call a farm," Zero said years afterward, "because we had land and a goat." The land couldn't have yielded a great deal, however, for the Mostels were unable to hold on to their property.

Celia, Israel, and their brood moved to a tenement on the Lower East Side soon after Sammy's birth. There they became acknowledged as spiritual leaders of the Jewish community, which respected them for the breadth of their learning—Israel was consulted on religious matters, while Celia often wrote letters for neighbors who were not fluent in English—and for their piety, for Celia's orthodoxy was no less passionately felt than was her husband's. Israel continued to put his expertise at wine-making to good use, working for his cousin as a wine chemist.

Relatives of Israel's and Celia's began arriving from Europe at a steady rate during and shortly after the First World War. Feeling a responsibility to keep the extended family together and to provide a more gentle introduction to American life than could be provided in the chaotic environment of New York City, Israel and Celia bought a farm of several hundred acres in Moodus, Connecticut. All of the Mostels and their relations went to Moodus for several years. Some of the new arrivals settled in the small Connecticut town permanently, while others lived on the farm until they became acclimated to their new country, then moved elsewhere. During the years Israel spent at Moodus, he practiced wine-making, producing sacramental wine as well as wine to be sold to the general public. As the expense of maintaining the farm required that he supplement his income, he also became superintendent of a kosher slaughterhouse.

Israel Mostel was "a very productive guy," as his son Aaron characterized him, but the necessity of maintaining a farm and looking after an ever-growing number of relatives, while running a slaughterhouse and a winery, soon began to exhaust him. Besides, Celia wanted to return to New York, where her children would be exposed to the lively and intellectually stimulating Jewish culture. After three years, Israel approached one of the farm's residents, his sister Sadie's husband. "Sam," he said, "you want to have a farm?" Sam Banner, whose business career had been less than distinguished, said that he'd love to have a farm. "All right," Israel told him, "you take over the mortgage, you've got a farm."

Sam Banner took the farm but was unable to meet the mortgage payments without Israel's help. At least, however, Israel had managed to shed some of his responsibilities. When he moved his family back to New York, they returned to the Lower East Side, this time to a house on Columbia Street. For the next several years, Israel took Celia and his children back to Moodus for the summer months; there they stayed as "guests" on Sam's farm. They continued to visit after the farm was converted to a resort known as Banner Lodge, which eventually became one of the most prominent resort hotels in Connecticut. Sam Banner turned out to be a shrewd businessman, after all.

Zero told *Holiday*'s Hugh G. Foster in 1963 that his father could have made a fortune during Prohibition by illegally making his sacramental wine available to the general population, but that he threw out the bootleggers who tried to enlist him. Possibly a true story, but, with Zero, who could know? He also told Foster that his father was a practicing rabbi—a "fact" that Israel Mostel's surviving sons dispute—and even supplied information concerning the supposed extent of his father's difficulties making a living at his rabbinical profession. According to Foster, "The earnings that miraculously kept Zero and his seven brothers and sisters fed, clothed and educated were their father's honorariums, and nothing more; a *bar mitzvah* here, a wedding there, and occasionally" a circumcision. It's a romantic picture, but probably one that Zero invented for the occasion. In reality, his father was steadily employed as a wine chemist and continued to run the kosher slaughterhouse in Connecticut during the summers.*

---

*Some of Zero's inventions may have begun as fictions created for his own amuse-

It could not be said that the Mostels were prosperous, however. The money to feed and clothe ten people was always in short supply at the home on Columbia Street. Still, the children did not seem to suffer. Israel Mostel invented games for the family to play, games that ordinarily ended with the parents making small sacrifices and the children reaping the benefits. Zero later described some of the games:

> On Chanukah we played a gambling game with a dreidl, which is a sort of a top, and father was most expert at cheating so that the children would get all the pennies. He was a very kind man. At the supper table, he used to ask us children: "What did you learn in school today?"
>
> Suppose I said "I learned about Joseph's dream . . ." Then my father would say: "Such a scholar deserves an extra piece of meat" and he'd take a slice from his plate and put it on mine. After going through the routine with the others, it wound up with the kids getting all the meat there was in the house.

Growing up with his family on the East Side, young Sammy Mostel gave no indication that he would one day gravitate toward a career as a comedian. Certainly his father would have objected to any such ambition, for, as Zero said many years later, "being an entertainer of that kind came under the heading of making fun of human beings, which is objectionable in the orthodox Jewish religion." Besides, he added on another occasion, "could you imagine my father, a Jew in a black hat with a long beard, sitting in a night club?"

Although Sammy may not have given any thought to a future in comedy, he was outgoing and had a lively sense of humor (his parents, he said, "thought I was funny"), qualities he had in common with everyone else in the family. Celia displayed a gift for one-liners at unexpected moments, as, for example, when one of the children in the crowded apartment stepped on the paw of the family cat. When the cat squealed, Celia looked down and said with mock sternness, "I *told* you not to go around barefoot!"

As if eight children, two adults, and a cat weren't enough, visitors abounded at the Mostel home: homeless unfortunates from the street

---

ment, but he eventually came to accept them as "fact." "Zero would really believe some of the stories he told. He enjoyed making alternate realities," said Mostel's nephew Raphael.

upon whom Israel took pity and invited in for a meal and a night's rest. "He brought home some poor man for almost every meal," Zero said. "I don't know where he found them—in the synagogue, on the streets, who knows? Most of them were dirty, and once I asked him why all the poor men he brought home were so dirty." His father, showing that he, too, had a dry wit, gently replied, "The clean ones, the rich get." Israel also displayed a commendable broad-mindedness. Zero's brother Aaron recalled one of the children pointing out to their father that the vagrant he had brought home one evening wasn't Jewish. "I didn't ask him if he was Jewish," Israel Mostel replied; "I asked him if he was hungry."

"I loved my pop," Zero said, looking back on his childhood. "He was a lovely, gentle man." Then, for emphasis: "He was a fucking saint."*

While Israel brought in as much money as he could from his wine-making and his slaughterhouse, Celia remained at home attending to the needs of her eight children. Even had they been capable of independence, it is doubtful she would have gone to work. Early in the twentieth century, wives—particularly wives in the Jewish community on the Lower East Side—seldom worked. Celia and Israel agreed that her "place" was in the home. When Sammy Mostel grew to manhood, he did not question that traditional wisdom, imposing the same convention upon Kate Harkin, his second wife.

---

*Zero was a master of invective whose speech invariably contained profanity, regardless of the subject under discussion. The words took on a different meaning depending upon their context—in the case cited above, "fucking" is a term denoting the deepest admiration—but the point is that they were a constant in Zero's speech. If he had been told that his life depended upon getting through an entire day without resorting to his usual scatological vocabulary, it would have been interesting to see if he could have survived until lunchtime. If his language were quoted accurately when he was ordering a sandwich, it would read something like: "I want a goddamn pastrami sandwich on fucking rye bread! And if you forget the !@$&!?! pickle I'll dip your !@?#&!! head into the fucking pickle barrel!" In the interests of saving space and sparing those few readers who may be prone to blush when confronted with such language—if not by the repetition—this biography will henceforth quote Zero's four-letter words only when they seem to be *absolutely* essential to his meaning. Recognizing that I am omitting much of his vocabulary, however, those readers who wish to savor the flavor of his language to its fullest may feel free to supply a "fucking" any time they wish.

Early on, Sammy showed an intelligence and keenness of perception that encouraged his father to think he had the makings of a rabbi. Israel's assessment was flawed, however, for of all the children in the household, only Sammy was relatively indifferent to religion; his enthusiasm was reserved for painting and drawing. As his father would later disapprove of his career as an entertainer, so—as an Orthodox Jew—he would be forced to object when Sammy showed an interest in art. As Maurice Sterne has pointed out, "Religious Jews took very seriously the Biblical injunction against 'graven' images." Remembering his own childhood, Sterne said, "I was badly punished one day by the rabbi . . . for drawing his picture on the ground with a stick." Indeed, Israel did not sympathize with Sammy's regard for art, but Celia did. Although she shared her husband's belief in Orthodox Judaism, she seems to have been more comfortable with her son's interest in painting and encouraged him to go to New York's many museums. Several accounts of Zero's early life claim that Celia regularly dressed him in a velvet suit and sent him with colored pencils and drawing pad to the Metropolitan Museum of Art to copy the masterpieces hung there. His favorite painting was *Study in Black and Green* by John W. Alexander, which he copied on every visit. Often the boy, with his obvious talent, attracted a crowd.

The adult Zero was quite a different person—far quieter and more studious—when he painted than at other times. When he was being observed, he seemed to feel (even if others didn't) that it was incumbent upon him to be the center of all attention. Even as a boy, that duality seems to have been present, for when crowds would gather around the serious young artist, he became puckish and outgoing. Occasionally, he amused the assemblage by copying paintings upside-down, placing heads at the foot of the canvas.

"Look at our Sam," Celia said about her son; "a child and he draws like a man." Later on, when he was painting regularly, she looked wryly at one of his abstract canvases and commented, "Look at Sam: a man and he draws like a child."

Celia "had a fervor about education," in the words of her son Aaron. If the story about the velvet suit is an exaggeration, as it might well be, there can be little doubt that she would have encouraged Sammy to learn everything he could about every subject that interested him.

The Mostel house was well stocked with books and the route to the public library was well traveled. All the members in the family spoke Yiddish and English; Italian and German were also used frequently. Like Israel, Celia possessed a love of learning that she transmitted to her son.

When Zero spoke about his mother and father, he generally said that his mother stood with him against his father, who urged him to be a rabbi. At least three times, though, he claimed that it was the other way around: "My mother wanted me to be a rabbi," he said on one such occasion. "They were going to send me to Prague to study. . . . [My father] asked me, 'Do you want to go?' I said, 'No.' He said, 'I'll put up a fight,' and he did." Obviously, little about Mostel's life can be accepted as precisely and absolutely factual, for Zero gave different accounts of the same event to different people, as it suited him. It wasn't only with the press that he varied his stories; his friends, his brothers, even his son Josh heard different versions of the same events. The only consistent aspect of this particular story is that one of his parents wanted him to be a rabbi while the other defended his right to make his own choice concerning his future.

All of the Mostel children felt warmly about their parents. "You could talk to them," Aaron Mostel said. "You could do a mathematical problem with your mother. Or a chemistry problem with your father. You could discuss things. You had parents who were parents."

One of Zero's favorite memories of his childhood was when his father and mother read the Yiddish stories of Sholem Aleichem to the children, "and we would roar with laughter." One suspects that there was a good deal of roaring at the Mostel household. As Raphael Mostel, the son of Zero's brother Milton, told me about the Mostel family gatherings he attended years later, "When the whole family was together it was like a carnival experience. Everybody was grabbing for the center of attention. They were all alike." When I asked if Zero's argumentative, volatile, comically grotesque manner was unique among the family, Raphael answered, "No. He was just the one who was doing it for a job." That same highly charged emotional climate undoubtedly prevailed at the home of Israel and Celia Mostel in the 1920s and early 1930s.

In March 1921, Sammy entered Public School 188 on Houston

Street. Typical of that time, the school was composed largely of Jewish students. Sixteen years before Sammy began school, some 65,000 pupils attended thirty-eight elementary schools on the East Side. Of the total, 61,000 were Jewish. Although a later generation would have objected to the segregated nature of elementary education in New York, most Jews of the early twentieth century regarded the situation without any sense of indignation. Indeed, it seemed only logical to most of them that Jews should attend school with other Jews.

Sammy's grades at P.S. 188 were uniformly excellent; he was an A student both in work and in conduct. "I was a good student," Zero said fifty years later. "I was interested in everything." His brother Bill agreed: "He could sop up knowledge and books," he recalled. "He had a photographic memory; he was the smartest of the whole family." When Sammy was promoted to junior high school in 1926, he continued to do well, skipping to the rapid advancement class.

In addition to his education at public school, Sammy also attended the Educational Alliance, an institution housed in a large building on East Broadway and Jefferson Street, where he received his training as a painter. The Alliance, founded in 1889, was designed to provide Jewish immigrants in New York with cultural enrichment. As the social historian Irving Howe described it, the Alliance was a "curious mixture of night school, settlement house, day-care center, gymnasium, and public forum." Classes in many languages—primarily Yiddish and Hebrew—were held throughout the day and evening, offering instruction to children and adults in such subjects as the English language, Greek and Roman history, cooking and sewing, and physical culture. And, after 1917—just in time for Sammy Mostel and other aspiring artists of his generation—classes in the arts were offered, as well.* One large room doubled as an art studio in the daytime and a rehearsal room for the orchestra at night. As a result of these classes, art exhibitions and concerts were offered, as were theatrical performances.

When Sammy first began to participate in the Alliance's art classes, he was overwhelmed by the size of the work space, especially in comparison with the crowded apartment where his family lived. "The Al-

*The art school had operated in the nineteenth century, but was closed from 1905 until 1917.

liance gave me a new life," he said. "I had never seen such *big* rooms before."

Prominent artists, such as Chaim Gross and Moses Soyer, taught at the Educational Alliance. Students who later made their mark in the art world included Louise Nevelson, Ben Shahn, Mark Rothko, and Adolph Gottlieb. Clearly, the schooling they received was superior. Sammy Mostel was fortunate to be trained by the same institution.

Aaron Mostel, who shared a bedroom with Sammy, recalled that the room was always cluttered with his brother's easel and paints, and that he—Aaron—often posed for portraits when Sammy was twelve years old or so.

In 1928, Sammy began the first of three years at Seward Park High School, where his aptitude for painting and drawing was encouraged. His graduation yearbook lists "Art" as his primary activity; and the printed inscription beside his picture calls him "A future Rembrandt." Significantly, the inscription goes on to say: ". . . or perhaps a comedian?" His selection as secretary of the Senior Council would indicate that he was also popular with his classmates.

Sammy must have been a potentially fine student. His essay, "If I Were an Eagle," was the winner in a contest at Seward Park High; his prize consisted of tickets to matinee performances at the Metropolitan Opera. The boy, who had already shown great interest in the plays presented on Broadway and in the Yiddish theatres on the East Side, now became familiar with and enthusiastic about a new theatrical form, reveling in the opportunity to see the great singers of the day: Kirsten Flagstad, Bruna Castagna, Titta Ruffo, Rosa Ponselle. "Of course, I annoyed people sitting next to me because I sang along with everybody," he claimed.

Despite his winning essay, Sammy's grades at Seward Park were little better than average, ranging from a low of 55 in history to a high of 95 in foreign languages. Surprisingly, his scores in mechanical drawing and in elocution gave little indication of any particular excellence, although he later distinguished himself as a draftsman and an actor.

Afterward, when asked how he got his professional name, Zero frequently answered that he was named for the average of his grades at Seward Park High. Not true. But if his academic performance was less than dazzling, it didn't prevent the high school from honoring him with its "Hall of Fame Award" after he achieved stardom on Broadway in 1962, "in recognition of his contribution to the culture of our times as artist of many talents—acclaimed in the dramatic arts and gifted in the graphic arts—who has brought honor and distinction to Seward, his classmates and fellow alumni." As the program commemorating the event makes clear, he had been an active member of the Alumni Association for years. "Zero has not forgotten his own hardships while a student at Seward Park," it said. "He experienced the same trials and tribulations which confronted most poor boys of that era. He is presently working with the Scholarship Fund Committee to raise funds for the needy and underprivileged children attending Seward Park High School."

Sammy Mostel graduated from Seward Park in 1931 and went immediately into the City College of New York, where he majored in fine arts and English. His family probably could not have afforded to send him to college if tuition were required, but City College was free in the early 1930s. Almost forty years later, CCNY was forced to consider requiring tuition and restricting admission to students with distinguished high school records. Had those requirements been in effect in 1931, Mostel would have been deprived of the experience of going to college. For that reason, he came out firmly against both proposed changes. "City College is free," he said in 1969, adding, "I hope it always stays free."*

City College, like all the schools Sammy attended, was predominantly a Jewish institution, particularly during the Depression; Jews constituted as much as 90 percent of the student body. The college was highly regarded, described by the New York *Times* as a "Jewish, proletarian Harvard."

At CCNY, Sammy was eager to enroll in every art class available, but, unfortunately, few were offered. So, after taking two freshman art courses and finding the instructor a sympathetic and knowledgeable soul, he repeated the courses even though he had passed them with an A and a B. It was typical of the adult Zero that he could not resist exaggerating this story. In its ultimate version, he claimed to have taken the same course eight times.

---

*Eventually, CCNY was forced to accept the inevitable and impose a tuition charge.

His favorite class, perhaps, was George Eggers's course in "life draw-ing," where the model was one Honey Bee Keller, a stripper from the Irving Place Burlesque House on Fourteenth Street. Dun Roman, a classmate of Mostel's, observed that Sammy "managed to paint not only stunningly well, but at the top of his lungs," particularly in this class. "As the Junoesque blonde vision mounted the stand, shed her kimono and seated herself on a high stool, Mostel emitted a whistle more penetrating than a fire siren," Roman recalled, "blasting us out of our chairs, except for Miss Keller, who in the course of her regular work had become used to it."

The outgoing, zany side of Mostel's personality grew stronger each year; his two selves—serious artist and frenetic comic—had already begun to assert themselves with equal strength. Dun Roman remem-bered his disrupting the art class with various imitations: Franklin and Eleanor Roosevelt, Mussolini, the entire Barrymore clan, Frank Mor-gan. Mostel supplied improvised dialogue that not only convulsed his fellow students but, at least once, also caused Honey Bee Keller to fall off her stand and into the arms of Professor Eggers.

Sammy's serious side did not disappear, however; it only became less public. His commitment to painting, which must necessarily be a sol-itary, contemplative discipline, increased. His love of literature was also sharpened while he was at college. In particular, he recalled having read James Joyce's *Ulysses*, which was then banned in the United States. Sammy somehow managed to get a bootleg copy, which he read in the college's bathroom. He held on to the book, illustrated with Matisse prints, reading it over and over in later years.

Sammy also adored the poems of Robert Browning, and he reveled in a class taught by a former president of the Browning Society. When asked to read aloud in class, Mostel and his classmates discovered—perhaps for the first time—how much potential this young man had as an interpreter of literature. "I venture that Browning was born expressly to be read aloud by Sammy Mostel," said Dun Roman. Browning's poetry, like Joyce's novel, remained significant to Mostel throughout his life. On more than one television show—to the dismay of his sponsors—Zero Mostel would suddenly cease his buffoonery and give a serious reading of a Browning poem.

Mostel once told an interviewer that he played Hamlet at CCNY.

The school has no record of it, but it's not an impossibility. An acquaintance recalled that Mostel had told him in the late 1930s that he had been in *Hamlet* (not necessarily playing the leading role) when he was in college. Although Sammy was gaining weight, he was still a relatively trim, good-looking youngster with a full head of hair, so he would not have been eliminated from consideration for the role on physical grounds. Moreover, after he became a professional actor, he aspired to play such Shakespearean roles as Falstaff and King Lear. However, another article about him (for which he presumably supplied the information) said, "He had no ambitions along dramatic lines, never appeared in college plays." It seems that Zero, the famous actor, amused himself by telling reporters conflicting stories about his early life.

A professor for whom Mostel had little regard—"an idiot with a huge Adam's apple" is how Zero later recalled him—assigned him to attend a speech clinic "because I had a low 's'—whatever the hell that is." But Mostel disregarded the assignment, earning himself a summons to appear before Morton Gottschall, the dean of liberal arts and sciences. Zero described the scene: "Dean Gottschall said he was going to kick me out because the professor had told him I had cut speech clinic 22 times. But I told him the professor was a liar and that I had cut only 21 times, so the dean let me stay in school."

Sammy had to work at odd jobs during the time he spent at CCNY. At night, he worked for a baking company; as a bonus, he was given one-day-old bread to take home. Although his jobs would have left little time for extracurricular activities, he claimed that he was on the swimming team and that he joined ROTC. It's difficult to imagine the determinedly individualistic Zero Mostel of later years in anything as regimented as ROTC, although predictably—if his story is to be believed—he was a spectacularly unsuccessful recruit. On one warm afternoon, according to Zero, his ROTC unit was holding a review in honor of the college's Charter Day. As the captain walked smartly down the line of uniformed students, he paused when he came to a disreputable-looking trainee who appeared to be wilting in the heat. "Attention!" shouted the captain, "not at ease!" Mostel responded lamely, "But Captain, it's not me at ease. It's my uniform." Eventually, Sammy became such an embarrassment to the Corps that he was kept out of sight whenever a public drill was held.

After graduating from CCNY with a bachelor's degree in 1935 (Zero later called it "the year of the miracle"), Mostel took night courses at New York University, studying for a master's in art. During the day, he worked at several jobs in succession: one was in a shop owned by a brother-in-law, turning the sleeves of overcoats; but the job lasted only four weeks. He intended to teach after he received his M.A., but he dropped out of NYU after one year. Many years later, he explained why: "Anyone can talk," he said, "but the artist must *do* things. . . . I decided that [becoming a teacher] was a kind of talking without *doing* anything." He had done a good deal of work on his thesis, a critical evaluation of the work of the great caricaturist Honoré Daumier, a project he intended to complete and publish later on, but—although he still spoke of doing so as late as 1943—he never finished it. Mostel was drifting: from school to school, from job to job, without any genuine sense of purpose. He knew that he wanted to be a painter, but he had little idea how to realize his ambition.

His own inability to settle upon a course of action was compounded by the economic condition that gripped the country. Even if he had wanted to do otherwise, the Depression would have made it all but impossible for him to do more than pick up a series of odd jobs. For a while, he and his brother Aaron worked as longshoremen at the Conover Street docks in Brooklyn, but the work was dangerous as well as intermittent. Sammy, who had joined a movement to reform the longshoremen's union, was beaten up twice by hoodlums. Still, he took whatever manual labor he could get, in one instance unloading bananas from steamboats. By and large, he preferred this sort of work to less strenuous activities. "I had a snobbery against white-collar workers," Zero said later. "If I couldn't do what I wanted to do, which was paint, it had to be manual labor."

Periodically, whenever he accumulated enough money, he would do what he wanted: he painted his way through Louisiana and Mexico, for example. When the money ran out, he took jobs in factories and in mines wherever he could find work. Then it was back to New York, and more manual labor.

His parents were upset at his drifting. "They thought I was a bum, a hobo," Zero said. "They thought anybody who wasn't a lawyer or a doctor was wasting his life. My mother used to crack her knuckles in protest." But, in reality, Mostel had little choice in the matter. There were few jobs available, and those there were offered no security and no real chance of advancement. However, if the Depression was responsible for Mostel's joblessness, it turned out that a government program created specifically because of the Depression would lead directly to his success in painting and performing.

2

Starting from Zero

When Franklin D. Roosevelt swept into office in 1932, he carried with him a mandate to create programs that would provide assistance for those who were ill clothed, ill housed, and ill fed. After experimenting with various alternatives, however, the administration came to feel that relief in itself was not the answer. Instead of simply providing government handouts, the administration determined to put millions of unemployed Americans back to work. Since jobs were unavailable in the private sector, the government would have to create them. Such programs were subject to criticism, particularly by those who believed that the government should not interfere with the economy; but Roosevelt, who had already established similar enterprises as governor of New York, was convinced that they could be made to work—and that jobs could be created not only for manual laborers and white-collar workers, but for artists as well: painters, sculptors, dancers, writers, actors, and others.

In 1932, during the waning days of Roosevelt's tenure as New York's governor, the state had hired more than one hundred visual artists to paint murals—often depicting laborers at work—in New York City's settlement houses. It was George Biddle, an artist who had known Roosevelt since they were schoolmates together at Groton and Harvard, who proposed to the president that a similar program be undertaken on the federal level. According to Biddle's plan, thousands of visual artists throughout the country could be put to work at government expense. The works they produced—principally murals in public buildings—would then become a national storehouse of works of art. Roosevelt encouraged him to pursue the idea.

Against the opposition of such organizations as the National Commission of Fine Arts, which had been created by Congress in 1910 to advise the president on artistic matters (and whose members were distinctly conservative in their artistic attitudes, favoring "classical" art and distrusting any hint of the modern),* but with the help of supporters such as Eleanor Roosevelt, Secretary of Labor Frances Perkins, Secretary of the Interior Harold L. Ickes, and Assistant Secretary of Agriculture Rexford G. Tugwell, Biddle eventually succeeded.

Especially significant was the support of Assistant Secretary of the Treasury Lawrence W. Robert, for the Treasury Department was the official custodian of all federal buildings, with the authority to decide how and by whom the buildings should be decorated. When the Treasury Department agreed to support Biddle's proposal, the idea was on its way to becoming reality. Ickes proposed to Relief Administrator Harry Hopkins that a project to employ artists be established.

As a result, Hopkins allocated $1,039,000 for the new Public Works of Art Project (PWAP); that money was used to pay fifteen hundred artists from $35 to $45 per week, one thousand artists $20 to $30 per week, and five hundred laborers $15 per week. Many complications ensued. Who would select the artists to be hired? What criteria should be used to establish that an individual possessed the talent to be described as an "artist"? Should the emphasis be placed on the artist's economic need or on his ability? The Republican National Committee,

---

*The National Commission of Fine Arts was only one of many organizations (not to mention individuals) that looked upon the notion of providing jobs for artists with skepticism. The American public might accept the notion of a job being created for a bricklayer—his work could be seen and felt, and it was likely to endure—but great numbers of people would object to the same consideration for an artist, whose work was, in many cases, ephemeral. Besides, many Americans distrusted artists; their work somehow didn't seem to be *work*. As one congressman put it, "Why don't they get a pick and shovel?"

moreover, accused the Treasury Department of wasting public money by hiring "hundreds of individuals belonging to the belly-ache school of artists to daub our public schools with so-called murals."

Despite the objections, the PWAP, during its four and a half months of existence, hired thousands of artists across the country (many of them located in New York City, which was firmly established as the artistic center of the United States), whose output, ranging from Indian blankets to murals, exceeded fifteen thousand pieces.

The PWAP was short-lived because the Roosevelt administration, under the false impression that the Depression would soon be over, recommended to Congress that the Civil Works Administration (of which PWAP was a part) be liquidated in 1934. Thus the PWAP had to release the artists it had hired. However, the following year saw the establishment by Congress of the Works Progress Administration, which proceeded to constitute a Federal Art Project (FAP) as well as several other projects in the arts, including programs for music, writers, and theatre. In addition to providing salaries for painters and sculptors, the Art Project sponsored classes and paid lecturers to give free tours at art galleries and museums. More than five thousand artists and teachers were hired by the project, which continued until June 1943.

As had been true with the PWAP, the FAP concentrated much of its effort upon New York City, where, according to Richard D. McKinzie,

> 80 percent of [those] reached by the art teachers were children. . . . In boys' clubs, girls' service leagues, orphanages, day nurseries, hospitals, churches, and settlements, FAP art teachers showed youngsters how to secure "canvases," usually pieces of brown wrapping paper, and mix their paints in muffin tins. Students seemed to like it, for at the end of the first year FAP boasted that in New York City and its vicinity 50,000 children and adults were being reached weekly through the teaching force.

One of those hired by the FAP in 1937 was twenty-two-year-old Sam Mostel—the youngest of all the painters on the project. Again, as had been the case at the Educational Alliance, he was in good company. "I worked with Pollock and Kline and de Kooning, all of them," he recalled. "Most of the good artists were on the project, teaching and working." The project subsidized Sammy's painting but also required him to teach art to children on occasion. Thus—despite his avowed distaste for teaching—he was given a job instructing youngsters at the Ninety-second Street Young Men's and Young Women's Hebrew Association. In 1937–38, Mostel taught evening classes in elementary drawing and painting and intermediate drawing and painting ("Tuition is free to the public," the catalogue announced, "with the exception of a nominal supply and equipment fee of fifteen cents per week"); in 1938–39, he taught a life drawing class four mornings a week. According to Aaron Berkman, the director of the Art Center, Mostel "was a very satisfactory teacher, highly intelligent," and popular with the students.

On one occasion, Mostel offered one of his pupils a detailed criticism of his work. The student seemed confused at first but ultimately said that he understood. Mostel must have been frustrated at hearing himself expound, however. "That's impossible," he said. When the student asked why, Mostel answered, "Because I haven't the faintest idea of what I was talking about myself."

Still, Mostel continued to think of teaching only as a stopgap measure, designed to support him until he could paint full-time. Perhaps because of that attitude, "he was clowning all the time," according to Berkman. "He was just incorrigible; sometimes he'd drive you to distraction because he would never stop."

Mostel enjoyed telling the following story: one evening while teaching at the "Y," he decided in the middle of a class that he needed to relax by taking a dip in the swimming pool. When an administrator walked into Mostel's classroom and inquired where the teacher had gone, the students directed him to the pool. When he found his man, the administrator demanded to know why Mostel was swimming when he should be teaching. "I'm studying water colors," Mostel answered.

Berkman has no recollection of the incident, but says, "That sounds like something he would have done." Zero did like to embellish—or invent—stories about himself, so one may accept it either as something that happened to Sam Mostel or something that Zero thought *should* have happened. His brother Aaron also remembers some incidents that no one else can recall. For example, Aaron claims that Sam Mostel followed his tenure at the YM-YWHA with another teaching stint at the New York School of Industrial Arts. The school has no employment records from the 1930s and the current principal had not heard that Mostel might have taught there until I inquired about it. Although he could not be certain, he doubted that Mostel had ever been employed at the school, for he thought it likely that Industrial Arts would wish to boast about having once had so famous an individual on its faculty. Nor do any of Mostel's friends recall Zero ever mentioning this job to them.

The income provided by the Art Project was meager but steady: $23.86 per week (a figure Zero never forgot). Periodically, when his services were required elsewhere, Mostel was dropped from teaching and painting on the Art Project, but he continued to be paid by the WPA: for a while, he was assigned to the New York Public Library and told to organize their art collection; at other times, he worked as a snow shoveler.

Mostel found it difficult to make ends meet, in part because he was supporting a wife. He and Clara Sverd, who were in the same class at CCNY, were married in mid-1939. The couple lived briefly together in what Aaron Mostel described as "a very nice apartment on Parkside Avenue in Brooklyn," but the marriage proved to be disastrous. Clara, who could not understand her husband's artistic aspirations, wanted him to quit the Art Project and take a job at the Post Office, which he refused to do. He did agree to work part-time for her father, who ran a restaurant near Grand Central Station. But Mostel was unable to get along with his in-laws and they disliked him, a situation that made for constant arguments. He was able to persuade Clara's mother to lend him money so that he could rent an artist's studio; Mrs. Sverd later claimed that Sam convinced her "that he could support [my] daughter on the scale she was accustomed if [I] would advance the capital." The loan enabled him, two other painters, and a sculptor, Herbert Kallem, to rent a small room without heat on the north side of West Twenty-eighth Street and use it as a studio. The rent was only $20 a month, but the four tenants nevertheless had trouble making the payments on time. Paying for utilities was out of the question. "We learned how to jump the meter so we could get electricity for nothing," said Kallem.*

---

*The same district was once known as Tin Pan Alley. In the building Zero occupied, George Gershwin had once plugged his songs. A nearby structure used to be the home of the vaudeville team Weber and Fields.

Mostel used his studio all too frequently for Clara's taste, often remaining there overnight. The couple began to have frequent arguments over his absences and his failure to bring home sufficient money to allow Clara to quit her job. Zero later said, "My wife had a temperament and habits of a spoiled daughter, which weakness was constantly kept at a high pitch by her doting mother."

Eventually, the arguments became more heated and in September 1941 Mostel arrived home to find that Clara had left him. One day his brother Aaron went to Sam's studio and finding Sam deep in dejection, suspected that the marriage had gone sour. "Sammy, tell me the truth," he said. "Are you living with Clara?" Mostel admitted that his wife had walked out and that he was too embarrassed to inform his family. Not only had she gone but, according to Aaron, "she took everything, even the chandeliers, which my parents had bought." At last Aaron persuaded his distraught brother to inform the other members of his family. "You didn't do anything wrong," Aaron told him. "What have you got to be ashamed of? Go home, tell it to your parents." Sam summoned the courage he needed and, after revealing his separation to his mother and father, moved back into their house.

But Zero Mostel must have remained ashamed for the rest of his life, for rarely has there been such a well-kept secret. In later years, he almost never spoke of his first wife, and only then to refer to the marriage as a great mistake. Many of the close friends whom I interviewed were astonished to find that he had ever *had* a first wife. While aware that his father had been married to another woman before marrying his mother, Zero's son Josh knew nothing about her—not even her name—and little about the marriage except that Zero was sensitive about the subject and preferred not to talk about it. All he could recall his father telling him, Josh said, was that "he got married and then got un-married as quickly as possible."

* * *

Another of Mostel's duties as an employee of the WPA was to give gallery talks at the Museum of Modern Art, the Frick, and the Museum of Science and Industry. His lectures were spiced with jokes and incongruous ad libs. By this time, there were two clearly defined sides to his personality: the committed artist, who could work patiently, calmly, with complete seriousness as long as his attention was focused upon his paintings and as long as he wasn't expected to be funny; and the compulsive performer, who simply could not (and seemingly had no desire to) subdue the impulse to entertain a group of people by employing his special brand of humor—and "a group" consisted of two or more. The museum lectures—he referred to them as "chalk talks" —represented an intriguing instance in which the two sides of his personality seemed to be constantly at war with one another. Not only was Mostel a gifted artist, but he was also genuinely knowledgeable about the subject; the learning he had absorbed at the Educational Alliance, CCNY, and NYU was continually supplemented by his own reading and contemplation. He was capable of delivering an edifying, illuminating lecture on art. Often, throughout his life, he would stroll slowly through a museum with a friend at his side. On those occasions, he offered brilliantly penetrating insights into the intentions and accomplishments of the artists whose work he discussed.

On the other hand, he was also a gifted comic, whose high school shenanigans had been refined to the point where he could create laughter by means both extravagant and subtle. Blessed with a fertile imagination and an irrepressible nature, he would blurt out remarks that were risqué or otherwise injudicious, and do so with the certainty of the born comic that everything he had to say was *funny*. And he was right.

As an amateur comedian, Mostel ventured into territory that others avoided, and became more outrageous by the minute. Explaining Picasso's *Girl Before a Mirror* to a group of elementary school students, he expounded: "This one is all woman, you gotta believe me. Look at her. Look at what she's got. More than one of everything. . . . You know tits, right? But Picasso's girl got four of them. Why shouldn't she? That's the way he saw her, and he has a right as a citizen of the world to see anything the way he wants to. Everybody sing with me, 'America, America.' That's enough!"

Zero's verbal facility, combined with what can legitimately be described as an embryonic pantomimic genius (the theatrical caricaturist Al Hirschfeld said that during Mostel's museum "routines," he "used to imitate wallpaper, a percolator, all sorts of abstract things. You could *see* the steam coming from the top of his head"), nearly always reduced his audience to helpless laughter. It seems likely that each of Mostel's museum lectures began with the intention of edifying rather than amusing the onlookers. But as he found himself the center of attention, he could not resist switching from his "scholarly" persona to his comic one. Invariably, then, what had begun as a serious lecture ended as a travesty—but one to which the museumgoers responded with unrestrained delight.

Mostel's unique comic routines soon became known outside the confines of galleries and museums, and his reputation as a funny man began to bring him invitations to entertain at parties. He received no more than $5 (and as little as $3) on those occasions, but he always stipulated that he be given all the pastrami sandwiches he could eat. Together with his salary from the WPA, Mostel's party money helped him buy paints, canvas, brushes, and the other paraphernalia he needed.

By this time, Sam Mostel was six feet tall, beginning to lose his hair, and gaining weight rapidly, as photographs from the time attest. In the early 1940s, he probably weighed about 210 pounds; eventually, he would balloon to over 300.

When Congress threatened to withdraw funding for the Federal Art Project in 1941, a committee of artists, Mostel among them, was formed to register a protest, and journeyed to Washington that summer. Mostel sat in the Senate gallery observing the politicians below. When he returned to New York, he included, for the first time, imitations of pompous politicians in his comic routine.

A new audience responded enthusiastically to these additions. Social clubs organized by labor unions were beginning to form all over New York City. The clubs, invariably left-wing in their political orientation, wanted entertainers who could incorporate social criticism into their acts. Sam Mostel was ready and willing to accommodate them by mocking the conservative politicians he had studied in Washington. Thus, his act began to be seen in union halls and at political meetings as well as at parties and in museums and galleries.

In late 1941, Mostel was delivering one of his comic monologues when someone approached him to suggest that he become a professional entertainer. The "someone," depending upon who was telling the story, was either Himan Brown, a radio producer; Ivan Black, a press agent representing a nightclub called Café Society Downtown; or Barney Josephson, who operated Café Society. Mostel's monologue was being given in a museum, at a party, at a fund-raiser for China Relief, or at the Artists' Ball, again depending upon whose account is to be believed.

Ivan Black's story was that he heard Mostel perform at a private party and approached him immediately afterward, saying, "You're wonderful. Where are you working?"

"In the studio," Sam replied.

"Which one?" said Black. "Paramount or Twentieth Century?"

"Are you kidding? In my own studio. I paint pictures."

"How would you like to work at Café Society Downtown?" asked Black.

"And get paid regularly, you mean?" inquired Mostel. For a man who worked for pastrami sandwiches, this was an irresistible offer.

In any case, whoever made the initial discovery, Mostel was encouraged to get his material together and do a formal audition for Josephson. He did so in November of 1941, but the club owner turned him down. Although Josephson used comedians occasionally at Café Society, he was primarily interested in presenting jazz musicians such as Hazel Scott and Teddy Wilson.

But after the Japanese attack on Pearl Harbor, the tastes of the audiences at Café Society—and throughout the country—were changing. People wanted to laugh and forget the war, however briefly. Josephson soon realized that the successful nightclubs emphasized comedy. Ivan Black reminded him of the fat, balding comic whom he had turned down in November. Still, Josephson wasn't at all sure that Sam Mostel was the right comedian for his cabaret. A second tryout was arranged, and either on that occasion or after Mostel's sixth audition—again, the stories vary—Josephson agreed to hire him. Asked what salary he would like, Sam responded, "A thousand dollars a week." Josephson said that he was thinking more in the range of $25; they compromised at $40.

Josephson was still not certain that he had made the right decision in hiring Mostel, so he asked Jack Gilford, who had been the first comic ever to play Café Society, to take a look at the newcomer's routine. Gilford suggested that Mostel's material tended to be overlong, but that he was a gifted comedian.

Encouraged by Gilford's endorsement, Josephson worked with Mostel to cut his material to reasonable length, then turned his attention to the next problem. Sam Mostel, he thought, was not an appropriate name for a comic, and—after rejecting Mostel's suggestion of "Fagel Bagel"—he turned to Ivan Black, who promptly came up with the name "Zero." "After all," Black said, "here's a guy who's starting from nothing." In a day when the Marx Brothers—Groucho, Harpo, and Chico—were the kings of comedy, Zero sounded about right.*

Café Society Downtown was not just another nightclub. It was begun in 1938 because of the discrimination against blacks practiced in most bistros of the time. Although black performers might be hired, they invariably earned less than white entertainers. Furthermore, black customers were generally denied entrance to the clubs where such performers as Lena Horne, Sarah Vaughan, and Josh White were playing. Barney Josephson intended to change that by treating all entertainers and all customers alike. "I wanted a club where blacks and whites worked together behind the footlights and sat together out front," Josephson said—an unheard-of practice in the 1930s. "There wasn't, so far as I know, a place like it in New York or in the whole country."

Josephson gave a variety of entertainers their first New York exposure, among them Billie Holiday, Kay Starr, Big Bill Broonzy, Imogene Coca, Jim Backus, and Carol Channing. His club, attractively decorated with murals by artists Adolf Dehn and Abe Birnbaum, featured pointed satire and the latest jazz.

During the club's first year, Josephson lost $28,000, but in time, Café Society, located at 2 Sheridan Square, began to attract its share of customers. It not only provided first-rate entertainment, it also soothed the conscience of those who objected to the discrimination that prevailed at most nightclubs. The enlightened social outlook of Café Society even drew so unlikely a customer as Eleanor Roosevelt. According to Barney Josephson, "She had never been in a night club in her life, and she never went to another one." Even so, Café Society was rarely full enough to cover expenses.

In 1940, still losing money, Josephson applied a novel approach to his financial difficulties: rather than close the café, he expanded, opening

*Zero's friends often shortened his nickname to "Zee" or just "Z." A few called him "Zook."

Café Society Uptown on Forty-eighth Street. Ivan Black, his press agent, sent a release to all of New York's newspapers stating that Café Society Downtown was doing such good business that Josephson had decided to open an uptown branch. Perhaps because its location was better suited to a nightclub clientele, customers flocked to the Uptown; and Josephson, who had planned to close the Downtown, suddenly found that the crowds there had doubled. To his surprise, both clubs had become moneymaking propositions. Perhaps he was even more surprised when Zero Mostel, the fat comic he had initially rejected, became his biggest attraction. Mostel, with his growing social consciousness and his dynamic style, was the ideal comedian for Josephson's establishments.

*   *   *

After acquiring his new name, Zero gave up his job on the Federal Art Project and made his debut as a professional comedian on February 16, 1942, less than two weeks short of his twenty-seventh birthday. Inhibited by all of the conflicting advice he received about how to perform in a nightclub, Zero gave meek and tentative performances at his first two shows that night. But when the audiences failed to respond, he decided to do his material in his own zany way. His act, made up of impressions (he did Charles Boyer, Jimmy Durante, Adolf Hitler, and his own invention: Professor Chamberlain Remorse, a seemingly meek ornithologist who ended his "lecture" with a lascivious whisper: "Birds mate, you know"), pantomime (the percolator coming to a boil), general silliness (he managed to hold a cigarette between his lower lip and his chin, creating the uncanny impression of a man with two mouths), and political satire, began with seeming indifference and progressed to ferocious intensity. Perhaps no other comedian threw himself so thoroughly into his act; perhaps no one else performed in such an extravagant manner. In any case, his decision to perform in his own unique fashion immediately proved correct, as the enthusiastic audience reaction at his late show confirmed.

His depiction of the pompous segregationist Senator Polltax T. Pellagra, a southern isolationist, was considered to be extraordinarily daring (because it was so openly political) at the time. As the senator, Zero combined southern oratory with double-talk and nonsense; he began by roaring at the audience:

> Mah fellow Americans, ah yield to no one with respect to 100% Americanism, BUT—in this great land of Dee-mocracy, where we have a past, present and the sacred principles of *fawnisawandfranisong* in midst of plenty, our forefathers showed us the way, and we must look into the future. And what do we see? Ah may be vague, but, when a man of my character impugns the character of another man, he must prove it in cold hard facts, and Ah have the information right here in mah pocket. This information was given to me by a malingerer whose name Ah'm not at liberty to divulge at this time because he happens to be *stravinadaplad* . . . BUT, Ah can tell you the name of the carrier pigeon who brought the message to me. Her name is Eunice! They say no poor man can vote in mah state. Ah wish to say that is a Red trick to besmirch the fair name of Southern womanhood. That is why we believe in all these principles on the one hand and on the other.

The routine, during which Senator Pellagra tried to fix the blame for America's entry into the war on progressive forces, ended with a line that was soon being quoted everywhere in New York: "As to the most grievous problem facing America today—the so-called Japanese attack on Hawaii—Ah'd like to ask: WHAT THE HELL WAS HAWAII DOING IN THE PACIFIC OCEAN ANYWAY??"

The nightclub critic for the New York *Herald Tribune* caught one of Zero's earliest performances and reported to his readers on February 28, 1942, "This comedian borrows from no other funsters I know of."

Zero's physical appearance alone was enough to provoke laughter. As his wife-to-be, Kate, described him: "In those days comics didn't wear funny clothes, they dressed like real people in dinner jackets, black bow ties and patent-leather shoes. But Zero had on a rumpled navy-blue suit, red tie and huaraches [sandals]. His hair was combed in the first upsweep for men, parted just over his left ear and brushed up and over to cover his bare dome." *Life* magazine in 1943 described him as looking like a boneless shad, a whale, and a balloon. And *Current Biography* in 1943 called him "an elephant in pants." But if he was an elephant, he was a remarkably graceful one. He included in his routine an impression of a jitterbug at Roseland, which, again according to *Current Biography* (in what one assumes was an excess of praise), "has been called by professionals one of the finest interpretative dances of modern times." He also had the ability

—which he put to good use during his act—of rolling his eyeballs in opposite directions. When he simultaneously seemed to lose his hands inside the sleeves of his jacket, audiences went limp with laughter.

Even Congressman Hamilton Fish, an isolationist who bore some resemblance—in his ideology if not in his manner—to Senator Polltax T. Pellagra, enjoyed Zero's routines. One night, he called the comic to his table and told him, "You were very good tonight."

Never one to conceal his opinion of a politician's record, Zero answered bluntly, "Thanks. I wish I could say the same of you."

Not everyone found the political content of Zero's act to their liking. Conservatives and isolationists were often outraged. One such was the New York *Sun*'s columnist George E. Sokolsky, who heard Zero's Senator Pellagra sketch on the radio later in 1942. Sokolsky found that the satire hit too close to home. "Frankly, I resented this number because my son enjoyed it," he wrote. "He laughed all the time. He thought it was the funniest thing he had ever heard. . . . And I saw the leaven of antagonism to Congress working. That boy, when he reads some of the anti-Congress propaganda, will visualize a Congressman in terms of Mr. Mostel's burlesque. His respect for the greatest American institution was not improved."

Zero could laugh at such sentiments in 1942, and undoubtedly he did. But the strong social content of much of his material won him some influential political enemies, including the Federal Bureau of Investigation, which entered Mostel's routine—and Sokolsky's objection to it—into its files.

Café Society Downtown became so popular that Barney Josephson asked actor John Randolph and director David Pressman to begin a series of "Sunday Satires" at the club. They agreed, and took Zero on as one of the entertainers, even though Randolph had some reservations. He had seen Zero do a benefit performance with disastrous results. "When he used to lay an egg, he could lay it bigger than anybody else," Randolph said. On the other hand, he added, "Zero was very, very talented," so Randolph and Pressman felt that it would be foolish not to utilize his skills.

After doing three shows a night, six nights a week, plus the "Satires" on Sunday, a normal individual would be exhausted. Not Zero. When he wrapped up his last show (at about 3:30 A.M.), his evening was just beginning. Among the customers who most enjoyed Zero's performances was Sam Jaffe, the actor (best known, perhaps, for his performance as the ancient wise man in the film *Lost Horizon* and for his work on the television series, *Ben Casey*). Jaffe and Zero immediately became the closest of friends, a relationship that endured until the end of Mostel's life. After Zero's last show, he and Jaffe would go out on the town together. As Jaffe's widow, Bettye Ackerman, told me,

> Being out on the town for them would be just playing around on Fifth Avenue. At one point, Zero was climbing one of the light poles and a policeman stopped and said, "What are you doing up there?" Zero said, "Somebody left a letter for me." Another time they were at St. John's [Cathedral] on Fifth Avenue. They were running around playing [on the outdoor steps, where many birds roosted]. The policeman said, "What are you doing?" They said, "We're cleaning up from the pigeons."

Zero's $40 salary was an improvement over his previous income, but it still didn't provide enough to pay the rent and utilities and keep him in paints—especially because his three-show-a-day schedule at Café Society gave him no time to eat elsewhere, leaving him no alternative but the expensive meals served at the nightclub. (At least they were expensive by 1942 standards; a dinner at Café Society cost $1.50.)

But Zero was about to go through "the most meteoric rise in entertainment history," as more than one writer phrased it. Perhaps the words originated with press agent Ivan Black, but, at least in terms of commercial success, they weren't far from the truth.

In early April of 1942, Josephson moved Zero to the Café Society Uptown, raising his salary to $100 a week. Mostel was such a hit that he was soon headlining at the Uptown and the Downtown simultaneously, doing six shows a night. As a reward, his weekly earnings increased to $450. On April 8, he appeared for the first time on *The Chamber Music Society of Lower Basin Street*, a nationally broadcast radio program that combined music and satirical comedy in much the same way Barney Josephson did at Café Society. His appearance was so successful that he went on to become a regular on the program. On April 24, he opened in *Keep 'Em Laughing*, a Broadway revue. A month later, he was starring in another Broadway musical, *Top-Notchers*. In July and August, he played at New York's Paramount Theatre—at

$1,250 per week—with great success. In September and October, he was in Hollywood, appearing in a Metro-Goldwyn-Mayer film called *Du Barry Was a Lady*, earning $3,000 per week. During his spare time, he appeared on radio shows with Fred Allen, Tommy Dorsey, and Kate Smith. He was booked into the famous La Martinique in New York, where his salary neared $4,000 weekly. After his first year as a professional in show business, Zero was performing in topflight nightclubs all over the country, entertaining on the radio, and earning close to $5,000 per week. And he remained loyal to Café Society, where he returned whenever his schedule allowed. Even in the late 1940s, he was still a regular performer at Barney Josephson's clubs.

Zero also occasionally made unscheduled—and unpaid—visits to a Broadway play called *Café Crown*, which opened in January 1942, and in which his friend Sam Jaffe was appearing. The café of the title was based on the Café Royale, a gathering place for Yiddish actors at Second Avenue and Twelfth Street, opposite the Yiddish Art Theatre. At the Café Royale, the actors and their friends would eat, drink, relax, and often play a game of cards. It was only to be expected that *Café Crown* would feature a card game in one of its scenes. What was unexpected was that Zero Mostel would often walk over to the theatre between his nightclub performances, stroll on to the stage and take a seat on the set. Not only would he play cards with the actors, he would insert outrageous ad libs into the otherwise scripted scene, wander about the stage as the spirit moved him and generally wreak havoc. On one occasion, Mostel encouraged his friend, the actor Philip Loeb, to accompany him to the nightly card game at *Café Crown*. Mostel and Loeb walked onstage together holding newspapers in front of their faces. When they lowered the papers, they were seen to be wearing the beards and earlocks of Hasidic Jews; understandably, the other actors broke up. One might think that the management of *Café Crown* would have posted guards to keep Mostel offstage, but they evidently felt that Zero was the most entertaining feature of an otherwise undistinguished comedy, so he was allowed to drop in whenever he wished.

*　　*　　*

Zero's performance style, complete with improvisational trimmings, may have been influenced by the Yiddish theatre. Although the organized Yiddish theatre was a relatively new phenomenon, having begun with the plays and productions of Abraham Goldfadn in Rumania in 1876 and having been introduced to the United States in 1882, it was already a thriving institution among Yiddish-speaking audiences in New York when Sammy Mostel was growing up on the Lower East Side in the 1920s and 1930s.

Mostel certainly saw Yiddish plays on Second Avenue. "The first time I saw [*King Lear*] was in Yiddish played by [Boris] Thomashefsky," he said. And, according to Mostel's brother Aaron, he performed in some Yiddish theatre productions as a supernumerary when he was a boy. "Sometimes we'd appear as extras in the Second Avenue houses for a dollar or two," Aaron said. "But it wasn't the money. We did it because we liked it."

Yiddish theatre was perhaps best known for its aggressive, larger-than-life, highly energetic performance style, the actors seemingly throbbing with emotion; passionate outbursts were frequently intermingled (or alternated) with songs, dances, and jokes that seemed to exist for their own sake rather than emanating from the dramatic material. In other words, a performance in the Yiddish theatre often resembled a vaudeville show whose separate components were bound together only by a loose strand of plot. Melodrama, tragedy, farce, musical numbers, expressions of lamentation and joy, all were likely to be intertwined in a single play.

The great actors of the Yiddish theatre—Boris Thomashefsky, David Kessler, Jacob P. Adler, Maurice Schwartz, et al.—generally performed in a style far removed from the understated, subtle methods pioneered by Stanislavski in Russia in the late 1890s and largely adopted by American actors in mainstream entertainment (although the Yiddish performers were capable of delicate expressions of feeling when the occasion called for it). For the most part, Yiddish actors took for granted their audience's desire for extravagant, joyous, lavishly decorated performances—even in somber tragedies.

Improvisation was also integral to the Yiddish theatre; often, it was a necessity. Most productions were given few rehearsals and the actors were hard-pressed to memorize their lines. Therefore, it was vital that an actor have the ability to improvise at those inevitable moments when his memory failed him and he was unable to speak the words of the playwright. Moreover, the richness of the actor's imagination, as demonstrated in his or her flights of improvisation, was fully appreciated by the spectators.

The atmosphere within the Yiddish theatre was unique, quite unlike the staid environment of mainstream American theatre. As historian Nahma Sandrow has written, "From the beginning audiences were passionately responsive to what went on onstage. . . . When the show displeased the audience, they were ready to yell comments and hiss . . . if they were bored they yelled, 'Get the hook!' which they had learned from American vaudeville. When the show pleased them they showed their pleasure lavishly. They might wait outside the stage door to carry an actor on their shoulders through the city streets."

Those actors who succeeded in the Yiddish theatre necessarily met the audience on its own terms; that is, with the extravagance the occasion demanded. Irving Howe said,

> Almost all the early Yiddish actors shared the view that man had been given a voice to shout, curse, whisper, weep. . . . Life on stage should be grander than on the street . . . what counted in Yiddish theatre, as it counted in Italian opera, was the sheer display of virtuosity, a talent driving past its material in order to declare itself all the more vigorously. Hit the high C no matter what happens to the plot of the opera. . . . What counted, as perhaps it always must in popular art, was the exuberance of the occasion, available every evening as cast and audience joined in a magical interchange of pleasure. . . . The leading Yiddish actors tended to be men of vitality and heft, accustomed to filling the spaces of the stage.

In describing the Yiddish theatre briefly, one must be careful not to suggest that its actors were incapable of discipline or subtlety. Indeed, New York's Yiddish theatre—the most prominent in the world in the 1930s—was dominated by actors and playwrights who wished to reform the style that had prevailed in the past and establish a more unified tone, less subject to sudden swings of mood, less given to bursts of improvisation. Still, it is fair to say that Yiddish-speaking audiences generally favored a broader, freer style than was the norm in mainstream American theatres, and that most successful Yiddish actors gave the audiences what they wanted. Moreover, Yiddish actors at their best were intensely exciting. Many non-Yiddish-speaking observers were deeply moved by the performances they saw but could not understand, as was James Agate, the British dramatic critic, who, after seeing a production of Maurice Schwartz's company, observed, "The performances by these Yiddish players contain more great acting than I have ever seen on any stage in any place."

Howe's description of "leading Yiddish actors" as "men of vitality and heft, accustomed to filling the spaces of the stage" also describes Zero Mostel. It is not inconceivable that Zero, having seen many productions of the Yiddish theatre, and—according to his brother—having participated in some of them, patterned his own style after the Yiddish actors with whom he was familiar.

Zero's son Josh and many—although by no means all—of his friends doubt that he was influenced by his experiences as a participant or spectator in the Yiddish theatre; they believe that his performance style was uniquely his own. One can agree with their assessment of Zero as an original in his choice of items to ridicule and people to imitate—and yet it is difficult to ignore the similarities between his style and that of many Yiddish theatre performers.

One of the finest Yiddish entertainers of the early twentieth century in New York was a comic named Sigmund Mogulesko, whose performance style, as described by Nahma Sandrow, sounds similar to Zero Mostel's. Sandrow wrote, "Mogulesko's presence could make a play, his winks and nuances could make a song. He was gifted musically. . . . He seems to have had an unusually flexible range, from sensitive character portrayal to nimble—often obscene—improvisation . . . he was not above . . . ad-libbing so as to confuse an actor he didn't like." Did Zero see Mogulesko perform, and might he have been influenced by him? There is no evidence either way. But if he did not see Mogulesko, he almost certainly saw Ludwig Satz and Menasha Skulnik, Yiddish clowns who were successors of Mogulesko's. He may even have shared the stage with them.

Over the years, Mostel maintained his interest in the Yiddish theatre, attending meetings of the Yiddish Theatrical Alliance in the 1960s and 1970s—and receiving an award from the Alliance as the "outstanding actor" of 1964 for his performance in *Fiddler on the Roof*. In a documentary made for television in 1973 that traced the history of Jews in America, Mostel narrated the section devoted to the Yiddish theatre.

Zero's friend Sol Kaplan recalled an occasion when Zero was playing at the Concord Hotel in the Catskills. "He found an elderly Jewish actor from the Yiddish theatre [in the audience] and he called him up on the stage and the two of them improvised brilliantly. It was just unbelievable. And the audience stood up to cheer; there was no stopping them."

*   *   *

Zero's guest appearances on *The Chamber Music Society of Lower Basin Street* brought him national attention for the first time. Several executives of the Blue Network had seen him perform at Café Society and immediately signed him to a radio contract. The format of *Lower Basin Street* was made to order for Mostel's brand of humor, and he didn't waste the opportunity to make a favorable impression on a nationwide audience. Indeed, the opportunity was a promising one: several performers who began with the program as unknowns went on to stardom, Dinah Shore among them. The show provided the same impetus for Zero's career. As a result of his success on the program, he was selected as the "Number One New Star of 1943" by more than six hundred editors of radio columns in American newspapers and magazines.

Although Mostel was physically and emotionally capable of keeping up the pace of his continually accelerating career, he was running out of material. One weekend, however, he stayed with friends who introduced him to another of their guests: Joseph Stein, then a psychiatric caseworker with ambitions to break into show business as a comic writer. Stein offered to write a sketch on speculation for Zero. Mostel liked it and bought it for use on *Lower Basin Street*. Stein continued to write Zero's material for the program for the remainder of the season.

Stein and Mostel did not work together again until the 1960s, when Zero appeared in *Fiddler on the Roof*, for which Stein wrote the book. But they almost collaborated on another radio show immediately after *Lower Basin Street*. As Stein tells it, "Some months later I was still working at my regular nine to five job. I was called by the William Morris Agency and they asked me if I would be willing to work on a half-hour pilot for a radio program for Zero. They asked if I wanted to work with somebody else, and I said, 'Sure,' and I met with the other writer; it was a fellow named Alan Jay Lerner [who later wrote

My Fair Lady, Brigadoon, and several other successful Broadway musicals]. And Alan and I did a half hour pilot for Zero, which I think was called the *Zero Mostel Hour*." The Blue Network announced that the program would premiere in September of 1942. But, as Stein said, "it never saw the light of day. Maybe it wasn't good enough."

Keep 'Em Laughing, Zero's Broadway debut, was performed concurrently with his appearances on *The Chamber Music Society of Lower Basin Street*—a considerable feat, for the stage show at the Forty-fourth Street Theatre was given twice daily with three performances on Saturdays and Sundays. Incredibly, Zero also continued to play the late shows at Café Society while performing on Broadway and on the radio. In addition to Zero, *Keep 'Em Laughing* featured Paul and Grace Hartman, Victor Moore and William Gaxton, Hildegarde, Jack Cole and his dancers. *Keep 'Em Laughing* was no more than a variety show, but one that had considerable appeal. Brooks Atkinson said in the New York *Times* that it was "overflowing with hilarity," thanks in part to Zero's "messy drolleries." Atkinson described Mostel as "a roly-poly zany with a voice that rattles in the cellar, eyes that cross and a face that gets foolishly distorted when he is making a political speech. For a first appearance in a large theatre he is doing remarkably well." George Freedley, writing in the *Morning Telegraph*, was even more enthusiastic. "He seems to be a first-class comic and a welcome addition to the top-flight buffoons. . . . He works hard and perspires both profusely and humorously. Mostel is a real find." Freedley commented that much of the audience had been drawn to the theatre particularly in order to see Zero, "whose night club clowning has become a Broadway legend." If the claim that Mostel's rise to the top of the show business ladder was the fastest in history seemed to be exaggerated, this statement would appear to confirm it. Zero had first opened at Café Society on February 16, 1942; Freedley's column was written on April 27. To become "a Broadway legend" after little more than two months as a professional entertainer must be something of a record.

Zero's first Broadway appearance brought him nearly universal acclaim, although some critics had reservations. Richard Watts, Jr., said, "I suspect that he still has quite a bit to learn about being funny," and Richard Lockridge praised with faint damns when he said, "You can find many pleasant things if you pick and choose," but, all in all, *Keep*

'Em Laughing was a triumph for a comic who had been completely unknown less than three months before.

Top-Notchers, which opened immediately after *Keep 'Em Laughing* closed, was an extension of that production, produced at the same theatre. Gracie Fields, who received top billing, was new to the cast, but most of the others, including Zero and the Hartmans, were hold-overs, using new material. Again, as with the earlier show, there were two performances daily, but this time a third was added only on Sundays, rather than on both days of the weekend.

Zero's engagement at the Paramount Theatre, where he was billed as "Broadway's Newest Comedy Sensation!," lasted from July 21 until August 4. The stage show, which also featured Ann Miller and Phil Harris and his band, was supplemented by an obscure wartime movie, *Priorities on Parade*. But the last night of Zero's run was also the world premiere of Irving Berlin's *Holiday Inn*. On that gala occasion, Berlin himself joined the stage show, as did Connee Boswell, Carol Bruce, Xavier Cugat and his band, Skinnay Ennis and his band, Alice Faye, Benny Goodman and his band, Betty Hutton, Jan Peerce, Marjorie Reynolds, and Phil Spitalny and his "Hour of Charm Choir." Movie-goers at the Paramount in 1942 certainly got their money's worth.

When Zero went to Hollywood to make *Du Barry Was a Lady*, he signed a long-term contract. The expectation was that he would appear in a series of films for MGM, but the studio released him from his contract after only the one movie, probably because Mostel's predilection for becoming involved in social causes gave the executives second thoughts. While he was making *Du Barry Was a Lady*, MGM was also filming *Tennessee Johnson*, a picture about President Andrew Johnson. The purpose of the filmmakers was to pay tribute to Johnson (who succeeded Abraham Lincoln and, in his efforts to rebuild the Union, became the only American president ever to be impeached) as a deeply principled, misunderstood man, maligned by history. In creating this portrait, the producers placed Johnson's opponent, Thaddeus Stevens, in an unsympathetic light.

After the filming of *Tennessee Johnson* was completed but before it was released, an angry group of MGM employees—of which Zero was one—petitioned to have the picture withheld from distribution. They argued that Andrew Johnson had been a reactionary who favored the return of slavery; and that Thaddeus Stevens was the truly heroic figure of the period because he had stood for civil rights and against the president's efforts. They claimed that the film was a distortion of history. The picture was "less liberal-minded than it should be," Zero said. MGM eventually conceded that the film's portrayal of Stevens was too harsh and agreed to reshoot some scenes. That did not satisfy the protesters, however, who continued to agitate for the film's suppression.

When *Tennessee Johnson* was released, many people found it difficult to understand what all the controversy had been about. Bosley Crowther wrote in the New York *Times* that the film "may not be inspired drama [but] all allegations aside [it was] a thoroughly guileless and uncommonly sincere attempt to tell the story of Andrew Johnson." However, MGM did not forgive Mostel for having sided with the protesters, and canceled his contract.

In *Du Barry Was a Lady*, the studio also revenged itself upon Mostel by cutting nearly all his scenes. In the version of the film (starring Gene Kelly, Lucille Ball, and Red Skelton, with music and lyrics by Cole Porter) shown to the public, Zero was ostensibly playing the dual roles of Taliostro and Rami the Swami; in fact, he did little more than perform a portion of his nightclub act, which had no relation whatever to the rest of the picture. MGM's clumsy editing effectively sabotaged Mostel's career as a film actor; it would be eight years before he appeared on the screen again. *Time* magazine commented that Zero's routine "seems to need an intimate audience." Mostel took the advice, returning to New York and his high-paying engagement at La Martinique, where he reinforced his reputation as "just about the funniest American now living," as *Life* magazine described him in 1943.

Then, as suddenly as his star had risen, with his salary rocketing from $23.86 to $5,000 per week, his career came to a sudden (but temporary) halt. In March of 1943, he was drafted by the Army and his salary was reduced to that of any other private: $21 monthly.

Zero's length of service and his duties as a private are something of a mystery—even to the members of his family. His brother Aaron said that Zero was a military policeman whose job was to bring prisoners of war from Europe to America, and that he continued to serve for three years. Aaron recalls that Zero "used to come to New York. He'd come in to the house, we lived in the Bronx, and he would eat like there's no tomorrow. He used to say that the people who guarded the German prisoners were given sandwiches and coffee, but that the German prisoners ate three meals a day." On the other hand, his son Josh believes that Zero spent all of his time in the army entertaining the troops and a clipping from a New York newspaper of April 30, 1943, seems to support this view. The paper says, "Pvt. Zero Mostel tonight received a Page One Award from the Newspaper Guild of New York for using laughter as a weapon in this war." A comment from Mostel's roommate at Camp Croft in South Carolina, where both men were stationed during and after basic training in 1943, also suggests that Mostel was more active as an entertainer than in any other capacity. The roommate said that Zero spent "a good bit of time at the U.S.O. giving free entertainment."

Mostel's press agent, Ivan Black, was not specific about Zero's duties, but asserted that the comedian remained in the army until 1945: a total of two years. In a 1961 interview, Zero himself claimed that he had served in the infantry; but if he did, no one else knew about it. The record shows, however, that he did complete basic infantry training at Camp Croft. What can also be verified from his army files is that Zero applied to be an entertainment director overseas for Special Services. That request prompted the chief of the Special Services Branch to ask the army to investigate Mostel's background. For a time the army kept close watch over the mail Zero received and sent out, noting the names and addresses of Mostel's correspondents. Army investigators also questioned several soldiers in Mostel's company to see if—as they seemed to believe even before they asked the questions—he was spreading Communist propaganda. Although they were told in every case that he wasn't (one soldier said, as reported in the army's typical bureaucratese, "that he has never heard Subject make any disloyal statements and considers Subject to be a loyal American"), the files they collected on him indicate that they remained convinced he was a member of the Communist party, and that—when he performed his Senator Pellagra sketch on *The Chamber Music Society of Lower Basin Street*—he had taken "advantage of his position [as an entertainer] to inject politics into his broadcast . . . with an idea of ridiculing isolationist senators." This, they claimed in a separate report, represented "a deprecation of American democratic principles," and—in yet a further report—alleged that the sketch was "an attempt on the part of the Subject to place Congress and the American System in an absurd and comical light."

In one of the interviews the army conducted with a civilian, they were told what they evidently wanted to hear: "Informant believed Subject to be an extreme Leftist, and in his opinion, Subject was attempting to bore from within through comedy, a form of the usual Communist technique."

During his tenure in the service, Zero never behaved in a way the army could find objectionable; indeed, his conduct while in the army was all but irreproachable. A report undertaken by the Military Intelligence Division of the War Department in June 1943 offered this summary of his behavior while in the army: "Good soldier; well educated, intelligent, independent . . . apt and willing soldier, gets along well . . . does his part without complaint . . . good man, never complains, very popular." The only negative aspects of the report consisted of the allegations that Mostel was "quick tempered," "in arrears on payment of separation allowance to his wife," and "lacking in military courtesy, probably because he [is] a natural comedian."

Despite the generally favorable summation of Zero's attitude, the army refused to alter its belief that he was a dangerous radical. A report issued from Camp Upton (where Zero was inducted) to the Post Intelligence Officer at Camp Croft said, "Subject was under surveillance while at this station and no evidence of Communistic activity developed; although he definitely is a Communist." The army thus determined that Zero was "not qualified" to be an entertainment director and rejected his plea to be transferred to Special Services.

Interestingly, Mostel was aware of the army's investigation. On a visit to Washington during a furlough in June 1943 he went directly to the Special Services Division, requesting a transfer to an overseas entertainment unit. He was told, in the words of Camp Croft's Post Intelligence Officer (in a confidential memo to the Officer in Charge), "that a possible overseas assignment would be held up because Subject was under suspicion as a radical." The Intelligence Officer went on to say that he was puzzled who would have given Mostel this information but that Zero would not reveal his source.

Why Mostel was discharged from the army is also in dispute. Perhaps it was because he had developed colitis (his brother's version) or an ulcer (as Kate said); or—as Zero himself suspected, with good reason judging by recently obtained documents—the army was convinced that he was a subversive.

The army itself officially stated that Mostel was honorably discharged for an unspecified physical disability. However, given the fact that the file they compiled on his alleged Communist political activities consists of more than one hundred pages, and that it was included in a folder entitled "Military Personnel Suspected of Disloyalty or Subversive Activity," one can easily draw the conclusion that the unofficial reason for Zero's discharge was based on their dislike of his politics. In any case, the army's record clears up any confusion concerning his length of service: he was released on August 12, 1943, having served for less than six months.

In September, no longer a member of the armed forces, Zero finally managed to accomplish what the army prevented him from doing while he was a member of the service: he went overseas for the U.S.O. to perform his comic routines for American troops.

3

A Man of Many Parts

As the army repeatedly observed, although Zero had come to be looked upon as a zany, he was, in fact, a man of many parts, one of which was political. As a Jewish son of immigrant parents growing up in New York, it would have been impossible for him to escape the impact of the Jewish Socialists, known as the Bund, activists who dominated political thought on the East Side for many years. Irving Howe described their influence in his book *World of Our Fathers*:

> Intense and excitable, with a loftiness of spirit that even its opponents envied, the Jewish Socialist milieu gave people a sense of home and of mission. Spurred by the example of their parents or by the eloquence of orators . . . , young sons and daughters of the immigrants would turn "naturally" to the idea of socialism; it became their initiation into the world, for a few the belief to which they would pledge their lives and for most a first inoculating touch of idealism before passing on to other, worldlier affairs.

The Russian Revolution of 1917 was of special significance to immigrant Jews in America, who hoped and believed that the Bolsheviks would put an end to the pogroms in Russia and that a new spirit of tolerance would spread throughout Europe. Israel and Celia Mostel, who are remembered by their children as liberal and politically active, would have had strong feelings about the Soviet Union and would have been knowledgeable about the Bund, although Aaron Mostel recalls that his father was "not a Socialist, but a registered Democrat, and a member of the local committee up to the time he died." Aaron believes, however, that his brother Zero was a committed Socialist. Politics, especially the politics of liberalism and socialism, would have been discussed frequently at the Mostels' dinner table, and Zero, along with the other children, would have been affected by it. Being a reader of Yiddish, he would also have been aware of the *Freiheit*, the influential Yiddish Communist newspaper that began operation in 1922 and was sold widely throughout the East Side.

Jewish culture in general tends to be sympathetic to liberal social thought. It is no accident, for example, that *Awake and Sing*, one of the finest American social plays (and a play that presents an impassioned argument in favor of communism) was written by Clifford Odets, a Jew. As Sarah Blecher Cohen pointed out, the author's—and the characters'—desire in *Awake and Sing* "to better society at large is clearly Marx-inspired, but it can also be traced to the universalist concerns of Judaism, for the title Odets chose is taken from Isaiah 26:19, which prophesies the resurrection of all peoples: 'Awake and sing, ye that dwell in dust . . .' Thus the Jewish prophetic tradition as well as Marxism were responsible for Odets's commitment to social reform in the theatre." These same forces operated on all Jews who were aware of their heritage. As the son of devoutly Orthodox Jews, Zero certainly was acquainted with Biblical teaching. And he "had certain beginnings and origins during the Depression which he remained faithful and true to politically because they had meant a lot to him," said his friend, Frances Chaney.

Mostel's political thought would have been further developed at the City College of New York, where the Young Communist League, composed primarily of Jewish students, was a powerful influence. Perhaps he took no part in Communist activities, but Dun Roman, his schoolmate at CCNY, confirms that there "was a strong politically liberal inclination even then, not at all uncommon in those times, and at that college particularly, but stronger in [Zero] than in most." John Randolph, another classmate at CCNY, also recalls Zero as a political activist. Thus, even in the 1930s, along with other young artists and intellectuals, Mostel took public stands against authoritarianism and social injustice.

In the America of the 1980s, it has become fashionable in many circles to be nonpolitical. In the 1930s, however, the opposite was true. It could hardly have been otherwise in a country mired in a devastating Depression. Many Americans of the thirties believed that the social and economic systems had failed. The passionate drive of many, therefore, was to participate in the restructuring of American society, and in the process to expunge the most glaring social inequities. To be nonpolitical in the 1930s was an anomaly in many circles; to Americans who had social consciences, those who were *not* politically minded were considered frivolous and irresponsible. Moreover, political debate, although often heated, was more commodious fifty years ago; all points of view were represented and openly expressed. Jack Gilford, like Zero Mostel a young performer whose career was beginning in the thirties, put it well when he said, "We were all political, and we [his friends] were all left. But as anybody from that period will tell you, being left was no crime—not until [Joseph] McCarthy showed up and put fear into everybody's hearts and lives."

It is probable that many artists gave little thought to any consequences that might result from their political activities, unaware that taking controversial social stands might have unforeseen and undesirable repercussions. As one journalist remarked, the scandal sheets of the 1950s that purported to reveal the Communist affiliations of artists twenty years earlier were really citing the most gregarious people in their field—those who tended to be joiners—rather than listing committed Communists.

Writer Ring Lardner, Jr., a former Communist and a close friend of Zero's, was uncertain whether or not Mostel had ever joined the Party, but suspected that he had. "I think Zero believed pretty strongly in Marxism and he was fairly knowledgeable about it theoretically. He had read a good deal of Marx," Lardner said. "I have a strong impression that he had joined the Party at some time, I think when he was in the Artist's Project or in the early forties." A prominent comic, who first knew Zero in the 1940s, was more certain: "Sure," he said. "Zero was a Red and everybody knew it."

The Office of the Provost Marshal General of the War Department certainly believed that he was. A report prepared by that office in April 1943 states, "Information has been received from a reliable government agency [probably the FBI] which indicates that one 'Zero' Mostel, New York City, a nationally known comedian, is a member of the Communist Party. . . . In Communist Party circles, there is frequent mention of the 10% of his income that he must pay to the Party as dues." In June of the same year the Military Intelligence Division of the War Department stated that Mostel "was reliably reported" to have been a Communist. The army cited a number of specific activities that they considered evidence of Zero's communism: entertaining on behalf of the *New Masses* magazine; exhibiting paintings "in conjunction with a conference of the radical organization known as the Artists League of America"; speaking at a meeting favoring Russian War Relief; performing at Café Society, which the army categorically branded as "a Communist-owned and operated night club"; entertaining for the Veterans of the Abraham Lincoln Brigade supporting the Spanish Loyalist cause; and similar activities. Furthermore, the reports claimed that Zero's various performances were looked upon with favor by the Communist newspaper the *Daily Worker* and noted that he had been "one of many Communists who signed the protest against the release of [the MGM film] *Tennessee Johnson*." The reports further noted that he belonged to such allegedly subversive labor unions as the American Guild of Variety Artists, the Amalgamated Clothing Workers of America, the International Longshoremen's Association, the International Ladies Garment Workers Union, and the WPA Teachers' Union.

But in the 1960s, Howard Rodney, who was Zero's dresser in *Fiddler on the Roof*, asked him directly, "Were you ever a Communist?" Rodney recalled that Mostel answered with equal forthrightness: "No. When I first joined SAG [Screen Actors Guild] and AFRA [American Federation of Radio Artists], anyone who asked for more money or complained about working conditions was called a Communist, and that's how the label got stuck on me." Burgess Meredith was emphatic: "I don't believe he was ever a member of the [Communist] party. I'm sure he wasn't. I think he was just a radical-minded fellow, and he liked to swim in those waters."

If Zero did join the Communist party when he was in his twenties, as a considerable number of artists and idealists did in New York in the 1930s, he would have done so because he wished to be part of a movement that would move the world toward freedom and equality. The "Popular Front" policy of the Soviet Communist party, announced in 1935, called for Communists, Socialists, democrats, and other progressive forces to stand together against Fascists and other social reactionaries—a policy that seemed to many both virtuous and honorable.

As Eugene Lyons wrote, many idealists joined the Communist party in the 1930s because they were "genuinely angry at Nazis and genuinely concerned for Spanish democracy, Spain's orphans, Chinese freedom and sharecroppers. They had not the remotest idea of what communism was in terms of economic structures or political superstates. For nearly all of them, it was an intoxicated state of mind, a glow of inner virtue, and a sort of comradeship in super-charity." Indeed, for many idealists, the choice seemed to be between communism on the far left and fascism on the far right, and given the choice, they unhesitatingly chose communism. It is also important to recognize that the Communist party's avowed aim after 1934 did *not* include the revolutionary overthrow of the American government.

Many Americans became disillusioned with the Communists when the party line shifted and Stalin and Hitler signed a nonaggression pact in 1939. Some Party followers maintained their membership because they could not bring themselves to believe that the alliance was genuine. Surely the Communists must have had a trick up their sleeves, they felt. But many dropped their membership as soon as communism became allied with nazism.

During the years in which the United States was involved in World War II, the Communist party line changed once again. For some, the shift repaired the damage that had been done in 1939. Beginning in June 1941, the Soviet government urged the formation of a "Second Front" in Europe, supporting an American-British-Soviet coalition against the Fascist powers. Zero Mostel approved of this policy; he took pride in saying, "I was the first radio comic to demand a second front." As John Cogley, the former editor of *Commonweal* and the author of a study of blacklisting has noted, "The Communist Political Association (wartime name for the Party) became an attractive outlet for the liberals' stirring hopes for the postwar world. As an ally, the

Soviet Union—whose resistance won general admiration—came to be endowed, even in conservative circles, with enormous virtues. Intellectually, socially and politically, it was highly acceptable to be pro-Soviet from 1941 to '45."

Whether or not Zero ever joined the Communist party, he made his progressive inclinations known to all during the war years. It was characteristic of Mostel throughout his life to assert his opinions loudly and vigorously. As Karl Malden said of him, "He had a viewpoint about everything and it was a strong viewpoint. And you could disagree or agree, but it was a strong viewpoint." However, different individuals perceived the strength and legitimacy of Mostel's commitment to left-wing causes differently.

Some who knew him thought that he became involved with liberal issues primarily as a social activity: because he was eager to be a part of his friends' milieu. Lou Peterson, an actor who became friendly with Zero during the 1940s, was one. He doubted that Mostel was a committed social activist. "I was married to a white girl," Peterson, who is black, told me; "and when we came to New York there was a great deal of proselytizing in an effort to have us join various causes, including Communist causes." Mostel, however, was not one of those who attempted to persuade Peterson to join the Communists or any other political organization. "I think he was involved in politics only because most of his friends were politically active," Peterson said.

On the other hand, Zero's friend Madeline Gilford disputed this view. She spoke of Mostel as "serious, very bright, and a very good [political] theorist. He was not just somebody who says, 'I believe in peace and democracy.' He really had some fine, sophisticated political understanding of class structure, and why he believed in socialism, and what he felt that capitalism did or didn't do for the arts."

Zero was certainly active in the political arena throughout the 1940s. He was one of the first stand-up comics to bring a distinct social slant to his routines. "I always did a lot of political stuff in my nightclub performances," he said; "I used to knock Hitler and Mussolini and all the things that humor should attack." He also performed enthusiastically and often for various social causes, giving benefits for the Joint Anti-Fascist Refugee Committee, United China Relief, and the Trade Union Division of Russian War Relief. Many of these performances

were cited years later in an attempt to prove that Mostel was a subversive. It should be noted, however, that he gave hundreds of benefit
performances in the forties, many of them for such nonpolitical and
noncontroversial organizations as the Police Athletic League, the Committee for the Care of Young Children in Wartime, the Stage Door
Canteen, the Free Venereal Clinic Fund of the Community Hospital
in New York, the Guild for the Jewish Blind, the Armed Forces Radio
Service, the National Foundation for Infantile Paralysis, the AAF Con-
valescent Center, and the Israel Orphan Asylum; he received a letter
from the captain of the U.S. Naval Hospital at St. Albans, New York,
thanking him for a performance "that not only entertained the men,
but also raised their spirits immeasurably." The public relations officer
of the New York State Guard thanked him for participating in a radio
broadcast to raise money for the Guard; his letter concluded, "Please
accept my very deep appreciation for your generosity and patriotism
in this work." Still another letter, this one from the War Finance Committee of the Treasury Department in February 1944, echoed those
sentiments: "We have been told by various people that have been guests
of your club [at La Martinique, where Zero was then playing] about
the wonderful appeal you are making for the 4th War Loan Drive."
When one looks at the complete list of benefits at which Mostel performed, the impression is one of political impartiality—or perhaps of
a man who was eager to please, had a difficult time saying no, and
accepted nearly every request to give of his time and energy.*

---

*However, in 1942, Zero failed to keep a benefit engagement for the Industrial
Workers Order, Lodge Number 620, for which he was berated in an angry letter. The
lodge had asked him to appear at a party to raise money "for the boys in camp" and
"to assure your being present we sent you a deposit of $2.50 (we have the money
order receipt for same) and we were assured that you would be with us without fail.
Publicity was sent out, tickets sold, and a crowd gathered eagerly awaiting your presence. You never came. Since that time we have written you and have called you . . .
but with no results. We feel that you owe us an apology, besides the $2.50 we advanced
to you and any money you would like to donate to this cause which you greatly
mistreated and to which you caused great inconvenience and embarrassment." Zero
was clearly thoughtless in this instance. Given all the other benefit performances at
which he did appear, however, it would seem unfair to accuse him of neglecting his
duty. In all probability, his failure to notify the lodge that he would not appear can
be attributed to his lack of decisiveness. Throughout his life, Zero avoided confron-
tations, and this seems to have been an occasion when, rather than simply saying no,

Still, there can be no question that Zero's politics were progressive. "He was a backer of the Spanish Civil War," John Randolph recalled, adding, "I don't think there was anything [concerning left-wing politics] that he didn't help participate in raising money for."*

In 1948, Zero became more directly involved in politics, campaigning for Henry Wallace for president. At Wallace rallies he sang a song called "Who's Going to Investigate the Man Who Investigates the Man Who Investigates Me?" It was to be the only time he would actively participate in a political campaign, perhaps because the mechanics of politics conflicted too harshly with the ideal. Zero recalled, "I remember one night when [Wallace] was feeling hopeful and we were sitting around talking about the future and he asked some of us what we wanted when he became President. Paul Robeson wanted to be ambassador to Moscow. 'What do you you want, Zero?' Wallace finally asked me. 'I want a part in a play,'" Zero answered.

Political statements can also be made obliquely. Such was the case when Zero was filming *Panic in the Streets* in New Orleans in 1950. He discovered that the set, as well as the city, was segregated. He demonstrated his resentment at having to work under such conditions as well as his contempt for segregation with an elaborate pantomime, performed while a large group of people watched. Passing up the drinking fountain from which a sign labeled "White" was hung, he drank deeply from the "Colored" fountain, following which he licked his lips vigorously, the look on his face conveying pure ecstasy. Then he drank from the "White" fountain; the taste of that water produced the most acute nausea, judging from Zero's look of revulsion. Finally, after looking quizzically at each fountain in turn, he elaborately switched the signs.

---

he accepted the engagement and could not bring himself to cancel it. By not showing up, he made the situation worse, of course, but he probably gave no thought to that until he received the reprimand. Until then, he would have justified his lack of decisiveness by reasoning, "If I say no, they'll be angry with me. So I won't say no and then everyone will be happy."

*As early as August 1942, an entry in Mostel's Federal Bureau of Investigation file claimed that he was "reliably reported to be a member of the Communist Party." However, the FBI's source for the allegation is not cited. Later entries indicate that the Bureau accepted the innuendo of right-wing newspaper columnists as "evidence" of Communist activities.

*   *   *

Kathryn Cecilia Harkin's parents ran a boardinghouse in Philadelphia, whose tenants included the members of Fred Waring's Pennsylvania Orchestra. They were in the first show Kate ever saw, *Hello, Yourself*, an experience that left her permanently stage-struck. When she was eight or nine years old, she began performing with a group of four other little girls. They called themselves "Broadway Varieties" and played four shows a day at movie houses around Philadelphia on the weekends. The act lasted for a year. Kate also attended Catherine Littlefield's dancing classes and—when her father died and the family needed additional income—began working regularly as a dancer at the age of twelve. Shortly before her high school graduation, her dancing teacher organized a ballet company, inviting Kate to become a member. She received more money than she had thought possible: $8 per performance. The Littlefield Ballet was astonishingly successful. They grew from fourteen members to sixty; they played at the Paris Exhibition and the Champs Elysées Théâtre, in 1936, performed in Deauville, London, and Brussels. By the time Kate was eighteen, the ballet was regularly employed as the resident dance company at the Chicago Civic Opera.

Kate's theatrical enthusiasms were less classical, however. As a teenager, and later as an adult, she preferred the showier, more popular forms of musical entertainment. She began performing as a chorus member at Chez Paree, Chicago's most prominent nightclub. That served as a springboard for her to dance in various clubs from the Midwest to the East Coast. But Kate, never a solo performer, much less a headliner, found nightclub jobs to be scarce and irregular, so, when she had the opportunity to join the Rockettes at Radio City Music Hall in New York—"the only steady job in show business for a dancer," she called it—she accepted eagerly. The work was tedious and unsatisfying, but it provided a paycheck steady enough and large enough for Kate to support herself and send money to her mother in Philadelphia.

On the night at Café Society Uptown in 1942 that Zero met Kate, then twenty-three years old, he walked her home and made a date for the following night. Not uncharacteristically, he promptly forgot all about it; but he called the next day to apologize and ask her out again. This time, he remembered the arrangement and took her to dinner.

She expected Zero's conversation to be that of the typical nightclub comics she had known: limited to show business news and gossip. But he spoke to her about politics, art, and literature. Nothing could have been more impressive to "a culture vulture [who] had a big inferiority complex about people who had gone to college," as Kate described herself. Zero also told her he had been born in Italy and several other inventions, many of them romantic. She fell for him immediately.

"Zero was only twenty-seven when I met him, but he was a man," Kate said. "All the other guys I went out with were boys, interested in sports, popular songs, me or other boys. Never once had a political discussion crossed their lips." More than anything else, Zero's understanding of politics impressed Kate. That knowledge, combined with his intelligence, his urbanity, and his zany sense of humor, overwhelmed her. "It wasn't until I met Zero that I got sophisticated," she said. "He even used to claim he taught me to read. If Zero provided me with a feeling of security, it was mostly because he was so smart."

Zero was equally smitten. He and Kate saw as much of one another as possible; and when he went to California to make *Du Barry Was a Lady*, she visited him there. He may have wondered how this rather naïve Irish Catholic girl would fit into his circle of New York Jewish intellectuals, but when he introduced her to Sam Jaffe and his other close friends, she had no trouble adjusting to them, nor they to her— although one of them told Zero that he shouldn't contemplate marrying Kate unless she was willing to convert to Judaism; but he dismissed the idea. In mid-1944, Zero and Kate decided to get married.

An obvious complication stood in the way of the wedding, however: he was already married. And now that he was a well-known comedian, his first wife had no intention of letting him go unless he agreed to pay dearly for his release. She demanded a large sum of money in exchange for a divorce, and Zero, recently discharged from the army, was unable to raise the sum. One day, as Mostel stood glumly in front of Radio City, Karl Malden, who had met Zero through Sam Jaffe, offered to lend him the money, but Mostel turned him down. Instead, Zero agreed to give Clara a percentage of his earnings for the rest of his life. In return, Clara went to Reno for a quick divorce.*

*For many years, the financial arrangement worked out by Zero and Clara continued

Zero and Kate were married on the morning of July 2, 1944, in the mayor's office at Long Branch, New Jersey, with several of Zero's cronies in attendance. After the wedding breakfast, Zero and his male friends went off to play a game of golf, leaving Kate to herself. If this seems callous treatment of a new bride, it was a preview of the future.

Zero compartmentalized his life, giving some time to his family, some to his performing work, and a great deal to his friends and his art. Nearly every day Zero would paint at his downtown studio, where he would usually have lunch at a nearby delicatessen. He might come home for dinner, but he was just as likely to go to a restaurant for a raucous meal with his friends from Twenty-eighth Street: other painters and sculptors.

Kate said:

> Of course, I knew that Zero had been a painter before he went into show business. I knew that he had a studio . . . where he still painted every day. But I didn't realize that this would go on after we were married. I grew up reading . . . love stories in which when people got married they did nice things together. They went to museums and movies, or they just strolled around New York hand in hand. . . .
>
> I had looked forward to that. But Zero hadn't been reading the same stories. He'd read books in which a man gets married and keeps right on doing what he wants, with the little woman fending for herself.

Zero's Twenty-eighth Street friends were all male; once in a great while a woman would be invited to attend the twice-weekly sessions at the studio when a model came to pose and all of the painters assembled to work on their individual canvases—but Kate was specifically excluded. "If my wife Kate came there, she would be shot on sight," Zero said. A friend of Kate's told me, "She felt left out and she resented it. She resented his spending so much time at the studio and not coming home for dinner and not letting her share in that part of his life. And years later, when he died, it pained her so much that she really hadn't

---

in force; but in the mid-1950s, when Clara needed $20,000, she agreed to forgo any portion of Zero's future earnings if he would immediately provide her with the settlement she wanted. He went to court. The Appellate Division ruled that he should only have to pay $5,268. He did—although raising even this amount forced him into considerable debt during the time when he was on the blacklist—and the matter was ended at last.

learned enough from Zero about his painting and hadn't shared his feelings about his painting."

Kate's exclusion from Zero's involvement with painting was not the only disappointment she had to face, for marrying Zero meant accepting life under his conditions. According to Kate, Zero told none of his New York friends about his marriage for what seemed to her an unreasonable length of time. "Not long after we got back to New York we were sitting in Toots Shor's with Frank Loesser and his wife," Kate wrote, "and Frank, noticing my wedding ring . . . asked Zero, 'Did you finally get married?' Zero said no." Whether this was just Zero's typical buffoonery or indicative of something deeper (a fear, perhaps, that his marriage to Kate would end as his marriage to Clara had ended, with her walking out on him) is open to conjecture.

The marriage also created problems with the mothers of both the bride and the groom. (Kate's and Zero's fathers were both deceased by the time the marriage took place.) Zero's mother, already upset by her son's divorce from Clara, took a strong dislike to Kate, an attitude that remained constant even after Joshua and Tobias, the Mostels' sons, were born (Josh in 1946, Toby in 1948). Neither of the boys ever met their paternal grandmother, who lived until they were adolescents. Zero continued to see his mother periodically after his second marriage, but the children were always excluded from the relationship.

It is worth mentioning that Aaron Mostel, Zero's brother, tells a somewhat different version of this story. According to Aaron, Kate "did not want to be part of the group. You'd try to gather her into the group but she combated it in some way." Aaron insisted that Celia was "not upset [by Zero and Kate's marriage] at all. She figured that was his business."

When another family member was asked how Celia reacted when Zero married Kate, he responded, "It was a very difficult time for everybody, including Zero. Of course there was a great deal of hullaballoo and rancor" concerning the marriage (as well as Zero's divorce from Clara), partly "because that was the first time that someone in the family had married outside the faith. And Kate, of course, resented that—as did Zero. But there was no estrangement from the family. There was never any exclusion of Kate—actually, quite the opposite.

There was just some bad feeling, basically between Celia and Kate."

On at least one occasion, Zero said that he thought it was one of his brothers who had provoked his mother's hostility to Kate. Unfortunately, none of the principals in this relationship—Celia, Kate, or Zero—are living, so the matter cannot be firmly settled.

The nonrelationship between Kate and Celia was nearly paralleled by the situation that existed between Zero and Kate's mother: she and her son-in-law almost never spoke to one another. The specific circumstances, however, were quite different. When Mrs. Harkin first met Zero, she invited him and Kate to dinner. She served creamed beef on toast—and it was her misfortune that Zero, a gargantuan eater who loved Jewish food, detested this particular dish. The evening was a disaster, and Zero never forgot it. He seems to have interpreted Mrs. Harkin's dinner as an act of insensitivity, perhaps even as a sign of hostility. Some time later, after the Mostels' children were born, Mrs. Harkin came to New York to live with her daughter and son-in-law, but another calamitous event occurred. One day, shortly before Christmas, Toby did something to make Mrs. Harkin angry and she said, "Well, I'm not going to give you a Christmas present." Zero was so furious with her for what he took to be a lack of sensitivity that he simply stopped trying to communicate with her. Evidently, she was equally disdainful of Zero, and in Josh Mostel's graphic phrase, returned his "brute hostility." Although she lived with the Mostels for years, she and Zero managed to ignore one another.

Her mother's presence in the household was not much easier for Kate than it was for Zero. Little things annoyed Kate—and became big things. She confided to a friend, for example, that every Christmas she would choose her mother's gift with great care, hoping desperately to please her. But her mother would invariably put the present back in the box, put the box in the closet, and never look at the gift again. Kate also told of sitting at the breakfast table each morning and listening to her mother pad from the bedroom to the kitchen in her carpet slippers, taking precisely the same number of steps every time. Kate realized that it was irrational to become irritated because her mother never varied the number of steps from bedroom to kitchen, but she couldn't help it; clearly, it was only a symptom of a larger problem. The remedy, perhaps, would have been to move Mrs. Harkin elsewhere, but, as a daughter who was genuinely dutiful, Kate could not contemplate that solution.

*　　*　　*

The relationship between Zero and Kate Mostel was composed of love and affection on the one hand and a substantial dose of vitriol on the other. Clearly, both partners needed one another, and each provided the other with warmth and companionship, but the rivalry and the barely concealed hostility of the relationship cannot be ignored either.

Those who believe that Zero and Kate's marriage was essentially a happy and healthy one are clearly in the majority. Burgess Meredith put it this way: Zero "adored" Kate, "with whom he fought most of his adult life. She was the closest and best part of him; and he of her, though their love was often boisterous." Joseph Stein said, "They had a great relationship. They used to scream and yell at each other but they really were extraordinarily fond of each other." Bettye Ackerman described the relationship between Zero and Kate as "stormy and exciting and great fun; part of the fun of the marriage was the stormy fights. They were so dramatic." Jack Gilford added, "Kate was a very good wife and very good for him." Frances Chaney maintained, "For all its trials and tribulations it was a real love story." Kate's close friend Wilma Solomon agreed: "They were essentially very close and needed each other very much. And I think they were crazy about each other. They stayed together because they had something very important for each other." Sol Kaplan, a close friend of the family, summed it up: "They used a lot of four-letter words, but that doesn't mean that the good four-letter word of 'love' wasn't there. It was, enormously."

Mary Yohalem, who was particularly close to the Mostels in the 1950s, said, "They were the most interesting people I ever knew in my life. They were complete originals. There's never been anyone to replace either one of them. They were both feisty, they fought, they yelled, they were selfish. But they were also generous. They were big, big people. They were always angry at each other. But it wasn't a sullen thing. They fought the way children fight—loud, but not sulky. And they loved each other."

If there was one predominant quality that saw them through their battles and kept them together, it was their sense of humor. Once, early in their married life, Kate and Zero decided to separate. As Kate lay in bed, staring at the wall, she heard the thundering sounds of packing behind her. At last the sounds stopped and Zero said, "Aren't you going to turn around and say good-bye?" She did; but when she saw her husband dressed only in a hat, shoes and socks, and carrying a suitcase, she couldn't resist laughing and welcoming him back to bed. "How can you leave a guy like that?" she asked.

Zero knew that he wasn't an easy man to live with. In 1964, he said about Kate, "Twenty years with me, she should get the Medal of Honor."

When Kate went to work to help support the family during the blacklist, Zero wasn't particularly happy. His view of marriage was entirely conventional: the husband worked, the wife remained at home taking care of the children and seeing to it that the husband's needs were met. One of the problems Kate had with this arrangement, however, was that she had no fondness for domesticity. A cook was hired to prepare the meals, and once Josh and Toby were old enough to look after themselves, Kate was often at loose ends. She read a good deal, visited friends, played poker, saw a great many plays and musicals— but one gets the feeling that she found it difficult to fill each day with satisfying activities. She expressed her resentment in flippant terms, but there is no doubt that the resentment was real: "Whenever Z was in some exotic or exciting place, where was I? Home with somebody's chicken pox or packing the place to move or attending the kids' Christmas play."

As Zero became progressively more famous, his time was increasingly taken up with interviews and other activities from which Kate was generally excluded. Wilma Solomon said, "Kate was depressed and bored. She complained that she felt lonely. He would come home in the late afternoon and go directly into his studio. He'd look at his art books and do whatever else he wanted to do, and there she was, and she'd been waiting for him all day."

Kate tried to participate in her husband's professional life when possible, and she had an opportunity to do so whenever he was required to learn music. Here, too, however, her contribution was not sufficiently appreciated (she felt) and Zero's attitude fed her bitterness. Wilma Solomon remembered being invited, along with some of their other friends, to an album Zero was taping. Kate stood there with him, cuing him. He was watching her and she was helping him in the nicest way. It needed to be done because he was insecure musically and she was very good. I'm sure she helped him whenever he did anything that required musical knowledge. Then once at my house Zero said that he had invited Sol Kaplan [a professional musician] to come to a rehearsal to help him with his music. And Kate was very hurt; she was in a fury—because he had asked Solly and didn't ask her. I don't think it would have bothered her whomever he asked if she hadn't been omitted.

At times, Kate appeared to retaliate by punishing Zero in front of friends. On Thursday nights, she and several other women had a regular poker game at the Mostels' apartment.* Rebecca Kramer Stein recalled one evening when Zero came home after a performance of *Fiddler on the Roof.* "He was tired and he wanted to talk. But Kate didn't say, 'Oh, Zero, how was the show?' She said, 'No, shut up! We've gotta finish the game.' And this big bear says, 'Oh, oh, okay,' and he goes to his room." Mary Yohalem has a similar recollection. Whenever Kate was angry with her husband, she'd say, "Zero, go to your room."

Kate shared with Zero the tendency to be "on" in public. All who knew her commented on her energy and vitality. But when the Mostels were at home alone their lives were far quieter, less "theatrical." This suited Zero perfectly; the public side of his personality needed to be balanced by the private side. But Kate felt that she was being ignored. Josh remembers a typical day at home, when no outsiders were present: "I remember Zero, he'd be reading the paper or something, and Kate would walk in and say, 'Watch this. Hey, Zero, the house is on fire. Zero, it's the doorbell.' And he'd just read his paper, he wouldn't notice."

Zero and Kate's relationship, volatile from the beginning, grew stormier as the years passed. They often raged at one another—"They were both screamers, and the marriage of two screamers has got to be mercurial," said Wilma Solomon—and more than once they contem-

---

*Zero also hosted a weekly poker game—for men only—at his studio on Friday nights. Sol Kaplan, who played once, never returned because the players "yelled so loud I thought I'd lose my eardrums. I never heard such screaming in my life."

plated divorce. The Mostels' friend Speed Vogel recalled several occasions "when I'd be with Zero in his studio and he'd be sleeping there instead of home, and drinking a lot and complaining a lot."

Rather than compete with one another directly for the attention of their friends, Kate and Zero, who were intensely competitive with one another, created two separate circles, one of them revolving around Kate, the other around Zero. As Wilma Solomon said, "At parties he would be in one room with his coterie while she would be in another room with hers. And that way, nobody stepped on anybody else's toes."

Kate and Zero often insulted one another in public. He called her "Snakemouth" and "Fat-Fat the water rat," among other terms of endearment. Since he always accompanied the language with a grin or a look of mock ferociousness no one knew whether his affection for Kate outweighed his hostility at such moments, or vice versa. But it was certainly a complex relationship, on her part as well as his. She was one of the few people who could take his insults and return them in kind. In fact, Kate was probably even more skilled at invective than Zero, and usually got the better of him. "Kate was very smart, very quick, very opinionated," said her son Josh.

Some of the anger Zero and Kate felt for one another was hard for their friends to fathom. The concert pianist Lucille Ostrow, a longtime friend of Mostel's, recalled that when Zero was staying with her in California after he received a subpoena from HUAC in 1955, "every time he'd call Kate, or she'd call him, I'd go out of the room because I could hear her over the phone just screaming at him. I don't know why, but she didn't give him any solace."

On such occasions—when Kate tore into Zero mercilessly—it was typical that he became quiet and subservient. Whenever a conflict of significant proportions arose between them, Kate proved to be the stronger of the two. Madeline Gilford called it "a complicated relationship," adding, "He was scared of her in many ways." Lucille Ostrow was even more emphatic: "He was scared to death of her. He made no bones about that."

But if Zero was reluctant to confront Kate directly, he took revenge upon her in other ways. Don Richardson, who knew the Mostels from 1946 until Zero died, recalled going backstage to see Zero after a performance of *The Latent Heterosexual* in Los Angeles in 1968. On his way out of the theatre, he said, "I had to go through the dark part of the front of the theatre. And on the stairs I found Katie, sitting huddled up in the dark, crying. I said, 'Katie, what's the matter?' She said, 'I'm hurting.' I don't remember exactly what it was but I think she had something wrong with her kidneys." Kate asked Richardson to tell Zero that she was in pain and wanted to go home. "So," Richardson continued, "I went to get Zero and tell him that his wife was very sick. I finally pulled him away from a bunch of people he was with. I took him aside and told him that Katie was hurting. And he said, 'Fuck her. She's the party-pooper of all time.' And turned away from me."

Richardson was particularly astounded at Zero's behavior because he had never observed anything remotely like it in the Mostels' relationship before. In general, he said, Kate "adored Zero, she absolutely worshipped him. And Zero worshipped her, too. Like most theatre people he got involved with other girls, but he would say things to me about Katie with the greatest reverence. He would say, 'She's the most beautiful woman in the entire world and the most beautiful human being in the world.' There was a great love story between the two of them. That's why I was so shocked."

Rebecca Kramer Stein, who was Kate's closest friend, felt that "Kate was the only one who could handle Zero. Kate was a force, absolutely a force—if she was sitting here the room would be vibrating—but the kind of force that, no matter what happened, Zero always respected everything about her. She was strong and extraordinarily bright and witty. She had such respect for the language. She always had an ambition to be educated. When she met Zero, she said he was the smartest man she ever met, and that was so important to her."

"Kate was very open about everything," said Wilma Solomon, "more than almost anybody I ever knew. It was as though she was prepared to share her whole life with you at all times. She would talk about her husband, her children, her mother, everything."

Although there were conflicts built into his relationship with Kate, Zero could say, "I'm a family man," and mean it. As much as he enjoyed being with his artist friends or being treated as a star at Sardi's, he genuinely liked Kate's company. "Though I can't think why, with *her*," he would say with a growl.

Zero and Kate also shared moments of pure fun, untouched either by hostility or by competitiveness. She used to do Zero Mostel imitations, to his great enjoyment. And she and Zero would perform routines together for the amusement of their friends—such as singing directly into one another's mouths while imitating Jeanette MacDonald and Nelson Eddy. She was, according to Julie Garfield (who knew the Mostels from the time she was a child), "an extremely funny woman in her own right."

That the Mostels' relationship was not entirely tumultuous was demonstrated poignantly to one observer in the 1970s. He saw them walking slowly hand in hand away from the Museum of Modern Art. Had they known they were being watched, they would very likely have begun to exchange loud banter, but—being, as they believed, unobserved—they were content to share a quiet, intimate moment together.

The same sort of feeling, perhaps expressed even more poignantly, can be seen in the written correspondence they exchanged whenever they were separated. Because Kate suffered from asthma attacks, she rarely accompanied Zero when he toured in a production. Instead, they wrote letters to one another. Kate told Frances Chaney that she and Zero "wrote to one another every single day when they were apart." The devotion involved in maintaining a daily correspondence seems difficult to reconcile with the stormy relationship they maintained in one another's company, but it was just one more surprising aspect of their complex partnership. "I thought it was so remarkable," Chaney said, "that through arguments, through fights, through disagreements when she would say, 'I'm going to kill you,' and he would make fun of her, putting her down, that this [correspondence] went on all the time."

When I asked their close friend Joseph Wilder about the Mostels' relationship, he replied, "I thought, considering Zero's self-centeredness and his eccentricities, that it was extraordinary that anybody could put up with him. Or that he could put up with her. This was not a 'How are you, darling?' syrupy, hand-holding relationship. I've occasionally seen it happen to a woman who's married to some famous guy that she decides to be subservient and spends her life in his shadow. Kate did not do that. Kate was her own woman. She was tough and strong and stood up to Zero—and that's how they went through life. They were in the ring together, but I felt that they were good together."

Kate strongly influenced Zero's performing career, helping him make the choices that led to stardom, and took intense pride in his achievements. Perhaps she was more aware of the immensity of his talent than he was, or perhaps she realized that his desire to become a full-time painter was unrealistic. Zero seemed at times to resent her ambition on his behalf, but he took her advice so frequently that it may have been a tacit admission on his part that Kate was just the sort of skilled and astute adviser he needed.

"Being Mrs. Zero Mostel was enormously important to Kate," Mary Yohalem told me. "That life was exciting, it was stimulating. Wherever they went, they attracted interesting people: artists, intellectuals. And Kate loved that. She had very ambivalent feelings toward Zero. If you ever said anything against Zero, she would knock you down. She was fiercely loyal to him. But she reserved the right to complain and yell at him when they were together." In one sense, Yohalem felt, Kate resented Zero because "she never managed to make a complete life for herself."

Kate's character underwent a substantial change when Zero became a famous performer. As Frances Chaney noted, "She changed with a lot of money. *Things* became important, although they had not been that important to her originally. She became somebody who cared about possessions. We all use money to replace other things, and maybe when life gets hard in a marriage, you run out and buy something and it makes you feel a little better."

Another element that may have added to the strain in the relationship was Zero's incorrigible flirtatiousness with women of all ages, all shapes and sizes. He frequently grabbed breasts and bottoms, probably to get attention and to heighten his well-established reputation for outrageous behavior rather than to establish a sexual liaison. Bill Schelble, the press representative for *A Funny Thing Happened on the Way to the Forum*, said, "He was always pinching. If you heard somebody scream, you knew that Zero had just pinched somebody." Ruth Kobart, who appeared with Zero in *Forum*, added, "It was always done with a sense of play; there was nothing serious or deep about it; it was a kind of joyousness." Orel Odinov Protopopescu, who, as production assistant for a film Zero made in 1974, was often in his company, remarked, "Sometimes there were young girls working on the crew whom he'd feel almost obliged to flirt with. He would do that with me occasionally, but once he'd gone through his obligatory period of flirting, he'd calm down and be himself. He somehow felt he had to put a show on."

I asked Howard Rodney, Zero's dresser in the 1960s and 1970s, about Mostel's flirtatiousness. "He used to *run* after them," Rodney replied. "He always reminded me of Harpo Marx. If a man and a woman came to his dressing room, he turned to the woman and said, 'What do you need him for when you could have me?' Or he'd run after one of the actresses and grab her. I'd say, 'Zero, what are you going to do *after* you grab her?' He didn't know. He just grabbed them as a joke." Rodney insisted that Zero "adored Katie" and that he would "never in a million years" become involved with another woman. Rebecca Kramer Stein was equally certain: "Zero was not a chaser. He may have given a little pinch, but, really, he was not a chaser." Other friends of the Mostels agreed, emphatically, that Zero had no genuine interest in other women.

In some cases, however, Zero's intent was more serious. As a theatrical and film star, he was often surrounded by attractive women, and some of his friends are certain that he occasionally slept with these women. But these relationships evidently had no deep significance for him. Joseph Wilder said, "Zero was not a lover of women; Zero was a lover of life. I can't conceive of Zero having the time for affairs. Affairs mean meetings, going on trips together, some kind of commitment. I don't believe it."

Some women who were members of the Mostels' social circle told me that Zero had made propositions to them—but always in a heavily conspiratorial manner, so that they were never certain whether or not he was serious. Invariably, they said, they laughed off the suggestion; but if they hadn't, would Zero have followed through or would he have played the incident as a joke?

There is good reason to believe that he would have been incredulous if any woman in his social circle had taken his proposition seriously. Mary Yohalem was married to Waldo Salt, a blacklisted screenwriter, when she was closest to the Mostels. "The years that Waldo and I were close to Zero and Kate and saw them socially, Zero was a terrific flirt," she said. "He had an enormous amount of fun flirting with women: pinching bottoms and kissing and really making a spectacle of himself.

You would think he was the biggest lady-killer in the world. But this was always in a roomful of people. I remember a few times sitting alone in a room with Zero and he was utterly embarrassed, ill at ease. He wouldn't come anywhere near me then. When we were alone he was quite the opposite of being flirtatious." Yohalem felt certain that Zero's flirtatiousness was only a pose and that he would have run swiftly away from any woman who took him seriously. "In front of a lot of people, he would pretend to flirt. But if there was not an audience, no."

Josh Mostel, Zero and Kate's son, elaborated on the same theme. "I always thought that Zero was a prude underneath it all; that a lot of this braggadocio was just that," he said. "I mean, a lot of his song and dance and his sexual hitting on women was a cover-up for being scared of women in a lot of ways. I don't think his behavior, his flirting, was designed to get laid. I think probably just the opposite—designed in some way to push them away . . . I don't think Zero had the famous wandering eye. I think there was this closet conservative rabbinical Judaism coming out."

Zero's sexual relationships with women other than his wife offer a good example of how people allowed their perceptions of Mostel to become the reality. Those who preferred to believe that he was faithful to Kate simply swept aside the evidence to the contrary. However, one friend of the Mostels said that "Kate didn't trust Z because he fooled around a lot, and her jealousy was crazy." Zero's affairs were "an open secret," she said. Others saw less evidence that Mostel was involved with many women, but acknowledged the existence of infrequent affairs.

A particular source of friction between Zero and Kate was Zero's drinking. Kate, who was a teetotaler much of her life (the fact that her father had owned a saloon in Philadelphia had a great deal to do with her attitude, she maintained), believed that Zero drank to excess, and it worried her. "I think she was a little too strict about it," Jack Gilford said. But, Frances Chaney explained, "alcohol terrified her; really scared her to death. When Zero would drink, no matter how much or how little, she would just go crazy. And Kate was never one to keep her mouth shut about anything. So she would berate him." Josh Mostel added, "She resented him drinking any alcohol. She'd yell at him . . . They had big fights about it."

Whether or not Zero had a problem with alcohol is open to question.

His brother Aaron maintained that Zero never drank: "Because he had colitis, he was not allowed to drink." Zero himself never made that claim, but he liked to tell interviewers, "I never had a drink before a show in my life." If he meant *immediately* before a show he was perhaps correct, but his son Josh recalled many occasions when Zero would have several drinks between matinee and evening performances. Josh believes that his father was dependent on alcohol. "Toby [Mostel] said that when Zero would go walk the dog, he'd stop at every bar along the way and have a drink," he said, adding, "I saw Zero drunk a few times. He was a maudlin drunk, bellowing."

Two of Zero's closest friends were physicians, and neither felt that his drinking was excessive, although both stated, "He loved to drink." Dr. Norman Pleshette added, "He loved good food and he loved alcohol." And Dr. Joseph Wilder noted, "Zero loved the good life, he loved to drink, he loved to eat, but he was most certainly not an alcoholic." Nor did Speed Vogel believe that he could be characterized as an alcoholic. "He would drink, and get drunk, particularly if he were unhappy," Vogel said, "but he did not *need* to drink."

Vogel summed up Kate and Zero's relationship with this story: "I was having trouble with my marriage at one time, and, because I was crazy about Kate and I thought she was terribly smart, I used to consult her about my problems. She would give me an analysis of what was happening from the woman's point of view, which I felt I was lacking. I remember Kate looked at me and said, 'Speed, let me tell you something. Every day of my life I have to fight like a tigress not to get pushed off the face of the earth by Zero, so stop complaining.' Kate and Zero were two mammoth human beings, always in a contest; it was a stormy existence. But very rich."

*　　*　　*

After his army discharge, Zero's career picked up where it had left off: near the top. His engagement at La Martinique in November 1944 demonstrated that he had lost neither his ability to make people laugh nor his following. *Cue* magazine described the act, which included his impressions of Jimmy Durante and "an almost obscenely real electric percolator" as well as a new sketch about a lunatic member of the Board of Education, as "comedy in the great tradition."

Mostel returned to Broadway in *Concert Varieties* in June of 1945. As its title would indicate, the show bore some similarity to the two earlier Broadway productions in which he had performed. But this was a variety show with a difference. Billy Rose, the producer, wanted to enrich the comedy with serious dance. Katherine Dunham received top billing, and Jerome Robbins was featured in a ballet with his company. The lives of Robbins and Mostel would intersect frequently from this time on. In 1945, they had a good deal in common, sharing a belief in the political left as well as performing in the same production.

Concert Varieties was different in another way. For the first time, Mostel received indifferent notices. Lewis Nichols in the New York *Times* said, "It is in the department of comedy that *Concert Varieties* . . . slows down. . . . Zero Mostel, Eddie Mayehoff and Imogene Coca appear at various times, and their styles are more satisfactory in the night clubs than on a large and lonely stage. Each of them goes on a little too long for comfort." Several other reviewers concurred. Burton Rascoe wrote in the *World-Telegram*, "Many found [Mostel] very funny indeed. I didn't." Robert Garland was emphatically negative in the *Journal-American*: "Zero lives up to his . . . name." Perhaps the critics had seen Mostel's act too frequently and were registering their belief that he needed to explore fresh material. George Freedley made the point explicitly: "His present material, some of which is all too familiar, is not particularly inspiring." Possibly as a result Zero began to think seriously of moving in a new direction. For several years, he had wanted to go beyond nightclub performing and into acting, and the cool reception he received in *Concert Varieties* helped to provide the impetus he needed to change the course of his career.

"I really wanted to be an actor," Zero said in 1961, "but everyone wanted me to be a gagman. I was a comic. Most comics never bother to equip themselves as actors. Most of the young comics today have the misconception that if they do a series of gags in a certain pose, that's enough. But the best comics are also good actors. Chaplin is a wonderful actor. W. C. Fields and Willie Howard and Bobby Clark were real actors, and so are Bert Lahr and Joey Adams and Shelley Berman. In France, the word *comédien* actually means both 'comedian' and 'actor.' "

Mostel felt that his own work qualified as acting of a kind and that the transition to performing in plays would be eased by his particular approach to comedy. "Everything I've ever done involves characterization," he asserted. "Even when I did a night-club act that was a high-class piece of characterization. Unfortunately," he added, unable to pass up the chance for a gag, "it was admired only by my family and my analyst."

Zero may have wanted to become an actor, but he was evidently too insecure about his ambition to confess it to anyone else. Early in 1946, Kate was taking weekly classes from an acting teacher named Don Richardson, and she spoke to Richardson about her belief that Zero had the makings of a good actor. But, she warned Richardson, Zero would not admit to any such interest. "He's a painter," he recalled her telling him. "He hates acting. He wants nothing to do with acting. But he's very funny and people are very amused by him. He works in nightclubs but otherwise he's done no acting."

Richardson thought that Zero "didn't sound like a very good prospect to me since he wasn't interested in being an actor, but I said, just to be nice to Katie, 'Well, bring him around.' When the next class ended, Zero arrived to pick her up. He was enormously heavy, he had bangs, a torn umbrella and a torn raincoat. Katie said, 'Zero, this is Don. Don't give him any shit,' and walked out. I was left alone with Zero. I said, 'There's the stage. Get up and do something.' He said, 'You're the teacher. *You* get up and do something.' He was very hostile. So I said, 'Katie told you not to give me any shit, so if you want to work with me, get up there and improvise a situation and let me see what you look like on the stage.' "

What followed astounded the acting teacher, as Zero gave a remarkable demonstration of his talent. In 1988, Richardson could still recall the incident in vivid detail:

He said "Okay," and he went up on the stage, took off his raincoat, put down his umbrella and he improvised a scene—making it up as he went along—in which he was a tailor, and he was very poor, and he decided to burn down the store in order to get the insurance. So he set fire to the store and then realized that his child, his little boy was in the back room and that the wife had gone out to shop or something. He tried to get to the back room through the smoke. But by the time he got to the child and brought him out into the street the child was dead. He sat on the curb, at the edge of the stage, crying. I found myself very moved by it. I thought he was a very impressive person on the stage. Suddenly, he stopped crying and he looked up at me and he said, "Would you like to see it funny?" I said, "Yes, I would. I'd like very much to see it funny." So he did the same improvisation funny—with a kind of black humor because at the end when he had the kid out on the sidewalk he was trying to sew the kid together again. So I said, "Okay, I'll take you on as a student." So he studied with me, on and off, for three years.

Zero thus redirected the focus of his professional life. Once determined to become an actor, he persevered despite many years of lukewarm receptions from critics and audiences alike."* His first opportunity to appear in a play—albeit a musical play—occurred in October 1946, when he was offered the role of Mr. Peachum in a modern version of the eighteenth-century ballad opera *The Beggar's Opera*. This step would ordinarily have involved taking a sizable pay cut, from nearly $4,000 per week when he worked in nightclubs to $750 per week, but after the play opened, he also performed in the late shows at the Embassy; still, one imagines that he would have embarked on his new career even if he could not have continued with the old one.

Duke Ellington and John Latouche's jazz version of *The Beggar's Opera*, first called *Twilight Alley*, then retitled *Beggar's Holiday*, was directed by George Abbott (who replaced John Houseman midway through rehearsals) and featured Alfred Drake in the leading role. The play opened in December to mixed reviews. Zero's performance was not entirely successful; Duke Ellington, who was too polite to speak out, left the theatre when Zero roared his tunes off-key. Critical response tended to one extreme or the other: utterly disdainful or highly enthu-

---

*When Zero wanted something, he didn't stop until he got it. It could be an item as insignificant as a tie that someone was wearing—in which case Zero would just remove the person's tie and say, "Don't worry, I'll send it back." Or it could be something as valuable as his friend Aube Tzerko's handmade eighteen-karat-gold $3,000 pocket watch. Tzerko made the mistake of showing Zero the watch one day. From that moment on, they never saw one another without Zero's saying, "Let's see the watch." He would stare at it for several minutes, then invariably say, "What the hell do you need it for? You don't wear it. I would wear it." After several years of this, Zero said, "You can have one of my paintings if I can have the watch." Tzerko, knowing when he was beaten, made the deal.

siastic. Louis Kronenberger of *PM* was among the naysayers, commenting, "Scoundrelly Peachum . . . became a mere zany whom Zero Mostel absolutely mauled with his intemperate practices," and Brooks Atkinson castigated his "grotesque and sweaty posturing," which, he said, was "no substitute for comic skylarking." On the other hand, George Freedley clearly approved of the shift in Mostel's career. "The joy of the evening," he wrote in the *Morning Telegraph*, "was the inspired clowning of Zero Mostel, who was extraordinarily funny as Peachum," and Rowland Field in the Newark *Evening News* expressed his enjoyment of "that droll buffoon, Zero Mostel, who has quite a knockabout field day as Peachum."

The reviews may have been less than satisfactory, but Zero was clearly hooked. Although he often returned to nightclub comedy in later years, he never wavered from his preference for acting. "I wanted to play in the classic comic literature," he declared. "I wanted to act in plays by Molière, the daddy of all comic invention. I felt that I had to study everything if I wanted to act. I felt that an actor was better if he knew what was going on, if he was aware of the literary stage tradition. I wanted to know how to do Lear and Toby Belch and Falstaff."

Mostel had always read widely—"I had read all of Shaw and Molière by the time I was nineteen," he averred—and was knowledgeable in many areas, but his new determination to "study everything" fed his already impressive erudition. In addition to his interests in show business, painting, and social theory, he became a voracious reader of philosophy, fiction, and drama. Dostoyevski and Proust were among the authors whose work he most appreciated. Hermann Hesse's *Steppenwolf* was a favorite novel, Sean O'Casey and Samuel Beckett were among the playwrights he most revered. He considered Edmund Wilson's *Axel's Castle* the finest collection of criticism he knew. His knowledge of art and artists was formidable, his understanding of Jewish history and theology profound. Mal Warshaw, a close friend of Mostel's, said of him, "Zero had an enormous range of interests. He was interested in people, he was interested in the theatre, he was an accomplished painter, he was interested in food, he was interested in politics, he was interested in what was going on in the world." His friend Aube Tzerko added, "He was knowledgeable in many areas. And not superficially. He wouldn't expound on anything unless he knew about it in depth."

Mostel also possessed a sophisticated understanding of classical music. He constantly played classical recordings in his studio, and he
himself was a gifted (although untrained) musician. "He knew so much
about music—and about all kinds of music—that he would just amaze
me," Sol Kaplan said. Zero's nephew Raphael Mostel, a composer, also
commented: "He hadn't learned to read music, but he was a very musical
person and he was able to deal with serious problems in music."

Sheldon Harnick was another who noted Mostel's aptitude. "Although far from being an educated musician, Zero had a first-rate
musical sensibility," Harnick said. "It was a pleasure to give him musical
material, because he handled it so adroitly. I don't know that I ever
saw him more proud and elated than when he got 'If I Were a Rich
Man' [from *Fiddler on the Roof*] right on the first take at the recording
session."

Mostel owned a large collection of opera recordings and tapes, which
he took with him whenever he was on tour. "I've heard every opera
twenty times, but I've never learned a libretto because I have too much
fun making up my own words," he said. His love of opera was evident
when he consented to give an interview to William Glover of the Associated Press. Bill Schelble, the press representative for the show in
which Zero was then appearing, took Glover to Mostel's studio. "When
we got there," Schelble said, "Zero was sitting in a big wicker chair,
listening to an opera. We walked in and he said, 'Ssh. Quiet. Wait until
this act is over.' Glover got sort of impatient because it wasn't until
after about fifteen minutes that the act ended" and Zero agreed to begin
the interview.

Mostel, who attended concerts frequently, conducted the Symphony
of the New World in a fund-raising performance of the *Semiramide*
overture in New York's Philharmonic Hall in 1969, and, although the
evening was not intended to be taken seriously, Zero clearly enjoyed
the musical side of the entertainment. Donal Henahan's "review" in
the *Times* evoked the proper spirit of the occasion: "He knew the Rossini
score backward and forward, even if there were times when there was
some doubt as to which way he was conducting it."

Another discipline about which Zero was well informed was medi-
cine. Pretending to be a doctor, he once engaged a physician (who
obviously didn't recognize Mostel) in a lengthy conversation. So thor-

ough was his knowledge and so convincing his impersonation that the physician completely accepted him in his role of medical practitioner.

"Zero was very informed about certain things," his son Josh told me, citing his "intellectual understanding [of] the philosophy of religion. . . . And he knew a tremendous amount about art. You could cover up a postcard except for a little corner and he could tell you all about the painting: where it was from, when it was painted, and the title—just from a few brush strokes. The curator of the American Museum of Natural History used to send him some pre-Columbian works of art to authenticate. Zero had the eye. He could usually tell a fake."

There were two distinct sides to Zero's personality, and the intellectual side was never seen in public. Madeline Gilford noted the remarkable change that came over Zero depending upon how many people were in the vicinity. "When I was alone in the studio with him, when I would visit him there, or when I was trying to get him to be in a play that I was trying to cast or produce, alone he was lovely and very vulnerable. The minute a third person came into the room he became what we know as his public personality: a braggart and a bully and overbearing and, at times, very insulting. Alone, he loved me, and I really felt his love and support. The minute it was in front of anyone —even Kate or Jack—he had to tell Jack I was a pain in the ass or tell Kate that I had a big mouth. One day I was in Zero's den when he got home—he didn't know I was there. A friend of theirs was sick and was in the hospital. They were very solicitous and very involved if someone were ill or had bad luck; they were very devoted in that way. And he came in and said, in a normal voice, 'Kate, Ed's sick again, they had to take him to the hospital—' And then he spotted me and said, 'WHAT'S SHE DOING HERE? BIG MOUTH!' "

When an individual spent an afternoon with Zero in his studio or strolled with him through an art gallery—where Mostel offered remarkably incisive comments about the works of art—he observed a sensitive, serious, studious man. Bettye Ackerman said of him, "When he spoke about art, his whole persona changed, and so did the tone of his voice." Deborah Salt, the daughter of Zero's friends Waldo and Mary Salt, recalled visiting Zero in his studio when she was a teenager. When he was painting, she said, "He was very quiet, pensive, and thoughtful, and totally into the work." Lucille Ostrow also discussed his intellect and his thoughtful nature. "In his studio," she said, "he was completely serious. He was probably one of the most knowledge-able persons I've ever known, about art, art history. Actually, he was a knowledgeable person in everything. He never gave that impression when you met him on a social level, or when he was fooling around, but he was a studied man, a learned man."

As soon as Zero set foot outside the studio or the museum, however, he resumed his clownish behavior. On the street, in a restaurant, at a party, he had to be the center of attention, even if it meant competing loudly to get what he wanted. Ordinarily, his public personality was an extension of the performer: boisterous, unpredictable, obstreperous, lovable, often hilarious. But to some it could be embarrassing. At times it was both hilarious *and* embarrassing.

Such an occasion occurred in the mid-1930s, when Zero and his then-wife, Clara, went out to dinner with John Garfield, a struggling young actor at the time, and his wife, Robbie. Neither couple had much money, so this was a rare night out. Robbie Garfield wore her one good dress, a satin gown of which she took great care, for it was almost impossible to clean satisfactorily. After the foursome had eaten their dinner, the waiter walked by with a dessert topped with an enormous mound of whipped cream. Robbie, nearly drooling, could not conceal her desire for the confection. Mostel asked, "Do you want it?" She shook her head sadly, as it was clearly beyond the Garfields' budget. "If you want it, it's yours," said Mostel, grabbing the dessert from the waiter's tray and shoving it in Robbie's face. Then he took a napkin, tied it around her neck and pantomimed shaving her with his knife. Everyone in the restaurant was helpless with laughter as Mostel com-pleted his routine. Only Robbie's laughter was mixed with anger. She was a rather pathetic sight—and her one good dress was ruined.

Every prank needs a victim, of course, and the victim will inevitably find it difficult to see the humor. Ordinarily, Mostel picked on those who, in his view, deserved to be picked on. But it is difficult to see Robbie Garfield as anything but an innocent victim, who in no way deserved to be humiliated.

Many of Zero's public displays of zaniness were far less dependent upon placing others in embarrassing situations. Most of them begin with Mostel eating in a restaurant—which may be indicative of the importance of food in the corpulent comic's life.

When Zero dined one night at Maxim's in Paris, he was amused by the pretentiousness of the staff. When the *sommelier* came to his table to take the wine order, Zero asked with mock innocence for a Coca-Cola. The *sommelier*, astonished but unflappable, returned to the table with a bottle and a glass. Zero insisted that he pour out a small amount. Then he swirled the soft drink in the glass, sniffed deeply of its bouquet, and took a small sip into his mouth. He continued to treat the Coke as if it were a delicate wine by letting it linger in his mouth while making faces that registered first ecstasy, then dismay. At last he spat the drink back into the glass and handed it to the waiter. "Take it back," he shouted. "Too young!"

At more than one restaurant, Zero performed an elaborate panto-mime: he took a piece of bread in his left hand and, with his butter knife in the other, proceeded to spread the butter on the bread, up the sleeve of his left arm, over his balding head and—deftly switching hands—down the right arm, ruining his suit in the process but reducing the astounded customers to gales of laughter.

Zero had a standard line for waiters. Near the end of most meals, he would call the waiter to his table, hold the plate (with a small portion of food) out to him and announce, "Give my compliments to the chef. And throw this in his face." When he reached the cashier, he would invariably fix the poor creature with a sneering look and say, "My lawyers will be here in the morning," after which he would march with pretended anger out the door.

Deborah Salt recalled two dinners with Zero when she was eleven years old, "both of which were just hair-raising experiences. When he walked into a restaurant he would do things that were just outrageous. It would make the other eaters stop and almost be unable to eat. He just bellowed and howled." Asked if she enjoyed Mostel's impromptu performance, she said, "It was partially funny, but it was embarrassing—because it was so outrageous, so loud; he demanded so much attention."

Wilma Solomon's description of Zero captures the extremes of his personality. Mostel was "a force, like a natural element," she said. "And it did lead him to be loud, vulgar, cruel, all those things sometimes. But I think his basic nature was very sweet and warm."

"Mostel is a wonder of nature, an elemental force," said critic Julius Novick; "you would not think that much abounding, astounding energy could be given to any one man." Robert Alan Aurthur, watching Zero emerging from his apartment one day, swinging his cane wildly in front of him and from side to side as he walked, thought, "Here may be the only existing performer who on stage or screen has always been smaller than life."

"He roared and rumbled and tried to intimidate anyone who wandered near his territory," Burgess Meredith said. "As far as I could tell, his behavior was genetic, like the hiss of a cat, but louder of course, maybe like the snort of a rhinoceros or the subsonic rumblings of a whale. Furthermore his craziness appeared to go on for most of his waking hours. For instance, going into a restaurant with Zero was like assaulting Omaha Beach. People's first instinct was to dive behind their tables like bunkers. After a while they generally recognized him and were amused by his actions, but not at first."

When an acquaintance encountered Zero on the street or in a room, he never knew what to expect. He was certain to be greeted in an extravagant manner, but how? With a bellow of outrage or a bear hug? He might suddenly find himself forced to his knees, the victim of an impromptu duel with Zero's cane. Lou Peterson said, "He was the kind of a man who would see you across the street and he would yell, 'Lou, baby!' and he'd run across the street and unbutton your fly—which would embarrass me no end. But when he realized that he was embarrassing you, he would try to make it up. Then he could be really gentle and caring and concerned."

Zero's conversation was punctuated by animal sounds, bursts of operatic song, invective in many languages and dialects, extravagant gestures, meticulous pantomimes. "Like Niagara," Sam Jaffe said, "his exuberance . . . just keeps on overflowing."

Nephew Raphael Mostel said, "Zero took an interest in everything. It was like having a searchlight on. When he was focused on something, he was *very* focused." Raphael thought that much of Zero's success as an entertainer emanated from that same source. "He was one of the most amazing people I've ever known: just the power of his presence and the ability to focus energy in whatever way he wanted was astounding. Time after time in performance he had the entire audience in his total control from the smallest gestures or sounds. The same thing walking down the street or dealing with him personally; it was very focused energy."

Some people were understandably embarrassed by Zero's effusive behavior in public, and wished to avoid it. Stella Adler, a prominent drama teacher in New York, was one. She strove to maintain her dignity at all times and evidently found Mostel something of a boor. One day she and a companion were out for a walk and saw Zero, at some distance, walking toward them. Adler said something to her friend and the two of them prepared to turn in the opposite direction. Suddenly Zero was on his knees, giving a graphic imitation of Marlon Brando as Stanley Kowalski in *A Streetcar Named Desire*, roaring "STELLAAAHHH!!!!" and crawling inexorably closer. Doing her best to ignore the crowd that formed to stare at her and the crawling man, she accelerated her pace and fairly ran away from him.

But Zero's outrageous manner could be balanced by unexpected interludes of delicacy and sweetness. One of Frances Chaney's fondest recollections of Zero demonstrates precisely those qualities: "Ring [Lardner, Jr., her husband] and I were living in New Milford, Connecticut, and Zero came over to visit. Our daughter was there with her fifteen-month-old baby. We were all in our living room, and Zero began to play with Carlo, our grandson. Zero and this baby played together for a good hour, hour and a half. Zero would do something and Carlo would imitate him. Then Carlo would do something and Zero would imitate. It went on and on. It was absolutely enchanting to see this great big guy doing just what the baby was doing. The baby was fascinated by him and he was fascinated by the baby. It was a beautiful sight—really lovely. He was putting as much of himself into his relationship with Carlo as he did in his work as a performer."

"Zero was a very sensitive and very understanding type of person," said Ngoot Lee, an artist whose studio was in the same street as Zero's. "He was a serious person, a more serious person than people thought he was. I mean, he'd joke around, but he'd worry, he always worried about his sons. Outside maybe Zero was a big bully but the guy was very sensitive."

Zero bullied those who were servile or authoritarian. He tested the limits of servility, often discovering—with disgust—that there were *no* limits. When Zero and Sam Jaffe were in a restaurant one evening, they were discussing just this subject. Zero: "I said, 'You know, people will put up with anything. You can do the rudest things and they won't mind.' So Sam asks me what, for instance, and I say, 'Well, for instance, I'll wipe my mouth with that man's necktie . . .' So I leaned over and then I did it. And what happened? The idiot thanked me."

Zero was as disdainful of authority as he was of servility, regardless of whether the authority was manifested by power, position, or wealth. He was gleeful when he was able to puncture the pomposity that, he felt, inevitably accompanied authority. There was the evening when he and Sam Jaffe attended a party that was being dominated by a Very Important Artist, who was taking great pleasure in being the center of attention. Mostel and Jaffe decided they would remedy that situation. From that moment on, every time the Artist opened his mouth to speak, Mostel or Jaffe would "accidentally" bump into the furniture or jump in loudly with a vocal contribution; the Artist never managed to say another word.

"The great thing about me," Mostel said immodestly, "is that I don't take myself seriously. Everybody [else] in the world takes himself seriously. The jerky plumber thinks he's saving the world and he's working in crap. And that goes for every profession. I knew a chiropodist who said there were three saviors in the world: Jesus, Moses and Max Horowitz. Sonofabitch—he cut off a callus and took himself seriously."

"Have you any idea how much I hate rich people?" he asked Robert Alan Aurthur one day, then proceeded to explain his attitude toward the rich (whose wealth alone conferred on them a kind of authority):

A few Sundays ago my wife Kate dragged me to some afternoon party given by her rich friends. I didn't want to go, but you know Kate. So I made the best of it and swore I'd be dignified and charming. We got there early, and I asked for a tomato juice. The host says there's no tomato juice, only champagne. I said in that case I'll have a seltzer. The host said no seltzer, only champagne. Okay, I'll die with thirst—but with dignity. I go to sit on a chair. The hostess yells, "Don't sit there, it's an antique." I turn to another chair; same thing: "Don't break the antique!"

I wander into the television room, turn on a ball game, and just as I'm about to sit down, the host runs in, screaming, "Watch out for the chair, you'll break it!" So I scream back, "Watch out for *me*, I'm going to break every fucking thing in this fucking house!"

People lead me to a couch in the living room, I can't even see the ball game. Nothing to drink, not a mouthful of food . . . Kate takes me home early.

Mostel's egotism and his insistence upon instant gratification led him to behave in ways that might have been considered offensive if they hadn't been accompanied by good humor and clearly intended to be outrageous. Aube Tzerko recalled with affection the time when he "was playing tennis with someone in Beverly Hills and Zero was standing by. Zero said, 'You call yourself a tennis player? Let me have that racquet.' He didn't even know how to hold the racquet, let alone play." Tzerko's wife, Saida, added, "If it was dancing, he could dance better, if it was tennis, he could play tennis better."

When Mostel wasn't playing the buffoon at a restaurant—passionately declaring his love for the waitress, banging on the table, loudly cursing the maître d', turning the ties of the customers around so that they hung down their backs—he was arguing furiously with his companions. When Zero ordered a corned beef sandwich at a delicatessen, *everyone* at his table had to have a corned beef sandwich. Whoever dared to order pastrami or roast beef would run the risk of seeing Zero rise threateningly from his chair and roar, "Take the corned beef, goddammit!" Or he might simply overrule everyone else's orders and demand that he order for the entire group because *he knew what they should eat better than they did*. And it wasn't just food that served as the subject for furious debate: art, politics, the weather, all were fair game. The point wasn't what subject was being debated; the point was that Zero had to be the winner.

In most cases Mostel's antics were described as hilarious by those who witnessed them. But the difficulty of conveying that hilarity to the reader is daunting. Julius Novick of the New York *Times* made a similar comment in 1968, when he observed Zero at a party in Dallas:

. . . Burgess Meredith is persuaded to sing a Russian song, and Zero agrees to "translate." "Babushka Volga vodka narodny, ny, ny, ny," sings Burgess, or words to that effect. "All Russians have hemorrhoids," translates Zero.

Burgess sings another line of Russian. "They haven't got hemorrhoids, they've got piles," says Zero.

The marvel, the mystery, of which I despair of convincing those who have never met him, is that this was not gross and stupid, as it probably looks in print, but brilliantly funny and irresistibly charming; . . . the poetry of coarseness.

*　　*　　*

Zero's ambition to become an actor was not swiftly realized. After he played in *Beggar's Holiday* in 1946, more than two years went by before he was cast in another play. Meanwhile, he continued his nightclub activities, both in New York and elsewhere: the Chez Paree in Chicago, the Clover Club in Hollywood, even at the London Palladium. He added new routines, such as his impression of a lost airplane, a heartbreaking song about the moronic girl who had left him, and satires on folk singers and folk dancers. He also ventured into a new entertainment medium—television—in 1948.

The television program, created especially for him, was called (for no particular reason) *Off the Record*. The idea—a good one, it would seem—was that television, as a visual medium, required comics whose primary appeal was visual. This was certainly true of Zero. Although he had achieved success on radio, there could be no doubt that the listeners were being deprived of the essence of Mostel's humor; one had to see him in order to appreciate him fully. Indeed, when *Life* magazine reviewed *Off the Record*, it noted that the program "heralds the arrival on the air via television of visual comedy." Shown in November 1948 on the Dumont network, the show also featured Joey Faye and Mimi Benzell. One sketch featured Zero as an incompetent disk jockey; in another, he was seen at an easel, apparently painting Joey Faye's portrait. Using his thumb to maintain perspective, Zero applied brushstrokes both massive and gentle, grimacing with every addition. At last, he revealed the painting to the long-suffering model: a portrait of Zero's thumb. Mostel and Faye also played two inept cooks. Later, they were joined by Mimi Benzell in a parody of *Carmen*.

Off the Record, a "special," was only shown once. But it led to another television program, this time giving Zero the opportunity to act in a play. The vehicle was a one-hour adaptation of George S. Kaufman and Moss Hart's 1937 Broadway success, *The Man Who Came to Din-*

ner. Edward Everett Horton starred as Sheridan Whiteside and Mostel was cast as Banjo, a loony character based upon Harpo Marx. Telecast on CBS in January 1949, it seems to have had almost no impact whatever (television was still a novelty and not enough Americans owned sets for any single broadcast to leave a strong impression), except that it did further Zero's ambition to become an actor and it seemed likely to create other opportunities for him to display his talents in that area.

But a complication of major proportions would force Mostel's career to sputter uncertainly for the next decade. The citizens of Wisconsin had elected Joseph McCarthy to the United States Senate in 1946. His election coincided with—and helped to promote—a national mania for blaming all of America's problems on Communists, Communist sympathizers, and "well-meaning Communist dupes." But McCarthy did not assume a leading role in the drive to expose alleged subversives until February 1950, when he announced in a speech made at Wheeling, West Virginia, that he possessed a list (the number on the list varied when McCarthy gave subsequent versions of the same speech: sometimes 57, sometimes 205, sometimes 81) of names of "card-carrying Communists" in the State Department. By that time, the national paranoia was already well under way.

4

The Blacklist: I

The House of Representatives created the Committee on Un-American Activities (HUAC) as a temporary investigating committee in 1938. Under its first chairman, Martin Dies, HUAC conducted an investigation into the Federal Theatre, the theatrical equivalent of the Federal Art Project on which Zero Mostel had worked. The stated presumption behind the investigation was that thousands of artists and administrators employed by the Federal Theatre were engaged in a conspiracy to overthrow the government of the United States. Some members of the committee went so far as to call the Federal Theatre "a branch of the Communist Party." HUAC's investigation was anything but an impartial inquiry; the committee members' purpose was to humiliate those who supported or were involved in the Federal Theatre, and, using the national publicity generated by the hearings, they succeeded. As a direct result of the committee's work, the Federal Theatre went out of existence in 1939.

Republicans and right-wing Democrats could claim few significant victories after Franklin D. Roosevelt's landslide triumphs in 1932 and 1936. Desperate to reassert their power, they gloried in the defeat of the Federal Theatre—a project created by the Roosevelt administration.

HUAC's widely publicized activities seemed to offer a way for conservatives to seize the political initiative and thus had the fervent backing of the right wing for its investigations into alleged Communist influence in education, government, and the arts throughout the 1940s.

HUAC's purpose was not to uncover criminal behavior: in the first place, the Communist party was a legal entity; secondly, the Constitution forbids congressional committees from charging individuals with crimes. "Rather," as Victor Navasky said in his book, *Naming Names*, "the committee was in essence serving as a kind of national parole board, whose job was to determine whether the 'criminals' had truly repented of their evil ways." Those who denounced communism and cooperated with the committee in every way received HUAC's blessings; those who did not were stigmatized as unpatriotic and subversive. From the beginning, HUAC's hearings tended to resemble inquisitions rather than trials: witnesses were denied the rights to which they would have been entitled in a court of law, so any allegation, regardless of how vicious or unsupported it might be, was entered into the record, where it stood without challenge.

In 1945, HUAC became a permanent standing committee. But its investigation of educators, religious leaders, and others was beginning to have a diminishing impact upon the public's consciousness. In 1947, however, the committee announced that it would once again hold hearings involving the performing arts. This time, the subject was to be the influence of communism on the movies—a subject that was almost certain to make headlines. The way for that investigation was paved by the establishment in 1944 of the right-wing Motion Picture Alliance for the Preservation of American Ideals, which charged that American films were in danger of being taken over by Communist infiltration.

A weekly four-page newsletter founded by three former FBI agents in May of 1947 offered "evidence" to substantiate the charge. *Counterattack: The Newsletter of Facts to Combat Communism* published the names of individuals who, it alleged, were subversive to the United States. "To date," it said, "the efforts of our government to expose and combat Communist activities have failed." Therefore, a private organization was needed to do the job, and the publishers—calling themselves American Business Consultants—volunteered for the job. At first, they concentrated their attack upon officials in government and in trade unions, but soon their focus shifted primarily to those who worked in show business. Their newsletter encouraged subscribers to take action (such as writing to a program's sponsor or picketing outside a film theatre) that would result in loss of employment for the "subversives" they identified. In an early issue, they made their aims clear: "Communist actors, announcers, directors, writers, producers, etc., whether in radio, theatre, or movies, should all be barred to the extent permissible by law and union contracts."

Counterattack chose to include men and women of various political shadings under the "subversive" umbrella. Some were certainly Communists, but others were anti-Communists who had at one time or another expressed support for a position also supported by the Communists, such as civil rights. T. C. Kirkpatrick, one of *Counterattack*'s publishers, blithely admitted that the newsletter made no attempt to differentiate between the two. "It is impossible to do that," he said, "and do it accurately." Thus, anyone who had supported the civil rights movement, for example, was likely to be stigmatized as a "pro-Communist," "a Communist sympathizer," or "a Communist dupe" in the pages of *Counterattack*.

The following polemic is typical of its style:

COMMUNISTS HAVE CREATED A "LIVING MEMORIAL" FOR J EDWARD BROMBERG. About 1500 people were jammed into a hall in the Hotel Diplomat (NYCity) on night of Dec 23. A thousand people were turned away for lack of space.

And what had these people come for? To hear identified Communist Party (CP) members such as playwright CLIFFORD ODETS, actor MORRIS CARNOVSKY, film director JULES DASSIN, and writer ABRAHAM POLONSKY eulogize the late J EDWARD BROMBERG, actor and CP member, who refused to tell House Committee on Un-American Activities whether or not he would fight for US in event of war with Stalin Russia.

Other speakers at this obviously Communist-inspired tribute to J EDWARD BROMBERG were: [A list of sixteen names—capitalized and underlined —follows. Included are Curt Conway, Charles Skinner, and Sidney Lumet.]

The "living memorial" to BROMBERG created at this affair was a scholarship to the Drama Lab (NYCity) for some aspiring actor or actress. . . .

NBC and CBS should ask CONWAY, SKINNER and LUMET why they are giving their services to Drama Lab. Mere fact that they are on faculty doesn't mean that they are Communists or pro-Communist. But the record shows clearly that Drama Lab is run by Communists and fronters, and is helping CP.

Knowing this, would loyal Americans serve the Drama Lab?

How did *Counterattack* know that the individuals they named were "identified Communist Party (CP) members"? Although some of them had been identified by witnesses appearing before HUAC, those witnesses were not subjected to cross-examination. Rather, their testimony was accepted at face value by the congressmen who, in seeking to expose Communists in America, made no attempt to question the veracity of "friendly" witnesses (i.e., witnesses who cooperated with the committee, offering the names of alleged Communists and former Communists); hence, the witnesses' charges can hardly be said to have been proven. Other individuals were "identified" by virtue of having their names appear in previous editions of *Counterattack* or in similar publications. Some were referred to in the *Daily Worker*—the Communist newspaper that was otherwise referred to by *Counterattack* as utterly untrustworthy, the mouthpiece of a vicious political party that would lie without qualm in order to achieve its aims. To quote it as a reliable source in order to identify subversives was either incredibly naïve or deliberately deceitful, particularly when the publishers of *Counterattack* admitted that they did not check the accuracy of the reports.

Furthermore, to suggest that "NBC and CBS should ask" members of the faculty of the Drama Lab why they were working for an organization that "the record shows clearly" are Communists or pro-Communists was obviously a signal to those networks that the faculty members should be blacklisted: in effect, be deprived of their jobs. The unstated but clearly implied threat was that the executives of NBC and CBS would themselves be accused of pro-communism in a subsequent edition of *Counterattack* unless they fired those who did not meet the newsletter's standards of purity. It should also be noted that *Counterattack*'s use of such phrases as "the record" and "pro-Communists" was an important aspect of its devious technique. By failing to define their terms, the publishers made refutation of their allegations an impossible task.

The editors' desire to enforce censorship in all aspects of American life is apparent in this warning to their readers: "In buying books for Christmas and in deciding what books to recommend for purchase by public libraries, schools and college libraries, etc., *be very careful*. The following books [nine were listed, including Norman Mailer's *The Naked and the Dead*] are being plugged by the Communists."

Counterattack encouraged the production of "patriotic" radio shows and movies, but claimed that the networks and film studios were incapable of complying, even if they were well intentioned, because they did not possess "a REAL knowledge of Communism." And what was the remedy for such ignorance? "If radio or movie people have questions on this subject that need answering in connection with any script, *Counterattack* will be glad to help." Such a statement bordered on blackmail, implying that any producer who did not request help from *Counterattack* was obviously motivated by a nefarious purpose and would be castigated in a future edition of the newsletter. The approach seems so transparently blatant and self-serving that one finds it difficult to imagine how *Counterattack* managed even to survive. As David Caute has written, "Basically, American Business Consultants was in business to sell and withhold protection, having first created the [conditions] against which protection was necessary." Nevertheless, the publication quickly became so powerful that its success must have been a surprise even to its founders. Many advertising agencies, sponsors, and film executives quailed before *Counterattack*, going to any lengths to appease its editors and avoid their censure.

Counterattack's success demonstrated that the American public was intrigued and distressed by reports of Communist infiltration in show business. Undoubtedly, the congressmen on the House Committee on Un-American Activities—who were understandably interested in increasing their visibility, since all politicians realize the value of name recognition in reelection campaigns—were motivated by the likelihood of a blizzard of publicity when they announced early in 1947 that they would hold hearings on the extent of Communist influence in motion pictures later in the year.

In October 1947, under the chairmanship of J. Parnell Thomas, HUAC prepared to begin its investigation. Most of Hollywood was initially cool to the idea. The Association of Motion Picture Producers issued a statement denouncing the proposed inquiry. When Chairman

Thomas announced that the leading Hollywood producers had reached an agreement with him to establish a political blacklist that would deprive any witnesses who refused to cooperate with HUAC of their jobs, the producers issued an angry denial. Directors William Wyler and John Huston and screenwriter Philip Dunne organized the Committee for the First Amendment to support those who were subpoenaed to appear before HUAC, enlisting such luminaries as Humphrey Bogart, Katharine Hepburn, Henry Fonda, Gregory Peck, and Ava Gardner. The group asserted: "Any investigation into the political beliefs of the individual is contrary to the basic principles of our democracy. Any attempt to curb freedom of expression and to set arbitrary standards of Americanism is in itself disloyal to both the spirit and the letter of the Constitution."

Nevertheless, the hearings commenced on schedule in Washington. They were immediately plunged into controversy when each of ten "unfriendly" witnesses announced in the most adamant terms his refusal to cooperate with the committee. Witnesses and congressmen berated and shouted at one another; lawyers for the accused engaged in heated arguments with the counsel for the committee. Both sides employed inflammatory language. John Howard Lawson, the first witness to oppose the hearings, accused HUAC of compiling "so-called 'evidence' [from] stool pigeons, neurotics, publicity-seeking clowns, Gestapo agents, paid informers and a few ignorant and frightened Hollywood artists." Members of the committee were equally intemperate in their response to the witness's diatribe. Lawson refused to give direct answers to the committee's questions and was ultimately led out of the hearing room. Other witnesses were less provocative, but all challenged the committee's authority, attacked its integrity, and refused to answer when asked about their political affiliations. The ten "unfriendly" witnesses—seven writers, two directors, and one producer—may have supposed that their fierce defiance of the committee would win them support from the public, but it had the opposite effect. The sight of irate witnesses shouting invective at members of Congress led to the immediate collapse of the Committee for the First Amendment, whose stunned members left Washington after the second day of testimony. Some of them feared that *they* might be subsequent targets of investigation because they had joined an organization that criticized HUAC's methods.* And the public was equally shocked. Few Americans objected when all ten unfriendly witnesses were cited for contempt of Congress and sentenced to prison.

These men, who came to be known as the "Hollywood Ten," may have unwittingly performed a service for HUAC. Rather than focusing the nation's attention upon the arrogance of any group who claimed the right to define what is "American" and what is "un-American," the Ten aroused such antagonism that Hollywood, responding to the public's outrage, capitulated completely to the committee. Eric Johnston, who, as the spokesman for the Association of Motion Picture Producers, had earlier denied that the film industry would participate in blacklisting, announced the association's new policy:

> Members of the Association of Motion Picture Producers deplore the action of the ten Hollywood men who have been cited for contempt . . . their actions have been a disservice to their employers and have impaired their usefulness to the industry.
>
> We will forthwith discharge or suspend without compensation those in our employ and we will not re-employ any of the ten until such time as he is acquitted or has purged himself of contempt and declares under oath that he is not a Communist.
>
> On the broader issue of alleged subversive and disloyal elements in Hollywood . . . We will not knowingly employ a Communist or a member of any party or group which advocates the overthrow of the Government of the United States.

HUAC ended the hearings two weeks after they began, but promised that further investigations would follow. Nearly four years elapsed between the 1947 hearings and the next round. Still, a new era had begun: it clearly had become possible for a congressional committee to impose its standards of patriotism upon individual Americans. Those who refused to accept HUAC's standards might well end up in jail, as the Hollywood Ten eventually did.

In the interim between the 1947 and 1951 investigations, the success of *Counterattack* and the notoriety achieved by HUAC stimulated other

---

*They were right. A number of those who were members of the organization were later accused of "Communist sympathies" solely because they had joined the Committee for the First Amendment; some were blacklisted as a result.

organizations to issue lists of "subversives," often in newly created newsletters. The Catholic War Veterans and the American Legion were among those who issued bulletins asking their members to picket movies or boycott the products of radio and television sponsors employing anyone who was, in the opinion of these organizations, politically impure. In October 1949, an anonymously written article entitled "Red Fronts in Radio" appeared in the *Sign*, a Catholic magazine. It listed fifty-one "radio celebrities who have been cited in public records as having been associated with Communist causes or fronts."

In 1950, the American Legion's newsletter, *Summary of Trends and Developments Exposing the Communist Conspiracy*, printed the names of 127 alleged pro-Communists and advised its readers: "Organize a letter-writing group of six to ten relatives and friends to make the sentiments of Americans heard on the important issues of the day. Phone, telegraph, or write to radio and television sponsors employing entertainers with known front records. . . . Give Americans a break just for a change by giving pro-Communists the bum's rush off the air." More specific advice followed: "In writing or phoning radio sponsors and others MAKE NO CHARGES OR CLAIMS. Merely state that you buy their products or services and enjoy their radio or TV shows but that you DISAPPROVE OR OBJECT TO SO-AND-SO ON THEIR PROGRAMS AND DESIRE THAT THEY BE REMOVED. NOTHING ELSE . . . DON'T LET THE SPONSORS PASS THE BUCK BACK TO YOU BY DEMANDING 'PROOF' OF COMMUNIST FRONTING BY SOME CHARACTER ABOUT WHOM YOU HAVE COMPLAINED. YOU DON'T HAVE TO PROVE ANYTHING. . . . YOU SIMPLY DO NOT LIKE SO-AND-SO ON THEIR PROGRAMS . . . you are not interested in their products or show until so-and-so is canned from the air." The results were predictable: since no film studio wanted its product picketed and no sponsor was eager to face a boycott, most of those about whom complaints were received were fired.

Even individual citizens, such as Laurence A. Johnson, owner of a chain of supermarkets in Syracuse, New York, became active in the crusade to rid the mass media of those they disliked. Johnson and other members of his family monitored all network television programs and took down the names of actors, writers, and directors whose political opinions they found objectionable. Then, working in concert with American Legion Post Number 41, Johnson wrote to the sponsors of the offending programs, informing them that he would remove their products from the shelves of his supermarkets unless they agreed to fire the artists he named. Moreover, he would notify other supermarkets and other American Legion posts to do the same. Those sponsors who may have been disposed to consider Johnson a mere annoyance soon learned otherwise. His certainty of the rightness of his approach, his tenacity in pursuing it until he was victorious (with the backing of an American Legion post and the implied support of the national organization and its millions of members), made him into an extraordinarily powerful figure. By the early 1950s, his word was law in radio and television. No one worked without Laurence Johnson's consent. Sponsors, advertising agencies, and networks all sought his approval and feared his wrath.

Most of the trade unions representing artists in radio, television, and films capitulated almost immediately to the blacklisting fever. In 1951, the Screen Actors Guild said that it would not come to the defense of any member who could not find employment because of his or her political activities. That same year, the American Federation of Radio Artists agreed to deny membership to anyone who had been identified as a Communist by the Justice Department, the FBI, or in court. In 1953, Ronald Reagan, president of the Screen Actors Guild, announced that all new members and union officials would be required to take loyalty oaths.

Some groups, like AWARE, Inc., and American Business Consultants, the publishers of *Counterattack*, not only listed the names of supposed subversives in newsletters, but also offered their investigative services to any client who wished to pay for them. An advertising agency, for example, would submit the name of an actor to AWARE, Inc., before offering him a job; the actor's "employability" would depend entirely upon the report compiled and submitted to the agency by AWARE.

Competition among newsletters and groups was fierce, since each wished to be known as having the greatest effect in rooting Communist influence out of show business. *Counterattack*, for example, alleged that a rival newsletter "unintentionally helps the Communists." Since such charges sound authoritative, but can be neither proven nor disproven, they were exchanged freely and often.

American Business Consultants remained the leaders in the business of exposing "Communists" in the performing arts. In addition to the continued publication of *Counterattack*, the company issued a book on June 22, 1950, called *Red Channels: The Report of Communist Influence in Radio and Television* (compiled by the three publishers and an un-acknowledged contributor, a free-lance writer named Vincent Hart-nett). The 213-page book, a compilation of names of 151 alleged subversives (including 44 writers and 68 actors), listed each individual's objectionable activities, according to the standards of *Red Channels*, immediately after his or her name. The listings included everything from organizations identified as subversive or as Communist-leaning by a governmental body (such as the California Committee on Un-American Activities, the Special Committee on Un-American Activities, the Massachusetts House Committee on Un-American Activities, etc.) to organizations vaguely described as "Communist-affiliated," "Communist-dominated," "Communist-front," or simply "subversive." As with *Counterattack*, the "evidence" for the allegations was often unverified information culled from newspapers, including the *Daily Worker*. In fact, Theodore Kirkpatrick, one of the publishers of the book, told *Sponsor* magazine, "We've never said the 'facts' in *Red Channels* were correct or incorrect. We've just reported the public records."

Some of the listings referred to organizations that had not functioned since the 1930s. Many of the individuals accused of Communist sympathies were cited for activities in which they had taken part before 1945, when the Soviet Union was America's ally in the war.

A few organizations, which were not identified as either Communist or Communist-inspired, seem to have been included for no particular reason other than that they met with the publishers' disfavor.* Such, for example, was the End Jim Crow in Baseball Committee, to which, according to *Red Channels*, Sam Jaffe belonged. Jaffe was also identified

---

*Counterattack had often done the same thing. In 1947, for example, after the attorney general of the United States made public a list of alleged Communist front groups, *Counterattack* arbitrarily added thirty-four more organizations, because, they said, they "ought to have been" on the list.

as having signed an advertisement, "We Are for Wallace," that appeared in the New York *Times* on October 20, 1948, under the auspices of the National Council of the Arts, Sciences and Professions. This latter organization was identified as "Formed 1948 of elements of Progressive Citizens of America who did not desire to affiliate with Progressive Party." And the source that cited the organization as "subversive" was *Counterattack*, on June 18, 1948. In other words, the source for the allegation in *Red Channels* that the Progressive Citizens of America was a "subversive" group was *Red Channels* itself, under the name of its alter ego, *Counterattack*.

Despite such absurdities, *Red Channels* quickly became an immensely powerful force in the entertainment business, so much so that it was known as "the Bible of Madison Avenue." Its impact was heightened when the Communist army of North Korea invaded South Korea three days after *Red Channels* was published. To some Americans who had not yet supported the Cold War, the invasion of South Korea seemed to affirm the danger of Communist influence not only abroad but in the United States as well. The Korean War, the Cold War atmosphere, the perception by millions of Americans of Senator McCarthy as a national savior—all these events and attitudes were reflected in the world of entertainment. And that meant that anyone whose name was listed in *Red Channels* faced the imminent prospect of being blacklisted from show business.

The first performer to be deprived of employment as a result of her listing in *Red Channels* was the actress Jean Muir, who had been chosen to play a continuing role on *The Aldrich Family*, a popular television program. When NBC received a number of telephone calls—"more than twenty" but "less than thirty," according to a network official—objecting to Muir's employment on the basis of her listing in *Red Channels*, she was dropped from the program. General Foods, the show's sponsor, issued a press release stating, "The use of controversial personalities or the discussion of controversial subjects in our advertising may provide unfavorable criticism and even antagonism among sizable groups of customers. Such reaction injures both acceptance of our products and our public relations. General Foods advertising, therefore, avoids the use of material and personalities which in its judgment are controversial."

The announcement prompted a flood of mail to General Foods. A spokesman said that 3,300 letters were received opposing the firing of Jean Muir (or anyone who had been condemned without a trial) and 2,065 favoring the sponsor's action. The spokesman stated that General Foods believed that 80 percent of the anti-Muir mail was stimulated by pressure groups. Nevertheless, the company refused to alter its stance, although, according to the spokesman, her listing in *Red Channels* had "nothing to do with our . . . actions."

Jean Muir denied belonging to four of the organizations *Red Channels* claimed she belonged to and explained that the other five charges were meaningless. For example, of her membership in the Southern Conference for Human Welfare, she said, "Yes, and I'm very proud to have been a member of the conference. . . . At the same time as I belonged, so did Mrs. Franklin D. Roosevelt, Senator Frank Graham, officials of the YMCA and the NAACP and later Senator Estes Kefauver. The conference was a sincere effort to improve the lot of all people in the South, white and Negro." Accused of having sent a telegram to the Moscow Art Theatre on its fiftieth anniversary, she admitted having done so but questioned why it should have been interpreted as a subversive act. "I sent them a cable of congratulations—so did a lot of other theatre people—on the fiftieth anniversary two years ago," she said. "We all follow the Stanislavski method of acting; we were paying tribute to that and nothing else."

But she was unable to persuade General Foods or NBC to rehire her. She had become a statistic: the first individual who could trace her blacklisting to *Red Channels*, in spite of official denials. The denials were necessary, of course, for an admission might prompt a lawsuit or unfavorable publicity.

No blacklist existed, according to those who were in a position to hire and fire individuals who made their livings in show business. A "blacklist," per se, might have been judged illegal, so the captains of the industry simply denied its existence. They insisted that it was pure coincidence that Mr. X, who had acted steadily in films or radio or television for the previous ten years, had not received a single offer of employment since his name was listed in *Counterattack* or *Red Channels*. Mr. X simply wasn't "right" for any of the roles in movies, radio, or television, they said; he was too short, too tall, too fat, too thin, his voice was too high or too low, his hair was too gray or not gray enough. That he had been named by *Counterattack* as a subversive had no bearing on the situation at all.

In spite of these denials, names of individuals stigmatized as "politically unreliable" were widely circulated throughout show business and anyone who was named was unemployable. The blacklist may not have consisted of a single written document—books and newsletters other than *Red Channels* and *Counterattack* were influential and some people landed on the "list" not because their names had appeared in any book or newsletter but solely because of rumor and innuendo—but there is no doubt that it existed. At one network, a list of approximately one hundred names was circulated to all producers, with the seemingly innocuous notation: "For Your Information: Keep these names in mind when casting . . ."

Some individuals and organizations avoided the accusation of "blacklisting" by publishing "whitelists." One such was Mrs. John Buchanan, the wife of an army reservist in Syracuse. Mrs. Buchanan called her compendium, comprised of 188 names, "a partial list of actors and actresses who have never been supporters of Communist causes. . . . The entertainment world is crowded with competitive talent," Mrs. Buchanan stated. "Why not ask your entertainment promoters to support *exclusively* honest stars of the calibre of Ginger Rogers, Robert Montgomery, John Wayne, Lois Wilson, Adolphe Menjou, Robert Taylor?"

The individual who was blacklisted was all but powerless. The publishers of *Red Channels* had protected themselves against lawsuits by inserting a disclaimer in their volume: "The information set forth in the following report is taken from records available to the public. The purpose of this compilation is . . . to indicate the extent to which many prominent actors and artists have been inveigled to lend their names, according to these public records, to organizations espousing Communist causes. This, *regardless of whether they actually believe in, sympathize with, or even recognize the cause advanced*" (emphasis added). Besides, individuals who might have been tempted to bring lawsuits against *Red Channels* were dissuaded by the knowledge that such an action would make them, in David Caute's words, "even more controversial, and therefore less employable than ever." Neither the networks nor sponsors nor advertising agencies could be sued because all of them firmly denied the existence of a blacklist; most even claimed to be ignorant of the existence of *Red Channels* and similar publications.

Performers who were listed in *Red Channels* were especially vulnerable. A writer could continue to sell his scripts (under an assumed name and at a fraction of the price he formerly commanded), but an actor could not conceal his identity, and was therefore simply denied work. (After his listing in *Red Channels*, Zero Mostel said, "I am a man of a thousand faces, all of them blacklisted.") If, in fact, Mr. X *was* being denied employment because of physical characteristics, as potential employers insisted, he might alter the pitch of his voice or dye his hair; but how can one remove his name from a list that doesn't exist? One could plead his case before a film executive or an advertiser, claiming that he had been unfairly accused (and many did so), but it was a futile exercise. The response was always the same: since no blacklist existed, there was no way an employer could remove an individual's name from it.

The vice-president of one network did not hesitate to say, "We're in a business that has to please our customers; that's the main thing we have to do, keep people happy, and, to do that, we have to stay out of trouble." Staying out of trouble meant avoiding "controversy." And one avoided controversy by denying employment to anyone who had been accused, rightly or wrongly, of subversive activity. One producer-director admitted, "We quarantine everybody in [*Red Channels*]. We cannot take any chances."

An actors' agent, speaking anonymously, was asked by writer Merle Miller in the mid-1950s, when Red-baiting activity was at its peak, "What do you think has been the effect of *Red Channels*?" He responded by holding up a list of seventeen names, "some of the biggest names in the business. Why, I don't even bother suggesting them any more. I know better. I've had too many turndowns. They're in *Red Channels*.

"The other day I got a call from this producer, and he says he wants somebody for the lead in one of his shows. He asks me, 'Who've you got like————[the name of a prominent Hollywood actor named in *Red Channels*]?' I say, 'What do you mean, who've I got like————? I've got the boy himself. Why don't you use him.' And this producer says, 'We just can't do it. I'm sorry, but we just can't, and you know why we can't.' "

Most of the Hollywood studios required their employees to take loyalty oaths in order to get—or to maintain—jobs. In some cases, only "controversial" employees were required to sign, which occasionally led to ludicrous situations. One man, born in the mid-1930s, was denied work because, it was said, he had fought for the Loyalists in the Spanish Civil War. The man pointed out that he had barely begun to walk when the Spanish Civil War was fought. Nevertheless, the studio insisted that he sign a loyalty oath before they would offer him a contract.

Despite the reluctance of most blacklisted individuals to file lawsuits against their accusers, Fredric March and Florence Eldridge sued *Counterattack* for $500,000 after the newsletter named them as Communist sympathizers. Until *Counterattack*'s accusation, they had worked steadily—separately and together—in the various theatrical media for years; but in 1948, their tax return showed a net income of a mere $2.58. *Counterattack* settled with the Marches out of court.

Some of those who were listed in *Red Channels* made efforts to "clear their names." Several went to the American Business Consultants office and attempted to explain that the charges leveled against them in *Counterattack* or *Red Channels* were inaccurate. But the publishers rarely made public retractions, claiming, "It is up to the public to judge his case." Of course, the information on which the public was expected to make a judgment—or at least that segment of the public that could provide employment for artists in the mass media—was the information listed in *Red Channels* and *Counterattack*.

Those who were willing to pay—either in cash or the loss of integrity or both—could get off the blacklist. The procedure entailed seeking out someone of importance in right-wing circles (a lawyer, an official of the American Legion, an advertising agency executive, a newspaper columnist, a union official) and expressing a willingness to publicly apologize for past transgressions, real or imagined. Often this involved making a financial contribution to a conservative cause and appearing at events sponsored by right-wing organizations. Nearly always, it meant volunteering to appear before HUAC and giving them the names of Communists and former Communists. But what if the individual had not been a member of the Party and did not know any Communists? No problem: the lawyer, the columnist, or the committee itself would provide a list of names, and the repentant witness would simply be told to read the names into the record. This sort of public humiliation was simply too degrading for most blacklisted individuals to contemplate, even if they were entirely innocent of all the charges that had been leveled against them; and many of those who *had* been Communists were unwilling to bring the same sort of troubles to others that they had endured; so most of them chose to remain blacklisted.

It is interesting to note that Kenneth Bierly, one of the three founders of American Business Consultants and an author of *Red Channels*, left the organization to set up his own enterprise, Kenby Associates; one of Kenby's clients was Columbia Pictures, who hired Bierly to clear Judy Holliday of the charges leveled against her by *Red Channels* and *Counterattack*. Bierly thus profited both when he called her a Communist sympathizer and when he claimed that she was not a Communist sympathizer.

Zero Mostel was listed in *Red Channels*, as were many of his friends: Sam Jaffe, Philip Loeb, Jack Gilford, Madeline Lee [Gilford], Burgess Meredith, Himan Brown, Dorothy Parker. According to the publication, Zero had entertained for "Social Functions of the Communist Party," had been a member of American Youth for Democracy, had sponsored the May Day Parade in 1947, had performed at a benefit for the Joint Anti-Fascist Refugee Committee, and had supported the Civil Rights Congress by attending a "reception for 19 Hollywood Writers, Directors and Actors," including those who had become known as the Hollywood Ten, at the Park Central Hotel in New York on November 2, 1947.

Even before the publication of *Red Channels*, however, on the assumption that Zero's listing in *Counterattack* would make it impossible for him to find employment in the mass media for years to come—and perhaps for the rest of his life—Kate went to work. She had always aspired to act and was given a small role in *The Bird Cage*, an Arthur Laurents play that opened on Broadway in February 1950. But the play ran for only twenty-one performances and the Mostels again faced the prospect of prolonged unemployment.

Many of those whose names appeared in *Red Channels* were effectively blacklisted the moment the book appeared. Others had already encountered difficulty finding work in the mass media because of charges leveled by *Counterattack* and similar newsletters, and had given up hope. Zero's friend Sam Jaffe, for one, was regarded as unemployable on television and in motion pictures in the early 1950s. His career in ruins, he might have succumbed to despair if he had not run into the playwright Thornton Wilder, an occasional professor at Harvard and an enthusiastic supporter of the Brattle Theatre in Cambridge, Massachusetts. When he saw the despondent Jaffe in New York, Wilder said, "Well, you don't have to sit here. There's a company in Cambridge where you should go and work rather than twiddle your thumbs and complain." Jaffe accepted Wilder's challenge when the Brattle Company offered him the opportunity to appear in Molière's classic comedy, *Tartuffe*. Not being subject to the same commercial pressures as the mass media, the theatre as an institution did not blacklist (although particular producers might refuse to hire anyone named in *Red Channels*). Jobs on Broadway are scarce at any time, however; and in a period when professional theatre outside New York City was practically nonexistent, the Brattle offered a rare opportunity for a performer to practice his craft, albeit at a far lower salary than was being paid on Broadway or in television and films.

Zero traveled to Cambridge to see his friend's opening night. It appeared that Jaffe might need the support of his friends, for a right-wing Boston newspaper had carried stories calculated to inflame the public against his appearance. Jerome Kilty, who started the Brattle company when he was a Harvard undergraduate and played Damis in the production of *Tartuffe*, recalled the tense atmosphere on the first night. "Zero was there because of Sam," he said, "wearing a false beard [as a joke] and sitting in the front row. When Sam made his first entrance and began to talk, he looked at the audience and broke out in a sweat. He couldn't speak. Eventually, he walked off the stage; he couldn't go through with it. I went into his dressing room and he was just sitting, looking in the mirror, and sweating. So the curtain came down and the audience got its money back. The next day, we all had to talk Sam into going on again. During the afternoon rehearsal, we encouraged him: 'Time to get on the horse again,' 'You have to go on.' And he did. Fortunately, the audience was full that night, and sympathetic—they all knew that he was blacklisted—and they gave him an ovation when he came on and applauded him throughout the play. He got through it and, after that, resumed his career."

After *Tartuffe*, Jaffe said to Mostel, "Now it's your turn; you've got to do something here." Zero, who had been working infrequently in any case, and who had good reason to believe that he was blacklisted, accepted the Brattle's invitation to act in another play by Molière, *The Imaginary Invalid*, a farce he had long wanted to appear in. (While he was in rehearsal, *Red Channels* was issued, ending all speculation about the reason for Zero's recent career difficulties.) The main character, Argan, provided Zero with a role that would give him every opportunity to employ his comic gifts. But Mostel did more than play the leading role; he adapted the play as well, although he did not so much translate it from the French as reassemble the existing English versions.

Kate was hired to play the role of the soubrette, who serves as a foil for Argan. Moreover, she was also paid as director of the production, although she had nothing whatever to do with the direction. She received the salary because Zero's first wife, Clara, was still entitled to a sizable portion of whatever money he earned as a performer. In earlier years, Zero had been unenthusiastic about the arrangement, but he could afford it. In the summer of 1950, however, money had become very scarce and the salary he and Kate would receive at the Brattle Theatre had to be carefully managed; it might represent the Mostels' only income for months to come. To ensure that only a small portion of the total went to Clara, Zero himself was paid only a minimal salary while Kate received two sizable paychecks, as actress and director.

Blacklisted or not, Zero remained characteristically irrepressible while working at the Brattle. Jerome Kilty recalls the company eating lunch together "in our communal dining hall. Zero would always get up and entertain us, and if he felt like it he would dance down the center of the tables, carrying on, being very, very funny, and very, very obnoxious at the same time."

The biographical sketch of Zero that appeared in the program was written by the actor himself. It said, in full:

ZERO MOSTEL's real name is Talburnium Kohhaaran Von Ecclesex. He was born in upper Slbeesing Holstein and is part Schnanger. He traveled in a stock company with the immortal Keane [*sic*], Garrick, Ben Jonson and Birdie Tebbets to the far corners of the globe, until one day his brother smashed the globe to smithereens. He has appeared in many films: *The Great Train Robbery, Greed, Grass*, and Pathé News Reels. Mr. Mostel is doing a festival of plays in a diving bell for the submarine service. All he has to say is, "Heads Off to Talburnium."

Zero's performance in *The Imaginary Invalid* began with Sam Jaffe sitting in the front row, wearing a false beard, and hugely enjoying the production along with the rest of the audience. Mostel considered *The Imaginary Invalid* his most satisfying performing experience to that time. The essence of Molière's farces is improvisatory, allowing Zero to work within the framework of a well-defined character but not restraining his ebullient, larger-than-life comic style. The following week, the entire production was moved to Cohasset, Massachusetts, where the Brattle ran a second theatre. Zero said of the experience: "I'd never worked in a play before then, and I found it exciting, playing with an ensemble and in a part that offered the opportunity for me to do so much—acting, comedy, singing and dancing, as well as a complete character. The part utilized what I felt I had. And I didn't have to work with a microphone or wear a blue suit and a tie." More than ever, after *The Imaginary Invalid*, he was determined to act rather than to perform stand-up comedy.

Kate also found the experience gratifying. "She was talented and meticulous," Kilty said, "the ideal straight woman. She was like a nurse with a doctor. 'Scalpel!' It would be there. 'Syringe!' It would be there. She was really very good. And she was naturally vivacious, and she used that to good advantage in the role." Moreover, whenever Zero was tempted to draw out a scene too long or overindulge in "shtick," Kate was "the one person who could tell him to knock it off," Kilty said. But, he added, "she didn't always succeed, because Z simply *couldn't* knock it off sometimes."

One of Zero's favorite stories concerned an elderly woman who asked to see him after one evening's presentation. She told him how much she had enjoyed his performance, "but," she added, "I would have liked it better if you had done the play in the original French."

"Do you know French?" Zero asked.

"No," she said. For once, Zero was speechless.

Following *The Imaginary Invalid*, Zero was eager to do more work with the Brattle. He wanted to play the title role in Ben Jonson's satire, *Volpone*, but the Brattle had recently presented that play with Thomas Gomez, so they were unable to accommodate Mostel's wishes. Both sides agreed to wait until Zero found a play he wanted to do and that the Brattle was willing to produce.

Meanwhile, a most unexpected event occurred. Zero, who believed that he was firmly blacklisted and did not expect to work in the mass media ever again, was offered a contract to appear in *Panic in the Streets*, a Twentieth Century-Fox film directed by Elia Kazan, a left-wing acquaintance of Mostel's from New York. It was also surprising that Zero was offered a role that would not capitalize on his fame as a comic; instead, he was to play a vicious thug who ultimately turns coward. Mostel's role was not a large one—the featured actors were Richard Widmark, Paul Douglas, and Barbara Bel Geddes—but it *was* a paying job and it did offer Zero the opportunity to break out of his comic persona.

Panic in the Streets is a well-played, gripping film. As Thomas M. Pryor said in the New York *Times*, it was "directed with a keen sense of appreciation for violence and suspense." Zero's performance was praised and—to his utter surprise—resulted in Fox's offering him a one-year contract. A special guardian angel seemed to have been watching over him. In some mysterious, totally unexpected way, Mostel had apparently beaten the blacklist. While other actors whose names appeared in *Red Channels* were losing jobs, Zero was suddenly gaining them.

He could continue to work in nightclubs, too, as he did during the autumn of 1950. Clearly he had lost none of his skill. He "keeps the Riviera rocking with laughter," said one review. "Here's a comedian [with] keen characterizations and story-telling ability."

Late in 1950, the Mostels moved to Los Angeles, where Fox kept Zero busy in undistinguished films such as *The Enforcer* (again playing a hoodlum, this time in support of Humphrey Bogart), *Sirocco* (Bogart again led the cast; Zero played an Armenian spy), *Mr. Belvedere Rings the Bell* (a comedy featuring Clifton Webb), and *The Guy Who Came Back* (Zero, playing an ex-boxer who ran a popular restaurant, *à la* Jack Dempsey, was called "funny and properly brassy" in A. H. Weiler's New York *Times* review), all released in 1951, and *The Model and the Marriage Broker* (with Zero as a timid bachelor), released early the following year.

The artistic satisfaction he gained from these movies was minimal. His appearance in Molière meant far more to him; even his nightclub experiences gave him greater enjoyment. "I hated Hollywood," Zero said later. "Everything about it—the people, the climate, the business. Everything. My wife hated it. The kids hated it." But Fox was paying him a good salary, he was able to rent a studio and spend a great deal of his time painting, and, as it seemed likely that his good fortune in evading the blacklist would not last forever, he and Kate hoped he would remain on the Twentieth Century-Fox payroll for as long as possible.

With three months remaining on his contract, Fox allowed Columbia Pictures to borrow Zero for the film version of Samuel Taylor's play *The Happy Time*. This promised to be a picture of some distinction, and Mostel's role would be larger and more gratifying than those he had played for Fox. But his listing in *Red Channels* finally caught up with him and his luck ran out. When he arrived at the Columbia studio to begin work, he was informed—without explanation—that he would not be allowed on the set. The guard at the entrance gate refused to follow Zero's suggestion that he call the film's producer; he simply repeated his orders to turn Mostel away. Zero went home to await word, but no one called him with an explanation. Instead, he saw a notice in *Variety* that he had been replaced in *The Happy Time* by another actor. He then received word that Twentieth Century-Fox had canceled the remainder of his contract.

Perhaps the studios had received notice about what was going to happen at the next round of hearings by the House Committee on Un-American Activities. For the first time, on January 29, 1952, Mostel was identified to the committee as a member of the Communist party. His accuser was a screenwriter, Martin Berkeley, who testified: "Zero Mostel, I met him in Hollywood, I will have to say around 1938, at the home of Lionel Stander. There was a meeting of the writers' faction [of the Communist party] at which I was present, and he was among those who were there." The accusation was totally false. Mostel had never been in California until 1942. But Martin Berkeley was providing HUAC with all the names it could possibly want. He appeared before the committee more than once, naming a total of 160 people as Communists—more than any other single witness. Even William Wheeler, the staff investigator for HUAC, thought it was absurd for Berkeley to claim that he could recall 160 individuals who had attended meetings with him more than a decade earlier. But Berkeley nevertheless testified that he could positively identify all 160. He couldn't, of course. In addition to Mostel, Victor Navasky discovered, Berkeley misidentified approximately a dozen others. Ring Lardner, Jr., also confirmed to me that "Berkeley was not very reliable. He said that Lillian Hellman and Dashiell Hammett were at a specific meeting at his house. And I know they were not, because I was there."

Still, Berkeley's testimony made it certain that Mostel would receive a subpoena from HUAC, and that he would be pressed to offer the names of other "subversives" as the price of continuing to work in show business. The threat of such a subpoena was dreaded by all who had reason to fear it, for to testify before HUAC was to put anyone with a left-wing background in an untenable position.

For those whose principles would not allow them to name names, appearing before HUAC was a horrific experience, with the outcome predetermined: one would either be sent to prison or be blacklisted— and possibly both. When the committee posed its inevitable question, "Are you now or have you ever been a member of the Communist party?," only three responses were possible—to affirm that one was or had been a Communist, to deny membership, or to refuse to answer by invoking the Fifth Amendment right not to incriminate oneself. Each response, however, contained its own trap.

Witnesses who had been members of the Communist party and were willing to say so, but were unwilling to supply the committee with the names of others who may have been Party members, did not dare to make the admission unless they also were willing to run the risk of a citation for contempt of Congress and the probable result: a prison term. The trap in this choice occurred because witnesses could not answer one question about a particular topic (such as, "Have you ever been a member of the Communist Party?") without forfeiting their right to subsequent use of the Fifth Amendment on all related questions (such as, "What names of other Communists can you give us?"). The inquisitors were, therefore, free to follow up with related questions on the premise that full clarification and elaboration were necessary in order for justice to be served. Any refusal to answer once the witness had been responsive to the primary question could result in contempt of Congress. Thus, witnesses who answered that they were or had been Communists *had to answer* every succeeding question put to them concerning their Party membership. In the eyes of the committee, only by naming names could witnesses prove that their repentance was genuine, their conversion to "true Americanism" complete.

To answer "No" to the question about one's own membership, even if the response were truthful, acknowledged the right of the committee to inquire into such matters—an acknowledgment many witnesses were not willing to make. This second choice also involved the risk of being accused of perjury, since the reason individuals were called to appear before HUAC was because they had been named as Communists by previous witnesses. The committee, of course, would believe the testimony of a "cooperative" witness when it conflicted with testimony HUAC did not wish to hear. Thus, in the eyes of the committee, witnesses who answered "No" had perjured themselves. And if convicted of perjury, the witnesses faced jail sentences. Furthermore, a "No" answer also resulted in a waiver of Fifth Amendment immunity, so that those who truthfully denied membership in the Communist party would still be required to offer the names of others they had seen at benefits or social gatherings the committee regarded with suspicion.

The third alternative, to invoke the Fifth Amendment, also involved a cruel catch, for in the eyes of the public (which included film-studio bosses, television sponsors, and advertising company executives), "taking the Fifth" was tantamount to an admission of guilt. Thus, witnesses who invoked the Fifth Amendment would escape the likelihood of imprisonment, but would inevitably be blacklisted and lose their jobs.

Elia Kazan came to Mostel's rescue once again after Zero was fired by Twentieth Century-Fox and named before HUAC by Martin Berkeley. Kazan offered Zero a role in a play he was directing on Broadway,

*Flight into Egypt.** Playing the minor role of a heartless hotelkeeper, Mostel was "exactly right," according to Louis Sheaffer in the Brooklyn *Eagle*; but Elliot Norton of the Boston *Post*, reviewing a performance during the pre-Broadway Boston engagment, said that he was "overplaying ridiculously." Most of the critics thought that Mostel and the other performers acquitted themselves reasonably well, but the weaknesses of the play prevented it from achieving success. After only eighteen performances, *Flight into Egypt* closed. The final performance, in April 1952, marked one of the last times Zero would be offered a living wage to appear on a Broadway stage for a period of five years. A week's engagement in *Lunatics and Lovers* in 1955 was the only exception. Mostel had been fortunate to escape the blacklist for as long as he did, but there were to be no more reprieves.

Zero let the Brattle Theatre know that he was available to do a summer production for them and that he would like to appear in another play by Molière. Consequently, *The Doctor in Spite of Himself* was chosen for August 1952. Again, the play was a farce, well suited to Zero's abilities; and, once again, Kate appeared in a supporting role. This production, too, was a success.† The translation of the play was by Elmer Engstrom (who played the role of Leander) "with interpolations by Mr. Mostel." Zero hoped that he would eventually be able to play Molière on Broadway, but, as he said later, "producers go wild when

---

*Subsequently, Kazan would renounce his left-wing past. He became a cooperative witness before the House Committee on Un-American Activities, supplying them with the names of Communists and former Communists.

In Kazan's autobiography, he referred to Zero as "an extraordinary artist and a delightful companion, one of the funniest and most original men I'd ever met." After Kazan's testimony before HUAC, he ran into Mostel one evening in New York. "By that time," Kazan wrote, "I'd hardened myself against the disapproval some old friends were giving me and didn't much care what people a good deal closer to me than Zero thought. But for some reason I did care what he thought. He stopped me and put an arm around my neck—a little too tight—and said in one of the most dolorous voices I've ever heard, 'Why did you do that? You shouldn't have done that.' He took me into a bar and we had a drink and then another, but he didn't say much and I didn't say much. All he did was look at me once in a while, and his eyes were saying what his lips were not: 'Why did you do that?' "

†It was also the last production given by the Brattle Theatre Company in Cambridge. The group moved to New York and renamed itself the Brattle Shakespeare Festival a few months afterward.

they hear the name 'Molière.' They immediately start figuring out the cost of the costumes."

Jerome Kilty summarized his impressions of working with Zero on the Molière plays. "His creative energy was limitless," he said; "his problem was harnessing it. He would decide how to play something, and you'd think we were going to get on with it, and he'd go back and think of a new way of doing it, upsetting everything. Sometimes he would think of a new way during a performance, and he'd try to break the other actors up." Perhaps it was inevitable that Mostel's years as a nightclub performer—where the comic must think quickly on his feet and be ready to deliver a clever ad lib in the face of any emergency—would carry over into his stage work. His improvisational attitude certainly lent his performances an air of spontaneity, but at times it also proved troublesome to his fellow actors.

Although Mostel appeared at the Brattle Theatre for only two weeks in 1950 and one week in 1952, these performances had a significant impact on his future career. Not only did the productions give further impetus to his decision to work as an actor whenever possible, but also, in Zero's words, "from that time on, people began to realize that I wasn't just another stand-up comic."

Stand-up comedy seemed to offer Zero the most likely possibility of a steady income, however. But he soon discovered that the blacklist also affected nightclubs, and in a particularly insidious way. The owners of the clubs knew that Zero Mostel, to whom they had once paid $4,000 per week, was no longer appearing on television or in the movies. Consequently, his name was no longer as much of an attraction as it had been. Moreover, the club owners knew that Zero's blacklisted status would probably prevent him from working in the mass media again, and that he was therefore totally dependent on the income he could derive from nightclubs. So the owners, aware that they no longer needed Zero as badly as Zero needed them, offered him engagements (when engagements were offered at all) at a fraction of the salary he had once received.

Walter Bernstein, a writer and a friend of Zero's, recalled accompanying him to the Concord Hotel one night during the period when Mostel was blacklisted. "I drove Zero up to the Catskills that night," Bernstein said. "I remember it very well because he was so humiliated going to a place where he used to make, I don't know, two or three thousand dollars a night, and now he worked for five hundred." But when Bernstein and Mostel arrived at the resort, the manager informed Zero that he would have to accept $250 rather than the $500 that had been agreed upon. Mostel objected—loudly and emphatically—but the manager knew that he held the upper hand. Zero wouldn't have accepted the job in the first place if he hadn't needed the money badly. He had already driven up from New York and could not afford to return empty-handed. The manager held firm: $250—take it or leave it. Seething with anger but feeling impotent, Zero took it. "And he went on stage in a rage," Bernstein continued, "just furious. But he did his act with ferocious brilliance, cursing the audience as he did, calling them terrible names in Yiddish." The audience thought that it was all part of the act. "The more he did that the more they loved him. They just howled. He would assault them and they thought it was hysterical. Zero got no satisfaction from it at all. He was on for forty minutes and they wouldn't let him go, and then he came off in this rage and, I remember, drank up a whole bottle of liquor and just went to sleep."

So even nightclubs would not pay the family's grocery bills for long, and the prospects of future employment in show business seemed dim. Zero and Kate had to make several significant adjustments in their lives. He would have to find some other way to earn a living. Kate would have to work when money became scarce. The family would have to live more frugally. Zero's penchant for buying works of art for the apartment was just one habit that he would have to change.

Some of the enterprises Mostel hoped would help provide an income came to nothing. One such possibility occurred when the actor Lou Gilbert visited Zero in his studio one afternoon. Gilbert was taken by the portraits and caricatures he saw, how they seemed to capture the essence of the individual portrayed by concentrating on his most pronounced physical feature. An idea suddenly occurred to him. "Maybe that's what we could do about acting," he said. "You know, how a guy walks and how a guy with a hooked nose—does he walk with his nose first or his stomach or what? It would be marvelous to teach something like that." Zero agreed, and he and Gilbert placed ads in the Sunday *Times* and the Sunday *Herald Tribune* announcing the Mostel-Gilbert school of comic acting. Some sixty applications were received. Zero offered to interview each applicant in order to determine his or her fitness for the proposed course. But he must have been disappointed in the caliber of those who applied, for he turned down all but five of them—leaving too few students to make the school a paying proposition. The idea was dropped.

Fortunately, Zero was not without an alternative means of economic survival. He could return full-time to painting, which he loved beyond any other activity. He would not be able to earn the kind of money he and his family had become accustomed to, of course, but if he could sell one or two canvases a week, the situation might not be so bleak. During the next nine years, months would go by during which the sales of his paintings barely covered his expenses, but, because he was doing what he most enjoyed, he had few complaints.

5

The Blacklist: II

Zero was able to live through the blacklist because he could sublimate whatever bitterness he might otherwise have felt by immersing himself in his painting. He liked to say he was a painter who acted for a living, rather than an actor who painted as a hobby. There may have been a self-serving aspect to such a declaration, for, at the time he made the statement—in the 1960s—he was already regarded as one of America's leading performers. To suggest, as he did, that acting was only a secondary interest implied that he, with less than a total commitment to entertaining, could outperform others who specialized in that field. Nevertheless, most of those who knew him best believed that there was considerable truth in his claim. Once, when asked which art he would give up if he were forced to choose, he responded, "There's no way of knowing which I need more, painting or acting. It's just that I have a need to do both." Obviously, both arts meant a great deal to him, but whereas he could perhaps have survived without performing—he was almost forced to during the blacklist—painting on a daily basis was essential to his existence. "I have to paint every day," he said, "or I don't feel alive." Walter Bernstein added that Mostel "felt the true core of himself not on the stage, but when he was painting."

"From the first moment that I found I could manipulate paint, I was in love with it," Zero said, although he was equally happy when "looking at someone else's paintings. I don't really know whether I enjoy looking or painting better," he added. Of all painters, he probably loved Klee's and Dubuffet's works the most, but he was also taken with the canvases of Kokoschka, Ensor, Brueghel, Pollock, Cézanne, Bosch, Rembrandt, and hundreds of others, all of which he could discuss and analyze in infinite detail. And he had little patience with those who did not share his enthusiasms. To one close friend who could not understand Zero's passion for Miró, he responded, "Don't you see how sensuous it is?" When she answered that she was unable to see it, he ended the conversation abruptly: "Well, you're just too dumb."*

It was not just the act of creation that Zero loved; everything to do with painting held a fascination for him. He loved the smell of turpentine. He collected "old objects which he liked to have around him—old bottles of sun-thickened linseed oil, old handmade papers, pencils with Siberian lead, inks, nibs, brushes, glues, dyes," in the words of his son Tobias, who wrote an introduction to a catalogue of Zero's paintings.† When Mostel was in Los Angeles, he often went to the store owned by Ted Gibson, who framed his pictures, and hung around all afternoon. At times, he pretended to be a clerk and waited on customers, recommending specific colors, brushes, glazes, and frames.

"Painting is a much more creative field than acting," Zero said. "You take up an empty canvas; you fill it. In acting, you've got something to start with. You're not always satisfied with what you put on the blank canvas, and, as in acting on the stage, you have a chance the next day or the next night to do it over. The beautiful thing about being a painter is that you can continue to paint all of your life. Eventually every actor is washed up, and even a plumber has finally to give up

---

*Zero did not confine his impatience to those who were, in his opinion, uninformed about painters. When he was in the midst of a conversation, he was likely to become furious if someone disagreed with him or displayed what he regarded as ignorance. Walter Bernstein recalled a sudden display of anger because Bernstein had not read the letters of Berlioz. "He was always trying to educate me in art and music. He would yell at me a lot because that was his style," Bernstein said.

†Both of Zero's sons were drawn to one of their father's careers. Tobias is now a painter, Josh a successful actor.

plumbing, but a painter can go on and on, until the day he dies. And that's what I plan to do. I'll be the goddamn Jewish Grandma Moses.

"Even when I'm in a play, I try to go every day to my studio . . . on West Twenty-eighth Street," he said. The studio, in the heart of New York's wholesale flower district, was across the street from the one Zero had shared with Herbie Kallem during the Depression. He bought the building on the south side of the street after he became a successful actor, occupying the entire top floor himself. Other rooms in the building were rented out: to a bar, to a business, and to other artists. Herbie Kallem's studio was on the third floor, directly below Mostel's.

Zero said that his studio was originally "a junk heap of a loft," but he redecorated it almost entirely in white. In addition to the paraphernalia one would expect to find in an artist's studio—easels, drafting tables, mounds of paint tubes, brushes, a raised area for a model, an enormous table of paints—Mostel kept hundreds of expensive art books, a sofa and comfortable chairs, several sculptures, a lithograph machine—and a sturdy table where he and other artists from nearby studios met weekly for a poker game. Mostel's studio was a second home to many of his artist friends: Herbie Kallem, his brother Henry Kallem, a painter,* Ian McLellan Hunter and Waldo Salt, both writers who loved to paint, Ngoot Lee, Irving Glazer, Remo Faruggio, and others. Ideas were freely exchanged and criticism offered by all.

Some of Zero's nonartist friends were invited to drop by in order to learn about art. Karl Malden was one. "When I was just beginning to make a little money," Malden told me, "Zero said, 'You ought to buy some paintings.' I said, 'Zero, I don't know anything about paintings.' He said, 'You come up to my studio and you'll learn about paintings.' And I used to go up to his studio a lot. All of those people were there painting, and between all of them, and me sitting there for a couple of hours every day, I began to look at painting the way they looked at painting." Still other friends dropped by just for a visit: Joseph Heller, Sol Kaplan, Eli Wallach, Stanley Prager, Sam Jaffe, Jack Gilford, Speed

---

*Henry Kallem taught a formal class in painting at his studio on Twenty-seventh Street for a time. Kate, who was normally excluded from Zero's studio, enrolled in Kallem's class. She also studied sculpture with Herbie Kallem.

Vogel. Occasionally, an interviewer would be allowed to watch the artists at work. On those occasions, Zero would often resort to the clownish behavior for which he was known outside the studio.

Ordinarily, though, anything associated with painting was treated with reverence, not humor. Jack Gilford described an instance when "I did some watercolors. And one day Zero says, 'Let me see them.' So I signed one 'Van Gilford' and brought them to him. Zero Mostel, who would let his pants down onstage for a laugh, said to me, 'That is not funny.' With Zero, you didn't make fun of painters or painting."

As a painter, Mostel was tied to no particular style. "Painting need not be done in any one way," he said. "It seems to me that trying a variety of ways, and a variety of mediums, keeps the mentality fresh." His earliest works were academic portraits, but they evolved into more adventurous, less representational canvases. "I'm constantly trying new things in painting," he said. "After I'd done one thing, I'd go on to try something new. In the early forties, I painted socially satiric things [in 1943, *Life* magazine described his concentration upon "lusty human types—such as a fish peddler, his hands slithering with blood and fish scales; a thick-necked Negro coal miner; or a big-bellied bartender"], and later on I did more abstract paintings." Most of his abstract works were characterized by the use of bold, contrasting shapes and vivid color. He also did thousands of drawings, watercolors, and collages. In some paintings, he mixed his media, using oils, crayon, and pastels on the same canvas. He employed scumbling, sgraffito, and other methods. Because he was so versatile and so prolific (he frequently worked on twenty or more paintings simultaneously; he claimed to have completed nearly twenty thousand paintings during his lifetime—and as many as six in a single day), it is impossible to generalize about his work. However, the elements that seem to surprise people most are the delicacy and lyricism that characterize so much of his output. For someone who—both as a performer and as a person—was renowned for his boisterousness and his explosive, almost frenzied behavior, it does seem remarkable that he could produce such meticulous and controlled drawings and paintings, many of them no larger than eighteen by twenty inches. One is again reminded of the remarkable duality of Zero's nature. "To me there were two Zeros," observed Ian Hunter. "There was Zero the actor, and Zero the painter. The actor was temperamental, loud, and 'on' most of the time. The painter was a quiet, modest fellow, immensely knowledgable about all aspects of the medium. While I admired Zero as an actor, I always felt that my friendship was with Zero the painter."

Hunter often witnessed Mostel's change from artist to famous performer, a transformation that occurred with lightning speed. "On Saturdays we drew and painted together in the Twenty-eighth Street studio," Hunter recalled, "and in those sessions Zero was all painter. Then at six o'clock, let's say, we'd leave the studio to meet our wives in a Spanish restaurant, a block and a half away. We'd be walking down Twenty-eighth Street—Zero, Herbie, and I—and the florists and other habitués would greet Zero, the local celebrity. Zero had a bit of shtick for all of them. At the restaurant, the owner made a big fuss over him and Zero played his entrance to the hilt. Zee was like a quick-change artist: the painter had become the actor, and all in a block and a half."

Shortly after the blacklist period—when he was reestablishing himself as a major name in show business—some of his paintings took on a harsh tone. During that time, his colors became more violent, the consistency of the paint thicker, the canvas more fragmented than before. He worked on a series of tortured paintings he called *Mutations*; a portrait of a man's head with three mouths, called *The Informer*; another series showing the anguished faces of atomic bomb victims; and still another consisting of hundreds of canvases with religious themes—rabbis or men praying—that Ruth Kobart, a visitor to his studio, felt were suffused with anger. Walter Bernstein thought that these works and others like them were reflections of Zero's bitterness, an outgrowth of his experience with the blacklist. At the same time, however, he was working on gentle, whimsical canvases: a packed subway car on toy wheels, a portrait of a benevolent-looking rabbi, a humorous painting called *An Old Man Begging*. In 1964, *Newsweek* described his work as "intensely personal expressionism, divided into two alternative views of the world, positive and negative. He paints tidy, cheerful abstractions, in the warm purples, reds and browns of Oriental carpets, cryptically decorated with fragments of Hebraic calligraphy. . . . The other main group of his paintings expresses pessimistic doubts of man's ability to realize his ideals."

Zero felt that the one constant in his prolific output was his individuality. "A guy's painting, if it's true, is of himself, always," he said. Sidney Bergen, the owner of the ACA Galleries, who exhibited Mostel's work in the 1970s, said, "Zero has what every good artist needs—a good mind, technical skill, and a style that is completely his own. He has a magnificent sense of color." Although he was a fine draftsman, Mostel was particularly concerned with color. He once commented, "Painting comes from color, not from drawing. I'm a colorist."

Perhaps, however, Sidney Bergen was excessively complimentary when he called Mostel's work "completely his own." Elements of the paintings of Chagall, Picasso, Miró, and others inform his work, and some of the artists who knew him felt that it was his failure to develop a truly individual style that prevented Mostel from achieving greatness as a painter. But Zero might not have been upset by that criticism, for he maintained (or—depending upon one's point of view—rationalized) that "there is often much talk about an artist's painting being like this or that or the other painter. I see nothing wrong with that. People seem to be afraid to let things rub off. After all, in the end you take it out of your own hand, your own way of seeing."

One of Mostel's artist friends who felt that Zero's achievements never quite matched his potential told me, "I don't think he had enough studio time to bring out what was inside of him. You don't become an important artist unless you're there struggling with the problem nearly every single moment of every day. I think Zero had it in him; I think he *could* have been a very important artist. His drawings were incredible. But his interest was too divided." This artist expressed the notion that Zero would have been a better painter if he had incorporated into his work the brassy, expansive part of his nature that he reserved for his performances, on stage and off. "That was Zero's uniqueness. And I don't think the wildness he had as a performer came out consistently in his work."

Ian Hunter felt that Mostel "might have emerged as an important American painter had it not been for [his] other career. In a show like *Forum*, for example, Zee would do eight performances a week and be on stage [during each performance] at least ninety percent of the time. There just wasn't energy left for the studio. In terms of painting—when he had a gig—he was a dabbler. Between shows he was a full-time painter, a professional. And several times, during his intensive periods in front of canvas, I felt that I saw something emerging— something kind of original—something that might be an individual style in the making. But before Zee had explored it all the way, another Broadway show would come up—and the elusive prize that his creativity was seeking would die of neglect. He would never pick up the thread of it again."

Mostel used his skill as a painter to enrich his theatrical performances by painting study after study of the character he would be playing during the months leading up to a production. One might say that the reverse was also true: since the subjects of so many of his paintings were theatrical,* he used his understanding of individual characters and of the theatre as a whole to bring greater depth to his painting. Perhaps the methodology he employed when painting, incorporating the tiniest details into his canvases, accounts for the minute observations he included in his finest stage performances.

Zero painted hundreds of self-portraits—often because no other model was available—in which he might transform himself into a beast or an unidentifiable shape. When he did not use himself as a subject, he always worked from a model. Ian Hunter described the process:

Every Saturday morning, providing Zero wasn't in a show, he and I and Herbie Kallem would go to Zee's studio and draw, or paint, from a model. We liked twenty-minute poses separated by ten-minute intermissions. The intermissions would be used for frantic card-playing. On the radio would be an opera. Zero liked to sing along with it. It was *La Bohème* one Saturday, and Zee did his version of "My Tiny Hands Are Frozen." Not quite what Puccini intended—but mighty funny. The model was always made timekeeper, and it was she who would nag us back to work.

Zee would take this big canvas, immaculately prepared for him with sanded coats of Gesso. He liked these big, floppy, long-haired brushes and

---

*In addition to delineating his own character, he often painted other characters in the play. A number of his works were of a more general theatrical nature. One, for example, showed the audience from the actor's perspective—as a beast, ready to tear the performers to shreds. Another, called *An Actor Being Consumed In His Parts*, portrayed an actor, naked and vulnerable, in the process of being devoured by the characters he played.

he liked them loaded with paint. He'd make line-drawings of the model, in burnt sienna or in ochre. Soon there'd be like six sketches of the model side by side across the canvas.

Then he'd start to paint. He liked a pretty big palette and his colors were bright. (He'd glaze some of them down, later.) He'd use the shapes formed by the drawings and by the negative spaces between drawings. And soon a semiabstract painting would begin to evolve. And soon there was not a trace left of the original half dozen female shapes.

Models usually mind their own business, but one day a model walked over between poses and took a long look at Zero's painting. No traces of her poses remained. "What do you need me for?" she asked Zero. "For discipline, my dear," he explained. "For discipline."

Zero said, "I always start realistic, always with live models. Then I'll turn the real around, superimpose figures, fragment bits, then some idea comes to me and I try to get something out of it."

Even on most performance days—except those on which he had a matinee—Zero faithfully went to his studio. "I never stop painting," he said. "You can't do it by fits and starts. If you paint, you've got to paint every day." He worked from nine or ten in the morning until late afternoon—always with classical music playing on the phonograph—then had dinner with artist friends at a nearby restaurant, then went to the theatre, sometimes arriving on the back of a floral delivery truck. When he was touring with a production, he always took his easel and painting supplies with him, working whenever he could.

Zero sold paintings to hundreds of people, including Burgess Meredith, Mel Brooks, Martin Ritt, Bettye Ackerman, Joseph Stein, Larry Gelbart, Jack and Madeline Gilford. His work was exhibited in the Whitney Museum (in 1956, at which time Sam Jaffe expressed the hope that Zero would "be able to say farewell to the theatre and go back to your first love, painting"), the Museum of Modern Art, the Brooklyn Museum, the National Portrait Gallery of the Smithsonian, and the Bezalel National Museum in Israel. Their prices ranged up to $12,000. But when asked if, as a magazine article claimed, he "commands formidable fees" for his paintings, Zero responded, "If that's what I said, I must have been giddy from just having sold a picture, and consequently oversold myself. . . . I don't *command*, as the guy says, considerable fees . . . and anybody—if I respect his taste—can come down to my studio and become the owner of a Mostel at less than what he'd have to pay for a comparable Rembrandt."

Zero professed indifference to critical opinion about his painting. On one occasion, he said, the art critic Harold Rosenberg asked to visit his studio. According to Mostel's account: "I showed him a painting, and he said, 'I don't like it.' I showed him another, he said, 'I don't like that one either.' I pulled out a third, he said, 'I'm not crazy about that one.' I had it with him. 'Harold,' I said, 'I don't need you as a fucking critic. *Just look at the paintings!*' I took out another painting; he looked at it a long time. 'That one I like very much,' he said."

Mostel was equally disdainful of the opinions of prospective buyers. One who asked to see some paintings was told, "You can't afford me," and "Why should I sell to you now when my prices are going up?" A writer conducting an interview with Zero asked if he could see his paintings. "What for?" Zero asked.

"Maybe I'll buy a few," the interviewer answered.

"How do you know I want to sell them to you?" Zero countered, ending the conversation.

Jack Gilford said that during the blacklist he took a wealthy friend to Mostel's studio in the hope that the friend would buy one of Zero's works. "And I remember his objectivity about people looking at his paintings. When he showed them, it seemed like he didn't care whether my friend liked them or not. He was absolutely without emotion as he showed the paintings. He didn't smile or say, 'Hope you like it'; he would just look away and wait until my friend had a good look, then show the next one."

An artist associate of Mostel's told me, "I don't think Zero wanted to be judged [as a painter]. And, except for the time he was blacklisted, he avoided being judged. Acting gave him the freedom to work in the studio without having to compete and make it in the commercial world."

The art world recognized the quality of Mostel's work when he was awarded the Albert Einstein Medal of Art in 1970. Nevertheless, Zero felt that his paintings were generally underestimated, perhaps because the public tends to view famous personalities who paint as dilettantes. "He always felt neglected as a painter," according to his nephew, Raphael.

Painting saw Zero through the blacklist, although it never provided more than a small income. On one occasion, Jack Gilford, who was also blacklisted, offered to lend Mostel some money. When Zero declined, Gilford bought a painting, but he could only afford to pay fifty dollars, far less than he thought the painting was worth.

Zero told a story about an occasion on which another blacklisted performer purchased some of his paintings at bargain prices:

> During the blacklist, this actor, a well-known actor, came to me and said: "I can't sleep or rest." I said: "Why don't you come over to the studio and rest." So he does, he takes a nap, he snores away, and then he wakes up and says: "Can I see your paintings?" So I showed him some. He said: "I don't like your paintings." The *chutzpah!* And then he becomes a pain in the ass, coming up every day for his nap.
>
> After a month or two he says: "You know, I kind of like these paintings. Can I buy one?" Well, what am I going to do? Give him one? Sell him one? So I pointed and I said: "See those little paintings? They're for my blacklisted friends, $10 each." He said, "Really? I'll take two." I'd hit his price right. Later he came to me and said: "Look, Zook, you got any more of those $10 paintings?" I said: "No, I had a fire sale and sold them all."

Occasionally, though, Mostel would make a lucrative sale, as when David Susskind bought five of his paintings in one day. And although Zero's economic situation was normally precarious, he looked back upon the blacklist period as a curiously happy time, for it freed him to paint. "Maybe it was a good thing," he said. "If I kept on making lousy movies, I might have become very rich playing the fellow who never got the girl." There were material privations to be faced, but economic necessity also forced him into a deep, highly focused and undiluted concentration upon the work he loved best, and that gave him enormous satisfaction. He later remembered the period as the most artistically productive time of his life. "I was happy painting in those years," he said. "After all, I was living by my wits, my hands, doing the things I know how to do." Larry Gelbart said, "I think the painting probably saved his life. Some of the blacklisted actors who were so embittered and suicidal and reclusive were people who had nothing at all besides acting to do; but Zero had his painting."

When the blacklist began to crumble and Zero went back to performing, he often told his agent, Toby Cole, "Don't work so hard trying to get me jobs. Take it easy." It was not a pose. "Zero was not particularly eager to work," she said; "he was very happy painting in his studio." Despite his efforts to remain out of the limelight, however, he found himself more and more in demand. Walter Bernstein felt that Zero's characteristic contentiousness in the years when he was at his peak as a performer may have "stemmed from a feeling he once expressed to me that he was not doing what he should be doing, which was painting full-time." After Zero returned to performing and achieved enormous success, "there was a part of him that resented it," Bernstein said, because Mostel had grown accustomed to the luxury of total concentration upon painting. Sol Kaplan added that, while Mostel loved both painting and performing, "if push came to shove, I think he would have given up performing."

In some respects, Mostel found that the material rewards of success as an actor interfered with his ability to paint satisfactorily. After *Fiddler on the Roof*, he said, he rented "a huge loft with lots of room and perfect sunlight and everything. And I sat there day after day for three months. I couldn't paint a thing. So I went back to the filthy little hole I'd had before." Once ensconced back in his Twenty-eighth Street studio, he again began "painting like mad."

Zero never lost his enthusiasm for painting. If anything, it became stronger as time went on. Near the end of his life, according to his son Josh, "he was looking very much forward to retiring, he said. He hated show business, he claimed. He just wanted to paint. Zero was happy with a paintbrush in his hand."

*   *   *

By itself, the money Mostel made by selling his paintings would not have been sufficient to provide the family with life's necessities, but Kate also contributed by working periodically. Her background as a dancer had whetted her appetite for success as an actress. She hoped desperately to generate a career of her own, but that ambition, to her sorrow, was never fully realized. Especially when Zero began his come-back in show business, Kate was frustrated by her inability to achieve similar success. Still, in 1953, she did appear in *Ladies of the Corridor*, a Broadway play by Arnaud d'Usseau and Dorothy Parker, both friends of the Mostels. But the play did not succeed, and after six weeks Kate had to look for other employment. She took the opportunity to act outside New York on the few occasions when jobs were offered, but they were intermittent and did not pay well. Eventually, she took an "honorable withdrawal" from Actors Equity because the Mostels could not afford the yearly dues, although they only amounted to about thirty dollars.

For about fifteen years, Kate taught a modern dance/exercise class every Monday and Friday for her women friends, many of whose husbands were also blacklisted. Each of the seven or eight members paid a few dollars per session. After class, the members ate lunch, discussed what was going on in their lives, and, as Kate said, "cleaned up the world." In addition to its educational and social aspects, the class was clearly therapeutic for everyone involved.

Those who were blacklisted formed a tightly knit social group, an extended family, partly because experience had taught them not to confide in others, partly because they were frequently unwelcome at other social gatherings, and partly because no one else could fully comprehend the situation in which they found themselves. So many of them lived in the same apartment building, for example, that FBI agents maintained a constant lookout; often the agents could be observed talking to the doormen. The Mostels were intensely loyal to their blacklisted friends—as their friends were to them—and remained so long after the blacklist ended.

One winter when money was particularly scarce, Kate took a job as a salesclerk at Saks Fifth Avenue so that she could buy Christmas presents for the children. And Zero continued to perform his nightclub routine at cut rates whenever the opportunity arose—although it arose less and less frequently. As time passed, the Mostels' financial situation became more precarious.

Actual persecution gave rise to imagined persecution. One day when Zero was riding on the subway, a man handed him an envelope, saying, "Zero, I've always been a fan of yours and I'd like you to have this." Mostel thought the envelope contained a request for an autograph or a newspaper clipping, but when he opened it he found a hundred-dollar bill. Josh Mostel recalled, "That was a lot of money then, because there were always problems about the rent and we never had enough money.

When Zero brought the money home, I remember him and my mother discussing it and wondering: was it an FBI plant? Was it a trick to get them not to declare it on their income tax? That was the kind of thing that resulted from the blacklist—always thinking that the government was after you."

Many of those who were blacklisted could not deal with the emotional or the financial problems it created. John Garfield, for example, suffered a heart attack and died soon after he was subpoenaed by HUAC; none of his friends believed the events were unrelated. J. Edward Bromberg, blacklisted after he testified before the committee, died before he was fifty. Mady Christians, unable to find employment after having made more than sixty films, was a victim of high blood pressure. She died of a cerebral hemorrhage soon after she was blacklisted. Some blacklisted artists left show business entirely, but, discovering that their reputations as "disloyal Americans" followed them, they continued to be the target of right-wing attacks even when they entered other professions. One of the most tragic victims of the blacklist was the actor Philip Loeb, who had been a close friend of the Mostels for years.

Loeb, who rated seventeen citations in *Red Channels*, was a featured actor on CBS's *The Goldbergs* when the sponsor decided to drop him. Gertrude Berg, the show's star and chief writer, initially refused to accept Loeb's blacklisting, stating, "I will appear on every available platform from coast to coast [if Loeb is fired] denouncing General Foods and advising people not to buy its products." In answer to her valiant stand, the corporation dropped its sponsorship of the program (because, General Foods said, it was "dissatisfied with the show's rating") and *The Goldbergs* went off the air. NBC then announced that it would add the program to its schedule the following month but with another actor in the role Loeb had played, and this time the change in casting did not meet with opposition. The remainder of Loeb's contract was paid off, but, as he said, "I'm still blacklisted. . . . I am deprived of work because of a cowardly, furtive smear campaign. . . . I claim that although innocent I have been ousted from my work and hounded from my profession by a dirty, undercover job." Loeb went so far as to deny under oath that he was a Communist, but it did not alter the situation. Suddenly, the actor, who had worked professionally for forty years, was unemployed, with few prospects of ever working again. As one frustrating, demeaning month followed another, Loeb sank further and further into depression.

Kate described Loeb's state of mind: "Phil had had a rotten few years. The blacklist had not only kept him from working, it had humiliated and beaten him down. He had a son who was seriously ill, and it cost thousands of dollars to keep him in a good hospital. . . . In addition, Phil had just had operations for cataracts, and he was terrified that he'd never be able to see well enough to work, even if the bad times would eventually be over."

In 1955, Loeb had not worked regularly for several years and could not afford an apartment. The Mostels, hard-pressed to pay the $225 monthly rent on their own apartment on West Eighty-sixth Street, suggested that Loeb move in with them and pay a portion of the rent. He did so, gratefully. One day, he did not return to the apartment when he was expected. Fearing that he had determined to commit suicide, Zero, Kate, and Loeb's other friends called every hotel in town, asking if Philip Loeb had registered. Soon the unhappy news became known: he had checked into the Hotel Taft under an assumed name and taken a lethal dose of sleeping pills.

The entire period "was so goddam stupid," Zero said. "My politics are my business. Besides, what sabotage could actors be accused of—giving acting secrets to the enemy?" Mostel could not get over the idiocy "of going after actors instead of spies." He added, "It was just publicity for that committee, that horrible committee. To inquire into a person's private and political life is against the intent of our own Constitution. I'm not a lawyer and I know that. But those idiot congressmen didn't." Whether the congressman were idiots may be debatable, but at least one of them was certainly corrupt: J. Parnell Thomas, chairman of the House Committee on Un-American Activities when the committee investigated the movies in 1947, was convicted of padding his payroll in December 1949 and later served a prison term—in the same facility where Ring Lardner, Jr., and Lester Cole, two of the Hollywood Ten, were incarcerated.*

*In 1956, the chairman of the committee was Francis E. Walter. The sincerity of Walter's conviction in ferreting out subversives may be called into question by a sug-

Mostel was equally contemptuous of those who cooperated with HUAC, naming alleged Communists or Communist sympathizers. "When people did testify and turned in their friends' names in order to save their own necks, the committee tried to make a hero out of the informer," Zero said. "What kind of society is that, where the informer becomes a hero? That's sickening." Eli Wallach said that Zero's attitude toward informers was unforgiving. "He'd say, 'If you deviate from my moral standard, I don't want to know you; I don't want to spend time with you.' " Whenever Mostel ran into an informer, he greeted him or her with apparent cheeriness (and deep underlying sarcasm), "Hello, Looselips!"

Even after Zero rose to the top as a performer, he continued to feel disdain for those who had informed. Gene Wilder, who acted with Mostel in *The Producers* in 1968—four years after Zero's triumph in *Fiddler on the Roof* made him a nationally renowned star—asked him how he felt about those who had cooperated with HUAC ten to twenty years earlier. "It wasn't a consuming passion with him then," Wilder recalled. "It was a scar, but it had healed, and he was on to a very productive career and was happy in his life as far as I could tell." Still, when Zero spoke about the blacklist, "he didn't forgive," said Wilder. "He mellowed, but he didn't forgive. He may have had compassion for the people who informed because they were weak, but he didn't forgive."

Still, the blacklist did not turn Zero into a bitter man. His innate resiliency helped him to put the years of misery behind him. "I know that the blacklist wrecked some lives," he said, "but I'm not easily wrecked." Jack Gilford, who also returned to prominence after many years on the blacklist, thought that he and Zero were able to resume their lives without undue bitterness partly because "we were doing a principled thing. We couldn't think of naming names. It never entered our minds. It never occurred to us to do such a thing. And yet people we knew did it, and of course they did it out of fear. They must have been frightened to death."

---

gestion he made to Arthur Miller when Miller was summoned to testify. According to Miller in his autobiography, *Timebends*, Walter said that he would cancel the hearing if Miller would allow him to pose for a photograph with Miller's fiancée, Marilyn Monroe.

As the Mostels' supply of money steadily diminished, it became apparent that Zero could not remain in his studio indefinitely. In an attempt to get work as a comic, Lou Peterson recalled, "Zero would come to parties and entertain, but not for pay. It was demeaning. And it was unfair for people to ask him. It was taking advantage of him." I asked Peterson if he thought Zero felt the same way. "I'm sure he did," Peterson responded; "he must have hated it." And when asked whether that resentment came through in the performances he gave, Peterson said, "Yes. They were angry. He would be an angry coffeepot, if such a thing can be imagined."

Zero also attended some sessions at the Actors' Studio, where established professionals performed scenes for the famous acting teacher Lee Strasberg. Perhaps Mostel thought that acting in scenes at the Studio would lead to employment on the Broadway stage. But Zero did not take part in the scenes (even though Strasberg discouraged actors from observing classes unless they planned to participate), because he disliked Strasberg's teaching methods, finding them oppressively psychoanalytical and excessively critical.

An acting job off-Broadway might bring in only $40 or so a week, but that $40 was desperately needed. And off-Broadway not only tolerated blacklisted actors, it actually welcomed them; a blacklisted actor might encourage a picket line, and a picket line would assure publicity for what might otherwise be an obscure venture. So Zero returned to the theatre in late 1954, in the off-Broadway production of *A Stone for Danny Fisher*, an adaptation of a Harold Robbins novel. As he had in several movies, Zero once again played a mobster.

Before opening, *Danny Fisher* changed directors twice and went through several cast changes. Don Richardson, whose weekly acting classes Zero attended between 1946 and 1949, recommended to director Luther Adler that Mostel be cast in the role vacated by Everett Sloane only two weeks before the play opened. The production, obviously troubled to begin with, was not looked upon favorably by the critics and ran for only six weeks.

Mostel's return to the theatre was a moderate success at best. Brooks Atkinson's review in the *Times* noted that his role was "well played," and his performance was praised by *Variety* and the *Journal-American*, whose critic, John McClain, said, "Zero Mostel has never been funnier or more menacing," but Louis Sheaffer said in the Brooklyn *Eagle* that he was "miscast." More important than any review, however, was the fact that Zero was at work in show business once again.

Within a few months—in March 1955—he had another off-Broadway engagement, heading the cast of a revue called *Once Over Lightly*. Having stated his preference for acting in plays rather than performing in variety shows, Zero might have regarded his new venture as a step backward. However, the production was significant in that Stanley Prager, who directed, and Zero, Jack Gilford, and Sono Osato, who co-starred, were all blacklisted in the mass media. E. Y. (Yip) Harburg, the lyricist best known for *Finian's Rainbow*, suggested that the show be called *The Banned Wagon*.

If anyone wondered whether Zero's nature had changed after several years on the blacklist, during which time he focused all of his energies upon the serious and solitary art of painting, worrying where the money to pay the next month's rent would come from, he demonstrated beyond doubt that he was as boisterous, as highly charged, and as raucous a personality as he had ever been when he was introduced to Sheldon Harnick after a preview of *Once Over Lightly*. Harnick, a friend of Stanley Prager's, had never before seen Mostel perform. He watched the first two minutes of Zero's initial routine, an elaborate pantomime, with enthusiasm. "Then, somehow," he said, "it became incomprehensible and seemed to go on forever." After the performance, Harnick went backstage, where Prager asked him for his reaction to the show. When Harnick gave his opinion of the pantomime, the director asked him to repeat it for Mostel. "I was introduced to Zero, who started to help me off with my coat," Harnick said. "As I described my delight with the initial two minutes, Zero practically purred. Then as I described my unhappiness and mystification with the rest of the pantomime, I discovered that my coat (which I was only half out of) had become a straitjacket. Others were amused by my plight as Zero held me nose to nose with him, frowning maniacally and making the jacket tighter and tighter." Harnick realized that all who were watching found Mostel's actions irresistibly funny. "But," he said, "I felt only intense discomfort and embarrassment." Zero hadn't changed. He was still playing the aggressive and compulsive clown in public.

In terms of Mostel's career, *Once Over Lightly* demonstrated that his comic gifts were as sharp as ever. At least one critic thought they were sharper than they had been. Never before had Zero received a review as rapturous as Brooks Atkinson's in the New York *Times*, which was devoted almost entirely to his performance:

> Fortunately, Zero Mostel is a low comedian, not interested in the mind. He is noisy, ugly, bulky, messy and funny.
>
> Not being an intellectual, he has a sense of the theatre. His timing is cunning. He is willing to move; he likes to shout; he wears ludicrous costumes with enthusiasm. When he is on the stage of the Barbizon-Plaza Theatre, where *Once Over Lightly* opened last evening, you can hardly help noticing that something is going on. If you don't Mr. Zero would be only too glad to come down and hit you over the head.
>
> The best stuff in this attenuated revue is his, or at least has him prancing through it. His grotesque pantomime as an actor studying himself in the mirror of his make-up table builds up to an ecstatic custard-pie finish with admirable artistic logic. . . . Very funny, too, in a frank sort of way.
>
> Mr. Zero as an Italian singer bawling at Jack Gilford as straight man; Mr. Zero as a voracious trencherman overpowering Mr. Gilford's aversion to food in an odious restaurant; Mr. Zero as a precocious little boy in a parody of Menotti's *The Medium*; Mr. Zero with Sono Osato and Mr. Gilford in a sketch about love among the animals; Mr. Zero as a diplomat adjusting himself to the Washington version of the Kremlin musical-chairs ballet—those are the scenes when *Once Over Lightly* is most amusing. Mr. Zero would be willing to go among the audience with a baseball bat if no one laughed.

A number of the other reviewers, however, took quite a different view of Zero's performance, calling it "far off form" and "wearing." One critic was punished for his opinion *in absentia*. The show called for Zero to enter down the aisle of the theatre at one point, carrying a cane. On the night after the reviews came out, Mostel stopped by the seat where a critic who had written a negative review had sat the night before. Zero improvised a comic—and derisive—monologue about the critic and proceeded to whack the seat with his cane.

Once Over Lightly was not a success. For an entertainer, however, a good notice in the *Times* can cancel out mediocre notices in every other New York newspaper, and Mostel's performing career was given a distinct boost, leading him back to Broadway, even if only for a week.

Within two months, Zero was back at work. When Buddy Hackett, the leading actor in the successful comedy *Lunatics and Lovers*, took a brief vacation in June 1955, he was replaced by Zero, who was then hired to play the role in a West Coast production of the play. In Los Angeles, while in rehearsal, Zero stayed at the home of his friend Lucille Ostrow because, as she said, "he had no place to stay and no money. So I told him to come and stay with me." *Lunatics and Lovers* opened at the Cathay Circle Theatre in Los Angeles, but, on July 7, 1955, shortly after the opening, Zero received the news he had been dreading: he was subpoenaed to appear in New York on August 19 before the House Committee on Un-American Activities, along with twenty-two other show business personalities including Zero's friends Stanley Prager, John Randolph, Sam Jaffe, and Madeline and Jack Gilford.

The purpose of the hearing, according to the New York *Times*, was "to determine whether Communist propaganda has penetrated to American [theatre] audiences seeking relaxation and not Red ideologies." Having established its power over the motion picture and television industries, the committee was now attempting to bring the legitimate theatre under its control.* Because the hearings were scheduled for mid-August, during the run of *Lunatics and Lovers*, Zero requested and received a postponement; HUAC agreed that a subcommittee in Los Angeles would hear his testimony in October immediately following the run of the play in San Francisco.

When the producers learned that Mostel had received a subpoena, he was nearly fired from the production. They told him that he would have to clear his name and cooperate with the committee if he wished to keep his job. Zero responded that his Jewish upbringing would not permit him to cooperate, for "as a Jew, if I inform, I can't be buried in sacred ground."†

Victor Navasky, in his study of the blacklist, *Naming Names*, explains the Jewish attitude toward informing:

*All but one of the witnesses were decidedly "unfriendly" to the committee. But most theatrical producers did not respond to the hearings as their colleagues in films and television had. All of the witnesses continued to be employed on- and off-Broadway.

†After discussing the matter, the producers relented. Zero was delighted, of course, and even more elated when, as he said, "the cast [who] was marvelous in their devotion to me . . . cheered when it was announced I would remain in the play."

The Aramaic word for informer as found in the Book of Daniel is *Akhal Kurtza*, whose literal translation is "to eat the flesh of someone else." The so-called Minean curse, which was introduced as the twelfth benediction of the Amidah prayer, says, "And for the informer may there be no hope." Jewish law as found in the Halakah, the Talmud, and the responsa of various rabbis sees the informer as a threat to the entire community, the potential destroyer of a people. . . . Penalties for the informer range from flogging and imprisonment to branding the forehead, cutting out the tongue, cutting off the hand, banishment, and, most frequently, death.

The stand Zero would take before the committee was thus never in doubt. His religion, political beliefs, and his friends' unswerving support all made his appearance as an "unfriendly witness" inevitable, but he still found the period between the day he received his subpoena and the date on which he was scheduled to testify a terribly difficult time to be away from family and friends. In New York, Zero's companions prepared strategies for their appearances before HUAC. Although they were all concerned about the possible consequences of the hearing, at least they could rely on one another for moral support. But Zero in California had only Sam Jaffe, Lucille Ostrow, and her father, Seniel, to rely on, for most of his old California friends, terrified that they might be accused of guilt by association, deserted him.* He wrote to a friend in New York: "I'm sort of suffering a letdown. . . . It is unfortunate to be in this town when this sort of thing happens." Zero also wondered if the producers of *Lunatics and Lovers*, having almost fired him once, might actually do so before the San Francisco hearing was held. His letter continued: "The producers are fine now but all week long Mike Connolly [a Los Angeles newspaper columnist] would call them and threaten them. I must say they were not scared finally to tell him off. So the prospect is good for continuing in this job." The

---

*Lucille Ostrow related the following to me: "One night, Zero's—I put this in quotes—'friends' came over to see him, but they came after 11:30 at night, and they wouldn't park on the street, they parked in the driveway so that if anyone was watching the house they wouldn't be able to tell there were people there. And that was the only night anyone came. Z called other people. I remember he asked one of them, 'Please come over, it's on your way to work, it's on your way home, please come over and see me.' But he never came. My father was the only one who came every day. After he got through at the office, he'd come and play a couple of card games with Z. They'd have a few laughs before he went home. Nobody else came to see him."

tour, after its Los Angeles opening in August, was scheduled to play in Tacoma, Portland, Seattle, and, finally, the Alcazar Theatre in San Francisco. "So," Zero concluded his letter, "for at least ten weeks I can feed the family."

Mostel could not afford to hire a lawyer for his appearance before HUAC, so Seniel Ostrow, the West Coast president of the Sealy Mattress company and a supporter of progressive causes, went to San Francisco to hire one for him. Ostrow also helped Zero financially, as did Sam Jaffe. "Sam helped a lot," Lucille Ostrow said. "It was like Sam had twenty-five cents and Zero had five cents, things were that bad, but Sam gave him all he could afford."

Zero was depressed, but "the more depressed he was, the funnier he was," Lucille Ostrow observed. His bizarre sense of humor and his manic need to display it at every opportunity were never more helpful to him, for he used them to subdue his anxiety. Despite the tension they felt, Ostrow recalled, they shared a good deal of laughter.

The strategy determined by Mostel and his lawyer, Richard Gladstein, called for Zero to claim his Fifth Amendment rights before the committee when asked about his political history or when it seemed that he might incriminate others. Nevertheless, he would try, whenever possible, to communicate his belief that HUAC had no right to question him about his political convictions—a difficult proposition, because the committee rarely allowed "unfriendly" witnesses to make statements. Above all, Mostel and his lawyer agreed, Zero would not subdue his sense of humor, thereby refusing to give in to the solemnity the committee would wish to impose upon him.

The hearing of HUAC's subcommittee occurred on October 14, 1955, with Chairman Clyde Doyle presiding. The only other officials present were Congressman Donald L. Jackson, and staff members Frank S. Tavenner, Jr., and William A. Wheeler. After establishing a brief biographical record—who Mostel was, where he lived, what he did for a living—Tavenner asked whether he had ever worked in Hollywood. "Oh, yes," Zero replied. "I was signed to a contract with Twentieth Century-Fox. Or was it Eighteenth Century-Fox?" When Tavenner objected to Zero's mockery of a revered American institution, Mostel amended the company's title to "Nineteenth Century-Fox." But Tavenner wasn't amused and the chairman ordered the statement stricken from the record. Still, Zero refused to adopt the somber tone of the committee. He referred to the pedestrian film *The Enforcer* as "the greatest artistic thing that has ever come down the pike." When Tavenner asked him, "You are also known by 'Zero' as a nickname, are you not?" Zero responded, "Yes sir. After my financial standing in the community, sir."

At last Tavenner shifted to the expected line of questioning. When asked if he had been a member of the Young Communist League, Zero held up his right hand, wiggled his fingers at the television cameras and refused to answer on the grounds of the Fifth Amendment. He invoked the amendment again when asked if he had entertained for the Joint Anti-Fascist Refugee Committee, the Voice of Freedom Committee, the Southern Conference for Human Welfare, and if he had spoken at an event billed as "Artists Fight Back Against Un-American Thought Control." When Tavenner showed him a handbill of the American Youth for Democracy listing his name as an entertainer for a benefit given for maritime workers in 1946, Zero objected to the implication that he had voluntarily appeared on behalf of a Communist front: "My point is that the organization for which [I] appeared . . . was declared subversive by the Attorney General's list long *after* the inception of that particular organization" (emphasis added).

Zero offered a brief civics lesson when asked if he was a member of the Communist party in 1942:

MR. MOSTEL: I refuse to answer that question on the grounds previously stated, sir, constitutional liberties, which I hear are granted to every individual in this land.

MR. JACKSON: And which the Committee does not question.

MR. MOSTEL: I'm sure it doesn't.

Tavenner attempted to establish that "various persons" had aided the Communist party "by entertaining at Communist Party functions, at public meetings that have been initiated by the Communist Party, and at 'cause' meetings, as they have often been referred to, initiated by the Communist Party, as well as meetings held by organizations commonly known and referred to as Communist-Front organizations."

Zero added, "And many other types of meetings which were held for cancer, heart, common colds, and a host of other favorites."

When Tavenner asked whether Ivan Black, the press agent for Café Society, was a Communist, Zero responded, "I will be glad to answer any questions of that sort where I don't have to talk about other individuals." Doyle, in his best inquisitorial manner, stated, "We are not satisfied with that answer, Witness, as being sufficient, and therefore I direct you to answer the question." Zero took the Fifth.

Tavenner tried to establish a link between Mostel and Martin Berkeley, who had given his name to HUAC. "I don't recall ever meeting him," Zero said. But Berkeley had sworn that Zero had attended a Communist party meeting in Hollywood in 1938. Zero invoked the Fifth Amendment, then added, "I was not here previous to 1942."

The interjection, though truthful, nearly trapped Mostel in a legal quagmire. Jackson, pouncing upon the technicality that made testifying before HUAC such a delicate balancing act, said, "Mr. Chairman . . . if Mr. Mostel says he was not here at that time, it seems to me that would be a misuse of the constitutional amendment, because an answer to the question would not tend to incriminate him."

A lengthy colloquy ensued, with Jackson, Doyle, and Mostel's lawyer arguing whether or not Mostel had forfeited his right to invoke the Fifth Amendment. At one point when the argument became heated, Zero interjected, "Don't fight, boys." But from then on, coached by his attorney (who was undoubtedly concerned that the subcommittee was laying the groundwork for a contempt citation), Zero cited the Fifth Amendment when asked any question about organizations he had joined, performed for, or sponsored.

As the hearing neared its close, Doyle said, "We never look forward to this sort of hearing or any hearing where any American citizen is being cross-examined."

"I sure don't either," Zero concurred. But Doyle was only at the beginning of a lecture on patriotism—a lecture that Zero's rebelliousness would not permit the chairman to carry on without interruption.

MR. DOYLE: Now, you are in a great field—

MR. MOSTEL: Sometimes.

MR. DOYLE: You are in a great field of entertainment of the American public. From now on, why don't you get far removed from groups that are known to be Communist dominated or Communist controlled, that sort of thing? . . . Why don't you remove yourself far away from that atmosphere, sir? You can be a much better inspiration and joy to the American people if they just know that there is not a drop, not an inkpoint, not a penpoint, of a favorable attitude by you toward the Communist conspiracy.

MR. MOSTEL: My dear friend, I believe in the antiquated idea that a man works in his profession according to his ability rather than his political beliefs. . . .

MR. DOYLE: I am not asking about your political beliefs.

MR. MOSTEL: My dear friend, I believe in the idea that a human being should go on the stage and entertain to the best of his ability and say whatever he wants to say, because we live, I hope, in an atmosphere of freedom in this country.

MR. DOYLE: That's right, and we will fight for your right to think as you please and be as you please and do as you please, provided you do it within the four corners of the Constitution. Don't you think it is your duty, as a great entertainer, to at least find out hereafter where the money you help raise is going . . . ?

MR. MOSTEL: I appreciate your opinion very much, but I do want to say that . . . maybe it is unwise and unpolitic for me to say this. If I appeared there, what if I did an imitation of a butterfly at rest? There is no crime in making anybody laugh. . . .

MR. DOYLE: If your interpretation of a butterfly at rest brought any money into the coffers of the Communist Party, you contributed directly to the propaganda effort of the Communist Party.

MR. MOSTEL: Suppose I had the urge to do the butterfly at rest somewhere?

MR. DOYLE: Yes, but please, when you have the urge, don't have such an urge to put the butterfly at rest by putting some money in the Communist Party coffers as a result of that urge to put the butterfly at rest. Put the bug to rest somewhere else next time. . . .

MR. GLADSTEIN: Is the witness excused, Mr. Chairman?

MR. DOYLE: The witness is excused. Thank you, Mr. Mostel. Remember what I said to you.

MR. MOSTEL: You remember what I said to you.

Television cameras and reporters were awaiting him as Zero left the hearing room. "Ah," he said, "they're letting me back on television. First time in years."

Zero's testimony won him admiration in the blacklisted community. Many who had received subpoenas had spoken bravely of the things they would say when they appeared before the committee, but most of them meekly (although understandably) said nothing except to invoke the Fifth Amendment.* Some who had boasted how angrily and eloquently they would "tell off" the committee capitulated entirely when the moment came to testify, giving HUAC all the information it requested, including the names of others. But Zero had not only emerged from the hearing with his dignity intact, he had had the courage to assert his belief in freedom of speech and to oppose the committee's attempts to limit that freedom.

Zero himself was pleased with the way his testimony had gone. "Figuratively, he clicked his heels in the air," Lucille Ostrow said. He had neither cooperated nor been intimidated by the committee, he had not allowed HUAC to destroy his natural ebullience, and he had had the last word.

When Zero returned to New York, he received a hero's welcome from his family and friends. But no job awaited him, so he retreated once more to his studio, where he remained for more than a year.

In December 1956, he opened in another off-Broadway production, Bertolt Brecht's *The Good Woman of Setzuan*, playing the minor role of Shu Fu, the barber. Brecht's American reputation was not yet fully

---

*Zero had no quarrel with those who did so. The Fifth Amendment, he said, "only happens to be . . . one of the most dignified amendments to the entire Constitution because to [refuse to] testify against yourself has an ancient history. They tortured people to get confessions."

established. His plays, which are now widely regarded as milestones of twentieth-century drama, were little appreciated by American critics in the mid-1950s, most of whom dismissed *The Good Woman of Setzuan* as "interesting" at best, pointless at worst. The production may not have helped. Brooks Atkinson said, "Excepting the individual acting of Uta Hagen, Gerald Hiken, Nancy Marchand, Albert Salmi and Zero Mostel, the performance is toneless and unwieldy." Other critics also referred to the "uneven" acting. *Good Woman* ran briefly at the Phoenix Theatre, then faded from view.

Zero's notices had been good, however, and they led to his being cast in the comedy *Good as Gold*—the first time he had been contracted to appear in an original Broadway cast in five years. For a variety of reasons, the opportunity seemed as promising as the title of the play. Acting on Broadway carried with it a prestige Zero had not known off-Broadway or on tour. His salary would be higher than any he had received in years, and the play seemed to have an excellent chance of being commercially successful. The playwright, John Patrick, had recently scored a big hit with *The Teahouse of the August Moon* and his theatrical style was thought to be in tune with the tastes of most Broadway theatregoers. Moreover, the play was not simply comic fluff. In its satire of the FBI, it was making a social statement at a time when most entertainments, fearful of the various congressional and state committees investigating unconventional political thought, were playing it safe by excising any material that might be considered remotely political. Zero would not be playing the lead, but he had a juicy character role, a jailhouse philosopher whose wooden leg was equipped with a spigot from which he could draw an ample supply of whiskey. After nearly a decade of enduring a sputtering show business career, Zero hoped that *Good as Gold* would put his professional life in high gear once again.

But it was not to be. *Good as Gold*, which opened in Boston, was criticized for the boldness of its political satire. The producers persuaded the author to remove the satirical bite, which effectively eliminated the play's greatest virtue. When the comedy opened in New York on March 8, 1957, its reception by the Broadway critics was unanimously unfavorable. One of the milder reactions came from Brooks Atkinson, who wrote, "Things look promising when the curtain goes up . . . but *Good as Gold* starts falling apart at about the halfway mark, and never recovers." Perhaps the most inadvertently brutal description of the play came from Ring Lardner, Jr., who went backstage after seeing one of its four performances. Unable to think of anything even remotely encouraging to say, he blurted out to Kate and Zero, "This is undoubtedly the WORST play I've ever seen."

Mostel probably drew little comfort from it, but, significantly, all of the critical comments about his performance had been enthusiastic. "Very funny," said Whitney Bolton in the *Morning Telegraph*; "a grotesquely droll characterization," added Thomas R. Dash in *Women's Wear Daily*; and the other reviewers concurred. Zero had received many good notices in the past, but he had also had his share of bad ones. In fact, the ratio of favorable to unfavorable reviews for his theatrical performances was not much better than even. For the first time, the critics had given their unanimous approval to his work. Because *Good as Gold* was such a flop, it was easy to overlook this widespread acceptance of Zero's performance style, but it was of considerable significance. No longer would his stage acting win fervent praise from some and equally impassioned contempt from others. From this time on, critics all but universally held that he was a brilliant performer in total command of his craft. The praise for his performance could not save *Good as Gold*, but, in hindsight, one can see that it presaged a comeback that no one in 1957 could have foreseen.

That same year, Zero was contacted by Toby Cole, who worked for a theatrical agent in New York. She was in the process of recommending actors to the producers of a play called *Press on Regardless* when she recalled having seen Mostel perform years before at Café Society, and remembered, in her words, "what a remarkable comedic talent he had." She knew of his blacklisting troubles, but that only increased her interest. Strongly opposed to the blacklist herself, she sought to oppose it by finding employment in the theatre for actors who were unable to work in films or on television. It occurred to her that Zero would be a good choice to play a cameo role in the play, so she telephoned him to ask whether he had an agent. "No," he said, "I haven't had one for a long time." Cole asked if he would like to be considered for *Press on Regardless*. Mostel said, "Sure, send my name, see what happens."

The play was never produced, but when Cole told Zero that the project had evaporated, she added, "I'll call you again as soon as I can.

I'll look for something for you." A year later, having opened her own agency, she called Mostel to ask if he would like her to represent him. When Zero suggested that they meet and discuss the possibility, she invited him and Kate to her apartment, only a few blocks away from his. During the evening, she explained to Zero that her interest in the theatre was primarily artistic rather than commercial. Her credentials in that respect were well established, as she had written and coedited four significant books on the theatre. She was well aware of the extraordinary theatrical developments then taking shape in England and Europe: the emergence of playwrights like Pinter, Ionesco, Beckett, Osborne, and Genet, and the inventive productions their plays were receiving. It was her ambition to introduce those playwrights to audiences in the United States, matching them with equally gifted American actors. She "didn't have any idea of Mostel's range as an actor," she said, but having seen his nightclub performances, "I knew that he was a superb mime, that he excelled at improvisation," and that he possessed the potential to be the ideal actor for the avant-garde repertory she favored. Zero was intrigued. He, too, wanted to appear in challenging, innovative plays. At the end of the evening, he shook Cole's hand and said, "Well, let's go on together, you and I." It was nearly six months before anything concrete emerged from their professional relationship, but Cole immediately began to circulate his name among producers.

Meanwhile, Burgess Meredith had been asked to perform the role of Leopold Bloom in *Ulysses in Nighttown*, a stage adaptation by Marjorie Barkentin and others (under the supervision of Padraic Colum) of a portion of James Joyce's epic novel *Ulysses*. Meredith told the producer that he preferred to direct the play, which, he said, had "obsessed" him since he first read it in 1955. Marjorie Barkentin's obsession was of longer standing. She had been planning a stage version ever since she read Joyce's novel in 1933. No play could possibly contain all the incidents in the novel, and *Ulysses in Nighttown* limited its focus to a 160-page section in the second half of the book, re-creating the wanderings through Nighttown of Leopold Bloom, the Irish Jew who serves as a kind of Everyman, and his young friend Stephen Dedalus. (Padraic Colum, in his introduction to the published version of the play, described Nighttown as "The Night Town of a city, any city. But also the lair of the witch Circe, who can turn men into beasts. The place of transformation, degradation, phantasmagoria!") The play alternates between "reality" and hallucinations. A narrator is present throughout to tie the strands of dreams, illusions, and reality together. But even the "reality" is phantasmagorical. As an example, Bloom makes the following speech during a "realistic" sequence in the play. He is speaking to Bella, a whore.

> *Passée* [*sic*]. Mutton dressed as lamb. Long in the tooth and superfluous hairs. A raw onion the last thing at night would benefit your complexion. And take some double chin drill. Your eyes are as vapid as the glass eyes of your stuffed fox. They have the dimensions of your other features, that's all. I'm not a triple screw propellor.

"Joyce comes alive when he's spoken aloud," Burgess Meredith observed. "He is meant to be spoken, not to be read with the eye." But no producer, on Broadway or off, agreed with him. For two years, the script of *Ulysses in Nighttown* had made the rounds and was turned down in every case as unplayable and too esoteric. At last Barry Hyams, a producer brave enough to take the risk, agreed to mount the play. Meredith's problems, however, were just beginning: "When we got a production, we couldn't get a Bloom," he said. "I begged and pleaded with over fifty actors, everybody from Hiram Sherman to Burl Ives, but no takers. I was so desperate I would drag out the script and read it to anybody who would listen. . . . The idea of Zero Mostel just came to me when I was lying in bed filled with despair at finding the right Bloom."

Meredith and Mostel arranged to meet in Dinty Moore's restaurant, where the director formally offered Zero the role of Bloom—a role that *demanded* an actor who possessed great pantomimic skills. Near the end of act 1, for example, the narrator speaks the following lines, "accompanied by pantomime": "Bloom covers his left eye with his left ear, passes through several walls, eats twelve dozen oysters (shells included), turns each foot simultaneously in different directions, bids the tide turn back, eclipses the sun by extending his little finger." For an actor to suggest those images imaginatively in pantomime is a monumental challenge, requiring a performer of extraordinary ability.

The lines Bloom speaks are equally difficult. For example, to the accompaniment of a waterfall (represented by voices saying, "Poula-phouca Poulaphouca Phoucaphouca Phoucaphouca"), Bloom says, "I was precocious. Youth. The fauns. I was sacrificed to the god of the forest. The flowers that bloom in the spring. It was pairing time. Capillary attraction is a natural phenomenon. Lotty Clarke, flaxenhaired, I saw at her night toilette through illclosed curtains, with poor papa's opera glasses. The wanton ate grass wildly. She rolled downhill at Rialto Bridge to tempt me with her flow of animal spirits. She climbed their crooked tree and I . . . A saint couldn't resist it. The demon possessed me. Besides, who saw? Done. Prff." As Zero said, "Some part! It uses an actor's complete range."

Zero asked Toby Cole to read the script and give him her opinion of it. She thought it was "problematic whether the play could be brought off successfully," but she enthusiastically recommended that he accept the role. "I was certain that no matter how the play was received, Zero would be reinstated in the theatre," she told me. Cole's opinion confirmed Zero's own belief. "I was made to play Bloom," he said. "When Joyce wrote this character, he wrote it for me. It's typecasting putting me in it."

Some directors might have shied away from Mostel because of the blacklist, but Burgess Meredith, a *Red Channels* listee himself, had no such qualms. "It's true that he was under a cloud politically, but this was a very off-off-Broadway production put on with very little money," Meredith said. "My only reservation about him was that he had been a comedian and he'd never done anything of consequence on the stage before and we were now about to put him in the leading role of a classic."

I asked Meredith what qualities he saw in Mostel that led him to believe Zero would be capable of playing a role as complex as Leopold Bloom. "Zero was always recognized as an extraordinarily talented man, even as a comic," he answered. "He was daring and intelligent. In looks and feeling, he seemed exactly right for the character to me."

Zero signed a contract on May 3, 1958, and the production was rushed immediately into rehearsal so that it could open late that same month. However, the play proved difficult enough to require an additional week of rehearsal, and the opening date was postponed until June 5.

Mostel had loved Joyce's novel ever since he read it in college. Blessed with a phenomenal memory, he now discovered that memorizing his lines would not be difficult: he already knew entire sections of the play by heart. He admired the novel for its "elegant inventive language."

Rehearsing *Ulysses in Nighttown* was an extraordinarily stimulating experience for Zero. Meredith broke the script into fifty-six scenes, to each of which he assigned a color, an intention, a suggestion of physical characterization (created by referring to paintings by Rembrandt, Bosch, and Michelangelo), a theatrical style, and a metaphor—all for the purpose of helping the actors use their own reality to create the surreality of Joyce's world. The metaphor of the first scene between Buck Mulligan and Stephen Dedalus, for example, was "a conversation between Teddy Roosevelt and Lord Byron." For Lynch's and Dedalus's brothel scene, the metaphor was "two Harvard men in Harlem on Saturday night."

Burgess Meredith said that Zero's energy was so great while he was rehearsing Bloom that "sometimes the old Houston Street building shook like the scaffolding of Cape Canaveral. When this occurred, we called it Zero Hour."

Zero's opinion of directors was generally quite low, but he made an exception in the case of Burgess Meredith. "I've worked with all kinds of directors," Mostel said.

Some of the big-name directors destroy the most wonderful thing an actor has. Just because he has power and importance, the destructive director tries to bend you to what he calls his sense of production instead of letting you use your own configuration, your own way of merging your own personality with the character you're playing. A good director knows how to bring out your own talent. One of the best directors I've ever worked with is Burgess Meredith. . . . What a wonderful director he is. He can say "Aah!" suddenly to me in rehearsal and I'll get more of out of the aah! than months with those fancy directors explaining me my motivations or the other kind, the ones who say, "Take two steps forward and then turn with a gleam of ferocity in your eyes." You know why? Because he's a wonderful actor himself—very inventive and very creative—so he can do a lot of the things he wants you to do on the stage. We're on the same wave length. It's like two painters talking. You don't need explanations. Sometimes he can make a single little gesture when he steps into a part, and it rubs off on you. He sees things a cut above realism. He has a conception of what a thing is, what it means. He knows how to make use of you as an actor, but always in good taste. It's very stimulating. And I don't feel the breath of ambition on him, which is always disturbing to an actor. I feel that his concern is for the play.

No one expected that *Ulysses in Nighttown* would have popular appeal; nor was it likely that the critics would find the play accessible. Since the producer expected little or no financial return, the most economical possible production was planned. The play would be produced at the tiny off-Broadway Rooftop Theatre, on Houston Street on the Lower East Side, a theatre that could be reached only by an unsteady elevator that held no more than eight people at a time. On the ground floor of the building stood the National Theatre, which presented comedies in Yiddish (and had, in earlier years, been the home of Minsky's Burlesque Theatre); on the second floor was the bagel workers' union; the Rooftop Theatre occupied the third floor.

The financial outlay for the production was infinitesimal. The entire costume budget came to $150. When Burgess Meredith learned that the producer could not afford to purchase the scrims he felt were necessary, Meredith put up $500 of his own money. For the most part, the salary for each member of the large cast was kept to the off-Broadway minimum: $40 per week. That was the figure Zero initially accepted, but Toby Cole managed to renegotiate a salary of $240 for him. (During the course of the run, it was raised to $300, then to $350.) She also arranged that he would have top billing in all advertising of the play.

Despite budgetery constraints, *Ulysses in Nighttown* was meticulously and thoroughly rehearsed and presented. Choreographer Valerie Bettis assisted Burgess Meredith with the direction, staging the actors' movements—a wise decision in a play that emphasized nonrealistic activities so strongly. "I asked the producers to give me Valerie Bettis because I wanted the action of the play to have some of the form and pattern of dancing, of ballet," said Meredith. "Not that our production is formalized stiffly, but since the whole play is a feverish series of hallucinations, I wanted to get some of the organized unreality you can get with dancing." Meredith himself played the narrator during the first performance; Carroll O'Connor, Tom Clancy, John Astin, Beatrice Arthur, and Anne Meara were all prominently featured in the excellent cast.

Critics and audiences alike were stunned by Mostel's performance. Still remembering him primarily as a stand-up comedian, few suspected that he was capable of such range, combining comedy with tragedy, speaking with an exquisite sense of poetry, expressing the seemingly inexpressible with his body, face, and hands.

Earlier in 1958, Laurence Olivier had electrified the theatrical world with his performance in *The Entertainer*. But, Jack Kroll wrote in *Newsweek*, "later that season on a stifling summer night in the rickety, firetrap Rooftop Theatre . . . something unbelievable happened. A fat comedian named Zero Mostel gave a performance that was even more astonishing than Olivier's, as Leopold Bloom in *Ulysses in Nighttown*."

Even Toby Cole, Zero's agent, was astonished. "I shall never ever forget that opening night," she said. "Any doubts I ever had about Zero Mostel's range as an actor were completely dispelled that evening. It was for me the most memorable evening I have ever spent in the theatre. I think I've seen every important actor in my lifetime on the stage—Renaud, Barrault, Olivier, Scofield, MacGowran, de Filippo, I've seen them all. And I realized that night that Zero was right up there in that league. His performance was incredible." Cole felt that Mostel never quite matched his opening-night performance, but that no performance he gave during the run of the production fell short of brilliance.

One reason some people felt Zero was at his best on opening nights was that he would always play the script as written and directed on its first performance. Afterward, he would alter his presentation depending upon his mood and the inspiration of the moment. Burgess Meredith described one night in *Ulysses in Nighttown* when "his emotions got so huge that he bit his fellow actor, named Dillon. Dillon's screams didn't bother the audience because they thought it was part of the act, but in a calmer moment after the performance, Dillon asked me, as director, if I had seen what happened to him. I said I had, more or less.

" 'If he does it again,' he said, 'what should I do?'

" 'Bite him back,' I said.

" 'He is too big,' said Dillon.

" 'Well, then, I suppose the next best thing would be to get out of his way.'

"And this, I believe, was the advice Dillon followed for the rest of the run."

When I questioned Meredith about Mostel's tendency to stray from the direction, he said, "He was very much of a rascal in that department. So I'd sneak in to see him every once in a while, and I'd try my best to get him back to the play as it was directed. I objected to his improvising because it threw the other actors off sometimes. Another thing I worried about was the purists coming to see Joyce. I used to beg Zero not to do anything too untoward. But he didn't pay much attention to me. Still, he wouldn't ad lib; he wouldn't add words to Joyce. But he would do things unexpectedly when he got bored. In fact, I never saw him do anything that *was* expected. He rather disliked doing the expected. But whatever he did, the audience liked it. And you couldn't get mad at him, he was so brilliant whatever he did."

Meredith must not have been in attendance one evening when Zero did alter the words of the play. Frances Chaney recalled one such occasion when she attended *Ulysses in Nighttown* with her husband, Ring Lardner, Jr. When Mostel spotted them in the audience he ad-libbed, "Oh, here are the prince of O'Lardner and the princess of Chaney."

The unpredictable nature of Zero's performances had one great advantage, Meredith felt: "It kept him from getting bored. He had a mind that easily got bored with things, so, when that happened, he'd do some outrageous thing once in a while. But," he added, "he was never mean in what he did; always generous, in fact. He would never try to ruin another actor's laugh, for instance. And then, since Joyce had never been done on the stage before, most people didn't know whether anything Zero did was supposed to be in the play or not."

Eventually, Meredith recalled, Mostel's performance "became more important than the play," in the sense that those who purchased tickets came primarily to see Zero's highly praised portrayal.

Toby Cole felt that the performance should somehow be preserved so that it could be studied by other actors. She contacted everyone she knew in television, pleading with them to televise the performance and to preserve the tape, but she was unsuccessful. Although *Ulysses in Nighttown* was an enormous success on its own terms, it must have seemed relatively inconsequential to the decision-makers in television, who inevitably thought in terms of entertainments that would appeal to millions. For all its acclaim, this production was being given at a tiny off-Broadway playhouse and its approbation by a comparatively small audience did not demonstrate convincingly that James Joyce would appeal to the American public at large.*

Even the off-Broadway audiences sometimes behaved "like a pack of cucumbers," in Zero's phrase. "Some of them tell me it's too deep— as though that's a crime! Sure, it's no Norman Krasna [i.e., typical Broadway] comedy!"

Critical reaction to Zero's performance was overwhelmingly favorable. "Zero Mostel . . . fat, grotesque and completely believable, capers, struts, grimaces and cowers like the agonized heart of Bloom. . . . Through every shade of emotion Mr. Mostel handles himself with skill, feeling and occasional flashes of humor," said the *Herald Tribune*. Jack Kroll said that Mostel as Bloom "broke your heart with no trace of sentimentality." Gilbert Seldes, writing in the *Village Voice*, called the production "the most imaginative and absorbing . . . seen in years." Seldes said that any actor playing Bloom faced a special challenge. "Leopold Bloom is one of the universals of literature, which means that every man (and I suspect every woman) knows what Bloom looks and walks and talks like. I thought I knew . . . how tall he was and how much he weighed." But, he went on to say, "the moment Mostel appeared all my preconceptions vanished. This *is* Bloom—and Heaven help whoever plays it in the second company. . . . The utterly complete embodiment of Bloom into Mostel is a totally different thing from Mostel throwing himself into the part of Bloom—and it is a rare phenomenon in the theatre. It is magnificent!"

Brooks Atkinson described Mostel as "the perfect Leopold Bloom. Around him the dreams and hallucinations, the feeling of guilt, the delusions of grandeur spiral off into a mad rigadoon. But Mr. Mostel's Bloom provides a solid center of gravity. . . . he pulls the whole production together with his solid characterization of the amiable, commonplace Bloom." In his Sunday piece in the *Times*, Atkinson added, "The degree of success [at transferring the novel to the stage] . . . is extraordinary. Directors [Meredith and Bettis] and actors have found

---

*Even if they had been more favorably disposed to the material, television moguls would no doubt have been mindful of Zero's blacklisted status, and therefore unlikely to allow him to appear in a telecast.

ways to convey the imagery of Bloom's spinning mind as it leaps from one graphic allusion to another . . . the part of Leopold Bloom, the common man, is played flawlessly by Zero Mostel. His vulgar bourgeois of Dublin, sensual, outwardly respectable, inwardly epicene, secretive, cunning, cheap in self-esteem as well as infamy, haunted by a million vicious specters—is the core of the performance. Bloom emerges from the novel intact in mind and body, and gives the work earthy vitality." Richard Watts of the *Post* said, "Zero Mostel is a revelation . . . he seems born to the part." Frank Aston of the *World Telegram & Sun* called Mostel's performance "superb."

Harold Clurman congratulated the authors and director for having taken "a section of Joyce's *Ulysses*—barely intelligible to many—and converted it into a fascinating stage piece with a continuity that has both psychological and narrative coherence which can be followed by the audience with interest and, for the most part, pleasure." But, he conceded, without "the vividly pathetic clowning" of Zero Mostel "the enterprise might have proved a calamity."

John Gassner felt that Mostel's performance was so remarkably effective that it blurred the line between reality and illusion.

> In his performance—and this is what made it so right for *Ulysses in Nighttown* and so exemplary for theatre art in general—it was simply impossible to distinguish between what is life and what is patently theatre. Living and performing became one in his case, from his first appearance on the stage to his last as he stood guard over the drunken Stephen Dedalus against the whole world, immensely dignified after having been grievously humiliated in the brothel from which they had both fled. And throughout the nadir of Bloom's situation it was impossible to differentiate between the planned comic pathos of a superb clown and the unplanned, hardly conscious, pathos of an ordinary human being.

Some critics—John Chapman and Robert Coleman among them—detested the play, which they were frank to admit they did not understand, but the praise for Mostel's performance was unanimous.

Ordinarily, the narration was spoken by actors Denis Johnston (who had aided in creating the adaptation) or Sean Dillon. Occasionally, however, in order to boost the sale of tickets, the narrator's function was taken over by a well-known performer. Since each narrator gave the lines a slightly different flavor, Mostel would adapt spontaneously to each new reading. When Eli Wallach rehearsed the narration, for example, he spoke the lines, "Leopold Bloom had his heart in the right place, he used to go to the veterans' hospital and kiss the oozing, suppurated wounds of the veterans." Wallach told me, "And as I said this, Zero gave me a look as if to say, 'You expect me to do that?' There was a long pause, so I repeated the speech. Again he glared at me. Then he decided, okay, he'd have to do it, so he bent down and pantomimed kissing the wounds with a terrible scowl on his face of disapproval and distaste. But then he wet his lips with his tongue as if to say, 'Hm, it's not so bad,' and went back and kissed it again."

Mostel's gargantuan talent was allowed free rein for the first time since his performances in the Molière plays at the Brattle Theatre. Only roles as expansive as those in such imaginative plays as *Ulysses in Nighttown*, *The Imaginary Invalid*, and *The Doctor in Spite of Himself* could contain his talent and display his range.

Mostel was given an "Obie" award for the best off-Broadway performance of the 1958–59 season. The award was confirmation of an astonishing fact: Zero Mostel, who had begun his career in show business sixteen years before and had won considerable acclaim as an inventive buffoon, had become, at the age of forty-three, what no one had suspected—a great actor.

Ulysses in Nighttown played for 206 performances at the Rooftop Theatre, and would have run longer had not the theatre been torn down to make way for a new subway line.

Leopold Bloom always remained Mostel's favorite role and *Ulysses in Nighttown* his favorite play. Few other playwrights anywhere in the world were writing dramas of such vision, he felt. *Ulysses* was a play with "language, imagination, invention, madness," he said. "The others are still writing 100 years prior to modern art."

A few days after the off-Broadway production opened, Toby Cole set in motion a series of events that resulted in *Ulysses in Nighttown* being taken to Europe.* She wrote to Sam Wanamaker, a blacklisted

---

*She also wrote to every prominent Broadway producer, trying to drum up business for her client in New York. Her campaign paid off when David Merrick offered Zero the opportunity to replace Peter Ustinov in *Romanoff and Juliet*. But Zero declined the offer in order to continue playing Bloom.

American actor living in England and operating the New Shakespeare Theatre in Liverpool. Cole suggested that Wanamaker might wish to import the production of *Ulysses in Nighttown* to England. Wanamaker was unable to do so, but he contacted the Arts Theatre in London and arranged for them to sponsor the production. In February 1959, the deal was closed; Zero and many of the other actors would appear at the Arts Theatre under the auspices of Furndel Productions. Toby Cole negotiated with Viscount William Anthony Furness for Zero's salary and travel expenses, and arranged for British agent Adza Vincent to look after his interests in London. Mostel sailed on the Queen Elizabeth for England on April 15.

The production that opened at the Arts Theatre on May 21, 1959, featured some cast changes (Alan Badel, for example, was cast as Dedalus), but was substantially the same as the one that had been seen in New York. It—and Zero's performance—were equally successful in England, as Caryl Brahms reported in *Plays and Players*: "In Mr. Zero Mostel who plays Leopold Bloom, we find an inspired clown, granted that his face, a putty moon, does his tumbling for him. His broad loose hands, his ambling and his giggle, his large eyes swimming with self-reproach, or shining with absurd defiance, his squalors and his grandeurs are peculiar to himself."

The critic for the *Times* of London did not like Marjorie Barkentin's adaptation of the novel, but said, "Luckily Bloom is marvellously well played by the American comedian, Mr. Zero Mostel. . . . Mr. Mostel's stage metamorphosis is a kind of delicate clowning which carries its own humanity. Whatever happens to Bloom in his mind's phantasmagoria, whether he achieves deification, or is turned into a beast, may appear to us almost arbitrary; but whatever it may be, Mr. Mostel, with easy gestures of the nicest calculation, contrives to keep his character and the audience on terms of friendly understanding." Zero was described as "an actor of genius" by John Wain in the *Observer*. "Mr. Mostel has everything," Wain reported, "the mad, rubbery face, the unremittingly eloquent eyes, the perfect timing, the ability to mimic, to assimilate, and then suddenly to be unmistakably and shatteringly himself." But perhaps V. S. Pritchett paid him the ultimate compliment when he wrote in *Encounter*, "I am sure that Joyce's [literary techniques] found a quintessential expression in this play which, because of Zero Mostel, almost stands on its own feet without the book."

Although this was not Zero's first visit to England, it gave him his first extended opportunity to roam through museums, his favorite recreation. During the month that *Ulysses in Nighttown* played at the Arts Theatre, "I didn't miss one day . . . in the National Gallery," Zero said. Each day he would choose three or four paintings to study; then peer at them intently for hours.

Following the London production, the play became the British entry at the Théâtre des Nations in Paris, opening there on July 9, 1959. Zero once again astonished audiences with the power of his performance. He was voted the best actor at the festival—a much sought-after honor, for the award was given by the theatre critics of twenty-five countries, known collectively as the International Critics Circle. The presentation was made at a midnight ceremony held in the foyer of the Théâtre Sarah-Bernhardt on July 21.

Subsequently, the production was taken to Amsterdam for another series of performances. Only a larger salary could have made Mostel happier. As he wrote Toby Cole, the cost of living in Europe was higher than either of them had expected and his income—slightly more than £100 a week (the equivalent of about $280)—barely covered his expenses. But the recognition he received after so many years of neglect more than compensated for the low salary. He loved the "larger than life" quality he found in *Ulysses in Nighttown*, and the scope it gave to his imagination and abilities. "I played [Bloom] on and off for two years in New York, London, Paris, and Amsterdam," he said later, "and never got bored; there was always something new to do, something interesting, something alive."

Mostel's success in *Ulysses in Nighttown* had led to his recording selections from Joyce's novel for Washington Records in April. It also led to his being asked to appear in the London production of *The Gazebo* and a film called *The Public Eye*, as well as in some of the major works in dramatic literature, past and present. Associated Rediffusion offered Mostel the role of Goldberg in a television version of Harold Pinter's first full-length play, *The Birthday Party*; Oscar Lewenstein, a British producer, wanted him for the role of Berrenger in the English premiere of Ionesco's *Rhinoceros*; Peter Brook invited Mostel to play in Alfred Jarry's *Ubu Roi* and Brecht's *A Man's a Man* in repertory at the Royal Court Theatre in London; and Joan Littlewood, the renowned British director whose production of *The Hostage* also won an award at the Théâtre des Nations, asked Zero to play Falstaff in *Henry IV, Parts One and Two* for the Royal Shakespeare Company at Stratford-upon-Avon.

If Zero's ambition was to establish himself as an actor of great range, capable of appearing in the finest plays, that ambition was realized as a result of his performance in *Ulysses in Nighttown*. As it happened, however, none of these offers came to fruition.

Certainly, the easiest to refuse should have been *The Gazebo*, a play of no particular distinction. But Zero, whose ability to take decisive action had not improved over the years, could not bring himself to do so. Instead, he allowed his British representative, Adza Vincent, to spend countless hours negotiating the smallest details with the producer; then, at the last minute, he insisted on various perquisites that had not been discussed before. "Finally," in Toby Cole's words, the producer "gave up in disgust." It was neither the first nor the last time that Mostel would embroil his agents in fruitless negotiations rather than simply admit that he was not interested.

Plans for *The Public Eye* fell through when the producers refused to give him prominent billing, fearing that right-wingers would threaten to picket the film, thereby endangering its American distribution.

Toby Cole was "bowled over" when she read *The Birthday Party* and told Mostel, "she felt that it was very important for him to go and work with Pinter, because it would establish Zero's commitment to this 'new' drama." But Associated Rediffusion was offering a salary of only £100 plus air fare, and Zero rejected the offer, to Cole's dismay.

In hindsight, much of this seems unfortunate. The opportunity to act in Pinter's play—a drama that was on the cutting edge of the vital new theatre then emerging in Europe—or to work with Peter Brook, perhaps the world's most innovative director, would have given Zero an unparalleled opportunity to employ his full range as an actor. The work he did in the musicals that ultimately made him famous—*A Funny Thing Happened on the Way to the Forum* and *Fiddler on the Roof*—was certainly brilliant, but called upon him to tap only a small fraction of his talent.

Zero did agree to make a short film written by Samuel Beckett, the Irish author in whom some recognized the spiritual heir of James Joyce. Beckett, whose *Waiting for Godot* was then playing in Europe, specified that his film needed a clown as gifted as Charlie Chaplin or Zero Mostel—an indication of the high regard in which Zero was held by those who had seen *Ulysses in Nighttown*. Anthony Asquith directed Mostel in Beckett's screenplay. Entirely in pantomime, the one-character film ran for less than ten minutes. Based upon Beckett's *Mime Play Without Words*, the picture was eventually titled *Zero*, but—except for a showing at the Venice Film Festival in 1960—it was never released. Some potential distributors were afraid the film was too avant-garde and might not be understood. Others seem to have been concerned that Zero's blacklisted status would cause it to be picketed in the United States.

Mostel did not immediately turn down the opportunity to play Falstaff, suggesting that he might wish to return to England and perform the role in a year or two. And he was enthusiastic about the chance to appear in *Rhinoceros*, to which he made a verbal commitment. He would come back to London, he said, as soon as a rehearsal date was set. In the meantime, he returned to the United States.

*   *   *

At the same time that Mostel was receiving offers for stage work in England, Toby Cole was attempting to revive her erstwhile movie career. She wrote to the powerful Hollywood agent Paul Kohner, enclosing reviews of Zero's performance as Bloom, and asked if Kohner would like to act as Mostel's representative for film work. Kohner was interested, but wary of Zero's blacklisted status. He asked if Zero would be willing to undergo the humiliating process of "clearance." Toby Cole responded, "He feels he has nothing to 'clear.' " The blacklist was beginning to lose its power in 1959, however, and one of the first signs was the televised version of *The World of Sholem Aleichem* on educational television's *The Play of the Week*.

Six years earlier several blacklisted actors, including Jack Gilford,

Morris Carnovsky, Ruby Dee, and Howard Da Silva had performed in an off-Broadway production of the play, adapted by Arnold Perl (also blacklisted) from the works of Sholem Aleichem and I. L. Peretz. In 1959, Don Richardson, Zero's former acting teacher, was hired to direct a television version on New York's educational station. Richardson, who was firmly opposed to the blacklist, approached Henry Weinstein, the line producer of *Play of the Week*, about casting Mostel in a major role in one of the plays and supporting roles in the other two. "I know Zero and I think he would be excellent," Richardson told Weinstein, then asked, "Would you help me fight to get him on the show?" Weinstein agreed, and the two of them suggested to Ely Landau (who served as board chairman of National Telefilm Associates, which owned Channel 13) and David Susskind, the program's executive producer, that Zero be cast.

Landau's first reaction was negative. "I can't hire him. He's blacklisted," Richardson recalled him saying. "But you own the station," Richardson countered. Landau decided to take a chance and hire the blacklisted performer. But Richardson's goal was more grandiose: to hire a cast composed largely of blacklisted actors, so that a clear statement would be made: *The Play of the Week* would challenge the blacklist not simply by including one blacklisted actor in *The World of Sholem Aleichem*, but by involving several. In that way, no one could possibly think that a blacklisted performer was being employed accidentally.

Richardson returned to Landau, arguing that such actors as Lee Grant, Sam Levene, and Jack Gilford be included in the cast. When Landau began to demur, Richardson reminded him that the crucial decision to hire Zero had already been made. "Well, what the hell," he said. "If you're going to go to jail you may as well go seven times as one time." Ultimately, Landau and Susskind agreed to all of Richardson's suggestions, and the program was, as Josh Mostel terms it, "like a Who's Who of the blacklist."

Zero's behavior during the production showed him both at his best and at his worst. Nancy Walker felt out of place at the first rehearsal. In a play about Jews, she was the only non-Jew in the cast. "But," she said, "all during rehearsals Zero saw to it that we had lunch together and he would talk the whole time with a thick Jewish accent telling lots of Yiddish jokes and suddenly it dawned on me this was for my benefit. When we were being made up just before going on I said to him, 'I could be the dumbest woman in the world but I'd know enough to thank you for teaching me the right inflections during those lunches.'"

On the other hand, Don Richardson recalled, "During the rehearsal period, Zero was constantly off in corners telling people that he should have played the lead in all three plays. I had a hell of a time getting him cast and he was standing around in the corner whispering that this actor was no good and that one was no good and that he should have played the lead in all the plays." Zero's displays of temperament, either in rehearsal or in performance, would become a familiar occurrence from this time until the end of his career. They became the price that had to be paid in exchange for the prodigious talent Mostel lent to the productions in which he appeared.

The World of Sholem Aleichem was broadcast for the first time on December 14, 1959, and repeated each night for a week. Later it was shown in several other large cities throughout the country. Jack Gould of the *Times* called it "theatre of gentle beauty, compassion and social protest. . . . Its unifying theme is the dignity and humor of the meek everywhere. On the New York stage the program was an evening's uncommon experience; it is more so on television."

Zero's remarkable grace was evident when he performed a lyrical, whirling dance in the production. Five years later, when *Fiddler on the Roof* (also from stories by Sholem Aleichem) was being cast, the memory of Zero's dance helped to influence the producers to choose him as Tevye.

At any time in the previous decade, the inclusion of blacklisted performers on a television program would have galvanized the political right into firing off vehement protests. But the barriers to employment for individuals with "controversial" political backgrounds were beginning to crumble on all fronts. *The World of Sholem Aleichem* did not end the blacklist—it was only a local program telecast on an educational station—but it represented one link in a chain of events that brought about that result.

The first significant link, perhaps, occurred in 1955, when the Hollywood branch of the Writers Guild refused to expel members who had taken the Fifth Amendment before HUAC. Two years later, Dalton

Trumbo, one of the Hollywood Ten, won an Academy Award for the story of *The Brave One*. He wrote the story of the film under the pseudonym Robert Rich, and so was unable to accept the award, but afterward all Hollywood came to know who "Robert Rich" was. Then, in 1960, Universal Studios announced that Trumbo would be given credit as the writer of *Spartacus*.

Most important of all was a lawsuit instituted by a radio personality named John Henry Faulk—a suit that eventually destroyed the institution of blacklisting altogether. Because Zero Mostel's life and career were so fundamentally affected by Faulk's lawsuit, the story is worth retelling in these pages.

In 1954, following years of discord among members of the American Federation of Television and Radio Artists (AFTRA) regarding the issue of blacklisting, the board of directors wholeheartedly supported the practice. The board was in turn controlled by AWARE, Inc., one of the organizations that published an "anti-Communist" newsletter. In fact, some members of the board also served as officers of AWARE.

The tortured logic by which AWARE justified blacklisting was summarized by John Cogley in his *Report on Blacklisting*: "Communism is a conspiracy; therefore Communists and all those who collaborate with them, knowingly or not, are conspirators. A 'pattern' of Communistic associations is a pattern of conspiracy. So *not* to support political screening *is* to support political conspiracy. Those who oppose blacklisting, whether they know it or not, are supporters of the Communist conspiracy."

A slate of candidates formed to run against the AWARE-dominated board in 1954 lost decisively. AWARE, determined that the members of the losing slate must be punished further, circulated a special bulletin to all radio and television employers, attacking the patriotism of those who had run against the board. "Out of 26 candidates on the 'independent' slate, at least 13 have what are considered significant *public records* in connection with the Communist-front apparatus," the bulletin announced. The employers promptly extended the blacklist to include those attacked in the bulletin. As Faulk said, the action "served as a stern warning to other members of the union; anyone who wanted to run in opposition to the AWARE-supported slate of officers had better think twice."

At a turbulent meeting of the New York local in March 1955, the membership of AFTRA, by a margin of almost two to one, voted to condemn AWARE for its action. The board of directors predictably accused all those who voted against AWARE of being Communists or Communist dupes.

John Henry Faulk, the host of a daily one-hour radio show on the CBS outlet in New York, was persuaded to run for local union office that year. He was one of a slate of thirty-three "middle-of-the-road" candidates, running in opposition to the AWARE-dominated board. The "middle-of-the-roaders" were just that: individuals who were not blacklisted themselves but who disagreed with the practice of black-listing. Newscaster Charles Collingwood was the candidate for president on the middle-of-the-road slate, with Faulk running for second vice-president.

At last, the membership of AFTRA condemned the irresponsible behavior of AWARE by voting the right-wing board of directors out of office. Faulk and his allies earned a tremendous victory, winning twenty-seven of the thirty-five seats on the board and taking office in January 1956.

AWARE did not accept losing gracefully. As was its custom, it suggested that its defeat had been engineered by Communists. Then HUAC was heard from. In Faulk's words, "a couple of weeks after we had taken office, the House Un-American Activities Committee, in its annual report, let go with a blast aimed at the Middle-of-the-Road administration. It declared among other things that the issue of black-listing was being used by the Communist forces to reinfiltrate the union. This report was released to all the papers and was widely publicized."

In February 1956, AWARE issued a bulletin that made seven specific charges against Faulk in an attempt to link him with pro-Communist activities.* Faulk took the bulletin to two CBS executives, who assured him that the network would not be influenced by AWARE's charges. But when Laurence Johnson, the Syracuse grocery-store owner, applied pressure, and persuaded Libby's Frozen Foods to cancel its sponsorship of Faulk's program, the executives began to waver. Then Johnson issued

---

*By June 1957, tactics such as these paid off. The middle-of-the-road slate was defeated and the backers of AWARE once again took control of the board of AFTRA.

a warning to Tom Murray, the advertising executive in charge of the Hoffman Beverage account, that he would remove Hoffman products from his supermarket shelves unless they, too, withdrew their sponsorship; and, he added, American Legion Post Number 41 would write a letter in support of his position.

If there was a single moment when the blacklisters' power began to erode significantly, this was it. For years, those who controlled television had effectively denied the existence of a blacklist and no one was able to prove otherwise. Now, however, Tom Murray showed Faulk the letter he had received from the American Legion. Armed with this evidence, Faulk consulted attorney Louis Nizer about instituting a lawsuit against Johnson, AWARE, and Vincent Hartnett, AWARE's guiding spirit. Nizer took the case, and the lawsuit was filed in June. Although preliminary hearings were held shortly afterward, the trial itself did not take place until years later.

In the interim, a pattern of harassment developed. In 1957, CBS fired Faulk, assuring him that his dismissal had nothing to do with AWARE or the impending trial. The following year, Faulk was subpoenaed to appear before HUAC. (Subsequently, however, they delayed the scheduled hearing several times and eventually canceled the subpoena.) Advertising agency executives and directors who had expressed sympathy for Faulk's position in the past suddenly refused to testify in his behalf.

At last, in 1962, a jury was empaneled and the trial began. Louis Nizer's first task was to prove the existence of the blacklist. His most important witness in that regard was the producer David Susskind, who testified that it was necessary for him to get political clearance on every actor he intended to hire for *Appointment with Adventure*, the program he produced in 1955–56. "I had to submit the names of everybody in every category to an executive of Young & Rubicam," Susskind testified, "and nobody could be engaged by me finally or a deal made and consummated, before a clearance or acceptance came back from Young & Rubicam." This was the standard practice on all television programs, he said. He estimated that, of the names he submitted, "approximately 33%, perhaps a little higher, came back politically rejected."

Young & Rubicam executives had warned Susskind that he was never to let an actor know that he—the actor—had been politically rejected.

Anyone who asked was simply to be told that he was "not right for the part." Susskind testified that he complained to Young & Rubicam, "Human beings are suffering loss of employment without any substantiation, without any charges, without even their knowing that they can't be hired," but the agency was unmoved. Instead, a Young & Rubicam executive gave Susskind a "whitelist" of 150 names and told him that only the actors included on that list should be considered when casting.

Even children had to be cleared, Susskind said, and told this story in court:

> In the course of *Appointment with Adventure*, sponsored by Lorillard at Young & Rubicam Agency, we required the services of a, I believe, at least a seven- or eight-year-old girl actress, child actress. . . . We finally found a child, an American child eight years old, female. I put her name in along with some other names. That child's name came back unacceptable, politically unreliable.

Mark Goodson, another television producer, corroborated Susskind's testimony when he agreed that everyone whom he intended to use on any of his programs had to be politically "cleared." Several actors, including Tony Randall and Kim Hunter, testified to the harm done to them personally by the blacklist.

Tom Murray then linked Laurence Johnson directly to the blacklist when he told the jury that Johnson had threatened to remove Hoffman Beverage products from his supermarket shelves unless the company withdrew its sponsorship from Faulk's radio program.

In cross-examination of the defendants' witnesses, Nizer demonstrated that the charges AWARE had brought against Faulk in its bulletin were false or deliberately misleading. Paul Milton, who had written the bulletin, admitted that he knew—and had known from the beginning—that Faulk did not belong to any of the organizations the bulletin accused him of having joined.

When Vincent Hartnett took the stand, Nizer attempted to prove that he was operating not out of patriotic principle, but the profit motive. Hartnett admitted that he had written an article "in which I was critical of the past employment practices of the Borden Company," but that he had shown the article to Borden Company executives before it was published. In an apparent effort to prevent the article from appearing, Borden paid Hartnett $10,000, ostensibly for "security work." Subsequently, an article by Hartnett was printed, praising the Borden Company for "taking measures" to correct the employment practices to which Hartnett objected.

Nizer also forced Hartnett to admit that he had printed false information when he had knowingly taken an item about Faulk from the New York *Herald Tribune* and claimed it came from the *Daily Worker*.

While Hartnett was testifying, Nizer noticed that he was looking around the courtroom and taking down the names of performers who were in attendance—presumably for use in a later edition of his bulletin. Suddenly, Nizer asked Hartnett if he could identify Faulk's wife in the audience. After a moment, Hartnett pointed out the wrong woman. Nizer seized the opportunity to inquire of the witness, "Sir, is that an example of the accuracy with which you have identified your victims for the past ten years?" It was a decisive moment in the trial.

Laurence Johnson did not testify, claiming that he was too ill. A physician for Nizer was dispatched to examine Johnson and reported to the court that the grocer was "fully able to come to court." Nevertheless, Johnson refused to appear, leading the judge to instruct the jury that they were "entitled to draw the strongest inference against him." On the very day that Nizer was summing up the case for Faulk, Johnson died in a Bronx motel room, evidently of natural causes. However, the trial continued, with Johnson's estate replacing Johnson as a defendant.

In June 1962, the jury brought in its verdict: Faulk was the winner on every count. AWARE, Vincent Hartnett, and the estate of Laurence Johnson were required to pay a record libel award totaling $3,500,000. Eventually, the Appellate Division of the New York Supreme Court reduced the damages but affirmed the verdict. Faulk ultimately received $550,000. Soon afterward, AWARE, Inc., went out of business.

For all practical purposes, the blacklist came to an end when John Henry Faulk appeared on *To Tell the Truth*, a nationally televised quiz program on a commercial network, on September 3, 1962, the first in a week-long series of appearances.* At last it had become possible for

---

*But Faulk received few offers after that. "I . . . soon found that the broadcasting

Zero Mostel and others like him to be hired openly on television and in the movies. Beyond that, to deny employment to individuals with progressive political views had now clearly been found illegal. The blacklisting nightmare had endured for fifteen years, forcing many people out of show business entirely and causing untold anguish. But Zero had endured. Beyond simple endurance, because of his triumph in *Ulysses in Nighttown*, his performance in *The World of Sholem Aleichem*, and the offers that were now beginning to pour in, the future suddenly looked bright. Fate, however, had one more setback in store for Mostel.

On December 16, 1959, only two days after *The World of Sholem Aleichem* was shown on television, Zero accepted David Merrick's offer to appear as a Monte Carlo croupier in *The Good Soup*, an adaptation of a French play that was scheduled to open in Philadelphia late in January 1960 and on Broadway in March. Mostel instructed Toby Cole to tell Merrick he wanted star billing (although his role was not a large one) and $600 per week, demands they both thought Merrick would refuse. Indeed, when Cole relayed Mostel's conditions to Merrick he walked her to the door and said, "Thank you very much, Miss Cole, good day." Only because Garson Kanin, the play's director and adapter, insisted on having Zero did Merrick eventually accept Mostel's demands. Had Kanin not intervened, however, Mostel would not have been upset. He did not particularly like the play, and he did not wish to sign a long-term contract that would prevent him from appearing in *Rhinoceros* in London. That production, however, was continually being delayed, Zero had to earn a living, and *The Good Soup* appeared likely to have a long and profitable run, principally because of Garson Kanin's impressive record of achievement, particularly with the spectacularly successful *Born Yesterday*. So Zero agreed to terms—but only on condition that Merrick would release him from his contract after the play had run four weeks, freeing him to begin rehearsals for *Rhinoceros*.

The Good Soup began rehearsing on January 4. On the afternoon of January 13, a Wednesday, Zero emerged from the rehearsal studio into

---

industry had not taken kindly to my lawsuit," he said. "It had exposed their collaboration with AWARE and the ugly business of blacklisting. I was *persona non grata* with them." Ironically, the man who broke the blacklist was perhaps the only performer not to benefit from his action.

the sleet and snow and decided that he would not take a bus or subway home, as he normally did. His *Good Soup* contract and the promise of a steady income would allow him to indulge himself a bit, so he hailed a taxi to take him to his apartment. But when Zero arrived at his destination and stepped out of the cab, a bus skidded onto the curb, knocked him down, and crushed his leg. Taken to Knickerbocker Hospital, Zero pleaded with the doctors not to amputate. Despite the dreadful pain, he was even able to make a feeble joke, telling the physicians that he had grown accustomed to his left leg, having known and loved it ever since he was a little boy, and that he could not be persuaded to part with it.

Merle Debuskey, the press representative of *The Good Soup*, rushed to the hospital as soon as he heard about the accident. Debuskey called his friend, Dr. Joseph Wilder, chief of surgery at the Hospital for Joint Diseases, and asked him to give a second opinion. "We didn't know how serious it was at the time," Debuskey told me, "and I wanted to hold the job [in *The Good Soup*] open for him." Kate conferred with the attending physicians, who agreed to let Wilder inspect Mostel's leg. Wilder's diagnosis was not much more favorable than that of the other doctors. "His leg was black, knee to ankle," he told me. "I couldn't tell if we would be able to salvage it, but I was satisfied we didn't have to amputate immediately." After transferring Zero to the Hospital for Joint Diseases, Wilder immobilized his patient and performed a skin graft.

Meanwhile, David Merrick, Garson Kanin, and Ruth Gordon (the leading player) discussed Zero's continued participation in *The Good Soup*. They were willing to make every effort to keep him in the production, and agreed that if he could rejoin the company before the scheduled opening in Philadelphia, he would not have to be replaced.

Soon, however, it became apparent that Zero would be hospitalized for months, and on January 19 his role in *The Good Soup* was given to Jules Munshin.*

As a result of the accident, Mostel lost the use of the muscle that

---

*The production closed after just twenty-one performances, despite having the look of a success. The play, by Félicien Marceau, had already demonstrated its popularity in France; Garson Kanin was highly accomplished both as a playwright and as a director; and the cast, in addition to Ruth Gordon, included such luminaries as Mildred Natwick, Sam Levene, George S. Irving, and Diane Cilento.

raises and lowers the foot. "We had salvaged his leg," Wilder said, "and we hoped that he would be able to walk without being badly crippled, but we never dreamed that he would be able to dance again on the stage." Another operation was performed; then a third; and then still another. Zero remained in the hospital for five months. Slowly, gradually, the injured leg began to heal.

"His recovery was quite remarkable," Wilder said, "and that was a tribute to him; his courage. Zero was a very brave man. He suffered terribly in the hospital." He was also terrified. As Toby Cole wrote to Adza Vincent, "This is his first time in the hospital and he has many fears." But he concealed his anxieties well, making jokes and acting almost as ebullient as ever. "I have never laughed so loud or hard or consistently in my life," Wilder said. "Everybody at the hospital loved Zero, not only because he was so funny and charming, but because the man was fantastically brave."

During Mostel's hospitalization, Wilder was asked to give a presentation to an international meeting of surgeons, describing the innovative surgery he had performed on Zero's leg. Mostel agreed to be present and to show the results of Wilder's work. As in all such cases, the patient would not be identified by name. After Wilder delivered his paper, he turned to Zero, saying, "Patient X, please show the leg." Zero promptly pulled up his right pajama leg, demonstrating an appendage that was completely fit. As the surgeons rose to give their colleague an ovation, Wilder muttered to Zero, "You miserable bastard, I'll kill you!" "Oops," Zero said, dropping his right pajama leg and lifting the left one, showing a mass of grotesque scars. The surgeons, disappointed, responded with mild applause.

Although Zero quickly established himself as the hospital clown, he must have given a good deal of somber thought to his situation. His professional comeback had come to an abrupt end. His financial condition was even worse than before, now that he faced months of inactivity and mounting hospital bills. His future as a performer was very much in jeopardy: so much of his comic style was dependent upon the incongruity between a man of immense bulk and his remarkable physical agility. Even if his leg were saved—and that was by no means a certainty—it was likely that he would never again be able to move with the grace for which he had once been known. What blacklisting had failed to achieve—the ruination of his career—a five-ton bus seemed to have accomplished. As Zero Mostel lay in his hospital bed in 1960, the future looked bleaker than it had two years before. Then, at least, there had been reason to hope that his career would recover. Now recovery seemed unlikely—and not only his career was threatened but even his ability to lead a normal life. He would have had every right to despair.

But the operations were spectacularly successful. When he was finally released from the hospital, Zero had what Wilder described as "a perfectly viable leg," although it was heavily scarred and, according to Sheldon Harnick, "looked more like wax than flesh and blood." Jack Gilford described it as looking "like a thin layer of hamburger"; Howard Rodney, Mostel's dresser for *Fiddler on the Roof*, compared it to "a piece of raw liver."

Toby Cole told Adza Vincent that Zero was "downcast about the painfully slow progress he's making." It soon became apparent that the leg would never fully heal, and to the end of his life, Zero carried a cane—which also served him as a handy prop when he was in the mood to swing it jauntily or to use it as a mock weapon. He had to elevate the leg when he slept and after he had been on his feet for a long time, in order to keep the swelling down. The pain was frequently agonizing. James Bronson, the stage manager of *Fiddler on the Roof* when Zero was playing Tevye (1964–65), recalled, "I would often see him arrive at the theatre walking with such pain that I feared he wouldn't make it through the performance, but he always did—and without complaint. Most of the people on stage were never aware of his pain."

When on stage Zero did not use his cane, and, when he performed in strenuous musical numbers, the wound would occasionally open, causing dreadful pain. Because of poor blood circulation, the leg would become extraordinarily hot during every performance. When that happened, Zero lost all feeling in the leg; and, not having any way to determine its condition, he lived with the constant fear that it would break while he was dancing. Immediately after every show, his dresser would apply a soothing cream to reduce the temperature of the leg.

Zero said that he managed to dance by "cheating a little. When you get something like this you learn to live with it. So I make the good leg do more work than it would normally. Anyone watching can't see this, but that's how I get away with it."

A program of exercise, primarily involving the use of a stationary bicycle, was prescribed, and Mostel faithfully followed the routine. He also took weekly therapeutic treatments at the Hospital for Joint Diseases.*

Finally, when his leg had healed sufficiently so that he could perform again, Zero Mostel was able to return to work. No longer restricted to the off-Broadway stage by the blacklist, he began to put together a string of successes so spectacular that few American performers have ever matched it.

---

*Several years after the accident, when he had reestablished himself as a star performer in *A Funny Thing Happened on the Way to the Forum*, he filed a suit for $200,000 against Surface Transit, Inc., whose bus had mangled his left leg, claiming that he had lost that amount in income as a result of the accident. Toby Cole prepared a bill of particulars about entertainments in which Zero might have performed had he not been hospitalized. She testified in his behalf, his lawyers argued the case persuasively, and a jury awarded Mostel $130,000, a figure that was later reduced to $80,000.

6

Comedy Tonight

As Zero still lay in the hospital, Oscar Lewenstein was eager to begin rehearsals of *Rhinoceros* in London. Mostel was equally enthusiastic about appearing in the production—not only because of the opportunity to further his career but because the play, in its plea for individuals to resist the temptation to conform, was so in tune with his own philosophy. In addition, Toby Cole regarded it as a wonderful chance for Zero to appear in the work of Eugène Ionesco, one of Europe's leading new dramatists, whose plays blended farce with tragedy, irony with despair. But she did not know how to respond when Lewenstein telephoned her to ask when Zero would arrive for rehearsals. Since the doctors themselves could not predict when Mostel would be released from the hospital, she could only report that he would leave for England as soon as possible. Lewenstein became increasingly apprehensive that Zero, whose leg was then in a cast, might not have the stamina to play the long and demanding role of Berrenger, who is onstage throughout most of the play. On the other hand, *Rhinoceros*'s other main character, Jean, has only a few scenes, although they are so powerful that the role is nearly equal in importance. On February 18, 1960, Lewenstein, having decided it would be unwise to cast Mostel as Berrenger, offered him the role of Jean; Zero would play opposite Laurence Olivier at the

161

Royal Court Theatre. Toby Cole wired back, "Role switch disappointing but Zero will play Jean to Olivier. . . . Doctor thinks April 15th safe date" to plan the beginning of rehearsals. Lewenstein responded that his contract with the Royal Court stipulated that the production must open on April 29; could Zero arrive in London no later than April 1?

Several weeks of calls and telegrams followed. Meanwhile, Dr. Wilder determined that Zero's hospital stay would have to be extended and another operation performed. Lewenstein reluctantly concluded that he would have to proceed without Zero. *Rhinoceros* opened at the Royal Court Theatre on April 28, 1960, under Orson Welles's direction, with Duncan Macrae playing Jean to Olivier's Berrenger.

Meanwhile, Leo Kerz acquired the American rights to the play, which he planned to produce on Broadway. Kerz spoke to Cole about the possibility of casting Zero as Jean; she in turn arranged a meeting at the hospital with Kerz, Mostel, and Robert Lewis, who was then scheduled to direct the production. After being assured that Zero would be released from the hospital in time to begin rehearsals, Kerz and Lewis agreed to cast him as John (as the character was renamed for the American production) and to bill him as costar with Eli Wallach, who would portray Berrenger. Kerz was taking a risk by not casting better-known performers in a play by a dramatist whose work was known (to the relatively few Americans who knew it at all) as relentlessly experimental and uncommercial. The two leads were described in the New York *Herald Tribune* as actors "who, while they have loyal followings, are not big box-office names."

Cole and Mostel decided that they would ask Leo Kerz for a salary of $1,000 a week. Believing that the producer would attempt to reduce whatever salary she requested, Cole asked for $1,250, and—to her surprise—found that it was immediately accepted.

Rehearsals for *Rhinoceros* did not begin for several months, so Zero taped a production of Samuel Beckett's nihilistic comedy *Waiting for Godot* for educational television. *Waiting for Godot* was the most esteemed play in the new, experimental European drama known as the Theatre of the Absurd. It had won fame and prestige for its author but was generally regarded as an entertainment too intellectually challenging to achieve popular success; indeed, despite a brilliant production on

Broadway in 1955, featuring Bert Lahr and E. G. Marshall, few theatregoers had availed themselves of the opportunity to see it. Zero was
familiar with the play, however, and considered it "a classic of our time.
Beckett reflects the modern world for everyone who is willing to see it
with a clear mind, purged of preconceptions," he said. "He presents
the dilemmas of modern life; his play is the work of an artist." Appearing
in *Waiting for Godot* would also reunite Mostel with Burgess Meredith,
who would play Didi to Zero's Gogo.

But the experience was not a happy one, primarily because Zero
disagreed so strongly with Alan Schneider's direction of the play. When
Toby Cole spoke to Mostel on the telephone during the rehearsals, she
asked, "How does it feel to be back on television after all these years?"
He replied, "Oh God, I wish I was blacklisted again." Certainly the
final product was painfully lacking in excitement, especially when compared to the Lahr-Marshall production. Jack Gould faulted both Zero
("a decided disappointment") and Schneider (whose directorial style
was referred to as "heavy literalness") in his New York *Times* review.

At last, late in 1960, rehearsals for *Rhinoceros* began. Although John
was the smaller of the two leading roles, it had the potential to make
a tremendous impact. *Rhinoceros* is an allegory about conformity, set in
a small French town where most of the citizens willingly turn into
rhinoceroses—the symbol of "running with the herd." Berrenger, the
main character, is caught between the wish to retain his individuality
as a human being and the lure of transforming himself into a rhinoceros
so that he will be like others in the community. John, his dapper and
worldly friend, is the only character in the play who is seen in the
process of transformation from man to rhinoceros. In the London
production, Orson Welles had directed Duncan Macrae to run offstage
several times during the scene; each time he reentered with a slightly
altered makeup until at last he appeared with a horn on his forehead.
In the New York production, Joseph Anthony (who took over the
directorial reins from Robert Lewis before the play went into rehearsal)
originally intended that Mostel would do the same. But Zero had a
better idea. He would become a rhinoceros without the use of makeup
and without leaving the stage. Zero said that the idea occurred to him
because of his training as a painter. Allowing the audience to see each
step in John's progression was "a painterly thing to do," he asserted.

The transformation began with his brow furrowing. As his eyes narrowed and grew ominous, his lip protruded. Then his foot became a hoof and began to thump the stage. He tore off pieces of the houseplants on the set and began to eat them. As Al Hirschfeld later said, "The illusion took hold that he was no longer encased in human skin." With terrifying surreality, John began to disappear, replaced by a rhinoceros.

"In a strange way, the strength of Zero's performance distorted the meaning of the play," Eli Wallach accurately observed, "because the character that I played [with whom Ionesco wanted the audience to empathize] was a man who resisted becoming a rhinoceros. And Zero's performance was so strong that people came to see a man turn into a rhinoceros." But Wallach did not resent the attention Zero got as a result of his performance. Indeed, he described him as "a comedic genius."

Ionesco, who, like Beckett, was one of the patron saints of the Theatre of the Absurd, came to New York to watch rehearsals and attend the opening night. At a reception at the French consul's house in New York, Ionesco, who knew no English, began to speak. Zero suddenly shouted, "*Il n'est pas le vrai Ionesco*! He's not the real Ionesco! I am the real Ionesco! He's a liar!" Ionesco later told Zero that it had been the best speech of the evening, highly Ionesco-ish in its absurdity.

Later, however, the playwright returned to Europe, refusing to stay for the opening night. He may have been upset by the tumultuous nature of the rehearsals. Don Richardson said that several of his friends in the cast called him, knowing that he had been Zero's teacher, asking him to use his influence "to get Zero to behave himself because he was doing outrageous things, shouting at the other actors: 'You don't know how to act, I don't know how the hell you got this job.' There was enormous dissension. Zero was beastly to the cast, absolutely terrible to them," Richardson said. Or Ionesco's departure may have occurred because he objected to the production's interpretation—in which the focus had shifted from Berrenger to John.

Rhinoceros opened at the Longacre Theatre on January 9, 1961. New York's theatrical critics were astonished by Zero's performance. "Mr. Mostel is probably the only actor in the world who can believably transform himself into a rhinoceros before your eyes," said Richard

Watts, Jr., in the *Post*. Howard Taubman, writing in the *Times*, praised Zero as "a superb comedian" who "performs with brilliant resourcefulness to make the change [from man to rhino] seem inevitable, side-splitting and terrifying." Taubman also called the Broadway production far superior to the one he had seen in London, which was "a rather stuffy, subdued version." In contrast, the New York production was "a joyous revelation," he said, "a rowdy, knockabout pleasure instead of a heavy-handed satire." The play was a triumph, especially for "Mostel the magnificent," said Walter Kerr.

Kerr provided the most detailed description of Mostel's transformation from man to beast:

> Now the rhinoceros beneath the skin begins to bulge a little at the eyes. The Kaiser Wilhelm mustache that has earlier adorned [John] loses its spiky endpoints, droops, disintegrates into a tangle that makes it second cousin to a walrus. The voice starts to change. "I hate people—and I'll r-r-run them down!" comes out of a larynx that has stiffened, gone hollow as a 1915 gramophone record, and is ready to produce a trumpet-sound that would empty all of Africa. The shoulders lift, the head juts forward, one foot begins to beat the earth with such native majesty that dust—real dust—begins to rise like the after-veil that seems to accompany a safari. The transformation is on, the secret is out, evolution has reversed itself before your horrified, but nevertheless delighted eyes.

Robert Brustein, writing in the *New Republic*, said that Zero demonstrated "a great dancer's control of movement, a great actor's control of voice, a great mime's control of facial expression." Brustein praised "the gracefulness with which he executes a Chaplinesque back-kick; the ease with which he shifts his emotions from calm to fury to bafflement; and above all the rapidity with which he transforms himself into a rhino before your eyes. . . . the play enables Zero Mostel to demonstrate once again that he is a very great actor."

Mostel's performance, with its control and economy, surprised even those who had seen *Ulysses in Nighttown*. One individual who had been involved in the production of *Flight into Egypt* nine years earlier recalled Zero's performance as "bumbling" and "directionless" and said that his development as an actor had been astounding.

The play also achieved a significant success, although few observers would describe *Rhinoceros* as great drama. Its allegory is too pat, its scenes too unnecessarily extended. Nevertheless, in a poor Broadway season, many considered it the best play of 1960–61.

After *Rhinoceros* opened, Zero's transformation to a rhinoceros became the talk of the theatrical world. Spectators literally gasped at his amazing conversion. "The audience would jump out of their seats" when the change occurred, Eli Wallach said. It "made you laugh with terror," said critic Jack Kroll. Mostel seemed to grow larger before the audiences' eyes. Neil Simon, who saw the performance, said, "I thought the management should have removed the first four rows to protect the audience from the raging beast who trampled everything in his path on the stage."

Some skeptics maintained that Zero's style had always been to overwhelm the roles he played and that his rhinoceroslike behavior was not really so different from his earlier performances. One observer went so far as to say to his face, "What I thought so clever about your performance in *Rhinoceros*, Zero, was the way you were actually able to portray a *human being* in the early part." Zero responded with an equal mixture of anger and humor, "May all your teeth decay, and may I be the dentist!"

In helping Ionesco make his point about the need to resist the temptation to conform, Mostel was in his element, Eli Wallach said. "In real life, Zero was the complete opposite [of John], a man of conscience. To those who tried to confine the artist, to mold his thoughts, to make him a fearful puppet, Zero thumbed his nose in derision."

Wallach and his wife, Anne Jackson, who played Berrenger's girl friend, Daisy, knew of Zero's reputation as an actor who could be unreliable, capable of changing his performance to suit his mood. "Never in our experience," said Wallach. "His identification with the morality of the play kept him within the bounds of exquisite taste."

Zero himself was beginning to tire of allegations that he was an undisciplined actor. "You know what they mean by discipline, don't you?" he said.

They mean English acting, technique without any life. Stand up, look thirty degrees right, take two steps front, say the words, turn left, sit down. That's discipline? That's crap. I *relate*! Acting is living; it's experience. It's relating. Every night the actors come to the theatre different people than they were the night before. You look into their eyes, they look back, and you connect. Something happened that day: their kid is sick, they had a fight at home. Something. They lived that day, so of course it changes. But not with technical actors like the English. Play a scene with them, you can't make them look in your fucking eyes. No connection; they look *through* you, for crissake. Fucking zombies!

I'll tell you about relating. One night in *Rhinoceros* there was some drunken shmuck in the second row who kept talking back to Eli, making his life miserable, telling Eli he hated him. Between acts Eli was practically in tears, and I said, "Leave the shmuck to me." So when I became the rhinoceros, without breaking out of character, I lean forward and *roarrrr* right at him, blowing the poor shmuck half out of his seat. He's petrified. He wiggles his fingers at me, and he whispers, "I like you," and not a peep from then on. That's *relating*!

The bestial noises that issued from Zero's throat as he became a rhinoceros were so hideous, so grating, that those involved with the production were concerned that he would not be able to sustain the use of his vocal mechanism for long. But Zero insisted that he was doing himself no harm, because he was using his "false vocal cords." He must have known something about anatomy that other actors have yet to discover, for he was right: he never lost or damaged his voice. Ironically, Eli Wallach was the one who had vocal trouble. "Zero so dominated the stage and his voice was so big that I couldn't compete with him," he said. "I lost my voice about a week before we were to open, and I lost it again afterwards—always unconsciously competing with Zero."

Mostel's animal roar came in handy one night when he was walking his dog on Central Park West. A mugger appeared and demanded his money. Instead, Zero began roaring and transforming himself into a rhinoceros before the mugger's astonished eyes. When the transformation ended with a frightful bellow, the terrified mugger ran away.

Leo Kerz, the producer of *Rhinoceros*, had invested his life savings in the production. He had experienced great difficulty raising enough money to mount the play on Broadway; not until *Rhinoceros* was already in rehearsal did he manage to accumulate the final $40,000 he needed to meet the production budget. Kerz maintained that there was a conspiracy against him. Perhaps he was right, but he also created some of his own problems. He signed two actors—Eli Wallach and Ray Bolger—to play the same role, resulting in an arbitration hearing by Actors Equity. Bolger ultimately withdrew, solving the problem. Then Robert Lewis claimed that Kerz had violated *his* contract, a claim that led to his withdrawal as director. Kerz's volatility made him a difficult man to work for. He estranged some of the cast members to such an extent that they didn't speak to him. Eli Wallach was so alienated that he barred Kerz from his dressing room.

One of Kerz's stands, objecting to the tradition of quoting comments from reviews out of context in Broadway advertising, won him both friends and enemies. For many years, plays (as well as movies, books, and other entertainments) had extracted words or sentences from reviews in order to publicize their productions (as in: "Thrilling"—Atkinson, *Times*; "Wonderfully stimulating"—Kerr, *Herald Tribune*). Kerz detested the practice, for good reason. In thousands of cases, a critic's considered opinion had been distorted so that it appeared to be totally approving when it was not (for example, Brooks Atkinson might have written, "The first scene is thrilling, but the remainder of the play is leaden"). So, although Kerz could have excerpted such comments as "the play of the year," "an antic piece with overtones of gravity," and "cleverly crazy," he chose not to do so. The advertisements for *Rhinoceros* did not include any critical comment at all.

Most of the cast members strongly opposed Kerz's decision, although some supported him. Zero, who had received the most enthusiastic reviews, was understandably eager to see them publicized. At a meeting held backstage after the third performance, the disaffected faction of actors spoke of paying out of their own pockets for an advertisement that would include critical excerpts. They also discussed the possibility of setting up a picket line around the theatre and outside Kerz's apartment. Eli Wallach suggested that Kerz should run an ad quoting the reviews in their entirety. But the meeting ended with no action being taken.

Kerz had thought he would have the actors' support and was surprised when he did not receive it. "You stick to acting and I'll stick to getting the people into the theatre," he told them. As to their idea about purchasing their own advertisement, he threatened to seek a court injunction to halt any such possible action. He did concede that Wallach's idea had merit, however, and agreed to consider printing several entire reviews in his advertising. Instead, Kerz eventually assembled a pamphlet containing copies of *all* the reviews and made it available to prospective ticket buyers at the theatre's box office.

He took out a large advertisement headed "The Producer of *Rhinoceros* Is on the Spot!" The ad explained that while *Rhinoceros* had received " 'quotable' or 'money' reviews, . . . Leo Kerz, the producer, is steadfast in his decision not to use quotes. . . . Mr. Kerz feels that a review is an important comment only in its entirety and that it is insulting to the critic and to the public alike to reduce such comment to the level of a consumer's report." The ad thanked the critics for their notices, Wallach and Mostel for their "amazing performances," and the public for its patronage of the play.

Despite (or perhaps because of) the controversy over advertising, *Rhinoceros* became a hit and made Zero a star once again. He was given his first Antoinette Perry Award, for the outstanding Broadway performance of 1960–61. ("Gee! The fellows at the zoo will be happy about this!" he said at the award ceremony.)

Mostel stayed with *Rhinoceros* when it moved to Chicago for a month in August and then returned to New York on September 11 for three additional weeks. By that time, Alfred Ryder had replaced Eli Wallach and Zero, his salary more than doubled from its original figure, had moved up to top billing. Later—after 240 performances on Broadway—Mostel and the production toured on the West Coast, then returned for a final three weeks in New York.

Oscar Lewenstein proposed reviving *Rhinoceros* in London, this time pairing Mostel with Olivier. But, according to Zero, "Laurence Olivier refused to work with me in *Rhinoceros* because I wasn't a big enough star [in England]."

Once again, Zero gave serious thought to performing the role of Falstaff in *Henry IV, Parts One and Two*. The Royal Shakespeare Company paid his fare to England in 1960 so that discussions could be initiated. But, for a number of reasons, the production never came about. For one thing, the stipend offered by the Royal Shakespeare Company was infinitesimal compared with his salary in *Rhinoceros*. Understandably, the Mostels were not enthusiastic about returning to a cramped style of living, one from which the family had just emerged.

Zero thought that the project might be salvaged if after the plays were done in Stratford, they could be shown in London, where his pay could be increased, but that could not be arranged. Then, too, Mostel was dismayed by the intentions of Joan Littlewood, the director. She told him that she wanted the production to be "a statement for peace." "Okay," Zero said, "we're all for peace, but I asked where in the play does Shakespeare make such a statement? 'Oh, Zero,' she said. 'We'll just forget about Shakespeare.' *Forget about Shakespeare!* "

Still, Cole wished that Mostel would accept the role despite the low pay. "The satisfaction and prestige for Zero in playing Falstaff would [be] worth more—much more—than the money," she said. Later, after months of vacillation, he finally rejected the offer.*

Mostel's decision was especially upsetting to Toby Cole, who wrote to Adza Vincent, "I wished for him to do Falstaff and that is my great disappointment of '61. Let us hope we will get him back on the track before too long." This attitude characterized their relationship: whereas Toby Cole was principally interested in finding good roles and good plays for Mostel, Zero was always concerned (understandable, perhaps, for one who had had difficulty making ends meet for more than a decade) about the money. He often told his agent that he had never accepted less than $2,250 for a nightclub engagement and that his salary for working in the theatre should be commensurate.

That an agent should encourage an actor to take a low-paying job because it would bring him artistic satisfaction is so rare it can be called extraordinary, since agents receive a percentage of their clients' salaries. Many actor-agent relationships have foundered because the actor has wished to appear in plays that would challenge his abilities while the agent has insisted that money is the only standard by which success can be measured. The Cole-Mostel association must be one of the few cases in which the roles were, to a substantial degree, reversed.

Toby Cole hoped that Zero, "an actor who was in a position to call his own shots—play the roles he wished—could effect a great change in the course of the theatre in New York which in turn would awaken

---

*The Royal Shakespeare Company was so irritated with Zero's indecision—and with his eventual rejection of the offer—that it asked him to reimburse them for half the cost of his airfare (which he refused to do).

the theatre throughout the country." Her disappointment was evident in 1987, when she said, "What a dream that was! And what a miscalculation!"

A few years later, the Falstaff idea was revived, this time with Peter Hall slated to direct. Zero went to England to discuss the role with Hall, who was then married to Leslie Caron. Mostel found their house small and uncomfortable, but the most dismaying inconvenience, he said, was that there was "*no food*! For dinner maybe you'd get one chop like this [about the size of a nickel] and four peas." The conversation about Zero's participation in *Henry IV* ended abruptly when Hall, concerned that an English audience might not accept the idea of an American actor as Falstaff, asked, "Can you play Falstaff in the manner of an English gentleman?" Zero answered, with considerable logic, that he intended to bring other qualities to the role. "No, no," Hall answered (according to Zero), "I want you to play the English gentleman."

Zero continued, "I rose from the table and said, 'You want an English gentleman, *get an English fag*!' I then went upstairs, packed my bag and left. Fuck 'em."

The role of Falstaff continued to be attractive to Mostel, however. Periodically, he discussed the possibility of portraying the character "in a good Shakespearean company." But in 1963, when just that opportunity presented itself at Stratford, Connecticut, Zero turned it down, preferring to continue on Broadway in *A Funny Thing Happened on the Way to the Forum*, which paid a much higher salary.

Still, Zero never completely gave up the idea of acting the role. Late in his career, when he thought of doing a one-man show, he wanted to include some of Falstaff's monologues. But that show never took place, and—except for doing one of Falstaff's speeches during a television special—Mostel never played the role. Nor did he ever perform in any of Shakespeare's plays.*

---

*In 1960, before Zero's appearance in *Rhinoceros*, the Shakespeare company at Stratford, Connecticut, wanted him to play Sir Toby Belch in *Twelfth Night*. Mostel was enthusiastic, but the producers at Stratford began to have second thoughts. Three months earlier, Zero's leg had been mutilated in the bus accident and, although his doctors gave assurances that he would be ready, the producers decided not to take the chance. As it turned out, they were right. When rehearsals began in April, Zero was still in the hospital undergoing therapy.

*   *   *

Originally, Zero was not supposed to have been involved in *A Funny Thing Happened on the Way to the Forum*. The script, a lunatic low comedy about a Roman slave who wins his freedom by uniting his master with the girl he loves, was not written specifically for anyone, but, as coauthor Larry Gelbart said, "Phil Silvers, who was then enjoying great success playing Sergeant Bilko on television, was the one we wanted." Silvers turned the part down in 1960 or 1961, calling it "old shtick." In a sense, he was right: the musical was a modern adaptation of Plautus's Roman farces, written in the third century B.C. But Silvers failed to see how brilliantly Larry Gelbart, Burt Shevelove, and Stephen Sondheim had interwoven the many strands of the plot with clever dialogue, outrageous puns, uproarious sight gags, and a bouncy score.* As Sondheim, who wrote the music and lyrics, said about the writing of the book, "It took Larry and Burt eleven complete and distinct separate drafts [written over a five-year period], and everybody thinks that it was whipped up over a weekend because it plays so easily. The plotting is intricate, the dialogue is never anachronistic, and there are only two or three jokes—the rest is comic situation. It's almost like a senior thesis on two thousand years of comedy with an intricate, Swiss watch–like farce plot. The style of the dialogue is very elegant."

But Silvers was not the only one who underestimated *Forum*. The show drifted from one producer to another until Hal Prince stepped in. Jerome Robbins, the original director, pulled out before rehearsals began and George Abbott took over. Abbott recalled that everything was in disarray when he entered the picture. There were many different versions of the play, he said, and his first chore was to help pull them together. He also made massive cuts in an attempt to remove subplots and sub-subplots he thought were both extraneous and—to use his word—"sophomoric."

Hal Prince originally contacted Zero in 1961 to see if he would be interested in playing the leading role of Pseudolus, the conniving slave. But it was only an informal contact and nothing came of it. A year

---

*Silvers later realized his mistake. He appeared in the film version of *Forum* in a supporting role, then played the leading character in a number of stage productions.

passed while the script went through rewrites. When the time came to cast the production, Prince's first choice to play Pseudolus was Milton Berle, but Berle, after initially accepting, objected to Abbott's deletions and told Prince that he wanted the original material restored. When Berle also insisted upon final approval, not only of the script but of the costume designer, scene designer, and choreographer, Prince withdrew his offer, leaving the production without a leading player.

After Berle was out of the picture, but before his departure from the show was generally known, Toby Cole was having a telephone conversation about other matters with George Abbott's daughter Judith, who worked in Hal Prince's office. In passing, Cole said, "I see that Milton Berle is going to do your play. Whatever happened to the interest in Zero?" "Do you think he would still be interested?" Judith Abbott asked. Five minutes later, Hal Prince called Cole from Boston to inquire about Zero's availability, telling her that Milton Berle was no longer being considered and that he hoped Zero could be interested in the project.

Prince then recommended Zero to the playwrights, but they were skeptical. Except for *Beggar's Holiday*, sixteen years before, Zero had never done a musical—and his performance in that show did not inspire great confidence in his musical abilities. Besides, Zero was not a true vaudevillian, and *Forum*'s creators thought that only a vaudevillian could bring the proper qualities to the role. They suggested Red Buttons; Prince demurred. He felt that an actor, not a vaudevillian, should be hired, because only an actor would be able to create the believability necessary for the audience to accept the piece. The argument about whether or not to offer the role to Mostel "got nasty," Prince said, but he ultimately persuaded the playwrights to accept his choice, and sent a copy of the script to Mostel.*

Zero was no more enthusiastic about the script than Phil Silvers had been. "I read it and I didn't like it," he said. Even after hearing Stephen Sondheim play the score, he remained unmoved, and that, apparently,

---

*This is Hal Prince's version of the events. Larry Gelbart recalls it quite differently. "There was no reluctance about Zero whatsoever," he told me. "There was never any feeling that he hadn't earned his spurs as a musical comedy performer. He seemed very right for the role."

was that. But he had not reckoned with Kate's ambitions for him, which were by no means satisfied by his success in *Rhinoceros*. Kate reveled in Zero's fame and opposed him strongly whenever he seemed about to make a career choice that might, in her view, jeopardize it. *Rhinoceros* may have made Zero a star on Broadway, but his achievements were still not widely recognized elsewhere. Even on Broadway, he did not yet have the status of a performer whose reputation was so powerful that his mere presence could turn a show into a hit. The leading performer in a successful musical comedy stands to make a great deal of money—more money than an actor in most nonmusical plays can hope to earn—and Kate was naturally concerned with the size of her husband's paycheck. But her ambition for Zero and her love for musicals were bigger factors. She adored the script and the score of *Forum* unequivocally, and she left Zero in no doubt about her attitude. As the family ate dinner the night after Mostel heard Sondheim play through the score, she held up a carving knife and shouted, "If you don't take it, I'll stab you!"

As Kate said later, "Zero was an intellectual snob and I'm a lowbrow ex-dancer. . . . I loved *Forum*. . . . But Zero wouldn't commit himself. Instead, he sulked." The Mostels had dinner at Walter Bernstein's apartment, where the subject of the musical continually came up. "He didn't want to do it," Bernstein recalled. "He resented it, but he knew that he'd have to do it [because of Kate's insistence] and he was angry about it."

Kate exerted an unrelenting pressure. "If he does *Lear*, I'll leave him," she said. "There have been enough Lears in the world. What the world needs now is laughter, fun. Z's on this obscure kick. You know what he'd *really* like to do, deep down in his heart? He'd like to find a play in Urdu and do it, so that *nobody* would understand it, and he could play every night to an audience of one, applauding wildly."*

---

*At the height of Mostel's success he was so well known that the theatre at which he appeared featured a huge billboard containing only one word: "Zero." Several of Kate's friends told me that she relished looking at that billboard, and that when she did so her face glowed with satisfaction.

But Ring Lardner, Jr., felt that Zero's own inclination tended more toward the commercial than he liked to admit. "I think in the end he always made the decisions," Lardner said, "and to a certain extent he used Kate's preference for the commercial

Zero conferred with Toby Cole. She, too, disliked *Forum*; but she admitted to a dislike of all musicals, so her support of his position had no effect on Kate, who continued to pressure Zero to accept Hal Prince's offer. Acting on Mostel's instructions, Cole called the producer to negotiate terms. Then Zero went to George Abbott's office to sign the contract (complaining to Toby Cole as they rode in the taxi, "I don't want to do this play"). He squirmed, argued, fought—and finally capitulated. "All right," he told Kate, "but this is the last time I'm gonna do something for money for you! Next time I'm gonna do what *I* wanna do!"

Still, the crisis was not over. When Zero told Prince he would accept the role, the authors—according to Prince—again protested that he was an inappropriate choice. "They threatened to withdraw the play rather than accept Zero," he said. Only when George Abbott backed Prince, adding that he would leave the project unless Mostel was hired, did the authors reluctantly agree.

An outstanding group of farceurs was engaged to play in support of Mostel: David Burns, John Carradine, Ruth Kobart, and Zero's old friend Jack Gilford. Gilford had already auditioned twice and been turned down on both occasions. But Zero, certain that his friend would add a special touch of zaniness to the production, wanted Prince, Abbott, and the show's creators to see Gilford at his best. Consequently, he offered to read with him. Mostel and Gilford rehearsed together for several hours before the audition; a generous act—"relatively unheard of," Larry Gelbart said—for stars rarely treat actors auditioning for supporting roles with such courtesy. "Zero wanted Jack to have the part, and worked very hard to get it for him," Gelbart recalled. As a result of the audition, Gilford was given the important role of Hysterium.

Learning the songs for *Forum* was no easy task for Zero because he could not read music and because Sondheim's songs, which sound easy to sing, are, in fact, intricate and difficult. Kate taught them to him, the first of several occasions on which she would help Zero learn his

---

things as an excuse for himself, for the decisions he made." Frances Chaney added that he often "played the poor besieged man, pretending that his wife was forcing him to do what he did not want to do."

music: for a record album, for *Fiddler on the Roof*, for songs he performed on television.

Zero asked that he be given an air-conditioned dressing room during the run of *Forum*, but Hal Prince flatly refused, although the request would seem to be reasonable for a heavy actor with a crippled leg who had to wear a heavy woolen costume ("like a sauna with two pair of pants," Larry Gelbart said) during the intense New York summer heat.

Mostel may not have wanted to appear in *Forum* initially, but once he agreed to do it, he was totally committed, working with great discipline in the rehearsals. "He never displayed any sense of superiority to the material," Larry Gelbart said, "or that he was working 'down.' "

Zero respected the director, George Abbott, whom he had come to know when Abbott directed *Beggar's Holiday*, and they worked well together. Abbott, seventy-five years old when *Forum* was in rehearsal, was the most highly regarded director in musical comedy, a father figure who commanded respect without demanding it. Whenever Zero became temperamental in rehearsals (which was rare), Abbott would simply say, "Stop acting like a child," which proved to be all that was necessary. Still, the relationship was not without some friction. From the first rehearsal, Abbott said, Zero "would begin to act before I had finished explaining something."

Abbott stopped him. "Zero," he said, "you don't listen."

Zero had heard that before. "My wife has been telling me that for years," he answered.

In its first preview performances in New Haven, it was clear that *Forum* was in trouble. As George Abbott recalled, "The audience laughed at this show, but they didn't *like* it." Among many problems, the most significant was that Abbott's cuts, which had simplified the various plots, had also eviscerated the play—just as Milton Berle had maintained months before. As Larry Gelbart noted, "A lot of fun was in the organized confusion. So we put it all back—and probably a little more."

The restorations helped, but not enough. Two of the performers were replaced in an attempt to sharpen the production, but the problems continued. One rewrite followed another, in furious succession. Ruth Kobart, who played Domina, the character woman, recalled "line

The quintessential Tevye

At Café Society, 1942

Young Zero working

and reclining in his studio

In the army

Surrounded by his paintings during the blacklist years

With Kate, 1965

and during the filming of *Great Catherine*

With Bea Lillie, testing the authenticity of his Tony award for
Rhinoceros

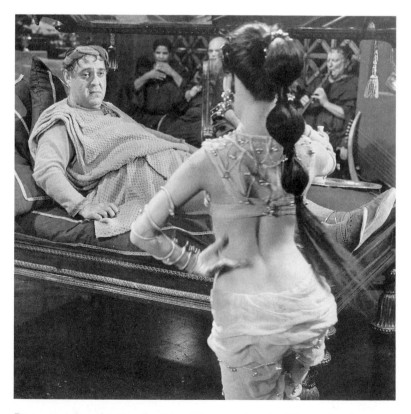

**In a scene from *A Funny Thing Happened on the Way to the Forum*.
Should Zero be looking so unhappy?**

Rehearsing for *The Merchant* with Sam Levene

and for *Fiddler on the Roof*

Zero, shortly before his death

changes by the pages every night." Her role was relatively set from the beginning, she said, but many of the other actors were remarkable in their ability to "get the script in the morning, rehearse it, swallow it in the process and spit it out at night. Then the next day there would be more changes and they'd do the same thing all over again." Pseudolus's role underwent more changes than any other. Kobart said her "greatest admiration was for Zero's ability to play the role perfectly, delightfully, imaginatively, ten different ways—and all of them superlative."

But when *Forum* moved on to Washington, D.C., audiences continued to dislike it. Abbott and the show's creators were stymied, unable to think what to do next. For a while it seemed likely that the play would have to close before it reached New York, as Richard Coe, the critic for the Washington *Post*, recommended in his review. One performance was given to a mere fifty people. But in a last attempt to save the production, two weeks before the scheduled Broadway opening, Hal Prince suggested that Jerome Robbins, who had originally been scheduled to direct, be brought in to evaluate the show and make whatever changes he thought necessary.

Prince's idea had merit, as subsequent events proved. Robbins was able to pinpoint the difficulties and remedy them, partly by choreographing an elaborate pantomime chase not unlike the Keystone Kops and partly by recommending that the opening number be changed. But the producer also knew that Robbins and Mostel were likely to be an explosive combination.

Jerome Robbins had been a "friendly witness" before the House Committee on Un-American Activities. One of those whom he had identified as a Communist was Jack Gilford's wife, Madeline. It was well known that Zero felt that Robbins's actions had been cowardly and detestable, that he had caused incalculable harm, and that he had betrayed his friends. As one individual noted, "Robbins was a choreographer. He could work with whatever ballet company he wished. His livelihood was not in the least threatened by the blacklist, but he played this very ugly role." Given the circumstances, how could Hal Prince persuade Mostel to accept Robbins's authority?

He took the most direct approach, telling Zero that *Forum* was in desperate trouble and that Robbins was the one person who might be able to save it. Prince was strongly backed by Sondheim, who had written the lyrics for *West Side Story*, an enormous success, which Robbins had conceived and directed.

Zero could not stand in the way of the only chance the production might have to survive; too many people's jobs were at stake. Mostel told Prince that he would not object to Robbins's participation, adding, "We of the left do not blacklist."

Zero Mostel was a man of many failings. He could be temperamental, vulgar, an exhibitionist, difficult to work with. But when the definitive history of the social milieu in the United States from 1947 until 1962 is written—the period of political witch-hunting—Mostel may be remembered for the nobility of that sentiment: "We of the left do not blacklist."

Mostel broke the news to Jack Gilford immediately after speaking to Prince. Gilford didn't think he would be able to work with Robbins and told his wife so in a telephone call to New York. But she persuaded him to stay with the show. "Why should you blacklist yourself?" she asked. "And why should all of us who fought against McCarthyism be further penalized?" Gilford remained in the production.

The relationship between Mostel and Robbins was never friendly, but—with one exception—it was businesslike and marked by an absence of hostility. "They functioned as artists," Larry Gelbart said, "and what they were doing had nothing to do with political ideology. The work on the show was what they were there to do." The single exception occurred during a rehearsal. As James Bronson, the stage manager, described it, "Tensions had been building and Jerry said something that blew the fuse. Zero stopped, walked down to the footlights, told Jerry how he felt about him and his politics. There was a long, embarrassing silence, and the rehearsal went on. As far as I know, the subject never came up again."

Robbins's insistence that the opening number be changed was based upon his observation that the first song, "Love Is in the Air," gave the audience the impression that they were about to see a romantic comedy; the rambunctious farce that followed was funny but disconcerting. A new number was needed immediately, he explained, one that would let the audience know what kind of show they were about to see.

Under normal circumstances, it would have been difficult for Sondheim to write a complex new song in two days. In this case, however, the composer did not have to begin from scratch. He had written a comic number called "Bless Our Play" before rehearsals began, but George Abbott rejected it, claiming that it was not "hummable." When Robbins asked Sondheim to replace "Love Is in the Air" with a new song, Sondheim played "Bless Our Play" for him. Robbins was delighted, saying that it was precisely the kind of song that was needed. He added, however, that Abbott (who still officially functioned as director) would be unlikely to accept a number he had already rejected. Consequently, Sondheim wrote "Comedy Tonight" (borrowing liberally from "Bless Our Play") during a weekend in Washington. The new song made it clear that the production would feature zaniness rather than romance. Robbins and Abbott both responded enthusiastically to the result and "Comedy Tonight" soon replaced "Love Is in the Air." Suddenly everything fell into place. As Sondheim said, " 'Comedy Tonight' played the first preview in New York and it not only brought down the house, but the entire show was clearly a hit . . . and it was all a matter of the opening number."

Even during the New York previews, changes continued to be made. Each day, Abbott rehearsed the actors at the Alvin Theatre (where the performances were given at night) while Robbins worked with the dancers and the participants in the pantomime at the Mark Hellinger. Gelbart and Shevelove continued to hand out revised pages of dialogue every morning.

At the opening night performance—on May 8, 1962—Zero was outstanding, playing within the boundaries of the script, focusing and disciplining his energies admirably. His comedy was broad where expansiveness was called for (as it was most of the time), subtle when subtlety was required. And the New York critics were ecstatic. Brooks Atkinson called Mostel, David Burns, and Jack Gilford "uproarious buffoons" who "have restored the era of good feeling by restoring low comedy to the stage."

"It is Mr. Mostel's evening," said John McClain. Walter Kerr, John Chapman, and Richard Watts, Jr., all expressed unreserved enthusiasm about the play and production. Of Zero's performance, Watts said that he "runs riot delightfully and delightedly as the conniving slave." Robert Coleman added, "Mostel . . . has a field day with the slapstick. He's on stage most of the time, dishing out the hoke with a relish that is irresistible, and prodding his vehicle along at dizzy pace. It's a terrific performance." And Richard Gilman, after praising the other actors for doing "superlatively well by their own uneven material," saved his highest praise for Mostel: ". . . as he does with everything he touches, [he] transfigures it."

Despite ecstatic reviews for Mostel and good ones for the show as a whole, *Forum* was not an immediate success at the box office. American theatre audiences do not often give their approval to slapstick comedies, perhaps because so many of them are tasteless. Not until after the production had run to moderate-sized houses for six weeks or so did the favorable word-of-mouth begin to make itself felt. From that point on, it was difficult to find an empty seat at the Alvin Theatre.

George Abbott had had only a few minor problems with Zero in rehearsal, but during performances Mostel began misbehaving to such a degree that the director could not contain his exasperation. The annoyance was still present when I spoke to him in 1987. "He was unfair to the other actors. He would not play honestly with them," Abbott said.

After the reviews of *Forum* made him an incontestable "star," Zero began to exhibit the temperament that often comes with stardom. He seemed to feel that he was more important than the play or the production, often departing from Abbott's direction to insert some piece of extraneous business. He tried to break up the other actors—often with success. Sometimes he altered the dialogue, tossing in phrases and sentences that were not in the script. He announced the result of the Sonny Liston–Floyd Patterson heavyweight championship fight from the stage, for example. On another occasion, he wished the audience a happy Halloween. When Jacqueline Kennedy attended a performance, he tossed in a joke about the White House; when he recognized John Randolph in the audience, he shifted all the action to stage right and spoke his dialogue directly to his friend. All of this infuriated Abbott and the members of the production team. Ruth Kobart, who had admired Mostel so deeply during the rehearsal process, was aghast: "I felt it was morally wrong for him to treat his talent that way. Other actors long to have the gifts he had—and then to abuse them as he did . . . After the first week in New York, after those fantastic reviews, the disintegration started. He would break the other actors' concentration, not give them what they expected, destroy the intent of the scene. I got so fed up that one night I made the only protest I felt I could make: I refused to take a curtain call." Several of the other actors, equally upset by Zero's behavior, congratulated Kobart, but when she tried to explain her feelings to Mostel, he was uninterested. He took his revenge upon her by forbidding her entrance to his large dressing room, which, as she said, "was the place to be. It was where all the smart talk was, and all the camaraderie. Generally it was open to everyone, but I couldn't get back in until I apologized."

Abbott returned to view performances periodically. On each occasion, he would speak to Zero afterward, trying to persuade him to stick to the script and to the rehearsed business. Mostel would generally accede to Abbott's wishes, at least for a performance or two. Occasionally, he would even seem genuinely repentant. Once, he said, Abbott had seen a new piece of business and "asked me to take it out. It got a huge laugh, but," he admitted, "maybe it didn't belong." In the long run, Abbott's attempts were in vain. Mostel might change his ways if he knew Abbott would be in the audience, but soon afterward he would revert to horseplay. Ironically, Hal Prince said, he had persuaded the show's creators to accept Zero in the role of Pseudolus because he wanted an actor; but "the actor . . . abdicated to the performer, pursuing laughs and ingenious bits of business, obliterating the story."

One musical number featured each courtesan in turn dancing for Pseudolus. Abbott wanted the audience's attention to be on the dancers, so he asked Mostel simply to observe the courtesans and not to do anything that might steal the focus. But Zero made certain that he would be the center of attention. He leered broadly at one dancer, looked shocked at the gyrations of another, moaned with lascivious pleasure at the dance of a third. The audience was delighted, but Abbott was livid. "He'd carry on with such business that the audience didn't look at the girls at all."

Because *Forum* is a comic romp, audiences did not object to Zero's mischievousness. Indeed, they relished it as much as he did. But the script is, in fact, as tightly structured as a play can be, and Mostel's additions wreaked havoc with the structure. The result might have been just as funny as *Forum*, but it wasn't the musical Gelbart, Shevelove, and Sondheim had written. No wonder they were irritated with their leading actor. "Irritated is a mild word," Gelbart told me. "It was very offensive. It was maddening."

Zero spoke to Craig Zadan, Sondheim's biographer, about his performance in *Forum*, attempting to justify the behavior that had alienated so many of his co-workers:

> There's a kind of silliness in the theatre about what one contributes to a show. The producer obviously contributes the money; the bookwriter, the book; the composer, the music; the lyricist, the lyrics; but the actor contributes nothing at all? . . . I'm not a modest fellow about those things. I contribute a great deal. And they always manage to hang you for having an interpretation. Why must it be dull as shit? I don't think theatre should be like that. Isn't that where your imagination should flower? But the producer, the director, the authors, all go on their vacations and they come back well tanned and I'm pale from playing the show, and they say, "It's altered a great deal since opening night." But I'm not the actor who can do it in a monotone all the time. Suppose you have a bellyache, can't you use it when you're on the stage? Don't you use what you have? Guys who call it shtick give me a pain in the ass. If you have the premise that a guy wants to be free, no matter what crazy things you do on the stage, as long as you feel that it's keeping with that premise, it should be accepted by the audience.

I suggested to the prominent comedian and student of comedy, Steve Allen, that Zero's tendency to improvise during the run of a play may have been a by-product of his possessing the comic's—as opposed to the actor's—temperament. Allen reflected that that might be the case. As a comedian himself, he said, "I do the same. I was in one Broadway comedy . . . called *The Pink Elephant* in the early fifties in New York. It was not that I *decided* I would be a little different every night. I never *decided* any such thing. There was even a conscious willingness *not* to be. I was willing to be cooperative. I'm not a temperamental performer. But every night funny lines would occur to me that never had before" and he would say them aloud. "I can understand Zero doing that, too."

Josh Mostel took exception to the idea that Zero's antics harmed the production of *A Funny Thing Happened on the Way to the Forum*—or to *Fiddler on the Roof*, as some observers would later allege. "I've seen many performances of both *A Funny Thing* and *Fiddler* in many different productions and Zero was brilliant every time," Josh remarked. "What made him a great actor was the fact that he was a master of his craft and a master of spontaneity. To see Zero work could be a very memorable and very powerful experience, and part of it was that he was relating in the moment. He did a performance on the Fourth of July in St. Louis where there were explosions from next door from fireworks and he put in some lines about the meal he had eaten and the gas he was having. Sure, that wasn't in the script, but there were explosions!" Josh maintained that had Zero ignored the explosions it would have given the audience the sense of watching a movie rather than a play. "And," he added, "to say that he got worse [as the run of a play progressed] I don't think is true. He just got different, and that's part of the nature of theatre. I just can't tell you the performances I've seen when he was absolutely brilliant. Whether he was sticking to the direction or to the playwright's words is just about irrelevant as far as I'm concerned. Brilliance is brilliance."

Even some directors would have applauded Zero's wish to incorporate unrehearsed business into his performances. Eugene Vakhtangov, the brilliant Soviet director, wrote in 1918 of his opposition to the theories of Gordon Craig and Vsevolod Meyerhold, who advocated actors without intellect or imagination. Craig, in England, and Meyerhold, in the Soviet Union, wished to turn their actors into robots who would unhesitatingly carry out the director's instructions. Vakhtangov, on the other hand, called for performers to employ "new devices" at every performance. "Every [performance]," he wrote, "is a new [performance] . . . I consider of the utmost importance the creation of conditions under which the actor . . . absolutely does not know how today a given line is going to sound at a given moment, not even approximately, that he be completely confident and at ease. . . .

"I do not want an actor to play a given spot equally strongly or equally humbly every time. I want that on any given day there be called up naturally, of themselves, those feelings and in those degrees of excitement in which on that day he feels true. . . . The worst thing of all is when an actor wants to repeat yesterday's success."

Vakhtangov's ideal actor would have performed the same play differently on every occasion, depending upon the stimuli of the moment.

In that way, Vakhtangov hoped, the actor would avoid giving lifeless and mechanical performances based upon repetition of the gestures and intonations he had employed the night before.

Thus, one could make the case that Zero's wish to leave himself open to flights of improvisational fancy during performances was a perfectly legitimate desire, justified by earlier theatrical theory and practice.

Nevertheless, many professionals in the New York theatre, uninterested in the historical nature of this controversy, were dismayed by Mostel's behavior, which became more pronounced as time went on. It is not unreasonable for a writer, who has labored for years over his dialogue, to want the actor to speak the lines as written; or for a director, who has meticulously rehearsed a production, to expect the actors to maintain its shape even when he is not in attendance. At times, the other actors who performed with Zero in *Forum* were terrified by his unpredictability, afraid that his departures from the script would leave them looking foolish before the audience. "He didn't have many friends in the cast," George Abbott said.

Zero even managed to alienate Jack Gilford by turning the generosity he had shown in helping Gilford win the role of Hysterium into a running joke spiced with more than a bit of malice. At every performance of *Forum*, during a big laugh, he whispered to Gilford, "Who got you into this show?" And he was abusive to Gilford in other ways. George Abbott recalled, "Gilford would have a piece of business and Mostel would pick it up and do it before he [Gilford] could." During one scene in which Pseudolus, having drunk a "passion potion," kissed and embraced the characters on stage, "Zero ran into me like a fire truck," Gilford said. "I had to brace myself against a board that was painted as a pillar. And even that bent when he'd crash into me." Larry Gelbart described another incident: "There's a moment in the funeral scene where Hysterium blows the veil that's covering his face up in the air, and they had a piece of business where Zero would put it back down in his [Gilford's] mouth. Well, eventually, Zero was putting his hand in his mouth—literally ripping the roof of his mouth raw." Gilford was enraged at Mostel's behavior and eventually stopped speaking to him offstage. For months, the two old friends did not exchange a word. But Zero—who couldn't bring himself to apologize—stopped abusing Gilford during the play. He went to the opposite extreme: not touching Gilford at all, even when the script called for it. When Mostel left the production in 1964, "we were not on very good terms," Gilford said.

Some—not many, but some—of his co-workers in *Forum* and, later, in *Fiddler on the Roof* were stimulated by what they referred to as Mostel's "spontaneity," his ability always to keep a performance fresh and vital, even if his methods were unorthodox. *Forum*'s stage manager, James Bronson, said, "He did embellish some of the situations, but I honestly think he added to the spirit of the performance." Audiences certainly didn't mind. With few exceptions, they loved Zero for the very reasons some theatrical professionals derided him.

Not only did the public respond warmly to his performance, the theatrical community gave it its highest accolade, when, in April 1963, Zero was given his second Tony award, for the best performance by an actor in a musical.* Mostel's acceptance speech followed Alan Arkin's and broke up the house. Arkin, who won for best dramatic actor, told the audience how supportive his producer in *Enter Laughing* had been. After one particularly bad rehearsal, the producer gave the cast three bottles of champagne. Zero began, "I had an experience quite unlike Alan Arkin's. One day when we had a bad rehearsal George Abbott brought in some tap water." Then he turned, saw an American flag at the end of the dais, saluted smartly, and exited to an ovation.

Zero also won *Cue* magazine's "Entertainer of the Year" award for 1962—another indication of the high regard in which his performance was held by most people. Critic Richard Gilman even suggested that the trappings of script and dramatic conventions were hindrances to the one truly momentous event: Zero's performance. In his review of *Forum*, he wrote:

> I could only have wished that Mostel had been allowed to have his head more often. [A] civil war . . . between him and the musical-comedy format . . . periodically cramped his style, so that you could almost see him fretting,

*Tony awards also went to *Forum* as the best musical of the year, to Burt Shevelove and Larry Gelbart for having written the book, to David Burns for his supporting performance, and to George Abbott for his direction.

as the rest of the cast also did, whenever those sterile injunctions had to be obeyed. There was one moment, though, when the full glorious possibilities of *A Funny Thing* were marvelously present. "Hide the girl on the roof," Zero tells someone, who replies, "Why?" "Why not?" Mostel answers, tiny hands trilling in the air, foot kicking backwards. . . . Why not throw away the plot, the logic, the surrenders to expectation, and really have a ball?

Larry Gelbart, after all the travails with Zero, still felt far more positive than negative about the experience of having worked with him. Gelbart told me in 1987, "He really was everything we wanted. I was very grateful to him for making the show work. He was a fabulous Pseudolus—he was wonderful. And I liked the way he worked: hard, diligently. I don't know if the years have put a rosier finish on everything, but I certainly liked him more than I didn't like him." Even George Abbott felt the same way. When I asked him if he regretted having cast Zero, he said, "Oh no, because he was wonderful. We were all happy that he was so good. I think he was much better than Milton Berle or Phil Silvers would have been."

Perhaps consideration should be given to Mostel's motivation when he deviated from *Forum*'s script. If his intention was to invigorate his performance so that the production as a whole would benefit, it could be seen as an admirable trait. If the intention was selfish, a wish to gain attention at the expense of everyone else, it can only be described as childish and worthy of censure. Zero claimed it was the former, his detractors claimed it was the latter, and there the matter rests. Or rather, "rested," for it was to become an even more heated issue during *Fiddler on the Roof*.

Regardless of how much Mostel embroidered the script, his performance in *Forum* never ceased being vital and compelling. In February 1963, nine months after the play opened, Joshua Logan, the veteran Broadway director, returned to see Zero for a second time. In the note he sent backstage he said, "You're even greater than I remembered. I'd rather see you dance or hear you sing or watch you react than any actor I know."

Pseudolus is a large and physically demanding role, one that would drain the energy of a performer in outstanding physical shape. The character is in perpetual motion, running, dancing, tripping, engaging in elaborate pantomimic business. For a 300-pound actor with a leg that barely functioned, the role was an overwhelming physical burden. For several months after the opening, Zero was unable to regain his full energy, even making what was—for him—the ultimate sacrifice: staying home each day rather than going to his studio to paint. The $4,000 per week he received (plus a bonus when the box-office receipts topped a specified level) may have softened the blow. On the other hand, it may have made him all the more resentful of Kate, who was getting what she wanted—stardom for her husband and a handsome weekly paycheck—while he was forced to abandon his chief interest, painting, in order to perform in a show for which he had no respect.*

Mostel continued to play Pseudolus until March 1964, nearly two years after he had opened. In the long run, everyone connected with *Forum* was rewarded. The creators got the hit they had worked so hard to bring about. The producer and backers reaped a sizable financial reward. Zero (who enjoyed playing Pseudolus, but whose opinion of the material never changed, in 1964 he called it "a bunch of junk") achieved immense popularity and recognition as a musical performer —without which he would not have been considered to play Tevye in *Fiddler on the Roof.* The stardom he achieved in *Forum* helped him win his case against Surface Transit Company by establishing how much money he might have made had he not been incapacitated. And Kate got a mink coat, her reward to herself for having persuaded Zero to play Pseudolus against his own instincts.

Offers were now coming in from everywhere. Until *Rhinoceros*, Zero had to seek out employment. After *Forum*, the producers of films, plays, and television shows courted him, pleading with him to appear in their productions.

---

*But Don Richardson, who came to see *Forum* at Zero's request when the musical was still on its pre–New York tour, tells a story that would seem to indicate that Zero quickly came to terms with the idea of performing only for material reward. Richardson was impressed with the production, and, as he went backstage, he told another actor, "You're going to have a very big hit." Then, he recalled, "I went into Zero's dressing room, locked the door, and told him to get the hell out of the show as soon as he could." He said, 'What are you talking about?' I said, 'This is going to type you as a ridiculous, fat, funny man, and you could be a very great actor if you really worked at it.' And he said, 'I've been poor long enough and I don't give a shit, I just want the money to paint.' And he stayed in the play."

*   *   *

Most comedians are instinctively funny. As they mature, they polish their gifts, of course, but few are interested in theories of comedy, why people laugh, what the uses of humor are. Zero, however, was vitally interested in such questions, and did considerable reading in his attempt to find the answers. He communicated his conclusions, based upon his reading, his observations, and his own experience, when he delivered the Theodore Spencer Memorial Lecture at Harvard University on May 20, 1962, less than two weeks after the opening of *A Funny Thing Happened on the Way to the Forum.*

When Zero was invited to give the lecture, he suggested a speech on the art of the Renaissance. But the topic had already been chosen, he was told; the speech would be billed as "Mostel on the Art of Comedy." The title must have been appealing. When the audience, composed primarily of students and faculty from Harvard, MIT, and Radcliffe, assembled at the Loeb Drama Center, they outnumbered the record crowd that had attended the previous year's memorial lecture, delivered by T. S. Eliot.

Zero not only discussed humor at Harvard, he *was* funny—although not necessarily at the same time. As he was being introduced to the audience, Mostel continually interrupted the speaker with ad libs, gurgles, snorts, and grotesque expressions. Within moments, the introducer as well as the audience was convulsed with laughter.

The speech itself, however, was an almost entirely serious affair, read directly from his notes without commentary, although he would deliberately mispronounce a word now and then to keep his audience amused. Zero began by acknowledging the impossibility of discussing comic theory without making even the most sidesplitting material seem unfunny. "There are few subjects, if any, which have produced for the past two thousand years quite as much rhetoric and pedantry as comedy," he said, "and this lecture will be no exception."

He passed quickly over the many theorists from Aristotle to Freud who have attempted to explain the meaning of comedy. The remainder of his speech focused upon his own ideas. He began by noting that "laughter is obviously in the very nature of man," but that comedy does not seem to travel well from one culture to another. All of the comic writers acknowledged by Americans to be masters of the form—Aristophanes, Plautus, and Terence, the actors of the *commedia dell'arte*, Molière, Goldoni, Shakespeare, Jonson, Cervantes, Rabelais, Swift, Dickens, Sholem Aleichem, Bernard Shaw, Mark Twain—came from Europe or North America, he observed. Comedy is also enjoyed in Asia, Africa, and South America, but the comic literature of those continents is all but unknown in North America. Therefore, he decided, comedy must be "a local thing, a home affair . . . [which flourishes only] in our own society or in a society such as we ourselves know. . . .

"Comedy is a commonwealth, a shared background of culture, of history, of a society, of experience. Therefore comedy is a unifying force. It brings people together. It is clearly social in its being. [But] if comedy is a unifying force, towards what end shall it unite us? If comedy is social, what purpose shall it serve in our society?"

Zero agreed with the belief expressed by George Meredith, the nineteenth-century British theorist, that comedy can only exist in "a society of cultivated men and women . . . wherein ideas are current . . . where there is . . . a climate of free intellectual activity." Under those conditions, Meredith maintained, "comedy shall bloom forth in a society, and people shall enjoy that commonwealth of laughter which serves to unify them."

The ultimate function of comedy, Mostel argued, was to serve as a tool for the perfectibility of mankind. He held that society is largely based upon the concept of piety, a concept he defined as "dutiful respect." But not all piety is constructive. "It is one thing for a child to render dutiful respect to parents who follow the principles of decency and fair play and honesty," he said, but "it's quite another thing for a child to give dutiful respect to parents who are willfully stupid, drunkards, deadbeats, and dolts. There must be two kinds of piety, one which deserves our dutiful respect and another which does not. On the one hand, this dutiful respect for parents or others, this is a matrix of an orderly society. On the other hand, blind and uncritical acceptance of filial piety can ossify the very tissue of society. . . .

"With George Meredith," Zero asserted, "I believe that comedy is a rebellion against that kind of piety which we may call *False* Piety. Comedy is a rebellion against hypocrisy, against pretense, against falsehood and humbug and bunk and fraud; against false promises and base deceivers; against all evils masquerading as true and good and worthy of respect. It is, therefore, the role of comedy to put to the test whatever offers itself as piety." Mostel used the era of Prohibition in America as an example. "Tens of millions refused to render dutiful respect to the Eighteenth Amendment to the Constitution of the United States. That rebellion found its full expression in the wit and comedy of the period. Comedy laughed [Prohibition] out of existence. Comedy put the pious experiment of Prohibition to the test and declared it a false piety and it was swept away. . . ."

A society without comedy is a society without freedom, Mostel observed. "In scientific formula, the freedom of any society varies proportionately with the volume of its laughter. That is called Mostel's Law."

Germany and Italy in the 1930s and 1940s offered examples of societies in which the true spirit of comedy could not exist. *The Threepenny Opera*, Brecht and Weill's comic attack on German society, opened in Berlin in 1928, but was banned in 1933 when Hitler was elected chancellor. "It was not again performed in Germany until just after Hitler was finished. Of what was this Hitler gang so afraid? Well, it was nothing more or less than laughter. Hitler's control of the German people was built on fear," and to sustain that fear, it was necessary to eliminate any possibility of laughter. "So Hitler closed *The Threepenny Opera*," Zero added. "He closed all the theatres where that kind of laughter might oppose his policy of creating fear. And he burned the books and then he burned the people."

Similarly, Charlie Chaplin's satire on Hitler and Mussolini, *The Great Dictator*, was not seen in Germany and Italy until after the war. Had Germans and Italians had the opportunity to see the film when it was made (in 1940), it might have had a beneficial social effect, Zero implied.

> What is needed is an atmosphere in which comedy can serve its purpose—spill the sawdust of the phony Caesar before he gets well mounted—an atmosphere in which comedy can help create a society devoted to truth and fairness. If such a society existed in Germany, could Hitler have reached power?
>
> Here we find the mission of comedy to correct those dangerous mistakes. . . . It is the task of comedy to label fools as fools, to make sure they do not get by as supermen. . . . It is the intention of comedy to promote

[the quality of goodness] in its audience. People who can laugh at provocation, who can laugh at irritation, who can be free of vanity and haughtiness and smoldering hatred; these people are blessed with the mildness of temper which is the climate of the perfect earth which we wish to inherit and abide in. The enemies of comedy are those who would keep us from that blessed state.

Who can be an enemy of comedy?.... It is these champions, these protectors of the false piety who hate the good feeling created by comedy. "Cut the comedy. Be serious," they tell us. The "tough minded," they call themselves, and then all flash their switchblades and whip their truncheons. They are found more and more in all regions of society, and especially in the hardening arteries of the outer extremities of ultra-conservative society.

... What shape, then, does their [ultra-conservatism] take? It takes the shape of an idiotic stiffening of the fear complex, a right-about-face, to-the-rear march of the human spirit. They are rebels against progress, any kind of progress, even against gently undulating, slow-motion progress. They are rebels against intellect; against the professors; against thinking; against experimenting; against trying; against newness; against strange shapes and forms; against sounds they've never heard before: Leon Kirchner's music. Against laughter. They do not understand. They prefer to hate than to love. They are sad rebels. They do not laugh away their fears. They do not restore their impoverished egos with steady supplies of gallant good humor which the rich comedy of the outcast, the bedraggled, and the put-upon gives us. This innate lack of good feeling says, "Cut the comedy. Be serious."

The alternative to comedy can be persecution or repression. When people cannot laugh off their difficulties or restore a sense of proportion, then affairs can swiftly deteriorate into tragedy.

So that his audience would not mistake Mostel's intention and believe that he wished to confine his censure to dictatorial societies such as those in Germany and Italy before 1945, he then applied his theory specifically to America.

The motto of the Pilgrims who landed at Plymouth Rock was "Cut the comedy. Be serious." Laughing on the Sabbath drew dips with the ducking stool. For general horseplay: all day in the public bath. For telling ghost stories, for laughing to yourself, for doing anything peculiar: a short, fast witch trial and a quick burning at the stake. ... They might call it piety, but I would call it sadism. Like all practical jokes, being burned at the stake is not too humorous. We all deplore the fool who enjoys giving us the hotfoot. How much more we should deplore the moral hotfoot called Puritan morality.

Comedy has come to America by the back door and has never been at home yet. To stage Shakespeare's *As You Like It* in Puritan New England, the players had to bill it as a "moral entertainment." . . . Puritanical America needed a good moral excuse to enjoy itself. In order to enjoy a good Falstaffian feast once a year, there had to be the moral and religious excuse of Thanksgiving. . . . This paradoxical Puritan behavior of putting on the hairshirt in order to enjoy oneself spread among the new immigrants. . . . We feel the necessity of enjoying ourselves and so we must attempt to do so while we wear this hairshirt. If we go to the opera, it is not for enjoyment, but to be improved. If we visit European cities, it is to be cultured, not to enjoy ourselves. . . . Everything else we do is because it is tax deductible.

Zero contended that America distrusted its humorists and ultimately co-opted them. "Dangerous humorists," such as Mark Twain, Eugene Field, James Whitcomb Riley, George Ade, and Ring Lardner, he said, "were saddled, bridled, and led into the stable of conformity."

Even in 1962, Mostel claimed, the American public was under the influence of Puritan attitudes, unwilling or unable to respond to true comedy—comedy that challenges false piety. "Who measures how much comedy is permitted [in America]? On television, this job is performed by the commercial sponsorship of comedy. Lest you be afraid to laugh, you are reassured at ten-minute intervals that these jokes are sponsored by U.S. Steel or Alka-Seltzer. Any one of us feels more comfortable about enjoying a joke when we know that we are chuckling along with a big outfit like General Electric or Alka-Seltzer. A comedian can go wrong, very wrong, in this country if his joke is not sponsored by some powerful instrumentality of the Hairshirt Society." But the result of reducing the comic impulse to what is acceptable to corporate America was the blandness of commercial television with its "safe topics": mothers-in-law, jokes about the Jewish garment center, "the sexless sex parody—all pretty plain stuff with very little appeal to the mind."

With few exceptions, Zero held, American humor was formulaic, unadventurous, dull. He pleaded for an environment that would encourage the reverse: "that thoughtful comedy of which George Meredith gives us permission. . . .

"Now what can we do [to bring about a golden age of American comedy]?" Zero asked his audience. His answer: "Fan the tiniest flickering flame of comedy with the good air of your laughter. Throw your hairshirt into the flame. Give your endorsement to that thoughtful comedy which follows your own line of rebellion. And for those of you who want to do more," he said, in conclusion, "put a hundred dollar bill in an envelope and mail it to Zero Mostel, c/o the Alvin Theatre, New York."

At the end of his hour-long speech, the applause, according to Gilbert Millstein, who was present, "was tumultuous." Zero was proud of his speech and its favorable reception. Although the talk broke no new ground—the ideas belonged to George Meredith—it expressed Zero's convictions admirably.

As Mostel flew back to New York with Millstein, basking in the afterglow of his success, he expanded on the subjects he had touched upon during the lecture. He began by speaking of the popular comedians of the 1960s, which led him into a more general discussion of his attitude toward art and artists. Millstein later reproduced Zero's remarks in an article he wrote for the New York *Times*:

> They're pretty sharp commentators, but I don't think they take a real stand. I don't think it has to be a stand that conforms to my opinions, but a stand. When Balzac committed himself to paper, he concerned himself with a genuine hunk of life. I don't think these boys do. Like most artisans, they fall short in their mentality.
>
> The interesting thing about an artist, whatever he does, is his mentality. We know Meissonier could paint Napoleon's whole damned army, but he didn't give you his feelings or the participants' about war. Whereas, if you look at Picasso's "Guernica," you are moved; you know the horrors of war; you feel it and you see it. What do you appreciate about Joyce and *Ulysses*? His mentality completely purges the mind. He strips Bloom down to his body, his soul, his sex, his feelings, his hurts, his aspirations; he makes a complete man of him.
>
> In the arts it is the things that strip themselves that are marvelous. . . . The most marvelous thing in the world is the taking of an identifiable attitude and tearing it out of you.

Mostel rarely saw that accomplished in the theatre, so he seldom attended. He was equally disinterested in film. "I hate movies," he said on another occasion. "The films I love I can count on two hands."

When he was asked why there were so few plays and movies that were worthwhile, he responded, "Fear, stupidity and a lack of talent." His refusal to attend the theatre and the movies was irritating to Kate, who loved nothing better. But he was adamant. So Zero haunted the museums and the art galleries while Kate went to plays with her friends.

Mostel regarded many of his own performances as insignificant because the plays in which he appeared did not express a strongly held point of view; in many cases, they did not even attempt to do so. "Acting is [only] important when you are in a play that makes people feel or enlightens people or elates people or cerebrates people or celebrates people," he said. Asked what an actor is to do if he is involved in a play that does not possess those qualities, Zero responded, "The actor has a . . . responsibility. Once you have agreed to do it, you have to do it, you do all you can to make it a true thing. And once you are in, you accept the fact that you are in for a long time, and each time you do it with everything you have."

Mostel's Harvard speech was so successful that WNDT, the educational television station in New York, intended to telecast a condensed version of it on September 16, 1962. Zero, who volunteered his services without pay, was to deliver the lecture before an invited audience. As it turned out, however, the abbreviated speech was not given because of a dispute between the Board of Education and the American Federation of Television and Radio Artists, which voted to strike against WNDT unless the station agreed to give the union—rather than the Board of Education—jurisdiction over the teachers who appeared on educational programs. When Zero, in accordance with union regulations, informed AFTRA that he planned to deliver his lecture on WNDT, the union told him that he was prohibited from appearing on the station.

Thus, television viewers never had the opportunity to hear Mostel's ideas about comedy, an unfortunate outcome; for the importance of comedy, in the view of all who have examined the subject, is enormous—and those who have examined it are among the most profound thinkers of the past two thousand years. Theorists have disagreed about whether comedy functions primarily on a social, psychological, or philosophical plane, but they all agree on its significance. The irony, of course, is that the casual observer believes comedy to be merely frivolous, a subject of no importance, whereas the most learned and serious thinkers regard it as a matter of immense importance in shaping human experience and values.

The comedian, as Zero implied in his speech, is often propagandistic, a crusader for a state of perfection. Seen in this light, Mostel's creation of Senator Polltax T. Pellagra—an incredibly ignorant politician who flaunts his stupidity proudly—was clearly based upon classic models; his routine was intended to expose "false piety" by means of ridicule, thus contributing to the betterment of society. Zero once put it this way: "The whole purpose of comedy is to expose the bad air, to knock off the fakes. A guy who mugs or scuffs his shoes makes 'em laugh as a reflex, but the real comedian clears out pomposities . . . and stuffiness by making people laugh at them."

Aristotle, the first significant comic theorist, would presumably have approved of Mostel's creating Senator Pellagra, for Aristotle maintained that comedy always deals with unworthy individuals, persons who are corrupt or cowardly, stupid or hypocritical, irrational or boastful. Comedy's function, Aristotle believed, was to expose these individuals to the community, thus advancing a more ideal society.

Henri Bergson, an important commentator on the subject, contended that comedy "depends upon the recognition of something mechanical encrusted on the living." When we perceive a human being behaving in a nonhuman fashion, our impulse is to laugh. Those who have seen the sequence in Chaplin's *Modern Times* when the tramp, while working on the assembly line, loses his humanity and becomes a cog in a vast machine, will know what Bergson meant. The routine in which Zero imitated a percolator was also representative of the idea. One might also include his transition from man to rhinoceros, which served in Ionesco's play to express the antithesis of human behavior.

Zero's own comic style did not demonstrate a slavish adherence to any particular theory, although the ideas of Aristotle and Bergson, among others, help to explain the principles underlying some of his work. But it is probably accurate to say that no comedian's style conforms to any specific theory, for comedians are not philosophers, but individuals who possess the knack of being funny.

*   *   *

There is a particular aspect of American comedy that must be taken into consideration when discussing Mostel's work. As Steve Allen observed, "About 80 percent of American comedians are Jewish." This was not coincidental, he felt. "To me the Jews are funnier, as a people, than any other group. Why? Because they have had more trouble. And trouble is often the heart of humor. . . . Traditional Jewish humor often converts a joke into a form of social comment or criticism. It must not be supposed, however, that the humor of the Jews is only a weapon with which they subtly strike back at a bullying world. A great deal of their laughter is directed at themselves. Self-criticism is one of the earmarks of Jewish comedy."

Stand-up comedy is rooted in the Jewish tradition; at least as early as the eighteenth century, the wedding jester, the *badkhon*, whose descendants can even today be found performing at Hasidic weddings, was a traditional part of every Orthodox wedding ceremony. The *badkhon* delivered a monologue in rhyme for the benefit of the wedding guests, jesting about marriage, religion, politics, any subject that came to mind. A number of twentieth-century Jewish comics, including Zero Mostel, clearly derived from the tradition of the *badkhon*. As Sarah Blecher Cohen described it, "It is a personal style, as if addressing wedding guests rather than an anonymous audience; in some cases it is even aggressively personal, insistently naked, and this is part of what people mean when they refer to a 'show biz' manner. Such comedians also retain the *badkhon*'s assumption that the universe is their material and that they should make their audiences not only laugh but think about their human condition."

A remarkable number of comedians and other entertainers came from Mostel's stomping grounds, the Lower East Side of Manhattan. Irving Howe wrote:

> The proliferation of entertainers—comics, singers, dancers—in the immigrant and other Jewish neighborhoods is a remarkable fact. There are the famous or once-famous names: Al Jolson, George Jessel, Eddie Cantor, Sophie Tucker, Ben Blue, Jack Benny, George Burns, . . . many others. And there are the hundreds who played the small towns, the ratty theatres, the Orpheum circuit, the Catskills, the smelly houses in Brooklyn and the Bronx.

. . . Forming each day a great fair of Jewish life, [the streets] became the training ground for Jewish actors, comics, and singers. You mimicked the hoity-toity Irish teacher who recited Browning in high school, you mocked the snarling rabbi who bored you in Hebrew school, and it made your friends hop with glee. . . . If your father was a cantor—Al Jolson's was; so were George Gershwin's, the songwriter Harold Arlen's, and Eddie Cantor's (part time)—you could imitate and parody his chanting.

Howe's description of the quality shared by Jewish entertainers could have been written specifically about Zero Mostel. "The distinctiveness of these entertainers, if it can be isolated at all," he wrote, "came through most vividly in the rhythm and tone of their work, the pulsation of their nerves, the unfolding of what we call 'personality.' . . . More important still was the almost hysterical frenzy with which many of them worked, their need to perform under the highest possible pressure, as if still heeding the Jewish folk view that for a Jew to succeed he must do things twice as well, or as hard, as a gentile."

Many of the Jewish comics, including Zero, used Yiddish words and phrases in their routines. This was particularly true when they performed in the Borsht Belt, those resorts in the Catskill Mountains that catered primarily to Jewish visitors. "Unashamed of being Jewish, [the performers] seasoned their acts to amuse, not malign, their people," said Cohen. "Many of these entertainers used Yiddish to establish an immediate intimacy with their Jewish audiences."

Some Jewish comics attempted to subdue their "Jewishness" when performing before Gentile audiences. They changed their names (Benny Kubelsky became Jack Benny, David Daniel Kominski became Danny Kaye, and so on) and were thought of not as Jewish comedians but as popular American entertainers. Zero, however, was one who asserted his ethnicity with a vengeance. As Irving Howe observed, "The Jewish entertainers moved, through the passage of generations, toward a rasping aggressiveness, an arrogant declaration of a despised Jewishness. Does the world regard us as vulgar? Very well, we will give you a bellyful of vulgarity."

Jewish humor was also influenced by Jewish politics. A truism of American politics is that Jews tend to be progressive in their social attitudes. Comedians, too, whether Jewish or Gentile, are usually of a liberal bent, since comedy's function (at least in the view of most informed observers) is to ridicule the status quo and to question established values in order to bring about a more perfect world. Thus, a relationship exists between Jews as political progressives and Jews as comedians.

Perhaps this link helps to explain why so many of the witnesses called to appear before the House Committee on Un-American Activities were Jewish. Indeed, HUAC was more than once accused of anti-Semitism because a preponderance of those subpoenaed to appear before it were Jews. Very likely more than a hint of anti-Semitism did exist among the committee members, but there is a kind of logic in their mistrust of Jews, for (1) comedy is in itself "subversive" to established values, and (2) Jews thoroughly dominate the field of comedy. (Perhaps, too, one can see why so many comedians—Zero Mostel, Jack Gilford, Lionel Stander, among others—were "unfriendly" witnesses, when one ponders this sentence in philosopher James Feibleman's treatise on comedy: "The comedian simply refuses to accept compromises and insists upon reminding each and every one of a duty to truth and value.")

Are most comedians aware of their function as reformers, as visionaries who point out the shortcomings of the social systems in which they operate? For the most part, probably not. But this does not diminish their importance. Zero Mostel *was* aware of his place in the history of comedy, as his Harvard speech made clear. Steve Allen believes that Zero was unusual in that respect, and that most comics have neither knowledge of nor interest in comic theory. He suggests that Mostel's understanding of comic tradition and theory did not necessarily make him a better comedian (although he acknowledged that, in his own case, "the more I acquire any technical knowledge the better I understand what I am doing"), "but it perhaps . . . set him more comfortably into his professional environment and gave him the confidence to know that he was doing the right thing because that's what the philosophers said should be done in that sort of context."

Allen observed that Zero's individuality also set him apart from other comics. "He was unique," Allen said, "and sometimes that could work to his disadvantage. It might seem strange that talent sometimes can be a problem, but there is a great deal of evidence, particularly in television, supporting the view that a certain easy-to-take blandness can carry you far in TV. It has done that in many cases. Zero's work was highly eccentric as compared to, say, a Bob Newhart or a Bill Murray or somebody of that sort. One does run into people like Newhart or Murray on the street, in reality. You practically *never* run into anybody like Zero Mostel. He was sort of a race unto himself, so to speak, distinguished sharply even from other Jewish comedians."

Zero possessed a number of attributes that made his comic style unique. His level of intensity on stage struck Neil Simon as the distinguishing element in his work. "Zero didn't embrace an audience," Simon observed. "He gave you a bear hug, squeezed unmercifully, then licked your face as he put you back down in your seat. Subtle gestures and nuances were useless props to him."

Brooks Atkinson suggested that what set Zero apart from most other comedians in the 1960s was that the essence of his comedy was visual rather than verbal. "Cleverness at the microphone [on the radio and in nightclubs] has been accepted as comedy for so long that we have forgotten a first principle," Atkinson said: "The true comedian moves." In other words, the "true comedian" employs pantomime and physicality as well as clever language. Atkinson believed that Mostel, Bert Lahr, Phil Silvers, and Red Skelton were among the last of the genuine comedians.

Gilbert Millstein distinguished between a "clown" (a comedian whose involvement is physical as well as linguistic) and a mere comic: "A comic may snap his fingers, bang his thigh with a rolled-up newspaper, clutch a telephone, sit on a stool and be markedly hilarious . . . but he is not a clown and usually not much of an actor.

"In the opinion of a good many people, Mostel is, with the possible exception of Bert Lahr . . . the finest clown in the business today, to say nothing of a great actor."

Mostel's ability to move his enormous bulk with grace and dexterity was perhaps the most obvious element in his visual comedy, remarked upon by all who saw him. But Zero's facial agility was as important as his physical prowess. He could, as Millstein described, "command his eyes, which are brown and glitter alarmingly, to move singly, in opposite directions (one up, one down, if he chooses) and with extreme speed. It is difficult to say what his face is like in repose, since it rarely is." The journalist Robert Musel recalled an occasion at a restaurant when Zero imitated a Picasso painting, "shifting his glasses so his left eye glared out of the right lens and the mobile mouth somehow twisted around to the other side of his face." As Musel said, to quote a funny line or a joke of Zero's does not satisfactorily communicate his humor. "The pay-off is often only a look, but such a look: an orchestra of emotions playing above the quivering chins. He is the most visual comic in the business."

Newsweek's theatre critic Jack Kroll thought the secret of Zero's comic success was that he "plays not so much characters as life itself. That overripe body, that seventeen-haired head with its eight-ball eyes and nostrils like the muzzle of a double-barreled shotgun, those cat-burglar feet and hands as graceful as a Balinese dancer—all this adds up to a consummate instrument, a Stradivarius of flesh which creates humors and incarnations like the classic actors of antiquity, like Shakespeare's Burbage, like Emil Jannings. It's not that Zero is funny—it's that he is ecstatic, intense, zealous—he makes us laugh because that is the quickest logical discharge for the stimulus he provides—the way a great kiss or a luminous thought can make us laugh."

After Zero's death, Kroll wrote, "He was a splendid example of one of his own favorite phrases—'the life force'—but he was an extraordinarily intelligent man and he had the actor's greatest gift, a genius for incarnation. Technically, he belonged to the great clowns . . . but, like Chaplin, his clownhood was only a disguise that enabled him to sneak into the realms of high art. He could do anything—sing, dance, shout, simper and soar. He was the most important kind of actor—a great popular performer who could be as profound as anyone—the kind that Shakespeare would have cherished. . . . Zero Mostel was, for me, the finest, most original inventive actor of the American stage."

Some critics and spectators admired Mostel's virtuosity but withheld total approval because they felt that he turned every role into a version of himself; he "brought the role to himself rather than bringing himself to the role," in the jargon of actors. Walter Kerr called Zero "one of the four or five funniest men of our time," but lamented that he was not "a completely honest performer."

Boston critic Elliot Norton felt that Zero's refusal to submerge his personality in the character he was playing was one of his greatest strengths as a comic performer. When he saw Mostel in *A Funny Thing Happened on the Way to the Forum*, Norton wrote, "He mugs, minces, pops and crosses his eyes, shouts, whoops, giggles and gurgles. Nothing is beyond him. Yet he is artful in his performance, even artistic. From first to last . . . he lets his hearers know that if Pseudolus is a nut, Zero is not.

"He plays the part as a game. He is not a buffoon, an idiot, an imbecile. He enacts buffoonery and idiocy. He knows what he does, exhibits his Pseudolus as a prank, and as he incites laughter, laughs along with the playgoer.

"There is a subtle and important difference between the acting artist like Zero Mostel, who plays at being a half-wit, and the half-wit who exhibits himself in the expectation of laughter. Only children laugh at helpless fools. The adult theatregoer looks for wit behind the seeming witlessness of the great buffoons and, finding it, is reassured."

Although Kerr and Norton suggested that Mostel's stage performances were more akin to clowning—using the word in its most complimentary sense—than to acting, others disagreed. Burgess Meredith and Charles Laughton both expressed the belief that Mostel was capable of becoming the finest classical actor in America—in tragic as well as comic roles. Meredith was unstinting in his praise: "He's the greatest interpretive artist in the theatre," he said in 1964, "the greatest in any performing medium . . . he's a genius."

When *Newsweek* profiled Zero in 1964, the magazine described him as a once-in-a-lifetime performer: "It is Mostel's totality, his scanting of no realm for the sake of another, his keeping in balance spirit, body, imagination, and mind, that lifts him above his fellow actors . . . he is restoring to the theatre its great and ancient power to sustain man's life."

Critic Clive Barnes was among the most avid enthusiasts of Zero's acting. But Barnes did not mean the kind of acting in which the actor merges his personality with that of the character he is playing. "Mr. Mostel never plays anything other than Mr. Mostel," he admitted. "This should be ghastly, but simply because Mr. Mostel happens to be so interesting, it works like a grand slam."

One attribute of a great actor is that, beyond communicating the work of the playwright to the audience, he adds to it, so that the finished product—his performance—transcends the intentions of the dramatist. When Zero performed in *Ulysses in Nighttown*, critic A. Alvarez sug-

gested that he had brought qualities to the role of Bloom with which
James Joyce had tried but failed to invest the character. "Mr. Mostel
has in abundance all the qualities—the warmth, pity, fallibility and
sadness—that make Bloom the Jewish Don Quixote of the twentieth
century. He is also immensely funny. Joyce always claimed that Bloom
was, above all, a comic creation, but in the book his comedy is often
weighed down by the author's obsessive encyclopedism. Mr. Mostel
leaves no doubts at all. He can imply as much in one expressive flick
of his hands and rolling of his eyes as Joyce crammed into pages of
tense prose."

Zero's comic brilliance came to him with remarkable ease. As Kate
said of him, "He could do anything you wanted him to do on the stage.
You'd say 'Laugh' and he'd laugh, 'Cry' and he'd sob. Ask him to do
a somersault, anything. He was completely uninhibited as far as acting
was concerned."

Perhaps, as playwright Joseph Stein told me, "Acting came *too* easily
to him. He didn't think of it as a very difficult art, and it wasn't to him.
And that was one of his problems, I think. It was child's play. As far
as I know, he never had an acting lesson. He wouldn't dream of it.
Acting came so naturally, so easily, to him." Indeed, Zero believed that
actors "are born, not made," so lessons, he contended, would have been
of no use to him.

But Zero *did* study acting with Don Richardson in the 1940s. For
some reason, however, he never acknowledged Richardson as his
teacher, preferring to be thought of as a purely instinctive performer.
Kate, too, went along with this charade, although it was she who had
brought Richardson and Zero together. "No one ever taught him. He
was just an actor. Without any acting lessons," she said in 1978.

Whatever the Mostels' motivation in denying Zero's study of acting,
they thoroughly persuaded the public and Mostel's friends that he was,
as they claimed, an untutored "natural."

Perhaps Zero wanted people to believe that he had never studied so
that he could justify his uninhibited, improvisational style. Certainly
his performances radiated self-confidence. Beatrice Arthur, who performed with Mostel in *Ulysses in Nighttown* and in *Fiddler on the Roof*,
said that Zero was remarkable because "he's not frightened or in awe
of anything: of his material, of his fellow actors, his producers, his

directors. . . . His great strength is [that he does not] question himself on stage . . . his talent, his taste, his choice. That's the secret of his genius."

Zero's approach to a role was instinctive, he said. "I feel it's right if my own inner censor knows what I am doing. Sometimes your intuition tells you certain things: to speak faster, or to speak more slowly, or to be less or more graceful. I think it's a matter of innate taste and intuition. . . . If I know the life of the character I am doing, I can use my inventiveness to eliminate or supplement an element of the character, and so create a spontaneity every night, every performance."

Mostel felt that truth was not in the details but in the larger view. He disliked actors who "tend to take the mundane, trivial things about" a character "and play those things solely," for "in that way they never expose the truth of the character." He said that one does not need to know anything in order to be an actor, but a *good* actor has to know "everything," because the words the actor (in this case, Zero) is given to speak "are somebody else's words, not mine. They do not form me. They do not help expose me to myself. I do that at other times with other things and then bring myself to the words I speak on stage."

"The best guide to acting is Bernard Shaw's phrase 'the life force,' " Zero said. "When all elements of art enter into it—the distortion, the reality, the naiveté—you have the life force."

His method during rehearsals, he said, was to "try everything. I go wild, or I try it with complete restraint. I supplement, eliminate, I shout, then whisper the part, then relate it to everyone else in the play. I listen to what the other characters say. I re-shape what I say to them. There comes a time when the inner censor says: You are speaking the truth; now you know the essence of the character."

On another occasion, he summarized his method of preparing for a role this way: "I eat it, I sleep with it, I misuse it, I dream it . . ." And, of course, he painted it as well.

Mostel was often compared to Charlie Chaplin, especially after *A Funny Thing Happened on the Way to the Forum*. Howard Taubman said Zero's "delicacy of touch is so charming and vulnerable that it calls to mind the little tramp." Richard Gilman, in his review of *Forum*, spoke of a gesture "whose only rivals are some of Chaplin's." *Newsweek*'s profile called him "the clear successor" to Chaplin, "a performer in whom the comic is indissolubly wedded to the serious and, beyond that, to the tragic."

Zero undoubtedly savored such comparisons, for he idolized Chaplin as he did few others. He revered W. C. Fields and the French actor Raimu, about whom he said, "In his every performance, you always felt that whatever character he created he seemed to have lifted it out of the abyss of humanity and made it a symbol of meaning for all men. And through the distortion that he brought to his portrayals, you felt he gave them the proper proportions and as a result they possessed a great truth." He also admired the American actress Laurette Taylor, whom he saw in *The Glass Menagerie* eleven times during its Broadway run. In general, however, Mostel's opinion of actors was not high. His son Josh said that he "held actors in a kind of contempt," saving his admiration for painters and sculptors. Zero's friend Aube Tzerko added, "He had a peculiar kind of disdain for most actors. He didn't think they were worthy of their reputation." Undoubtedly, his contempt was based largely upon egocentricity, for Zero never for a moment questioned his own superiority to most performers.

For Chaplin, however—whom he met and knew slightly—he had unalloyed admiration. "In everything he has done in the films you are always aware of his tremendous imagination, his artistry, his sympathy, and that marvelous natural grace of his," Zero said. When Chaplin returned to America (Chaplin, like Zero, was considered politically suspect by right-wingers, who campaigned to have him deported) after his European exile for an eighty-third birthday party and tribute given by the Film Society of Lincoln Center, Zero and Kate attended along with hundreds of others. At the conclusion of the tribute, as the crowd rose in a standing ovation, the Mostels' friend, Rebecca Kramer Stein, observed that Zero's face was aglow with affection and admiration.

Like Chaplin, Zero's comedy was noted for its underlying pathos. Offstage, too, Mostel was a complex mixture of opposites. When he seemed to be at his most serious, there was always an edge of humor underneath. When he was apparently clowning and saying outrageous things, one wondered if he might have been serious. Zero once described his comic style as "highly intellectual, underplayed" and "deadpan." He was joking, of course, for he knew perfectly well that his personality, on stage and off, was characterized by exuberance. But was the remark (however comically phrased) also intended to reveal a yearning to be taken seriously?

How is one to react to Zero's condescension toward most actors and to his constant references to the triviality of acting in comparison with painting? Probably by dismissing most of it as a pose. As Josh Mostel said, despite Zero's protestations, "he must have loved acting, he had such a good time doing it. Anyone who saw him work would know that. He reveled in it. He loved [it]. I just think Zero didn't believe he loved it."

7

On the Roof

In March 1963, during the run of *A Funny Thing Happened on the Way to the Forum*, Zero appeared on a television special for children; the following month, he presented what was essentially a one-man show on television, performing pantomimes, some of his old nightclub routines and revue sketches, reading Browning's poetry and a selection from *Ulysses*, doing a speech of Falstaff's—and managing in the process to subdue the outsize behavior for which he was normally known, adapting to the size of the television screen with admirable restraint, giving the finest performance he ever gave in that medium.

Zero used his influence to see that his son Josh was hired to perform a comic sketch with him on another television special. Josh, who was then in his freshman year at Brandeis, found it a bitter experience. It is not unusual for fathers to be impatient with their sons, but Zero's display of impatience was so pronounced and so public that it was humiliating for Josh. "There was a rehearsal and he yelled at me," Josh said. "I came in too soon, too fast. He kind of got hysterical and went into a tirade. 'No, no, listen, what's wrong with you?' and yelled at me. And of course I didn't say anything and I did it the way he wanted. But I decided never to work with him again. And I didn't."

In later years, after Zero became even more prominent because of his performance in *Fiddler on the Roof*, he occasionally suggested to Josh that they try to work together once again. Josh was adamant, however. "I could have played Motel in every road company of *Fiddler*—I could've done it forever," he said. "But I thought, 'No, I don't want to do it. I'll work without Zero.'"

In addition to Zero's television activities in 1963, he was photographed in various poses for a small volume of humor called *Zero Mostel Reads a Book* and he introduced the first concert of the Youth Symphony of New York (in which Josh was a second violinist) at Carnegie Hall; but these activities amounted to holding actions until his next major project came along.

That same year, Toby Cole attended a reading by Saul Bellow of a play he had written years before and set aside. The play, then called "Bummidge" (after its main character) and later retitled *The Last Analysis*, focused upon a great Jewish comedian who, obsessed by psychoanalytic theory and distressed by the feeling that he has been turned into a commodity, retires at the peak of his career in order to become the subject of a bizarre psychological experiment. Bellow's sardonic comedy impressed Cole immensely. A few days afterward, when the playwright visited Cole in her office and asked her to represent the play to Broadway producers, she agreed immediately, adding, "I have exactly the right actor for you."

"I was struck by how perfect it would be for Zero to play this role," Cole told me in 1987; she felt that the character of Bummidge reflected Mostel's "own deep-down feelings" about art and life, and saw the opportunity to bring together one of America's foremost character actors with one of America's greatest writers. Together, Cole and Bellow attended a performance of *Forum*, and Bellow agreed that Mostel would be ideal for the part.

On Zero's forty-eighth birthday, February 28, 1963, Cole visited him in his dressing room at the Alvin, bringing Bellow's play with her. It was, she said, "the best birthday present an agent can make to an actor . . . an absolutely extraordinary play." When she presented it to him, she told him, "Zero, you are a really lucky man. Here is a play almost written to order for you by Saul Bellow, one of our great novelists." But she was disappointed in Mostel's reaction. Although he did not reject *The Last Analysis* immediately, his response to the work was reserved at best. He thought the play needed major revisions. He also expressed doubt that he was physically capable of playing a character who was onstage practically every minute of the play. Although Bummidge is certainly no more physically demanding a role than Pseudolus, it is far more *linguistically* demanding. The actor who plays Bummidge is called upon to articulate the play's ideas in intricate—often convoluted—linguistic constructs. The play cannot succeed, moreover, unless the actor can persuade the audience that he is a magnificent comedian. All in all, the role is one of the most demanding ever written. Marilyn Stasio, who included *The Last Analysis* in *Broadway's Beautiful Losers*, her anthology of worthwhile plays that failed in New York, described the complexity of the main character in these terms:

> The comic of which Bummidge is meant to be a prototype is almost grotesque. He is a man whose private personality is so shaped by his clown calling that he seems in thrall to it. Obsessed with comedy; a compulsive laugh-glutton who will starve if he cannot provoke mirth; paralyzed by fears of silence, of "dying" before an audience; fanatically dependent on success; a virtual slave to his public; a helpless host dependent on the parasites who feed off his talent; a public exhibitionist with no private retreat—the portrait of Bummidge is the picture of a *tragic* comic . . . [whose] psychological pronouncements [are] his own corrupted, garbled, half-digested, and absurdly comic interpretations of Freudian theory. . . . Certainly it describes many of our great American clowns of past and present. And only one of them, one of the superclowns, could have done justice to this role.

Mostel spoke several times to Joseph Anthony, who was scheduled to direct *The Last Analysis*, making many suggestions for revisions to the play. Toby Cole also tried to arrange a meeting between Mostel and Bellow, but Zero kept putting it off. Cole said, "I got the feeling that Zero really didn't want to come face to face with Bellow. Bellow is an intellectual and Zero was very timid about being in the company of intellectuals." The proposed meeting never occurred.

Another reason for Mostel's reluctance to meet with Bellow may have been his glimmer of interest in a musical, then called "Tevye," that Fred Coe intended to produce. For years, Zero had spoken to friends about wanting to play the role of Tevye if anyone could create a satisfactory dramatic adaptation of the Sholem Aleichem stories in which the character appears. Joseph Stein, the author of *Tevye*, visited Zero backstage at the Alvin Theatre after a performance of *Forum* in late 1962 and gave him a copy of the script, which, according to Cole (and to Kate), Mostel disliked, finding it unworthy of the great Yiddish author upon whose stories the musical was based. Fred Coe later delivered another version of the script to Toby Cole, who passed it on to Zero. The following morning, Mostel again expressed his lack of enthusiasm. But when Cole, who hoped Zero would choose *The Last Analysis* and reject *Tevye*, suggested that she inform the producer Mostel was not interested, he told her, "Oh no, don't be so fast in refusing. Let him hang on a bit. Don't be so eager. He'll wait."

Subsequently, Fred Coe called Toby Cole often, asking whether Zero was ready to commit himself to the project. Jerome Robbins, who had been selected to direct the musical, made it known that he, too, hoped Mostel would play the lead, but he could not wait forever for Zero to make up his mind. At a meeting attended by Coe, Robbins, and Cole, the agent was asked, "What are we to make of these delays? Why is Zero not saying yes or no? We want to get the project under way." Cole was not authorized either to accept their offer or to refuse it. So, grabbing at the most convenient straw, she said that Zero wanted to hear the score before reaching a decision. Thus another meeting was arranged in March 1963, this time with all the principals present: Zero and Kate, Toby Cole, Robbins, Coe, Stein, Sheldon Harnick, the lyricist, and Jerry Bock, the composer.

Afterward, Zero told his agent that he had been favorably impressed by Bock and Harnick's score but still was not ready to commit himself to their musical. For fully eight months in 1963 Zero kept both Roger Stevens, the producer of *The Last Analysis*, and the team that represented *Tevye* dangling. He continued to profess mild interest in both projects, without committing to either one.

Several weeks after Zero heard the score for *Tevye*, Toby Cole was asked to meet Harnick, Bock, and Robbins at the Booth Theatre. They were bewildered by Mostel's behavior and asked Cole whether or not she thought Zero was sincerely interested in their project, since they wanted to begin rehearsing within the next six months. Cole, trying "to disengage [them] from their interest in Zero," said that Mostel had liked the score but that he had several other enterprises in mind and was deciding among them. The creators of *Tevye*, understandably impatient to get started, began to consider other performers.

In July 1963, during a month's vacation from *A Funny Thing Happened on the Way to the Forum*, Zero and Kate went to Europe. For Zero, this was a chance to visit all the art galleries he had long wished to see. In Paris, Zurich, Bern, Vienna, Copenhagen, Brussels, Ghent, Bruges, and Antwerp, Zero did little but look at cathedrals and paintings. Kate was restless to do other things, but she was unable to persuade her husband to change his itinerary. Finally, she asserted her independence, saying that she would visit no more museums. "I'm getting paint poisoning," she told him.

Mostel returned to *Forum* in August, but in October he took a two-week leave in order to tape the pilot for a new television series. Toby Cole did not know of Zero's plan until, to her surprise, she read about it in a newspaper article. The pilot, to be financed by Screen Gems, would feature a character named Zero, an actor and painter, with a wife named Kate (to be played by Kate) and two sons named Josh and Tobias (to be played by Josh and Tobias). For several months, Cole had felt a coolness from Zero, she said, but she had no inkling that he was about to embark on a project about which she knew nothing. The article stated that Screen Gems had negotiated for Mostel's services with Sidney Elliot Cohn, Zero's lawyer. Cole immediately called Cohn, who confirmed that a series was in the works and told her (as she recalls it), "You have nothing to do with it." The plan, Cohn explained, was that Zero would play in the series for two or three years, then "retire as an actor and live off the residuals for the rest of his life."

According to Toby Cole, Sidney Cohn had been trying to get Zero to sever his relationship with her for several years. After his success in *Rhinoceros*, Cole recalled, a meeting had been held in Cohn's office. Cohn advised Mostel that he had the potential to become one of America's foremost performers, but that he "had no future in the theatre." As Cole remembered the conversation, "Mr. Cohn said there were no parts for a character actor like Mr. Mostel and that his salvation was in television." Cohn also asserted that Cole was not the proper agent to handle an entertainer with a major television career. Cole vehemently disagreed with the notion that Zero "had no future in the theatre" and was shocked by Cohn's suggestion that Mostel should allow himself to be represented by the influential William Morris Agency—the very organization that had dropped him when he was blacklisted. When she and Zero left the meeting, Mostel told her to pay no attention to Cohn, that their relationship as actor and agent would remain the same as it had been in the past.

Clearly, the relationship had changed two years afterward, when Cohn told Cole in 1963 that she was to have nothing to do with Zero's prospective television series. Mostel's attitude toward the performing arts, and his place in that world, had obviously also changed. The thought of Zero Mostel, who was so critical of escapist entertainment—and particularly of television—devoting his energies to a standard situation comedy is staggering. Less than a year earlier, he had said about television that it typically presented comedy "with no virility at all. . . . They make a sap out of the wife. The husband is a god. This kind of thing never has any *substance*, which is what comedy is all about." Zero's sudden decision to appear in just such a comedy reflects the dichotomy of his personality. In one breath, he expressed bitter contempt for actors who accepted roles in escapist entertainments, insisting that no artist should waste his time performing in trivial material; then, without seeming to realize the contradiction, he announced that he was ready to concentrate all of his creative energies upon just such a trivial television series.

Zero finally announced that he was definitely not interested in *The Last Analysis*. Perhaps, as director Joseph Anthony later said, "Zero felt the verbal load was so huge that he himself would drown in the role. I think Zero's theatre sense told him he would have to carry it all on his back." Toby Cole, hoping that Mostel would have a change of heart, pleaded with Roger Stevens to postpone the production of the play until Zero became available, but Stevens decided to go ahead, casting Sam Levene in the leading role. The play was performed on Broadway, but it did not fare well, closing after twenty-eight performances.* Perhaps, as Toby Cole believed, Zero could have played Bummidge so

---

*An off-Broadway revival in 1971 did little better. Joseph Wiseman, a fine actor, played Bummidge, but it once again became clear that the role needed the qualities only a great clown could bring to it.

dynamically that his presence would have made the play successful. Even Sam Levene later commented, "Maybe I was wrong for the part. Yeah, I think maybe Zero Mostel would have been better. Maybe if Zero had played it, it would have been a big success." But that will forever remain a matter for speculation.

Burgess Meredith had agreed to direct the pilot for Zero's television series. From the beginning, the show, to be called either "The Zero Mostel Show" or "Zero Hour," was in trouble. The original concept had been to present a reasonably honest portrayal of Zero's life as an actor, painter, husband, and father, with ample opportunity for him to display his versatility as a performer. But the original script was found wanting, so Jerome Chodorov was brought in for a rewrite. Chodorov and Zero worked together on the draft, Zero's function being restricted to "kicking around ideas," according to Chodorov. Still later, Mel Brooks was called upon to make the script funnier. Each successive rewrite carried the script further and further from the original conception, however, with the final version being little more than a collection of routine gags that called upon all of the characters to behave in ludicrous and improbable ways.

At the last moment, Zero must have realized that the show, despite its potential to earn him a fortune, was creatively worthless, for he abandoned the project on the first day of taping. He claimed that he was withdrawing on the advice of his doctor, and, indeed, he was concerned about the demands of performing in a weekly program; but it is clear that he used his physical condition primarily as an excuse to get out of a show he no longer wished to do. He told Burgess Meredith that it would ruin him. "He didn't feel inspired by it," Meredith told me. "Finally, he just said, 'I don't want to do this; it's nothing.'" Mostel was never a decisive man; throughout his life, he vacillated when he was called upon to make a decision concerning his career. He had often driven his agent and various producers to the point of distraction with his inability to make up his mind.* But never before had he agreed to participate in a project, then pulled out after it was already under way.

---

*Sol Kaplan also remarked on Zero's procrastination, a quality that irritated many people. Kaplan, who arranged music for Zero and conducted the orchestra for an album of his comic songs, said, "He would kid around a lot, doing all kinds of crazy shtick,

Once again, Zero was available. Hal Prince, the producer of *Forum*, by this time had bought out Fred Coe's interest and become producer of the Sholem Aleichem musical, which had been retitled *Fiddler on the Roof*, after Marc Chagall's fanciful painting. Prince, in consultation with the play's creators, had, after considering Danny Kaye, Danny Thomas, Alan King, and others, decided that Mostel was their choice to play Tevye after all. Consequently, they offered him a contract through Toby Cole in October 1963 in order (as Cole was told) "to get Zero to make up his mind." Still, he avoided giving a definite answer.

Cole did not know it—because Zero never told her—but she was no longer functioning as his agent. Sidney Cohn had supplanted her. She finally learned about the new arrangement when Cohn called her late in January 1964 to say that she could remove Mostel's name from her roster of clients.

Recalling Zero's earlier assurances that he had no intention of dropping her as his agent, she telephoned him to see if Cohn's account was true. According to Cole, Mostel was evasive. He maintained a light, bantering tone—not an easy task, for Cole was angry and upset. Finally, in response to her declaration that Mostel's acquiescence in Cohn's plan had hurt her deeply, Zero asked, with childlike ingenuousness, "What's the matter? Didn't Sidney say it nicely?" He agreed to meet with her

---

but eventually, when the time came to really get down to work, then he would do it." Mostel worked on screenplays with Kaplan, but nothing came of them, partly because of Zero's tendency to put off getting to work until the last possible moment. Kaplan described the process: "We'd work in his studio mostly and we had to play one of those card games, hearts or something—with Herbie Kallem, always—then we'd talk about this artist or that artist, and then he'd show me what he was working on, and it would take a good two to three hours before we'd sit down finally and get to work on the treatment."

One of the screenplays Kaplan and Mostel worked on was sufficiently developed that Milos Forman, the director, became interested in the possibility of filming it. But Zero sabotaged the possibility before it could become anything more than that by behaving in his typically zany way. Kaplan: "Forman came to Zero's apartment with his producer. I don't know what happened to Zero: he suddenly got down on the floor and made like he was dead. Milos Forman didn't know what the hell was going on—and neither did I—and there I was saying, 'Hey Zero, come on, get up, for Christ's sake, get up, they're here.' And he didn't even flutter an eyelid for five full minutes. Well, with this behavior, Forman didn't know what the hell to do." It is perhaps unnecessary to add that the film was never made.

to discuss the matter fully, but he postponed the appointment, then traveled to London—and the meeting never took place. The next time they saw one another was at an arbitration hearing in 1965, when Cole sued Mostel for commissions she claimed he owed her.*

Sidney Cohn arranged with Hal Prince to release Zero from *Forum* so that he could make *The ABC Murders* in England, then return to New York in June 1964 to begin rehearsal for *Fiddler*, should he finally approve the project. Mostel would have become the first actor to portray Agatha Christie's fictional detective, Hercule Poirot, on film if *The ABC Murders* had been made as originally cast. As early as the 1950s, Zero had suggested a series of Poirot films to his British agent, Adza Vincent. But he disliked the script for *The ABC Murders* and began working on a version of his own. Eventually, MGM bought out Mostel's contract for $50,000, replaced him with Tony Randall, and released the film under the title *The Alphabet Murders*.

Having opted out of the television series and no longer able to use the Christie film as a reason to delay consideration of *Fiddler on the Roof*, Zero looked at the revised script Joseph Stein and Jerome Robbins had prepared. In Zero's estimation, they had improved it greatly, partly as a result of his—Mostel's—own contributions. According to Zero, "certain songs were written at my suggestion. . . . Jerry Robbins came to my home and we had a long discussion of what should be in there, how it should be played and so on." Just how much influence Zero had on the rewrite is uncertain, but the script was certainly different. Among other things, Stein and Robbins had enlarged the play's focus, from the character of Tevye the dairyman to the entire Jewish community in the village of Anatevka. Whereas the script originally called for the musical to open with Tevye's wife, Golde, and her daughters energetically preparing for the Sabbath, the new version began with "Tradition," sung and danced by the people of the village. More generally, the play now dealt with the disintegration of an entire way of life: the life of the closely knit community of rural Jews in czarist Russia, ending with their expulsion from Anatevka. Stein and Robbins had also turned what had been predominantly a comic play into one that mingled serious themes and poignant conflicts with warmth and humor.

---

*The events set in motion by those hearings are detailed in chapter 8.

Moreover, the character of Tevye had been deepened to the point where he was as multidimensional and challenging as any character ever written for a musical. In Tevye's desire to retain the traditional authoritarian role of the father, he resists his daughters' desires to marry the men they love. In his wish to observe Orthodox Jewish tradition, he firmly opposes his daughter Chava's marriage to a Christian. The tension of his inner struggle is such that he pronounces Chava "dead" and refuses to see her—or to allow his wife and children to see her—ever again after she marries. Tevye's ambivalence, conflict, and behavior are believable, heartbreaking, and extraordinarily complex, especially in terms of the main character of a traditional American musical. Stimulated by the challenge of playing such a well-written role, Zero finally told Hal Prince that he would appear as Tevye.

It is conceivable that Mostel's own background influenced him to accept the role. Zero's mother had objected so strongly when he married a Gentile that she rejected his wife and refused to meet Zero and Kate's children. However, the view of those closest to him is that his own experience had no bearing whatsoever on his professional decision to play in the musical; nor do they believe that it affected his portrayal of the character.

Zero insisted that he would not sign a contract calling for him to remain with the show for more than nine months. Prince agreed, partly because having watched Mostel's performance in *A Funny Thing Happened on the Way to the Forum* become less faithful to the script as time went on, he was wary that the same problem might recur in *Fiddler*. Jerome Robbins also thought that a nine-month contract would be wiser than an agreement for a longer period of time. He predicted to several people that Zero would be wonderful as Tevye for the first several months, and then his performance would begin to disintegrate. Still, both Prince and Robbins were eager to have Mostel play the leading role in their musical, believing that any difficulties he might create would be more than compensated for by the brilliance they expected him to bring to the early performances.

Following his usual custom, Zero did several paintings of Tevye and the other characters in *Fiddler on the Roof* before rehearsals began. He continued to work on these studies for years and in the 1970s, he authorized the Newmarket Gallery in New York to make prints of three of the paintings and to sell five hundred copies of the set for $325 each.

Rehearsals for *Fiddler* began on June 1, 1964, but only after an acrimonious dispute between Robbins and Prince. The director, who was notorious for procrastination, insisted that he was not ready to begin rehearsing, that he needed a month's delay. The producer, who had already signed contracts with actors and theatre owners, insisted with equal vehemence that a postponement was impossible. When Robbins sent Prince a telegram informing him that rehearsals would not begin until he felt he was ready, Prince responded by demanding that the director pay him $55,000 to cover the costs of the delay. Robbins capitulated and the musical went into rehearsal.

The process began with the cast participating in several improvisations, all of them aimed at creating a sense of how it feels to be a member of a persecuted minority. In one of the improvisations, for example, blacks attempted to purchase books in a white-owned bookstore in the South. That experiment clearly aided in the actors' emotional identification with the persecuted Jews of Anatevka. But some of Robbins's other rehearsal techniques were of less apparent relevance and left the performers wondering why they were being asked to experiment in such seemingly futile ways.

Robbins's inability to settle upon a specific way of approaching a scene was particularly upsetting to the performers. When arranging the actors' patterns of movement, he would block a scene one way, then, after the actors believed the blocking was behind them, he would make such drastic changes that the new blocking bore no relationship to the old. Later, as likely as not, he would throw out all that had been accomplished and begin again. Zero held his irritation in check but clearly did not like Robbins's approach. Nor did Robbins confine his constant alterations to the blocking; he applied the same technique to the actors' characterizations, asking them to approach their roles in all manner of ways, leaving many of them frustrated and angry.

Robbins, a stern taskmaster to whom the art of diplomacy was unknown, often insulted his co-workers when they presented him with work that was less excellent than he wished. His perfectionism and his tactlessness alienated many of his colleagues, according to Richard Altman, Robbins's assistant on the production, who suggested that they found the director to be demanding, merciless, and tempermental.* Before long Robbins and Joseph Stein were not on speaking terms. On the other hand, Robbins was also a powerful creative force, continually improving the production with his alterations. "I had absolute faith in Robbins," said Sheldon Harnick.

Mostel and Robbins were cordial to one another throughout most of the rehearsal process, although Zero continued to dislike the director, always referring to him as "that son of a bitch" in conversation with friends. But he respected Robbins's professional skill. Perhaps no other director could so effectively have persuaded Mostel to control his impulse to insert comic business into his characterization. Time and again, Robbins would veto looks or gestures that he considered inappropriate. Zero complied reluctantly but with growing irritation. In order to avoid a confrontation between the director and the star, Richard Altman was delegated to pass Robbins's notes on to Mostel. Altman described the process:

> Each evening . . . I would come to his dressing room to give him notes from Jerry, and the moment I appeared he would holler: "Four eyes, get outta here!" or, "Shmuck-face, out!" or, "You're Robbins's friend—out! I want no friends of Robbins in here!" Each time, I would start to leave and he would call me back, offer me a glass of vodka and listen to what I had to say—not entirely in silence, however. He would continue to pour out invective, cursing me or Jerry under his breath. This was one of the games Zero played, and he played it to the hilt. Since he couldn't, or didn't dare, get at Jerry directly, he was satisfied to get in his digs at me. However, despite his snarling protests, he usually did what he was told. He was quick and precise, and he realized, however grudgingly, that in Jerry Robbins he was dealing with a talent that was at least the equal of his own.

One day, Mostel engaged Robbins in a rather juvenile battle of wills. Zero habitually chewed gum during rehearsals, causing Robbins to

---

*A story, perhaps apocryphal, is told of Robbins when he was directing *West Side Story*. Robbins was standing on stage giving notes to the members of the cast, who were united in their dislike of him. As he gave the notes he began to edge backwards, toward the orchestra pit. According to the story, none of the actors spoke a word of warning, and it was only by inches that Robbins avoided falling into the pit.

become increasingly irritated. He asked Mostel to toss the gum away, but Zero refused. Eventually, the gum became a symbol of the conflict between the two men. Finally, Robbins shouted to Mostel in the middle of a rehearsal, "*Please* don't chew the gum," whereupon Zero elaborately stuck the gum behind his ear. Richard Altman, who watched the confrontation, recalled its aftermath: "During the next scene, whenever [Zero] was turned upstage [with his back to the audience], he would pop the gum back in his mouth and chew ferociously until just before he had a line; then he would put the gum behind his ear, say his line, turn upstage and repeat the whole process. One look at Jerry was enough to know that Zero was dangerously overplaying his naughty-boy routine. It was as though Zero wanted to provoke a battle, and I think Jerry sensed it. We all watched and waited to see what he would do. But he did nothing. He had no tolerance for insubordination, but he obviously had some sense of proportion, even if Zero didn't. To have an outburst over a wad of chewing gum seemed ridiculous and idiotic, and it never took place."

If Zero behaved mischievously at times, he displayed his creative brilliance at others, as when "If I Were a Rich Man" was being staged. Mostel asked Robbins if he could work out the number on his own—and he did. Although Robbins subsequently made some minor alterations, the impulse for the staging of that song, which became one of the highlights of the production, derived almost entirely from Zero. In later years, the actors who followed Mostel in the role of Tevye invariably followed his staging down to the smallest details.*

In other ways, too, Mostel improved "If I Were a Rich Man." For one thing, he was responsible for improvising the cantorial-like sounds that became such an integral part of the song. For another, he resisted the attempts of Harnick and Robbins to drop the serious verse that ends the predominantly comic piece. As Harnick said, Zero's resistance illustrated his "respect for and understanding of the Sholem Aleichem stories on which *Fiddler* is based." He recalled:

---

*As Howard Rodney, his dresser, told me, "Because of Zero's crippled leg, he sat on a milk can, he sat on his wagon, he sat on a bench, he always sat to get off his leg. But every [subsequent] Tevye with two good legs would do the same thing."

Well into rehearsals, we had a production meeting one day at which Zero was present. I had already begun to lose perspective on much of what I had written due to overfamiliarity with it. Consequently, I had begun to feel that the song "If I Were a Rich Man" got too serious towards the end. I now felt that the end of the song should be as amusing as the rest of it had been. I suggested that either the song should be shortened or I should rewrite the lyrics where Tevye sings, "If I were rich I'd have the time that I lack / to sit in the synagogue and pray," etc. Zero became indignant. "You can't cut *that*! That's the man! Not the jokes! That's the man who reveres the spiritual side of his life, the part he's too poor, too weary, and too uneducated to enjoy fully! That's what this man is *about*! You can't cut *that*!" Zero spoke with passion and authority. We didn't make the cut. He was dead right.

Zero claimed that he had consented to appear in *Fiddler* because "I knew I would have something to say about the way the show was shaped." He said that he had been responsible for inserting Tevye's one-way conversations with God. "I got in the line that's the whole essence of Sholem Aleichem," he boasted: "when Tevye says to God, 'With your help, I'm starving to death.'" But Joseph Stein has no recollection of writing dialogue specifically at Zero's behest. Whoever deserves the credit, Tevye's speeches to God, composed of equal parts devotion and sly irreverence, were a highlight of the musical.

The credit for not playing Tevye too sentimentally, however, goes unequivocally to Mostel. Zero felt that Sholem Aleichem "was incapable of [sentimentality]. Like all great writers tragedy and comedy are present [in his work] all the time. . . . [Tevye is] one of those characters who's bottomless. . . . In the darkest moments, he has lightness; in the lightest moments, a darkness." Although Tevye suffers one emotional blow after another in the course of the play, the quality of humorous defiance that Mostel brought to the part eliminated any possible sentimentality. As a result, Tevye was that rarest of phenomena in a musical: a fully rounded character, kindhearted but stern, highly amusing but deeply affecting.

The pre-Broadway performances of *Fiddler* were initially discouraging. Opening in Detroit on July 27, 1964, the show received generally favorable responses from its audiences, but it certainly was not thought of as a "blockbuster." Because of a newspaper strike, few reviews appeared, but those that did (in the weekly edition of *Variety*, for instance) were lukewarm about the play and production, although enthusiastic about Zero's performance. The Fisher Theatre was occasionally one-quarter empty during the five weeks of performances in Detroit, a disappointment to the producer and to the theatre owners, even though it could be attributed, at least in part, to the newspaper strike and to a heat wave.

The cast began to feel frustrated. The production did not seem to improve despite continual rewrites and constant rehearsals. Eventually, they came to believe that the show would not succeed.

But Robbins continued to refine the production each day, cutting material here, adding there, rearranging dialogue, playing scenes with different intentions. "Do You Love Me?," one of *Fiddler*'s finest songs, because it defines and clarifies the relationship of Tevye and Golde, was added a week after the Detroit opening. Gradually, the audiences began to respond more warmly; their size increased steadily with the passage of time; and the actors—when they were able to fight through the exhaustion brought on by constant performing and rehearsing, and exaggerated by the demands of Robbins's perfectionism—began to take heart.

Again, as he had in *Forum*, Zero showed his ability to adjust to the most sweeping changes with remarkable facility. Not fazed by new lines, new songs, or new approaches to individual scenes, he would simply digest the changes, absorb them, and perform them brilliantly.

Sheldon Harnick was particularly encouraged by the improvements made to *Fiddler* in Detroit. "During those five weeks, we did a great deal of work," he said. "By the time we finished the run, we had reshaped our troubled and overlong second act considerably: four songs that didn't work were gone." And the new songs "strengthened and enriched the show. These changes, plus much tightening and revising of the book, gave me good reason to feel optimistic."

After performances, the company would occasionally gather together in an attempt to relax. But Zero's compulsive behavior often made relaxation impossible. As Sheldon Harnick recalled, Zero and Kate "gave a party for the cast during our out-of-town tryout in Detroit. Zero entertained, improvising, singing, dancing, doing anything and everything under the sun to entertain and amuse us. He was brilliant. It was awesome. I even felt privileged to be a witness to his genius. But after forty minutes or so, it began to pall. Perhaps, now that he had entertained us, we wanted to relax with one another. People began to drift away from Zero. He couldn't bear it. The quality of his improvisations began to grow manic, strained. The situation was getting awkward. Zero worked harder and harder to get our attention. Kate suddenly intervened. She began to bawl him out. Her fury and scorn brought him under control and allowed the party to continue."

The story Harnick tells is unusual only in that it is so extreme. Zero normally behaved outlandishly when he was in a group. But he occasionally confounded expectations, surprising partygoers by lapsing into silence just when he might have been expected to be at his most manic.

Harnick did not see that side of Zero, however; nor did he know the private man. "I would like to think that with his old close friends he was the relaxed art lover, the cultivated philosophical humorist, the humanitarian," he said. "But I have no idea whether that person existed or, if he did, whether Zero could sustain that persona for any length of time. To use a phrase I have used often in describing Zero, the person I knew was a brilliant baby, unpredictable, hilarious, egocentric, compulsively driven to be the center of every gathering."

In Washington, the critical reception for *Fiddler* was overwhelmingly enthusiastic, largely because the show had been trimmed, sharpened, and generally improved. Audiences turned out in record numbers. Robbins remained unsatisfied, however, cutting dialogue here and adding other material there.

During the Washington run, Zero suffered a bout of laryngitis that prevented him from performing for four days. His colleagues were uncertain whether the show could survive his absence. Mostel himself had often implied that *Fiddler* would be unsuccessful without the electricity provided by his performance, and many of the cast agreed. It was with much trepidation among the members of the company, therefore, that Paul Lipson, Mostel's understudy, went on as Tevye. But audience response to the production remained favorable, if a little less enthusiastic than when Zero was performing. It was the first indication that *Fiddler* could stand on its own, without the aid of its "star."

During Zero's illness, Richard Altman continued to visit him daily, informing him of any changes that had been made. "He was never nicer to me," Altman said. "Though feeling weak and miserable, he thanked me graciously each time for coming. He was simply too weak to dredge up insults or expletives. It took a lot of energy for him to behave outrageously, and he was just too sick to bother," Altman commented astutely.

Even before *Fiddler* reached New York, Robbins began to lose control of Zero's performance, as Mostel took to altering the shape of his scenes. His impulse was to insert bits of business that were undeniably funny but that distracted from the focus of a particular scene. Robbins, fearing that Zero's tendency to interpolate material would increase unless it was checked immediately, continued to do his best to prevent it, but he became progressively less successful. Since he had been doing the same thing in other productions for years, it seems unlikely that Zero's motivation for improvising was to win points in his battle with Robbins. Nor does it seem that Zero had any intention of upsetting the other actors, although that was frequently the result. When he was onstage and a fresh thought occurred to him, it was evidently impossible for him to subdue the impulse to translate it into action. Audiences clearly loved Mostel's performance, and their approval fueled his improvisational tendencies. Mostel would have defended himself by claiming that his Tevye would have been less spontaneous and less electrifying had he held his impulses in check.

Zero's inclination to improvise was decidedly helpful at certain critical moments. Whereas other actors might have been thrown by an onstage accident, Zero was able to respond instantly and spontaneously. On one occasion, when Tevye's house was supposed to revolve during a tryout performance in Detroit, one wall failed to move. Zero improvised a conversation with God, saying "Just because I didn't pay the rent to the landlord, you don't have to punish me." Then, while the stagehands rushed to repair the damage, Zero continued, "If you were a decent God, you'd put my house in order." Whenever he entered the house in later scenes, he'd ad lib, "Hasn't the carpenter come to fix the house yet?"

News of the brilliance of Mostel's portrayal and the probability that *Fiddler* would be an overwhelming success reached Broadway well before the show itself. The advance bookings amounted to $650,000, a tremendous presale in 1964, nearly double the original investment in the production. So many theatre parties purchased tickets that brokers complained they were unable to get seats. Ticket-buyers formed a line from the day the box office opened.

Inevitably, everyone was tense on the day of the opening, September 22, 1964. But Zero defused the tension when he arrived for the afternoon rehearsal, weaving unsteadily along the sidewalk, nearly falling down, bumping into unwary pedestrians. "Oh my God, he's smashed!" one of the actresses moaned. But Zero stopped, laughed heartily, and strode jauntily into the theatre.

The performance at the Imperial Theatre that evening was an unqualified success, partly because of the play itself, partly because of Jerome Robbins's production, and partly because of Zero's performance, which was—according to the critics—astonishing.

After opening night, most of the cast went to the Rainbow Room. Zero stayed only briefly; after dancing a hora with Senator Jacob Javits, he said he was too tired to remain longer. He left before the reviews came out, apparently secure in the belief that they would be favorable.

They were more than favorable. They were—for the most part—ecstatic. "The new musical . . . is filled with laughter and tenderness," said Howard Taubman in the *Times*. "It catches a moment in history with sentiment and radiance. Compounded of the familiar materials of the musical theatre—popular song, vivid dance movement, comedy and emotion—it combines and transcends them to arrive at an integrated achievement of uncommon quality."

Of Zero's performance, Taubman said, "If Sholem Aleichem had known Zero Mostel, he would have chosen him, one is sure, for Tevye. . . . They were ordained to be one. . . . Mr. Mostel does not keep his acting and singing or his walking and dancing in separate compartments. His Tevye is a unified, logical conception. . . . When Mr. Mostel sings 'If I Were a Rich Man,' interpolating passages of cantillation in the manner of prayer, his Tevye is both devout and pungently realistic. When Tevye chants a prayer as the good Golde tries to convey an item of vital news, Mr. Mostel is not only comic but evocative of an old way of life. When Tevye hears the horrifying word that his third daughter has run away with a gentile, Mr. Mostel dances his anguish in a flash of savage emotion. . . . In Mr. Mostel's Tevye [the production] has one of the most glowing creations in the history of the musical theatre."

Nearly all of the reviews echoed Taubman's praise for Zero's performance. Richard Watts headlined his notice, "The Brilliance of Zero Mostel," and commented, "That [the musical, composed of diverse and unusual elements,] works out as effectively as it does is due . . . chiefly [to] the brilliantly resourceful and intelligent performance that Zero Mostel offers in the central role. . . . He emphatically reaches new heights in *Fiddler on the Roof.*" John McClain said that *Fiddler* was "a great tribute to the comic gifts of the star . . . it is a constant delight to observe Mr. Mostel in a role beautifully tailored to him." Norman Nadel wrote that Sholem Aleichem's stories "provided the people, plots and best of all, the abundant and gently heroic role that must have been waiting all these years for Zero Mostel."

The day after the reviews appeared, the line of ticket-buyers at the box office was even longer than usual, so long that the police erected barricades in front of the nearby Piccadilly Hotel in order to keep the entrance clear. Hal Prince instructed his employees to serve iced tea to the three hundred people in line on that hot September afternoon.

Seldom has anyone been as ambivalent about a work of art as Zero Mostel was about *Fiddler on the Roof.* On the one hand, he would sometimes tell his friends that he regarded the material as second-rate; on the other, he defended it fiercely against outside attack. He blamed Joseph Stein for the script when it was described as insufficiently serious; but he often took credit for the same material when it was praised. "I was raised on Sholem Aleichem," he said. "I read his stories in Yiddish over and over again. They weren't the same in translation. When Joseph Stein . . . brought the script to me, he said he knew Yiddish but he didn't." Stein claims that Zero was wrong on this point: he did indeed know Yiddish, although, being more comfortable in English, he used English translations of the stories as his source material. Zero continued, "He didn't have as deep an understanding of the lives he was writing about as I did."

It is certainly true that Zero had loved the Sholem Aleichem stories since he was a boy and that he had long wished to play Tevye, a character who, he said, "is universal. He has no nationality, really, because he symbolizes the underprivileged in every country—no matter what adversity he meets, he just puffs up his chest and goes on." Zero enjoyed playing Tevye more than any other role, with the exception of Leopold Bloom.

Mostel believed, however, that he had had to fight a lonely battle with everyone else connected with the production in order to maintain *Fiddler*'s integrity. All but he had sought to alter Sholem Aleichem's characters drastically in the fear that a "too-Jewish" production would appeal only to Jewish audiences, he contended. The original costumes were designed to be ludicrously colorful replicas of nineteenth-century peasant garb, Zero maintained; but he insisted that they conform to reality. He added, "They also wanted to have colored *Yarmulkes* and fancy *tsetse* as part of the costumes. Can you imagine that?" Hal Prince's version of how the costumes were conceived is quite different, however. "The colors of the peasants' clothes were beautifully controlled," he said, "then beaten and aged in a vat of dye, then shown to Jerry [Robbins], who would say take them back and age them, and they would be beaten some more and dipped in dye and returned for his approval." Still, Zero was certain that only his influence had saved the production from corruption. "I'd plead and cajole," he said. "I'm terrific at cajoling."

Mostel also claimed that he had originated much of the specific business that gave the production its authentic flavor. For example, Zero said that he had persuaded Robbins that the actors should observe the Jewish Orthodox tradition of kissing the *mezuzah* whenever they entered Tevye's home. According to Mostel, there was initial resistance to his suggestion. "What was that you just did?" Robbins asked. "I kissed the *mezuzah*," Zero answered. When Robbins looked perplexed, Zero explained, "Every Orthodox Jew would kiss the *mezuzah* before he entered a house." Mostel also claimed that he had demonstrated certain characteristics of Jewish dance to Robbins, which the director-choreographer then used in the production.

On other occasions, however, he showered praise and credit on his co-workers. "All of us worked together to keep the feeling and spirit and characters of the Tevye stories intact, and the show is all of a piece—the book, the music, the lyrics, the choreography, the acting," he said. "All of it is Sholem Aleichem. There has never been a musical like this one. The songs are never gratuitous; they're always part of the show. On the whole, if I do say so myself, it's great. . . . This show is one of the best things done on Broadway in years. . . . In addition to being a musical, it's a play. It's a show that's a cut above anything else ever attempted. . . . Our show is an honest piece of work."

Stein, Harnick, and Bock's intention from the beginning had been to create a musical play that would—within certain strictures inevitably imposed by the commercial theatre—be as faithful as possible to the material from which it was adapted. Some changes, such as reducing the number of Tevye's daughters from seven to five, were made for purposes of dramatic focus and economy; others, such as changing the matchmaker from a man to a woman and giving her a sizable role in the play, were made in order to balance the serious aspects of the musical with comic material; however, the *spirit* of Sholem Aleichem's stories was not violated. Harnick and Bock, for example, had not attempted to write songs that could be removed from the musical's context and turned into "hits" (although, ironically, many of the songs did become extremely successful on their own). Rather, each song was intended to support and further the play's mood and plot.

Stein made certain shrewd decisions about which incidents in the Sholem Aleichem stories should be dramatized. For example, Tevye's youngest daughters, Shprintze and Bielke, appear only as small children in *Fiddler on the Roof*, whereas their adult lives are chronicled in the original stories. Shprintze commits suicide and Bielke's husband meets with financial ruin, forcing her to leave America. Had Stein opted to include these incidents in the play, they would surely have tipped the balance too heavily toward the tragic, perhaps rendering the material unsuitable for musical adaptation.

Zero's love of Sholem Aleichem and his reverence for Jewish tradition undoubtedly were influential to some degree in shaping *Fiddler*. In the theatre, the most collaborative of art forms, it is often all but impossible to pinpoint who was responsible for a particular contribution. James Bronson, who as stage manager was present at every rehearsal, said, "Zero's contribution to *Fiddler* was great; he knew the subject matter better than anyone concerned with the production."

Walter Kerr, in his review of *Fiddler*, had said, "I think it might be an altogether charming musical if only the people of Anatevka did not pause every now and again to give their regards to Broadway, with remembrances to Herald Square." On those occasions when he felt contemptuous of the script, Mostel might have made the same comment himself, but he disliked hearing it from anyone else. When Kerr or other critics condemned the musical or Zero's performance as being unfaithful to the spirit of the original stories, Mostel responded angrily, "A few self-elected Sholem Aleichem experts want to give you this little twist of the arm, so they say the show is 'too Broadway.' " He added, "Or the guardians of culture describe some little thing I do as 'a Broadway gesture.' What the hell is a Broadway gesture? I goggle my eyes, they say. I've been in the business for twenty-two years, and for twenty-two years I've goggled my eyes, but now it's described as a Broadway gesture. . . . One critic [Robert Brustein in the *New Republic*, who wrote, "I cannot help but regret that he is draining his talents into a benefit audience musical"] said I shouldn't play in this play, I should play in some *other* play [*The Last Analysis*], but, unfortunately, he said, 'Zero has sold out to the ladies from the Hadassah.' What I want to know is: What's wrong with *them*? They're all nice ladies who collect money for Israel and do good work. What's wrong with that?"

Zero was quick to rise to the defense of those who enjoyed *Fiddler*. "You just can't beat our audiences," he said. "They get right into the show with us. I'm especially fond of the matinees. We call them 'the shopping bags,' because all the ladies come to the theatre from their shopping carrying these big paper bags. Every night, we're mobbed backstage—by Jews and non-Jews, by readers of Sholem Aleichem and non-readers of Sholem Aleichem. A lot of the people have some previous knowledge of the way of life written about by Sholem Aleichem; a lot of others had parents who knew, but they themselves, born here, never heard about the old country from their parents. However, whether they know or don't know, when they come backstage they're *all* overwhelmed by feeling. One man came back and immediately broke down. I had to give him a drink. . . . The audience responds the way an audience should. If theatre is not what the audience gets from the stage, what is it? It should enlighten, make you identify, make you feel better—all those things—and our show does that. We could have thirty curtain calls every night if we wanted them. The people don't want to let go. What more could you ask for?"

If Zero was ambivalent about *Fiddler on the Roof*, it is also true that the production's creators were ambivalent about Zero's performance.

On the one hand, they were grateful that Mostel had brought to the role precisely the qualities of warmth and humor they sought. Joseph Stein said, for public consumption, "This is one of the very rare occasions when an actor and a part are completely wedded to one another. Zero can change a mood in the middle of a line, or bring different shades and color to each performance—and they *all* seem right." Privately, however, Stein deeply resented Mostel's departures from the script.

Richard Altman also regretted the gradual change he observed in Zero's performance. "Once past the opening night, Zero began to let down," he said. "He felt free to step outside of Tevye—more and more often as the weeks and months went by—to become Zero the mimic, Zero the clown prince. . . . On opening night he had been the best he would ever be. Soon afterward Tevye would become just another oddity out of Zero's bottomless bag of tricks."

The difficulty was compounded because Zero was convinced that *he* was responsible for *Fiddler*'s success, that the show would have collapsed without him. Thus he took even greater liberties with the production than he had taken with *A Funny Thing Happened on the Way to the Forum*. That show, by its very nature, seemed to give its star a certain license for zany conduct, but *Fiddler on the Roof* was quite a different matter. On many occasions, the production nearly gave way beneath the weight of Zero's unpredictable antics. He made faces at the other actors when the audience could not see him; he whispered out-of-character comments when the audience could not hear him; he altered the blocking when it suited him, often throwing the other performers into a panic; he introduced elaborate pantomimes that were greeted with laughter but had nothing whatever to do with Tevye.*

Fiddler was a long play to begin with, and it got longer when Zero

---

*Again, Josh Mostel comes to his father's defense, claiming that there is no truth to the claim that Zero ever "kidded around" during a performance. "As far as I can tell, the ad libs he made were either inconsequential or very helpful and very astute," Josh said. "I think he wasn't out of control; I think he was just existing in the moment. Sometimes when you're on stage something happens and you're on your own. It's not that ad libs are necessarily wrong. There are ad libs and there are ad libs. The idea that he was brilliant on the first night and went steadily downhill is way off base, I think. Throughout the run of that show he was *working*."

interpolated material. There was concern in Hal Prince's office that Mostel's antics could extend the curtain beyond midnight—which, among other things, would have meant that the stagehands had to be paid overtime.*

Joseph Stein said, "There were times when we who had created the show felt uncomfortable going to the theatre, because we never knew what the hell we would see. He would extend a scene with a little ad-libbing and sometimes he would throw in Yiddish words just to get a laugh here and there, which absolutely did not fit the context of the show." In writing the script, Stein had consciously steered clear of Yiddishisms, feeling that the use of Yiddish would make the play too parochial. No wonder, then, that Zero's tendency to toss in Yiddish words and phrases whenever it suited him was particularly aggravating. It began, Harnick recalled, "one night in the tavern scene, at the moment when Tevye, while dancing, accidentally bumps into one of the Russians. Zero let out a stream of Yiddish ending with the word 'tuchus' [ass]. Sure enough, there were scattered giggles throughout the house. I was appalled. We asked Zero to take out the Yiddish. He refused. He kept it in for another two weeks or so, until he was 'good and ready' to take it out."

Some of Zero's most successful business became corrupted as time went on. For example, while talking to God, Tevye accidentally stuck his arm into a bucket of milk, then shook his arm, wrung his sleeve and dripped milk on his shoes, all the while carrying on the conversation. Zero performed this business so subtly that it added a poignant charm to the moment. But when he was unable to resist going for the biggest possible laugh, he would wring out his sleeve over the orchestra pit; the business would indeed get a bigger laugh, but it destroyed the believability of the scene.

Everyone tried to restrain him, of course, but to little avail. Zero admitted that he "couldn't care less about the people who say I'm difficult." His standard, he insisted, was: "I say to myself, 'Will Sholem Aleichem like what I'm doing?'" Clearly, he felt that he knew Sholem

---

*But it never happened. Every time Zero came offstage he'd inquire about the time and adjust his performance accordingly. Occasionally the curtain would come down at 11:59, but never at midnight.

Aleichem's intentions better than Robbins, Stein, or Harnick did, and that his knowledge gave him the freedom to do as he liked. Harnick recounted one representative occasion when *Fiddler*'s creators attempted to persuade Zero to give a more legitimate performance:

> Someone sent Hal Prince a review from a Kentucky newspaper. The theatre critic had seen *Fiddler* in New York and told his readers that it was a "darling" show but he advised them to wait to see it until some other actor was playing Tevye. This particular critic had obviously been put off by Zero's clowning. Well, in response to that article, Hal prepared a letter which he intended to send to Zero. But before he did he gave all of us on the creative staff a chance to read it and offer comments. The letter couldn't have been more diplomatically phrased. It said something to the effect that we recognized Zero's extraordinary abilities and his brilliant talent; we realized that it might be boring for a man with such gifts of invention to do the same thing every night; we expected that there would continue to be such inventions; all we were asking was the right to tell him when we thought any particular invention was inappropriate. Along with the letter, Hal sent a copy of that Kentucky article. Zero hit the ceiling. He cursed all of us. Nobody could tell *him* what to do! He had saved our *!!@#&!! show! Still, for a while he played the show as directed.

Every so often, Joseph Stein said, he could nudge Zero back to a more honest performance by visiting him backstage before the curtain went up and telling him that someone he respected—Isaac Stern, Pablo Picasso—was in the audience. But, of course, this technique could not be overused or Zero would have realized it was precisely that: a technique to make him behave onstage.

During the sequence in which the ghost of Fruma-Sarah appears to Tevye and Golde, Zero refused all entreaties to stop reacting to the ghost so broadly and inappropriately. Maria Karnilova, who played Golde, was especially upset with Mostel's antics during the scene. Robbins, feeling that he had no other alternative, ordered that Zero's spotlight be turned off. Mostel continued to behave as before, but he did so in darkness.

"Regarding his behavior onstage, there are two ways to look at it," Sheldon Harnick said. "The charitable way would be to acknowledge that Zero was endlessly creative and had such a fertile imagination that he tended to become bored doing exactly the same thing at every performance. So he would change business whenever the spirit moved him. And in his defense, I must admit that 95 percent of the audience (perhaps even more) adored whatever he did. The uncharitable way would be to acknowledge that Zero was an extravagantly gifted egomaniac who had to be in the limelight at all times. I didn't object to Zero's 'embroidering'; much of it was delicious. (Zero, after all, was a comedic genius.) What I objected to was the way he would distort the shape and intention of a scene by directing attention to himself when the focus should have been elsewhere." Harnick ruefully recalled overhearing an audience member say at the end of one performance, "That Zero Mostel is marvelous. He's the whole show. It wouldn't be anything without him."

The denunciations of Mostel's performances, especially in *Fiddler on the Roof*, were often based upon his inclusion of seemingly inappropriate material within a tightly structured framework. On the other hand, if the Yiddish theatre was his conscious or subconscious model, those interpolations would not have seemed to be intrusions but conventions firmly grounded in Yiddish theatrical tradition. And where better to incorporate Yiddish theatre techniques than in a play about Jews, created by Jews, and performed (at least early in its run) largely for Jewish audiences?*

Certainly no one could accuse Zero of giving anything less than a total commitment to *Fiddler*. Performing in the production was such a physical ordeal that he once again had to curtail his painting. In fact, for the first several months of the New York run, he stayed in bed all day, not rising until a few hours before he had to go to the theatre at night. He arrived shortly before curtain time, since he did not have to use a false beard—he grew his own—and did not use makeup.

Zero won his third Tony award for *Fiddler*, as best actor in a musical in 1964–65. This meant that he had won a Tony for each of the last

---

*Isaac Bashevis Singer said, "*Fiddler on the Roof* is really a sort of imitation of [the Yiddish theatres on] Second Avenue." And Tevye was first brought to dramatic life in a Yiddish play called *Tevye the Dairyman* in the 1920s. Maurice Schwartz made a film adapted from the play in 1939.

three plays in which he had appeared—a phenomenal achievement. On this occasion, however, the sweetness of triumph was mixed with rue. In all, nine Tonys were given to *Fiddler*: one to the musical as best of the season, two to Jerome Robbins (one for direction, one for choreography) and individual awards to Zero, Maria Karnilova for her Golde, Joseph Stein, Sheldon Harnick, Jerry Bock, Patricia Zipprodt for her costume design. In their acceptance speeches, each of the winners thanked those who had contributed to the show's success, as is customary. What was unusual, however, was that all of them pointedly omitted Zero's name. When Mostel, the last to receive the award, came to the podium, he commented with seeming humor but a clear trace of bitterness, "Since no one else has thanked me, *I* will thank me."

But many of the members of the chorus, seated in the balcony, resented it when Hal Prince (who accepted on behalf of the production) expressed his gratitude to those who had invested money in *Fiddler* and failed to mention the show's leading player. They cheered Zero's comment and applauded throughout as he gave the rest of his speech in Yiddish.

Mostel, along with others connected with the production, was also given the Sholem Aleichem Award by the Israel Histadrut Campaign. Zero won the New York Drama Critics Award and the Outer Circle Award for his performance; the Yiddish Theatrical Alliance honored him as the year's outstanding actor. *Fiddler* cemented his reputation as one of the country's great comic actors. Perhaps the ultimate confirmation of Zero's superstar status came not from the awards and medals and honorary degrees he was given, but when he and Kate, both of whom had been treated as political pariahs for so long, were invited to a reception at the White House in June 1966.

Eventually, *Fiddler on the Roof* became the longest-running show in Broadway history (until its record was broken by *A Chorus Line*). Those who invested in the production received more than ten times their money in return. Obviously, Zero's prediction that *Fiddler* would swiftly close if he were not in the cast was proven wrong.* But it is

*The musical was hugely successful not only in New York but also in professional and amateur productions throughout the world.

also true that every actor who played the role after he did was influenced by his performance to such a degree that theirs were invariably extensions of the one he gave.

The first actor to take over the part was Luther Adler, who played Tevye when Zero took a two-week vacation in January 1965. The simple fact that Adler was a heavy man indicates Mostel's influence on the casting. Sholem Aleichem had described Tevye as gaunt, but the image of Zero became so strong in the mind of the American public that nearly all succeeding Tevyes resembled him physically. If *Fiddler* were to be revived anywhere in the United States today, it would be all but unthinkable to cast an actor who looked like the Tevye of Sholem Aleichem's description. Even in the 1971 film, it is reasonable to conjecture that Topol was cast, at least in part, because of his physical resemblance to Zero.

And Zero's interpretation of Tevye also became the accepted standard. Paul Lipson, Herschel Bernardi, and Robert Merrill were among the actors who played Tevye on Broadway. Each of them brought a certain individuality to the role, but each of them performed within the framework established by Mostel. Theatregoers would probably not have accepted an interpretation that varied too drastically from Zero's.

Luther Adler, like Mostel, was also steeped in Yiddish culture. His father, Jacob P. Adler, had been one of the idols of the New York Yiddish theatre. Luther Adler made no conscious attempt to differentiate his performance from Zero's, knowing that the public would be disappointed if he did. "I hold no great brief for originality in acting when it means that you have to sacrifice the truth," he said, suggesting that Zero had discovered "the truth" about Tevye and that it would be pointless to tamper with his interpretation. In fact, however, the performance Adler gave was dissimilar in one important respect. He emphasized the poignancy of Tevye's character but was unable to bring out the humor. Most of the cast regretted the loss and were happy to see Zero return to the production.

After Mostel had played in *Fiddler* for six months, the physical and emotional strains began to tell. As Zero said, "*Forum* was a strenuous show from the physical standpoint, but it didn't demand much else. The part of Tevye not only calls for a lot of action, but the role requires a big emotional contribution by the actor. The combination is exhausting." As a result, Zero devised a scheme, approved by his physician, that he presented to Harold Prince: he would play Tevye for three months, then be replaced by another actor for the next three months, then return for another three-month period, and so on. To Zero's surprise and irritation, Prince responded that he could not possibly sell tickets on that basis and denied his request.

As Mostel's contract neared its end, Sidney Elliot Cohn, certain that Hal Prince would agree to any terms in order to keep Zero in the production, tried to renegotiate the contract at a much higher salary.* Cohn's certainty seemed to be well founded. Despite the friction Zero had created within the company, *Fiddler* was still known as "the Zero Mostel musical" and many observers believed that the production could not succeed without his presence. Among them were the owners of the Imperial Theatre, who pleaded with Prince to accept whatever terms Zero requested. After several conferences, however, the show's creators "decided to rely on the material," in Hal Prince's words, and to let Zero go.

A party was held onstage following Mostel's last performance on August 14, 1965. Sheldon Harnick said, "Despite our run-ins with him, it was an emotional occasion and I was feeling rather nostalgic. At one point, I went over to him and said, 'Zero, I'm sorry to see you leave.' He answered, 'You mean you're sorry to see the grosses fall.' Then he turned and walked away." Harnick added, "He must have been tremendously disappointed when the grosses *didn't* fall after Luther Adler [once again] took over."

Ironically, many of the actors who had dreaded performing with Zero were unhappy after his departure, because they felt that no one else was able to bring as much excitement and as many dimensions to Tevye—and therefore to the show as a whole. It is undeniable that Mostel was better able to balance the play's comedy and poignancy than any other performer. As the critic Abe Laufe observed, he "could

---

*Cohn also insisted that a chauffeured limousine bring the star to and from the theatre, but this request made perfect sense. After an evening's performance, it was essential that Zero rest his leg as much as possible. Moreover, it is extremely difficult to find a taxi in New York at that time of night—audiences from scores of theatres are all looking for taxis at approximately the same time—and it would not have been reasonable to expect that Mostel would have to return home by bus or subway.

be riotously funny one moment, and then suddenly heartbreaking in the more emotional scenes, as in his refusal to speak to Chava."

Nor did the show's creators regret casting Mostel. "I think we were very lucky to have had him open the show; I was enormously pleased with the work he did at the beginning of the production," said Joseph Stein. Sheldon Harnick felt that "Zero at his best was a superb Tevye. And certainly in the comic aspects of the show his Tevye was incomparable."

James Bronson, *Fiddler's* stage manager, felt that Zero's contributions to the production were far more positive than negative. "I think he had great respect for the material and certainly never abused the orthodox elements," Bronson said. "And he never 'walked through' a performance. In his own way, he was very professional. We had our problems, but I was always able to talk them over with him and try to find what was creating those problems—a sloppy orchestra, an indifferent performance by another actor. . . . I found that his irritation was almost always brought on by the other person on stage, and Zero was very slow to forgive and forget. He knew his craft far too well to tolerate petty unprofessionalism. Zero's performances were always vital and exciting for the audience. He was larger than life on that stage, and perhaps some of the other actors couldn't stand up to that."

* * *

A Funny Thing Happened on the Way to the Forum, which was released in 1966, was Zero's first film (excepting Samuel Beckett's *Zero*, which was not distributed) in fourteen years. His screen comeback was greeted so favorably that Mostel changed the course of his career, appearing far more often in films than on the stage from that time on, and generally receiving star billing. But *Forum* itself, although it made a small profit, was not a successful film. Zero attributed its failure to Richard Lester, the director, whose technique was so relentlessly manic (full of jump cuts, juxtaposition of unrelated images, etc.) that "you think [he's] shooting your toes and [he's] catching your left nostril." But Mostel had been offered his choice of directors, and Richard Lester had been one of the five men on a list of those acceptable to him. Presumably, he had been familiar with Lester's style from the beginning.

Zero believed, as did most observers, that *Forum* was terribly diminished in its film version. "The great thing about the piece on the stage was that it was one set, sixteen characters, three houses, and you did it very simply," he said. "You go to the movie and there's horses, zebras, peacocks shitting all over the place, your father's moustache, orphans, winos, donkeys with hard-ons . . ." Larry Gelbart was even more distressed, calling it a "terrible, terrible production. When they got Phil Silvers to play Lycas they started writing more for him. And you know that piece is like a Rubik's Cube. If you change one thing, that changes another, which changes still another . . . I don't even know what I think of Zero in the movie," he added; "I just know I was so crushed by it that I probably didn't pay much attention to what he was doing."

The producer, Melvin Frank, was at odds with Lester from the beginning. Frank was so upset by the final product that he withheld the film for more than a year after the shooting was completed. Zero's performance, while successful in the main, was limited by the director's frequent use of close-ups, in which Mostel's facial expressions often appeared grotesque. In addition, the close-ups gave little opportunity for Zero to demonstrate his physical grace.

Vincent Canby of the New York *Times* summed up the critical opinion when he wrote, "In transferring from stage to screen the show's low-down, knockabout antics, the movie makers seem to have allowed some of its madly theatrical spirit to escape."

Despite Zero's disappointment in the film, he enjoyed the time he spent in Spain, where *Forum* was shot. Initially, he had been reluctant to visit that country, where Fascist dictator Francisco Franco still ruled. Eventually, though, his desire to see the Prado, Spain's great museum of art, changed his mind. "I figured, why should he [Franco] see all those wonderful paintings and not me?" Once every week, Zero and Jack Gilford (who reprised his role of Hysterium) went to the Prado, where Mostel invariably reverted to his old position as museum guide, explaining each painting in detail to Gilford.

Just as Mostel helped Gilford win his role in the Broadway cast of *Forum*, he was instrumental in getting him into the movie. When Gilford went to Melvin Frank's office to confer with him about the possibility of playing Hysterium, he found Mostel already in the room. Gilford's and Mostel's friendship had been strained ever since they had acted together in the stage version of the musical and Zero had physically abused Gilford. But as soon as Gilford entered the room, Zero began shouting, "Hire him! He knows all the lines! He'll do a good job!" From then on, the two comics resumed their friendship.

Mostel's on-again, off-again relationship with Gilford reveals a good many sides of Zero's personality: his loyalty, his lack of reliability, his helpfulness, his willingness to take unfair advantage of another actor. Perhaps, too, there was an element of competitiveness that should be taken into account, for competitiveness is part of the makeup of most comedians. One comic does not like to be outdone by another and will go to nearly any length to prevent it—not necessarily by attempting to lessen the effect of his partner but by raising his comic sense to new heights. A good example is the film Mostel referred to in his Harvard speech, *The Great Dictator*. That movie, written, directed by, and starring Charlie Chaplin as a Hitler-like dictator, also featured Jack Oakie as a Mussolini clone. Chaplin's script gave some of the best lines and scenes to Oakie, but, during the filming, when Oakie received the more enthusiastic reception from the crew and visitors to the set, Chaplin could barely conceal his aggravation. His competitiveness clearly emerged as he struggled to top each of Oakie's laughs; Oakie did the same; Chaplin became even more determined not to be outshone. The film, a comic masterpiece, clearly benefited from this sense of competition. In a similar way, Mostel seems to have alternated between fondness and competitiveness in his relationship with Gilford.

Gilford recalled Mostel's last day of work on *Forum*. "Zero had just dubbed some of the sound track, and he was about to go home. What he said was very touching. He said, 'Two blacklisted actors, and we finished a movie.' Because in our blacklist experience, very often we would start on a project and not finish. But we beat them. We beat them. We survived."

When Zero returned to New York from Spain, he was eager to plunge back into the New York theatre. Since 1964, he had expressed a desire to form a repertory company in partnership with Burgess Meredith. In February 1966, Mostel, Meredith, and Paddy Chayefsky announced that they would form just such an enterprise, to begin operations the following year. The project seemed to offer the principals a way to satisfy their artistic yearnings without tying them down to a venture that was unlikely to yield much financial reward. Actually, the institution they envisioned had nothing to do with repertory (in which the same actors perform a series of plays in rotation), but it did borrow from the repertory idea a commitment to an ongoing organization that would produce several plays each season. Theirs would not be a permanent company, they explained, because prominent actors might be reluctant to devote an entire season to such a venture; rather, a separate company would be engaged for each of four plays, which would be presented for limited engagements of ten weeks each. Meredith and Mostel would also be free to work in films and television when they chose.

In the first year, the organization would produce two new plays—Chayefsky's *The Latent Heterosexual* (featuring Mostel and Meredith) and Guy Endore's *The Man That Was Shakespeare* (directed by Mostel with himself and Meredith in the cast)—and two revivals—*Ulysses in Nighttown* and *Waiting for Godot*. Mostel hoped to present a musical adaptation of Sean O'Casey's *Juno and the Paycock* in the second year. When asked why he had decided to embark on the project, Zero, then fifty-one, responded, "There's such a lack of imagination on Broadway . . . I want to do good things before I pass on." Chayefsky was motivated principally by the desire to see his plays live beyond the normal Broadway life-span; he felt that a company of the kind he envisioned would keep them in its repertory for as long as five years.

In June 1966, the threesome announced that, under the name "Actor-Manager Productions, Inc." (and with Arthur Cantor and Milton Sperling as producers), *Ulysses in Nighttown* would inaugurate their venture, opening on Broadway on November 1. By then, however, they were no longer committed to additional plays or to anything remotely resembling a repertory company. "We got confused trying to plan everything so far in advance," Meredith explained. "Consequently we came to the conclusion to do *Ulysses* first and then gradually make our future plans."

In August, however, *Ulysses in Nighttown* became unavailable, because James Joyce's estate had agreed to Walter Reade's proposal that a film be made from the original novel, and Reade insisted that the picture would have to be distributed before a Broadway play could be presented. Meredith announced that *Ulysses in Nighttown* would be postponed until the following season and that *The Latent Heterosexual* would be rushed into production instead. A Broadway opening in late December was anticipated. Meredith also let it be known that Arnold Sundgaard's *Forests of the Night* would replace *The Man That Was Shakespeare* and that *The Threepenny Opera* was under consideration for production. So was Molière, although no specific plays were mentioned.

But the project never took flight. Chayefsky said it was because the partners could not find enough new plays to produce. Mostel's version was different. He said, "We couldn't get a one-eyed honest man to head it up." Meredith was perhaps most candid; he told me that the venture collapsed because "we didn't have the stick-to-it-iveness to carry it through. It would have required a lot of hard work. None of us were organizers. If some practical-minded fellow had done it, we'd have gone along with it and lived happily ever after. But I don't think any of us were of the caliber that could raise all the money and do all the business necessary." Subsequently, Meredith did direct Mostel in *The Latent Heterosexual* and, years later, he revived his production of *Ulysses in Nighttown* with Zero as Bloom. But these were produced completely outside the framework of an ongoing organization. The other plays they announced were not produced at all.

As a result, after *Fiddler on the Roof*, Zero was absent from the New York stage for nearly a decade. He spent most of that time making films (a medium he detested), many of them of low quality. The paradoxical question must be asked once again: why did someone who professed such high standards willingly contribute his talents to such trivial projects?

Zero said, "I'll tell you why I haven't been around [i.e., on the stage]. After I did *Rhinoceros* everybody sent me scripts about animals. After . . . *Forum* all I got were plays about slaves. After *Fiddler* I was offered every Yiddish play that had a father of five or ten children." But of course this was nonsense. Zero could have played nearly any character role he chose. Producers would have been only too happy to star a three-time Tony winner in the kinds of plays he professed to love. He did not suffer from a lack of material, as he claimed, only from an inability to focus his attention on a specific project and from a willingness (born of laziness? or of the lure of money?) to lend his talents to unworthy projects.

He might have played Leopold Bloom in the film version of

Ulysses, which would have been a challenging venture, and—in all probability—an artistically rewarding one. (It would have been unlikely to be financially rewarding, as the plan was to show the film in the United States for three days only, except in New York City, where it would have an unlimited run.) As early as 1958, Zero spoke of his desire to play Bloom on film. When Jack Cardiff proposed to make a movie of *Ulysses* in 1962, Toby Cole and Adza Vincent campaigned to win the role for Mostel; Twentieth Century-Fox, the producers, wanted Peter Sellers, but, as it turned out, the entire project was shelved. In 1966, Zero again expressed interest in the role, but his enthusiasm seemed no more than half-hearted, and, in any case, Joseph Strick, the director, preferred the Irish actor Milo O'Shea, who eventually played Bloom in the film.

What happened to Zero's oft-expressed ambition to play Falstaff and Sir Toby Belch, to act in the comedies of Molière and the epic dramas of Brecht (he told Toby Cole that he aspired to play Azdak in *The Caucasian Chalk Circle* and "make Bertolt Brecht a big hit on Broadway"), to play challenging roles in good new plays (in the plays of Pinter, for example, which he said in 1964 he was eager to undertake)? On many occasions in the past, he had said he wanted to play King Lear. "I think I know the secret of it," he remarked in 1962; "and I have the energy for it. I know how to play the exposure of that man, a man who rips the skin off his body. . . . I have a kinship for it."

The point here is not that Mostel should have devoted his career to playing roles such as King Lear. Those characters might well have proven to be beyond his abilities, even though some people, including Burgess Meredith, thought he might have been capable of doing them justice. The point, surely, is that for years Zero was driven by an ambition to do good work, and his ambition, if it did not produce great classical performances, *did* produce his brilliant portrayals of Leopold Bloom, John (in *Rhinoceros*), Pseudolus, and Tevye. But when he should have been in the prime of his career, he all but lost his desire to appear in works of value or works that would stretch him as a performer, settling instead for whatever would pay him the most money and maintain his position as a "star."

He certainly was that. William Goldman in 1969 identified Zero as one of only two performers on Broadway (Gwen Verdon was the other) whose reputation was such that he could guarantee a musical's success simply by appearing in it. Goldman maintained that *The Education of H*Y*M*A*N K*A*P*L*A*N*, which played only twenty-nine performances with Tom Bosley, would have run for two years "if Zero Mostel had been in the title role." *Newsweek* said of him after he opened in *Fiddler*: "Broadway has a new king and divinity, and there are no rivals in sight." After *Fiddler*, Zero also had an unfortunate reputation as an actor whose performances in long-running plays lacked discipline, but that made no difference to producers, who would have been delighted to have him appear in their shows.

8

The Irreducible
Zero

Zero's character changed after he became a world-famous performer. Although his charm never deserted him, his riches and great success made him irascible on occassion. When he was asked by the New York *Times* on Christmas Eve, 1975, what good deeds he had performed lately, Zero responded facetiously, but with an edge of genuine perverseness, "I did half a deed. I helped an old lady half-way across the street at a very busy thoroughfare." Frances Chaney said, "As he got older and he became a big star, he got more opinionated and got to be willful. He would want his own way; he was egotistical. He would get cross and cranky."

Lou Peterson agreed. "He became very difficult to deal with. I think that was part and parcel of the humiliation he had been put through during the blacklist. I think it was indicative of the fact that he was an angry man."

*   *   *

On balance, Zero was liked far more than he was disliked; he amused far more people than he embarrassed; he was regarded as loyal and generous much more often than he was judged to be selfishly undependable. But one who did come to view him as unqualifiedly disloyal and unprincipled was Toby Cole, who felt betrayed when Zero suddenly dropped her as his agent. "It wasn't so much the money I cared about," she told me in 1987, "it was that I felt he had done a very wrong thing and that it would be important for him, morally, as a human being, to correct it." Shortly after Zero's lawyer, Sidney Elliot Cohn, told her that she would no longer have anything to do with Mostel's career, Cole put her case against Zero before the New York Supreme Court, claiming that he owed her thousands of dollars for her work as liaison between him and the producer and creators of *Fiddler on the Roof.* The court's Appellate Division ruled that the matter should be submitted to Actors Equity. Equity scheduled a hearing in 1965, but neither Zero nor his attorney appeared, in defiance of union regulations. Nevertheless, the hearing went forward, and Equity agreed that Cole had been unfairly denied money that was due her; they recommended that Mostel pay her $100,000. They could do no more than recommend, for their decision had no standing in law. On the advice of his attorney, Zero refused to pay. The case was then taken to the American Arbitration Association for a binding decision.

On August 8, 1967, the Arbitration Association met in New York. By that time, Actors Equity had changed its position; it supported Mostel, on the basis that Cole did not have a written contract with him at the time of the *Fiddler* controversy. Three arbitrators heard the case. One—Theodore Bikel—was selected by Mostel, one—Eric Bentley— was chosen by Cole, and the third—Sidney A. Wolff—was hired by the Arbitration Association.

The hearing began by establishing the fact that Cole had served as Mostel's agent from 1957 until 1964, which neither Mostel nor his lawyer disputed. However, Cohn claimed that the relationship had been based upon an oral agreement and Zero was therefore not obligated to Cole in any way. It was true that a written contract existed only for one year (1958–59) and that Cole and Mostel had otherwise operated on the basis of a handshake, technically a violation of Equity rules. Cole insisted that such arrangements were common and that Zero had given her no prior indication that he was about to seek other representation when she was suddenly informed by Sidney Cohn that Mostel no longer required her services. Cole maintained that she had negotiated in good faith on Zero's behalf during preliminary discussions about the casting of *Fiddler on the Roof*; therefore, even though Zero was not actually signed to a contract until after their relationship was severed, she was entitled to receive commissions from his *Fiddler* salary.

Cohn held "that Miss Cole did not obtain this employment for" Mostel and "she was not approached to obtain this employment for him." Cohn further stated that Cole had *never* found employment for Zero; that all of his jobs between 1957 and 1964 had been obtained as a result of his own efforts.

Cole freely admitted that she did not negotiate the *Fiddler* contract, but claimed she had been prevented from doing so by Mostel's decision to drop her. She conceded that Zero was approached directly by the producers of many of the plays in which he appeared, but said, "Important actors always find their own employment. Agents are needed to negotiate terms, etc."

Feeling betrayed by Mostel, with whom she thought she had "a particular kind of closeness," she attempted to convey to the arbitrators the extent of the work she had done for him during the time he had been blacklisted—when other agents refused to represent him—and while he had been recuperating from the operations on his leg. She spoke at length about her role in the "grueling negotiations" concerning Zero's salaries and perquisites in *Rhinoceros* and *Forum*.

The witnesses called to testify at the hearing helped to buttress Mostel's case. Carl Fisher, general manager for Harold Prince, testified that he had negotiated Zero's contract for *Fiddler* with Cohn, not Cole. Zero took the stand and stated that Cole had never obtained a single job for him. He implied, Cole told me, "that except for an occasional telephone call, I was almost a complete stranger."* The decisive testimony was given by the president of the Theatrical Artists Representatives Association, who stated that only written contracts between performers and agents were binding. Cole's lawyer attempted to rebut that assertion, claiming that when written contracts expire, oral contracts remain in force if the parties agree; but he failed to convince the

---

*Theodore Bikel asked Zero whether he had paid commissions to Cole for seven years simply because "you are a nice guy." Mostel answered in the affirmative. Eric Bentley asked, if Zero had decided during the run of *Forum* that he no longer wished to be represented by Cole (as Zero testified), why he had waited nearly two years to tell her so. Zero answered, "It is difficult for me to tell people *finito*."

arbitrators, who, when they met to reach a decision, agreed that Cole had a strong moral case but a weak legal one. Therefore, the tribunal found, by a two-to-one margin, that Cole was not entitled to receive any commissions from *Fiddler on the Roof.*

It is not at all uncommon for actors to change agents as their careers evolve. The arrangement between actor and agent is a business proposition; if either the actor or the agent feels that business could be improved by severing the connection, it is neither unusual nor immoral to do so. It may also be true, as some of Zero's friends have suggested, that Toby Cole, who suited Zero's needs admirably when he was a struggling blacklisted actor in the 1950s, was not the appropriate sort of agent to guide his career after his enormous success of the 1960s. By any standards, however, Mostel's handling of the situation was hurtful and inept. He was wrong to insist that Cole had not been involved in the initial stages of *Fiddler on the Roof,* and he was insensitive at best when he allowed Cohn to inform her of the break in the actor-agent relationship rather than telling her directly.

Zero's thoughtless behavior in this incident was not typical. But one could not call it completely out of character because Zero's character encompassed so many diverse qualities, most of them admirable, some of them disagreeable. It is impossible to generalize accurately about the man, for the different aspects of his personality varied so extraordinarily. As Walter Bernstein said of him, "To most people, he was all contradiction. Vulgar and delicate. Angry and gentle. Self-centered and generous. Even physically: so heavy in repose and so incredibly light-footed when he moved. People chose the extreme they needed. There were certainly enough of them. Perhaps he was too big to grasp whole."

Sol Kaplan recalled an anecdote that, for him, "summed up Zero in the truest sense," perhaps because it includes examples of both Zero's grossness and his sensitivity. Kaplan and Zero were riding in a crowded subway when they noticed an elderly black woman, loaded down with packages, who was forced to stand because no one would offer her a seat. Zero said, "Follow me" to Kaplan, and he began pushing through the crowd, groping awkwardly toward the woman, his eyes unfocused and apparently sightless. In Kaplan's words, "He became a blind man. People made way for him. Then suddenly he kind of lurched over and he almost fell into a man's lap. The man jumped up to give Zero his seat. And then Zero's eyes became very focused for everybody to see. He raised his hat and gave the seat to the elderly black woman."

But neither Mostel's actions nor his character were entirely laudable. Larry Gelbart mentioned that Zero "had an ego as big as he was. And it was inflated even further by the kind of adulation he received. And the end result of that was a very spoiled child saying that he could get away with anything."

Madeline Gilford felt that Zero's problem, after he became successful, was that "he really didn't believe the success. And he was very dependent, as was Kate, on very high-paid fancy people to take care of them. I mean, the amount of salary that he would give to Sidney Cohn and to his agent and to his accountant . . . Kate, especially, believed that a star should live a certain way. They should live in a certain way and they should be treated a certain way. And they were easily seduced, I think, by elegant treatment, like a producer having a car and driver at their disposal for twenty-four hours." Whereas Jack Gilford admired Zero's insistence on being given star treatment ("He wanted a certain amount of money or else he would not work, and he never came down in his price," Gilford said approvingly), Madeline was critical of the same attitude: "They didn't have a good business sense. After he did a certain number of guest spots on TV, the golden goose was dead because Zero wouldn't come down from this enormous salary he demanded. And they also didn't take the responsibility for some of their choices. They wanted Sidney Cohn and others to make their decisions for them, but if things didn't turn out, it was, 'That shmuck!' Oh, how Zero would blame people if something didn't turn out. There never was anything that [Zero and Kate] were culpable about. It was always that this shmuck did them in. If something went sour, nobody was ever smart enough or good enough for them."

Don Richardson felt that the flaws in Zero's character became painfully apparent after he achieved immense success. "During the period that he was blacklisted," Richardson said, "at various times people used to go to his house and bring groceries because the family was starving. Later, when he got famous, these same people tried to call to ask him for a favor or an introduction to somebody, and he refused to ever speak to any of them. He turned them all down. Katie became just as difficult. They both became very, very bad."

Richardson was particularly upset by Zero's treatment of Herbie Kallem, who rented the studio below Zero's in the building Mostel owned on Twenty-eighth Street. Kallem "was a helpmate to Zero," Richardson noted. "I mean, he cleaned his studio, he saw that Zero got food, he got Zero girls. He did everything he could possibly do to keep Zero happy. And Zero never did anything for him. So, after Zero got famous, I went and told Zero he ought to give Herbie a show [an exhibition of Kallem's sculpture] or do something for Herbie—and he just laughed. He never did anything for Herbie at all."

After Zero became recognized as a star, he was determined that no one would be treated better than he, and he spent a good deal of time trying to remedy any perceived inequity. When he was in Spain filming *A Funny Thing Happened on the Way to the Forum*, he was certain that the producers had not given him the best room in the hotel, so he systematically peeked into every other room to be certain it wasn't larger or more luxurious. When he was touring in *Fiddler on the Roof* in the mid-1970s, he believed, erroneously, that the producers were not booking him into the best hotels. As a result, he always instructed his dresser, Howard Rodney, who traveled with Zero and looked after him, to check out other hotels at every stop on the tour. Rodney would always comply, reporting his findings to Zero in detail. But Mostel would always end by saying, "Well, we're not going to move. It's too much trouble."

Mostel and Rodney developed a close relationship. If Zero behaved rudely to others, Rodney never noticed it. "You had to love the man," Rodney said; "he was the most fabulous man to work for. He was so good-natured and sweet. I've never in my life worked with anybody who was as sweet as Zero."

Perhaps Rodney was not aware of any change in Zero's personality or behavior because he did not know him until after Mostel had become famous. However, Joseph Wilder, whose first encounter with Zero occurred before he appeared in *Rhinoceros*, also found it difficult to accept the fact that Mostel had changed, and stressed his loyalty to old friends even after he became successful. "Zero was one of the most loyal men I've ever known in my life," Wilder said. "You went to a party at Zero's—he and Kate would throw at least one really big party a year—and you could almost write out the guest list. They were the same people who stood by Zero for all the years of his life. No matter that Zero went from almost having disappeared in a cloud of black-listing to becoming one of the notables in our culture, one of the most popular actors around, a man who had presidents, mayors, governors in his back pocket; all these people and other great celebrities were very available to Zero; but instead of having these big guns around to show them off, I never met a person at Zero's parties except for that old gang. And I thought that was remarkable. That made him very special to me, and to a lot of other people, because he stuck by his people throughout the good and bad days."

While Wilder was not blind to Zero's faults, he found them insignificant in comparison to his virtues. "I feel that Zero was my closest friend, and Zero, I believe, felt the same way about me. But if you had an ego which needed someone to massage it, to call you frequently, to remember your birthday, to do all the things that some of us want in a very close friendship, you were not going to get that from Zero. In other words, I knew Zero loved me, I knew he was a good friend, I knew he would kill for me; but Zero did not have time for any of the amenities. He was primarily a self-centered man marching through life to his own drum. He was an extraordinary character, and if you wanted to be part of his entourage, then you accepted him, you had to understand that this was a man different from other people. Zero was a real original."

Mostel himself claimed that success never changed him, that he remained the same free spirit he had been in the past. "I don't like to do a lot of things you have to do to become a success as an actor," he said. "I don't go to ladies' clubs. I'm not willing to make a business out of myself. If an actor gets that involved with himself, he's doing photographs in the morning, then the meeting with the publicity man, then his session with his psychoanalyst, then the hot lunch at Sardi's. If you do a lot of that kind of thing as an actor, you get farther, but then you don't have time to paint if you want to go to your studio and paint." Zero gave himself a bit more credit for independence than the facts warranted. He did his share of posing for photographs and meeting with publicists, but it is also true that he always reserved time for himself to paint.

One aspect of his personality that certainly did not change was his extravagance. He always tended to be cavalier with money, even when it was scarce. When he sold a painting during the blacklisting period, he would often treat one of his friends to a lavish dinner. Ngoot Lee remembers Zero's taking him to Luchow's for a dinner that cost "a few hundred dollars." Greater wealth only increased Zero's extravagant tendencies. He often bought expensive works of art to decorate his apartment; he occasionally decided on the spur of the moment to visit a museum in a foreign country for a day so that he could study a particular painting.

Kate did her best to keep Zero's extravagance in check. If he had his way, he would buy every work of art—and every art book—in New York. Consequently, she wanted to control most of the money and parcel it out to Zero when he needed it, a tactic that succeeded on some occasions but failed on others. "Every time I pick up something for a few bucks, a shabby little first edition of Vasari's, I have to smuggle it into the house under my coat, like contraband," he complained.

One way in which Zero did change emphatically was in his attitude toward social causes. Perhaps because he had endured the blacklist as a direct result of his involvement in political matters, he felt that he had "paid his dues" and wanted nothing more to do with social causes. He often made statements such as the one he gave to *Life* in 1964: "I hate all politics: right, left and center. Liberals can be as nutty as anyone else." On another occasion, he said, "I don't believe in any parties— Republican, Democratic, Socialist or Communist." Joseph Stein thought that some of this was camouflage. "I don't think he ever lost his very strong liberal or progressive attitudes," Stein told me. "I think he decided not to actively participate, but I think his heart was always where it had been." Karl Malden agreed: "I don't think Zero could become conservative about anything."

Sheldon Harnick said, "On those occasions when I or someone else tried to enlist Zero's aid for some political cause, he invariably sidestepped, leaving me with the feeling that he was terrified of sticking his neck out again and being penalized economically." Ring Lardner concurred. "It's quite true that Zero got cautious. And part of it was Kate, not wanting him to give his name to causes. His attitude was that he had given his name too freely in the forties, and Kate definitely encouraged that attitude."

When Toby Cole was still functioning as Mostel's agent, she frequently received requests for Zero to make contributions to social organizations. "I'd give him these letters, asking for money to good, worthy causes, and I'd say, 'Do you want to send them some money? I'll send it for you. How much would you like me to send?' He'd say, 'Throw 'em out!' He never, never wanted to have any contribution made to any cause or organization."

Zero's son Josh said, "He didn't talk about politics much at all. I think what Zero learned was that if you express your beliefs, you can get killed."

Although Zero refused to give time or money to political causes, he did demonstrate considerable generosity on a personal level. The actress Marian Seldes remembered an occasion when she and Zero emerged together from a theatre in Philadelphia in 1977. "My daughter Katharine was waiting for me," she said. "Zero had not seen her for many years. She was now a young woman. He stopped and greeted her, flirted with her, reminded her of his friendship with her father—and in less than five minutes completely captivated her. It was a lovely thing for him to do."

Various nephews and nieces who could not otherwise have afforded to live in New York stayed in Zero's huge apartment on Eighty-sixth Street; one of them lived there for five years. Saida Tzerko recalled that when Zero learned an actress who had once had a small role in one of his plays needed surgery, he immediately offered to pay for the operation. Madeline Gilford spoke of Mostel's being "incredibly sensitive and involved" about an incident concerning her son. James Bronson, who stage-managed *Forum* and *Fiddler*, said, "He was an easy touch for anyone who needed financial aid. He hired a stagehand who was totally inadequate, but he had worked with him years before and he was down on his luck." Thelma Lee, who played Golde to Zero's Tevye in the revival of *Fiddler on the Roof* in the 1970s, said, "He made himself aware, as very few stars do, of what was going on in the company. And if anybody needed any help financially or otherwise, he was there." Howard Rodney recalled, "I remember once they let a stagehand go [during the pre-Broadway tour of the *Fiddler* revival] because there were too many stagehands coming into New York. And I went and told Zero, 'Did you know they're letting this man go?' He said, 'Oh, no, they're not.' And he called all the bigwigs in. He said, 'We started with this many men and we're going to finish with this many men.' And the stagehand did not leave."

Rodney himself received many gifts from Zero during the tour. "I've never received gifts like that from any other performer," he said. "Three leather coats, beautiful rings on my birthday. Every night he took me home in a chauffeured limousine. He'd also take the doorman home. Whoever was still in the theatre—the doorman, the porter—Zero would tell them to get in the limousine and he'd take them home." According to Frances Chaney, "He was extremely kind and generous to people whom he had always known and loved. All his artist friends from back in the WPA days. And any struggling artist in that building down on Twenty-eighth Street would have his love and respect and admiration."

Ngoot Lee said, "He was one of the truly good friends. He's one of the few people who, when I traveled in the Far East, sent me letters and asked me how I'm doing and asked if I needed any money. He was just beginning to make money then—he was in *Rhinoceros*. And he really sent me money. That was amazing. When I returned in the fall, he was one of the first people who called up, came to my studio to see if I needed any money, which was one of the beautiful qualities about Zero. I had a lot of rich friends, but he was the only one to come around and ask me, 'Hey, you need any money, kid?' "

Deborah Salt, whose parents were friends of Zero's, tells a particularly affecting story demonstrating his generosity. "I was trying out for the High School of Music and Art, some time in the mid-sixties. Zero took the day off and I went over to his apartment." After telling the fourteen-year-old to spread her sketches and paintings around the room, he proceeded to give her a lengthy, detailed, and honest critique of her work. "I was really nervous about it," she said, "because I had so much respect for him. He spent hours with me. He went over each one, discussed every single drawing and every line. He really went into them in depth." I asked if Mostel's comments had been constructive and helpful. Salt responded, "Oh yes, definitely. He was brilliant. He knew about line, composition, all aspects of art. He was very loving and gentle and kind." When she was accepted into the High School of Music and Art, Zero "was very pleased," she said.

Bettye Ackerman said, "I never saw him do an unkind thing to anybody." Karl Malden noted, "If you were a friend of Zero's, you were always a friend no matter what you did. He was a very loyal man."

But it would be wrong to overemphasize either the generous aspects of Mostel's nature or his defects, for his character is a study in contradictions. The elements that made up Zero's character were so diverse and so often in conflict that some believed he was psychologically unbalanced. Eric Bentley summed him up in three words: "Zero was irrational." In describing her ambivalent feelings toward Zero, Frances Chaney said, "There were enormous variations in his personality—enormous—that I think were beyond his control." Jeff Corey, who worked with him in *Sirocco*, said with some affection that Zero "was not a fully qualified Homo sapiens." Mostel characterized himself this way: "I was analyzed for years of my adult life. I'm perfectly abnormal."

When the tensions in his life became difficult to deal with, Zero could retreat to his hideaway off the coast of Maine. He always claimed that he hated the country—which seemed to him to mean everything outside New York City. The dirt, the bugs, the clean air, the trees, the lack of noise all drove him crazy, he said. "I hate sand, sea, surf, all that *dreck*." Nevertheless, after renting a cottage on Monhegan Island for several summers, the Mostels built a home there in the 1960s. Kate said that Zero didn't really think of Monhegan as "the country" because it was populated by so many fellow artists—among others, Herbie Kallem and Henry Kallem had homes there. While Kate was able to enjoy the scenery and the attractions of country life, Zero's studio, which was inside the house, provided a Twenty-eighth Street environment transported to a different location. He spent at least eight hours every day at work in the studio. During one summer on the island, he completed seventy-eight paintings.

For a man who claimed to hate the country, Zero chose the most rural environment one could imagine. Thirteen miles from Maine, Monhegan's population at the height of the season was 450. There was no electricity on the island (although the Mostels had their own generator), only one telephone (at the general store), and only one car: a Jeep belonging to Jamie Wyeth. The island was so small that one could easily walk it in a day. But the same inconveniences that one might expect to exasperate Mostel also had the advantage of isolating him so thoroughly from the rest of the world that he could concentrate totally on his painting. Zero came to love his retreat on Monhegan Island, so much so that he told one person, "If I didn't have to make a living, I'd never leave."

When it turned cold, however, Zero was always eager to return to Manhattan, with a renewed appreciation for cement, dirt, the subways, the pounding of jackhammers—and the adulation of thousands.

*   *   *

When he was in New York, Zero often behaved compulsively. Exaggerating slightly, he claimed that he drank "about eighty-three cups of coffee a day." Once, while working in his studio, he fainted; the doctor later diagnosed his malady as caffeine poisoning. Zero recognized that he was also compulsive about food. When asked if he ate too many pastrami sandwiches, he replied with characteristic hyperbole, "I guess twelve of anything is bad for you."

Kate scolded him about overeating. "She tells me if I don't stop eating all those pickles and pastrami sandwiches I'm going to have a heart attack," Zero said. But Kate was only intermittently successful in persuading Zero to reduce, for his love of good food was legendary. As Robert Musel put it, "He generates more emotion reading a menu than Sir Laurence Olivier squeezes out of an evening of *Othello*." All the males in the Mostel clan—Zero, Josh, and Toby—were overweight. In 1964, in an attempt to keep Zero and the boys away from the refrigerator and freezer, Kate toyed with the idea of having keys made and wearing them around her neck. But she dropped the idea when she realized the probable consequence: "If they were *really* hungry, I'd be strangled to death." In time, Kate, too, put on considerable weight. Both Zero and Kate kept two wardrobes: one for when they were fat, another for when they were on diets.

Zero particularly liked traditional Jewish food, although the amount he consumed often resulted in indigestion and other unfortunate aftereffects. Still, when it was on the table before him he would invariably say, "What the hell, I'll eat it anyway."

Al Capp wrote about the impromptu performances Zero used to give in the 1940s when they gathered at the Carnegie Delicatessen each night after his nightclub performance. "It has taken an awful lot of

Carnegie's chopped liver and Greek salad to get Mostel in the shape he has now," Capp said, "and he used to get into shape every night at the Carnegie. What made this nightly training period an unforgettable spectacle was the way he gave the waiter his order.

"When he wanted chopped liver, he would imitate a chicken having his liver chopped; for a Greek salad, he imitated the entire cast of the salad—an anchovy, a head of lettuce, a bit of cheese, a herring and a couple of olives, getting together and greeting each other in Greek dialect."

One of Zero's favorite hangouts was Russ & Daughter's appetizer store on Houston Street. He and his friend Dr. Norman Pleshette made regular pilgrimages to Russ & Daughter's, where Zero ordered immense sandwiches of Nova Scotia salmon, sturgeon, sliced onion, and cream cheese with vegetables. And he introduced Calvin Trillin to the Parkway Restaurant on Allen Street, where schmaltz (chicken fat) was set out on every table for those customers who felt the need to add an extra touch of goodness to their meals.

The Sixth Avenue Delicatessen named a sandwich after him. The "Zero Mostel" consisted of chopped chicken liver, corned beef, tongue, and cole slaw.

Zero's excessive consumption of food and drink was part of a larger pattern. As Josh Mostel said, Zero, who thought of himself as a student of philosophy, counseled moderation in all things. "But you didn't see it [in his behavior] much."

Ngoot Lee was a gourmet Chinese cook. Zero often went to Lee's studio in the mornings to draw and paint alongside his friend, but one suspects that he was primarily interested in the lunch he knew would be coming. "I fed him for many years," said Lee. "One time he ate so much, somebody called him and he couldn't walk from the chair to the telephone. I had to tell them to call later. He couldn't move."*

Norman Pleshette felt that Zero's inability to moderate his eating habits was compulsive and debilitating. "He was a tremendous eater,

---

*One of Mostel's projects was to teach Yiddish to the Chinese-born Lee. But the brand of Yiddish Zero taught was peculiar indeed. Speed Vogel, an artist and writer who lived in one of the studios in Mostel's building on Twenty-eighth Street, said it took "careful deprogramming and two years of instruction" to "explain that the four-letter words our good friend Ngoot learned from Zero were not Yiddish."

and he had absolutely no control," Pleshette said. "Food had a lot to do with his life, no question about it." On the other hand, Joseph Wilder said, "I didn't think Zero ate too much. I always felt, as a doctor, that Zero was just that kind of fella. He was big, of course, but his fat became him. It was part of his whole being. And I always felt that physiologically this was the way he was put together and that any other shape would have been false."

Ngoot Lee told a story revealing Mostel's surprising sensitivity concerning his physical appearance. "One hot summer day I went sneaking up to Zero's studio to see what he was doing. I found him without a tee-shirt or anything—I could see all his fat hanging out there. He grabbed his shirt, covered his chest. I laughed, but he still felt embarrassed. Even after I knew him for so many years, he felt embarrassed."

This wasn't the only occasion on which Zero displayed sensitivity about his weight. Bettye Ackerman observed that he disliked seeing himself in films because he was ashamed of his corpulence. "I looked like a beached whale," he said when he saw himself in *The Producers*.

Although Mostel's "signature" was that of a fat man who moved with balletic grace, he made several efforts to reduce. From July until November 1962, while he was playing in *A Funny Thing Happened on the Way to the Forum* on Broadway, he lost sixty pounds. Dissatisfied with his progress, however, he would occasionally go for an entire day without eating. Throughout his adult life, Zero alternated between periods of drastic dieting and periods when he gained weight with equal rapidity. A compulsive man, he found it impossible to be moderate on stage or off.

* * *

Friends of the Mostels agreed that "it was probably very difficult to be a child of his because Zero could be so childish," as one of them put it. Another said, "Zero had great difficulty relating to his boys." And a third pointed out that, "it's difficult to be children of such dynamic people." Zero, who disliked authority in any form, generally refused to assume a disciplinary role with his sons—although he would occasionally assert his parental authority with a vengeance. Perhaps as a result, the Mostels' sons were widely regarded as spoiled when they were children. Some described them as holy terrors. As one of the

Mostels' friends told me, "They moved into a house in Los Angeles [in the early 1950s]. The kids were riding up and down the hallways on their bicycles. They wrecked that place. The walls in their bedroom were all chalked with different colors. Zero was permissive and Kate was sometimes permissive and sometimes a disciplinarian. The problem was that there was no consistent strain."

Zero saw—or pretended to see—the havoc the boys wrought in the Los Angeles house as funny and made no objection. He claimed that there was nothing wrong with his sons' upbringing, that he had set a good example for them, "exposing [them] to things, to museums, to concerts, to good books, and music. To hard-working people with ideas." All of that was true, but his failures as a father were monumental.

Josh Mostel attributed a great deal of the difficulty to the fact that Zero "was different in the family. He was much grouchier and less apt to show off. In the family he had his high moments, too, which were a lot of fun, but there was a sort of punishing and crabby and hysterical side that I found a tremendous pain in the ass sometimes."

Josh loved to be with his father when he was a small boy, he said,

because he was very childlike, Zero: playful, fun. I enjoyed going down to his studio with him, taking walks with him, doing things with him. He was very playful. When I was growing up, when I was a kid, I kind of feared my mother because she was always the disciplinarian. And Zero would always play a game: "Oh my God, let's watch out, it's Kate," you know. "Let's go hide." And we'd run from the authority figure. Then, when I got to be around high school or college age, I became much closer to my mother. . . . I got to appreciate my mother more. I could somehow rationally talk to my mother, but not my father.

He could also be very insulting sometimes. He was very competitive with me. He was very un-nurturing. He was very egotistical and concerned about himself, not about me. He was very humiliating and punishing. Whenever he introduced me he'd always grab my face and twist it around and cause me tremendous pain. There was a lot of resentment about my father. He tended to be very puppyish with people and get all excited and "acty," like a little puppy dog. Or funny and charming and the center of attention and excessive—whenever he saw strangers. And I kind of felt that I got dropped.

He also could fly off the handle. I once made eggs and put the omelet pan in the sink. He yelled, "YOU HAVE TO WASH IT RIGHT AFTER YOU MAKE THE EGGS!" You know, it's like I can't eat the eggs and *then* wash the omelet pan? He was hysterical, that's really the word for it. He'd kind of lose control for a few seconds. That would drive you crazy.

On the one hand, Zero often confided to Sam Jaffe that he was troubled by his relationship with his sons. On the other, he took genuine pride in their accomplishments, but found it difficult to tell them so directly, tending to be critical and undiplomatic when he appraised their work.

He did make some efforts to be supportive. For example, he flew to Washington when Josh was appearing in a production there. He also sent a telegram to his son, saying, "If you're going to follow in my footsteps, use Desenex." Furthermore, he boasted about Josh's success to his friends.

Still, it seemed to Josh that Zero always denigrated his ambition to be an actor. On one occasion, Josh received a negative review from John Simon. When Zero saw the review, rather than commiserate with his son, he used Simon's notice as a weapon to establish his own superiority, saying, "He's always loved *me*. He's always written wonderful things about *me*."

Josh summed up his conflicting feelings about his father: "You know, Zero was a lot of fun, and very intelligent and very funny. [Life with him] had its ups and downs. It was never constant. It was not boring. He was a ravenous person for everything. For life, for food, for drink, for attention, for laughs, money, anything. Zero wanted it all."

9

"Upward
and Downward"

From 1966 through 1975, Zero's career was marked by a fair amount of activity but little enthusiasm and little artistic progress. After *Fiddler on the Roof* and the film of *A Funny Thing Happened on the Way to the Forum*, he seemed to lose interest in acting except as a way to make money, and to ignore the value of the material in which he was performing. The results were uneven: the few successes were far outweighed by dismal films and television productions, and his Broadway career stalled almost entirely; only once during the decade did he participate in a Broadway production.

Many artists—and particularly those with personalities as frenetic as Mostel's—go through periods of a decline in their commitment to artistic excellence. Such periods can serve as a prelude to a rededication, and, indeed, the years immediately following 1975 demonstrated that the fires of artistic ambition within Zero began to stir once again. Nevertheless, one cannot ignore the mediocrity that characterized most of his output for a decade.

Great Catherine (filmed in the winter of 1966–67, not released in America until 1969) was the first film Zero made after reestablishing his movie career with *A Funny Thing Happened on the Way to the Forum*. An adaptation of Bernard Shaw's slapstick comedy, *Great Catherine*

259

gave Mostel the opportunity to play Patiomkin, chief counselor to the Russian queen, a character who is described by Shaw as "gigantic in stature and build, his face marred by the loss of one eye and a marked squint in the other . . . a violent, brutal barbarian, an upstart despot of the most intolerable and dangerous type, ugly, lazy and disgusting in his personal habits."

When the play was first produced in 1913, Shaw defied the actor who played Patiomkin to overplay the role, suggesting that it could not be done. Zero himself said that the problem was not that the actor might get out of control, but "to control Shaw." He needn't have worried. His raging, belching, cackling, leering, snorting, and bellowing extracted every ounce of grossness from the character; his performance was so unabashedly—and deliciously—vulgar that even viewers who prefer more subtle humor would be hard-pressed not to laugh. Mostel easily dominated every scene he was in, nearly obliterating the other actors from the screen.

But the scenes Zero was not in had little vitality. The end result was a moderately amusing piece. When the film was shown in New York, Howard Thompson said in the New York *Times* that "the glorious hamming of the portly American makes the picture. Surely Mr. Mostel's antics would have won the playwright's approval." However, Thompson added, "Mostel, who all but pulls down the palace with his bare hands . . . comes on so strong in the opening 20 minutes, and explodes thereafter with such wild, slapstick abandon that the rest of the picture pales and teeters uncertainly."

Thompson's notice was one of the most enthusiastic. Joseph Gelmis, writing in *Newsday*, called the film "noisy rather than funny," and lamented that Mostel, "one of the great comics of stage and screen . . . is squandering his abilities in a film such as *Great Catherine*." *Cue*, although approving "some wild clowning by the overpowering Mr. Mostel," said "the film falls on its face." The initial reviews were so tepid that the film was withheld from general distribution; in failing to win release, it served as a portent for most of the other films Zero made during the next decade. *Great Catherine* can now occasionally be seen on late-night television.

Peter O'Toole, whose production company sponsored the film, co-starred with Mostel and Jeanne Moreau.* O'Toole must have enjoyed the experience of working with Zero, for the two of them became interested in performing *Staircase* together on Broadway. The two-character play, about a pair of homosexual barbers, had already achieved success in London when Bill Freedman and Charles Kasher, the producers, announced in March 1967 that O'Toole and Mostel would appear the following season in New York. The announcement was another omen of the future, for, as on several other occasions when Zero planned to return to the stage after *Fiddler on the Roof*, he did not participate in the eventual production. In this case, according to Bill Freedman, "when it was found out that Peter O'Toole was not available, Zero decided not to do the show."

Coincidentally, the actors who did appear in *Staircase* on Broadway were Milo O'Shea, who played Bloom in the film of *Ulysses*, and Eli Wallach, Zero's co-star in *Rhinoceros*. Wallach later said, "I would have loved to have done [*Staircase*] with Zero." But he believed that acting in a two-character play with Mostel might have strained his vocal mechanism, just as he had chronically lost his voice when sharing the stage with Zero for two scenes in *Rhinoceros*.

Several months before *Great Catherine* began filming, Zero had become amused by the name of Emile Gaboriau's fictional detective, Monsieur Lecoq. Gaboriau has often been called "the father of the detective novel" and his detective has been described as the direct forerunner of Sherlock Holmes. But it was just Lecoq's name, rather than the adventures in which Gaboriau placed him, that intrigued Mostel. He proposed to producer Carl Foreman, whose Highroad Productions was associated with Columbia Pictures, that a film entitled *Monsieur Lecoq* be made with Zero as the title character. Furthermore, Zero said, he would like to collaborate on the screenplay with an experienced film writer. Foreman and Mostel decided to ask Zero's old friend Ian Hunter (whose credits include *Roman Holiday*, among other films) to work on the project. Hunter later recalled, "I was delighted to be working with

---

*In one scene, Zero had to carry O'Toole down a staircase, which proved to be too much of a strain on his left leg. The graft opened, and six weeks of bed rest were required to permit it to heal.

Zero and writing a comedy. The first thing we did was to look through the Gaboriau books. But that Monsieur Lecoq didn't seem to agree with anything Zero had in mind. So we just developed this wild, funny story."

The writers evolved an unusual working arrangement. Mostel and Hunter, who were living in the same building on West Eighty-sixth Street, met at Hunter's apartment at about ten o'clock each morning. "We would talk out a scene or a sequence," Hunter recalled;

> and then Zee would unfold his New York *Times*, and sit down at the poker table and do the crossword puzzle, and I would sit down at the typewriter. By the time Zee finished reading the paper, I'd have a rough of the scene we had developed together. And then Zee would do something quite remarkable. Any dramatist can benefit from a cast of actors putting his draft "on its feet"; that is, acting it out script in hand. Zero did just that. He would play all the parts, ad-libbing creative bits of business, pausing occasionally to throw in new ideas. And then I would man the typewriter again and incorporate into the scenario Zero's contributions, and that would be the scene. Then we'd go out to lunch.

Hunter emphasized that the work they did together was a genuine partnership. When I remarked that it sounded as if he had really done the writing of the screenplay, Hunter responded, "Well, I certainly did all the typing. But the writing was done when we talked out the scenes—and Zee was an equal if not dominant partner in that."

Hunter later joined Zero in London, where *Great Catherine* was shooting, to polish the script. The writer felt that the screenplay was very funny, but that some of the scenes might prove technically impossible to shoot. "I figured, what the hell, I didn't want to inhibit this crazy talent of Zero's, and I assumed that the producer and director would eliminate a few of the wilder, more impractical scenes." But, said Hunter, "Foreman went off to California, and the director was in the grip of the booze. He had a few conferences with me and Zero, went over the script in a quick and blurry way, and then went off to France to shoot it. I then lost touch until Zero came back [to New York], and what Zee told me was that the director had been so deep in the flagon that he had been falling asleep on the set. To Zero the ultimate indignity was when the director fell asleep during a take. A few scenes got shot, but finally the whole [film] collapsed because—to put it bluntly—the director was too drunk to shoot. I think there was some plan to resume, but that never happened."

Only some still photographs from *Monsieur Lecoq* survive. Published in *Playboy* in 1974, they showed Zero cavorting in a bathtub with several of the actresses in the film.

Mostel's next endeavor was a television special for ABC that was broadcast in May 1967. He appeared as many characters in a variety of sketches, sang "Sunrise, Sunset" from *Fiddler on the Roof*, and joined a chorus of fat, tuxedo-clad dancers in a satiric rendition of "Top Hat." Acknowledging what had by then become increasingly obvious, Jack Gould said of Zero's performance, "The home screen may not be his ideal metier. In the tight close-up of the camera, his pantomime and broad slapstick seemed disappointingly overdone." Harriet Van Horne, writing in the New York *World Journal Tribune*, was even more emphatic: "To viewers who admire subtlety in style, skillful shadings and cerebral humor, [the telecast] must have been—save for a few high moments—a thundering bore.

"There's no denying that Mr. Mostel is a man of huge vitality and precise—if circumscribed—comic gifts. But his manner is curiously hostile, so hostile that we are loathe to surrender our laughter. He punches at life too hard. Every stroke is a wild blob, every sound a hoarse scream.

"In television this technique is particularly unfortunate. We are not, after all, watching from the last row in Yankee Stadium. If we were, that Gargantuan manner would be ideal."

Mel Brooks's film *The Producers* offered Zero a role tailored to his oversized screen personality. The script, written by Brooks, concerned a young bookkeeper (Gene Wilder) who persuades Broadway producer Max Bialystock (Mostel) to join him in mounting the worst play in the history of the theatre, *Springtime for Hitler*, in the certainty that the production will close in a single night. Their scheme is to overfinance the play by several thousand percent, then pocket the excess investments after the closing. To insure the production's failure, they hire a transvestite director with an unblemished record of failure, and engage the rankest amateurs as performers. But, to the producers' consternation, audiences mistake *Springtime for Hitler* for a camp comedy and turn it into a runaway hit. Bialystock and the bookkeeper are caught and sent to jail—where, of course, they attempt to produce an overfinanced prison musical.

The picture called for two outstanding comedians. Brooks wrote Bialystock with Zero in mind, but had trouble persuading him to accept the role. "He didn't want to do *The Producers*," Brooks recalled.

> I gave him the script. He read it and said "No." I said, "Read it again," and he said, "No, I don't want to read it again." I said, "Read it again." He said, "All right." So he told me he read it again, and he said, "I liked it a little better but the answer is still no. I just don't want to do it." I said, "Why?" He said, "I'm not crazy about the character, I don't know if it holds together."

Brooks played his trump card.

> "Okay," I said, "one last favor and then I'll leave you alone on this. Give it to Kate, let her read it, that's all, just make sure Kate reads it. And I want Kate to call me." He said, "I don't know if I can do that," and I said, "You have to do that. This is very important. I've spent two years writing this thing and I had you in mind all the time. I bought your paintings when nobody else would, so you owe me this." So he said, "All right," and he gave it to Kate. Kate read it, she called me, she said, "It's marvelous, it's sensational, I'm gonna work on Zero until he does it." And she worked on him. He called me a week later and he said, "You son of a bitch, I'm gonna do it. My wife talked me into it."

Brooks offered the role of the accountant to Gene Wilder, whose only prior film experience had been a small role in *Bonnie and Clyde*. When Wilder was appearing on Broadway in *Luv*, Brooks visited him backstage with the movie's producer, Sidney Glazier, saying, "The only thing is, Gene, Zero doesn't know you at all. I'm sorry to put you through this, but you're going to have to do a reading for him."

Wilder, who had believed that no audition would be necessary, was intensely nervous about meeting and reading with Mostel. "My heart was pounding as I walked to Sidney Glazier's office," he said. "I went up the elevator and my heart was pounding harder. I knock at the door. There's Mel and Sidney and Zero. Zero gets up and walks toward me and I'm thinking, 'Oh God, why do I have to go through this again? I hate auditions, I *hate* them.' Zero reached out his hand as if to shake hands and then put it around my waist and pulled me up to him and kissed me on the lips. He gave me a big kiss on the lips. And all my fear dissolved. We sat down and read a scene from the script." Half an hour after Wilder left the audition, Brooks called him to say that Zero was pleased with his reading and that the job was his.

Wilder felt that Mostel took him under his wing from the beginning, for which he was enormously grateful. Before shooting began, a press luncheon was held in May 1967. At a long table, each person was assigned a seat designated by a place card. At the center were cards for Zero, Brooks, Glazier, Dick Shawn, and one or two of the other well-known performers. Wilder's designated seat was far from the center, indicating his relative lack of importance. Zero took charge. He rearranged the place cards so that Wilder would be sitting next to him. During the press conference, whenever Zero sensed that Wilder was nervous, he put a protective arm around the young actor's shoulders.

During the filming, the relationship between Mostel and Wilder grew closer. "You may have heard stories about how bombastic, aggressive, and dictatorial Zero might be," Wilder said. "It didn't happen with me. He always took care of me. I loved him. He looked after me as if I were a baby sparrow."

Wilder found Zero "a very generous actor," often subduing his own performance so that Wilder became the focal character in a given scene. Yet, he conceded, "Zero could also be selfish. If he had an *idée fixe*, he'd moan and groan," insisting that things be done his way. Mel Brooks added that Mostel took a dislike to one of the actors in the film and "was not at all nice to him. He barked at him a lot, chased him away."

Brooks shared many personality traits with Mostel. Both had manic tendencies; both constantly needed to be at center stage; both were intensely competitive. Brooks and Mostel were not strangers—Brooks had written material for Zero in *Once Over Lightly* and had done a version of the script for the television series that Mostel rejected in favor of playing *Fiddler on the Roof*; they had seen one another socially, and Brooks was enthusiastic about Zero's painting—but Zero had never worked *for* Brooks, and many expected the combination to be explosive.

Those who worked on *The Producers* offered widely differing accounts of the Brooks-Mostel relationship—a microcosm, perhaps, of the dissimilar ways in which people tended to view Zero as an individual.

According to Ralph Rosenblum, the film's editor, Mostel and Brooks began sniping at one another soon after shooting began. Brooks was especially insecure, Rosenblum felt, because the film was his first directorial venture. Since much of his previous experience had been on live television, he was accustomed to working at a much faster pace than can be achieved when making a movie; as a result, he became progressively more impatient with the film's slow progress, and took out his frustration on the cast and crew. Brooks "soon found himself in a head-on conflict with the mountainous Mostel," Rosenblum said. "The first time Zero couldn't perform with just the inflection Mel wanted, Mel saw the entire project slipping from his grasp. After several faulty takes, he started to shout, '*Goddamn it*, why can't you . . .' but Mostel turned his head like a roving artillery gun and barked, 'One more tone like that and I'm leaving.'

"By the end of the first week, Brooks and Mostel headed two enemy camps. On one side was the enormous booming actor with a presence, a range, and an inclination to go overboard with semicomic ad-lib insult that could wither an innocent recipient to his ankles. On the other, a short, sinewy, panther-eyed director whose operating temperature was each day rising closer and closer to the flash point. 'Is that fat pig ready yet?' Mel would sputter. 'The director?' said Zero. 'What director? There's a director here? *That's* a director?' "

Although Rosenblum was aware of the most intense conflict between Brooks and Mostel, Gene Wilder saw things from a wholly different perspective. In general, he said, "I didn't see friction." The exception was when Zero would "get these directorial notions about how the picture should be done." Zero would suggest, "Why don't you shoot it like this?" Brooks would reply, "I got this planned out. It's going to be better like *this*." And Zero would mumble, "Cocksucker! What the hell does he know about how to shoot." But, said Wilder, "there was never any animosity about it later. Zero would drop it right away. When it was over, it was over."

Brooks himself felt that his relationship with Mostel was productive. "Every once in a while we would have a fight," he said, "but it [the working relationship] was pretty damn good. I would remind him that even though he was bigger physically than I was and he had a bigger name and that he was a star, I would use the words of the director in the picture and say, 'You are ze actor, I am ze director, I outrank you,' and I would let him know in no uncertain terms."

Brooks continued,

> Every once in a while Zero would say, "My leg hurts and I want to go home early." I was making a movie for roughly $900,000, a full-length movie, and I *couldn't* let him go home early. The whole movie revolved around Zero's character. If there was any animosity, number one, it came out of the fact he always wanted to go home early and, number two, that he had his concept of the scene and how the scene should go and I had mine. I'd say that about 75 percent of the time we felt exactly the same way about the scene, but every once in a while he had a different, let's say a different dynamic, and every once in a while he was absolutely right. He would say, "Let me show it to you," and I would say, "You're right. Do it that way." And every once in a while I'd say, "No, Zero, you don't understand, because if you do that, that color is orange, and then you're going to be orange in the next scene, and orange in the next scene. I know where the tiles in this mosaic go. You're getting lost in each tile, but there is a mosaic and the tiles have to fit in. [If you do it your way] it's going to be too bright, too florid, a little too zany and crazy, and I want different textures out of you." That made sense to him because he was a painter.

Eventually, Brooks maintained, Zero came to accept his authority willingly. "When he'd see that the measure of my direction was not always to the loud and to the brighter colors, he saw me dealing with more muted colors, he figured maybe there was some other side to my intelligence and my nature."

Mostel also gained respect for Brooks one day when Zero discovered that the woman who was responsible for the film's titles was the grandniece of Ivan Bunin, the Russian writer. When Zero began to quote from Bunin, Brooks added, "You mean the fellow who wrote 'The Gentleman from San Francisco.'" Zero was "flabbergasted that I knew this obscure writer," Brooks said. "He realized that I was very well read and maybe as intellectual as he was, which amazed him."

Gene Wilder and Zero would frequently have dinner together and speak, often quietly and reflectively, about various subjects, including painting and—a topic Wilder was eager to explore—Zero's blacklisting experience. When they spoke about the day's work on *The Producers*, however, Zero would become agitated, revealing the irritation that

Wilder said he managed to conceal on the set. Zero would complain about whoever had annoyed him that day, shouting, "The son of a bitch doesn't know his ass from his elbow!" According to Wilder, "He might say it about Mel, or about the prop man or the cinematographer, or about me. But, although sometimes he meant it seriously, it wasn't a deeply felt thing."

The Producers has achieved the status of a cult film with some moviegoers. Others agree with Renata Adler's New York *Times* review, in which she called it "a violently mixed bag. Some of it is shoddy and gross and cruel," Adler wrote; "the rest is funny in an entirely unexpected way. . . . *The Producers* leaves one alternately picking up one's coat to leave and sitting back to laugh."

Zero's performance, too, is considered a comic masterpiece by some, a grotesque bit of overacting by others. Steve Allen enjoyed Zero's "strange, high energy, highly funny, powerhouse kind of vibratory level." Mel Brooks was delighted with the portayal, calling it "wonderful, a miracle of a performance. He was the Max Bialystock I wrote." Renata Adler, on the other hand, said that Mostel was "generally . . . as gross and unfunny as only an enormous comedian bearing down too hard on some frail, tasteless routines can be."

Adler's description of Zero's difficulties in projecting the same qualities on film that he did on the stage is a well-reasoned analysis:

> For some actors, used to working very warmly and creatively with theatre audiences, something goes quite wrong in movies. For them, the response of a live theatre audience is both warming and limiting; it defines a performance. Acting before a camera, on the other hand, is projecting into infinity. No soundings can be taken. There is no baffle. Zero Mostel seems to be that kind of performer. He swims through the celluloid like a great bat or fish without his sonar. The camera seems to affect him as the telephone affects men who do not believe in it. He roars and overdoes.

Even Mostel's friend Burgess Meredith observed, "I've never seen a person who transferred less well to the screen. He was good, but something was lost. The full impact of his personality somehow got filtered out by the film process."

Zero was not unaware of his problem. He confided to Martin Ritt, who directed him in his final picture, *The Front*, in 1976, that he was uncomfortable with the scale of most of his film performances. But he did not feel that he was entirely responsible, often blaming his failure to master the medium on his directors. "They don't know what to do with me," he once said, maintaining that movie directors can only "shoot guys who don't know how to move or walk. They [use] lots of closeups. They've got to back off a little. . . . My whole [body] does it, not just the eyes."

In films, which generally called upon Mostel to play realistic roles and invariably limited the use of his fertile imagination, he was confined, fettered, rendered creatively impotent. Few of his films showed him at his best, in part because the medium itself was inhospitable to his outsize talents, but also because most of the roles in which he performed did not allow him the scope to demonstrate the full range of his creativity.

Ironically, perhaps, Gene Wilder's performance in *The Producers*—which Zero so gently nurtured—is all but universally regarded as more satisfactory than Mostel's. The characteristic underplaying (interrupted by moments of fierce explosiveness) for which Wilder later became noted was not yet familiar to film audiences and was particularly effective in this otherwise manic, frequently uncontrolled picture.

* * *

In 1968, Zero returned to the stage in *The Latent Heterosexual*, Paddy Chayefsky's serious comedy originally intended to be one of the first projects of the aborted Mostel-Meredith-Chayefsky repertory company. Several commercial managements had wanted to produce the play after the venture collapsed, but Chayefsky held out for a repertory production. When the APA Repertory Company—the only organization in New York then devoted to repertory theatre—agreed to include his play in its 1968–69 season, Chayefsky was jubilant. Convinced that a pre–New York tour would help him to sharpen it, he suggested to Mostel and Meredith, who still wished to participate in the production, that they try the play out at Paul Baker's Dallas Theatre Center and then take it to various cities around the country. Beyond giving Chayefsky the opportunity to rewrite, the idea was to insulate the play from the intense pressures of the New York theatre by removing it to such a distance that the country's most influential critics would not have a chance to evaluate it until after its defects had been eliminated.

Mostel was set to play the leading role, as originally planned, but Meredith, who had earlier been scheduled to costar with Zero, instead served as director. Jules Munshin took over the role Meredith was to have played.

The Latent Heterosexual, a sardonic comedy, concerns John Morley, an extravagantly effeminate poet who, after twenty-five years of failure, writes a best-selling book: a steamy saga of homosexual life in Tangier. Because he has never paid any taxes, the government attaches Morley's royalties, his advance on paperback rights, and the money from a movie sale. Morley consults an accounting firm and is advised to avoid taxation by establishing a corporation and also by marrying one of the accountant's clients, an expensive call girl (so that Morley will be eligible for a second deduction). The poet takes the advice and unexpectedly falls in love with his wife, after which all traces of his effeminacy disappear. He learns that he is not a homosexual after all, but that his fear of impotence had driven him to assume homosexuality as a pose. He veers sharply in the opposite direction, behaving in stereotypically "masculine" fashion: treating people brusquely, wearing a ten-gallon hat, smoking a cigar.

Morley's corporation gradually brings him incredible wealth, but, as he becomes more and more concerned with making money, his human qualities begin to disappear. He is unable to take pleasure in becoming a corporate robot (a state his financial advisers have already achieved), however, because of his poetic sensibility. The comic nature of the play turns deeply pathetic as Morley recognizes his loss of humanity and tries, without success, to reverse it. As the play nears its end, Morley is a total invalid, no longer able to function physically or mentally. At the conclusion, gathering all his remaining strength, he commits suicide by plunging a pair of pruning shears into his stomach.

The role of Morley was written specifically for Zero. It gave him the opportunity, in the early scenes, to do the effeminate turn he enjoyed indulging in for the entertainment of friends and family. According to Josh Mostel, "Whenever Zero was with a homosexual, he'd dance and he'd giggle, he'd become one of the girls, flounce around and become all wiggly." Gay men would not be offended by Zero's parody, Josh claimed, because it was so clearly intended to be outrageous.

Another way in which the role of John Morley was tailored to Zero is that the most severe physical demands upon the actor are confined to the early scenes. Beginning in the fourth scene, approximately half-way through the play, Morley begins to limp, walking with the help of a cane. Afterward, he is generally seated or lying down. Thus, a role that might have been difficult for Zero because of his bad leg contained a number of devices to make it less physically demanding.

During a rehearsal for *The Latent Heterosexual*, Burgess Meredith, who must have thought that Zero could no longer surprise him, was astounded when, in the midst of a soliloquy, Mostel decided, in Meredith's words, that "the stage was getting too small for his emerging emotions . . . he crossed the proscenium line and began to rampage the aisles. Then, still roaring Paddy's lines, he disappeared through a far exit. We could hear him perfectly as he prowled the basement below. The other actors, bewildered, shouted their lines to the floor. And then, like a Minotaur from the labyrinth below, exactly on cue, he erupted from the wings back onto the stage as the curtain fell."

Paddy Chayefsky's plan—to work on the play before the glare of publicity was focused upon it—was destroyed when the New York *Times* began to track the production's progress. Clive Barnes, the *Times*'s drama critic, went to Dallas in March 1968 to view the work, despite Chayefsky's best efforts to prevent him from doing so. The producers, who knew that neither the play nor the production was ready for critical evaluation, called Barnes twice, pleading with him not to go to Dallas—to no avail. Barnes made the trip, saw *The Latent Heterosexual*, and subsequently wrote a review. He was ecstatic about Zero's performance, beginning his notice, "If Zero Mostel is not America's greatest actor I would be extraordinarily interested to know who is. Last night . . . he gave a performance . . . that was so rich, deep, comic and pitiable that he . . . seemed to be revealing a comic truth so gigantic that you almost wanted to cry at the sheer, damned honesty of it." But Barnes was far less impressed by the play, which he called "more interesting than totally successful."

Julius Novick followed up with an article for the Sunday *Times*, in which he offered several critical judgments: "Chayefsky has attempted that trickiest of all genres, serious low comedy, but he has actually written only a succession of unimaginative routines and set-pieces. Analogously, Mostel performs a series of bits that never coalesce into a character. These difficulties are compounded by Meredith's disjointed production."

Reviewers from *Life*, the *Christian Science Monitor*, and *Time*, among other publications, followed Barnes and Novick to Dallas. *Newsweek*'s critic thought the play was "not bad"—the kind of praise so faint that it is likely to drive prospective theatregoers away. The reviewer was enthusiastic about Zero's performance, however, saying, "Great hot Zero almost hatches this play, and it's wonderful to see him try. [He] creates a series of incandescent marvels—the transformation of Morley from a fairy with a beret, a book and a flower, undulating across the stage like a queer dromedary, to a virile husband with Texas hat, ithyphallic cigar, booming voice and crushing grip, to a human corporation signing contracts with the precision of an ecstatic machine . . . Zero radiates radical passion no matter what his love object is—a boy, a girl, a poem, a deduction, a phantom holding company, or death itself." But the supporting cast, except for Jules Munshin, was not up to the best professional standards, the critic maintained. The remark was both predictable and unreasonable. Some of the roles were played by nonprofessionals, so it is hardly surprising that they were acted with less polish than might have been expected from performers on Broadway. For that matter, all of the performances, including Zero's, were still in development, as was Meredith's production, as, indeed, was the play itself. Chayefsky called the production "entirely experimental on all our parts . . . We were just trying things out. . . . None of us regard this as a finished production." All concerned had hoped that their work would not be subjected to critical judgment until it could be refined and perfected—but harsh critical judgment was what it received.

Although audiences in Dallas seemed to enjoy the play and Zero's performance enormously, the critical commentaries in the New York *Times* and the national publications effectively killed the play's chances for success in Manhattan. Eventually, it was withdrawn from the APA's repertory and never seen in New York—partly because of the reviews, partly because Mostel and Chayefsky got into a bitter quarrel about the casting of one role; Chayefsky refused to approve the actress Mostel wanted and Zero refused to remain in the play unless she was cast. The production moved from Dallas to Los Angeles, then closed. Its only other notable performance was given later in 1968 by the Royal Shakespeare Company in London with Roy Dotrice in the role of John Morley.

Chayefsky called the entire episode "a very unhappy and bitter experience." Burgess Meredith was particularly disappointed that *The Latent Heterosexual* did not continue, for he thought that parts of the play "were brilliantly written" and that Zero "was superb," both in his comic and his tragic playing. Meredith believed that if circumstances had not combined to ruin the production, it would ultimately have become a great success.

Because *The Latent Heterosexual* was never shown in New York, it has had little impact on the American theatre. In the United States in the 1960s, before the regional theatre movement attained its current eminence, most people felt that New York *was* the American theatre. Thus, if a play was not produced on Broadway, it was unlikely to be produced elsewhere, either professionally or by academic and community theatres. This outcome is particularly unfortunate in the case of *The Latent Heterosexual*, for the play is brilliant in many respects. Imaginative ideas and dialogue crackle from the opening to the closing curtain. The play is dynamic, as the unfolding events lead to continual changes in Morley's character, a character that is stunningly developed by the playwright. The lawyers and accountants in the play do not change at all, but that is Chayefsky's satiric point: the preoccupation with material wealth and how to increase it has long since frozen their characters and prevented any development. It must be conceded that the play is overlong, excessively "talky," and relies heavily on the obscure language of which Chayefsky was too fond. But those are precisely the weaknesses that might have been excised had it been allowed to develop away from the glare of critical attention.

*　　*　　*

Nearly a year passed before Zero returned to show business. He was becoming increasingly reluctant to leave his Twenty-eighth Street studio. As Madeline Gilford said, "Zero just didn't want to go to work. He wanted to stay in the studio and paint." Only a serious financial setback forced him back into performing once again.

According to one of Mostel's closest friends, Zero's brother Milton, who was his accountant and financial adviser, assured Zero that he would see to the details of financing the house Zero wanted to build on Monhegan Island. Unknown to Zero, Milton used the money in Zero's pension fund to finance the building of the house—an illegal use of such funds. The government subsequently sued Zero and imposed a fine so heavy that the reluctant performer was forced to make as much money as he could as quickly as possible. "It was the only period I knew him after the blacklist when he was broke, because the government took so much," said Ian Hunter. "It was a big crisis. I guess if I had to figure a time when Zero was most upset it was that period, because you figure you're doing nicely and suddenly you find you owe the government a couple of hundred grand; it's a hell of a thing to face up to."

For a while, it seemed that Zero would return to the Broadway stage in a musical called *The Exception and the Rule*, which, judging from the abilities of the proposed participants, might have been a notable achievement. Inspired by a play of the same name by Bertolt Brecht, the book was to have been written by John Guare, the lyrics by Stephen Sondheim, and the music by Leonard Bernstein. Jerome Robbins was announced as the director and Mostel as the leading actor.

But the venture ran into trouble immediately. In order to disabuse potential customers of the notion that the musical would be a reverent, painstaking (and dull) adaptation of Brecht's drama, Bernstein recommended that the name of the piece be changed to "A Pray by Blecht." The musical was thereafter referred to by that awkward title. Then the announced opening of the production was postponed for six months. At last, it was abandoned altogether, in part because Zero had to leave for Hollywood to honor a film contract, and finally, because Sondheim was dissatisfied with his own work and decided not to continue.*

The film Zero made was *The Great Bank Robbery*, a comic Western of no distinction whatever. The New York *Times* called it "probably the least interesting movie of 1969 . . . so casually inept it can't even support negative superlatives." Although Zero's performance was the film's best element, the venture was so uninspired that it hardly seemed

---

*Ironically, when Robbins directed a showcase production of the Brecht-Bernstein-Sondheim-Guare musical in 1987—its first public showing—Josh Mostel was cast as the merchant.

worth the effort. *Mastermind*, also made in 1969, must have been even worse, for it was never released. The same fate befell several other pictures Zero made during this period, prompting him to call himself "the king of the unreleased movies."

A film that did find distribution, at least on a limited basis, was *The Angel Levine*, released in 1970. Harry Belafonte's production company took Bernard Malamud's short story about a middle-aged Jew named Manischevitz, changed him to an elderly Jew named Mishkin, and altered the tale in several bizarre ways, so that the film script was nearly incomprehensible. Belafonte, who, in addition to producing, played Levine, a black Jewish angel, introduced some plot complications that clashed jarringly with the events in Malamud's story, and inserted inner-city dialogue in order (in Belafonte's words) "to get some black reality in there." Two screenwriters, one black and one Jewish, attempted to wrestle this material into reasonable shape, but it was an impossible proposition. Zero performed with dignity in a role that called primarily for that quality rather than for comedy. He and Ida Kaminska, a former star of the Yiddish theatre, who played his ailing wife, managed to achieve some affecting moments; but the performances (including Zero's) were unexciting, the script confused and confusing. In addition, the mood of the film was overly sentimental, and the tone so subdued that it bordered on the soporific. The best one can say about the picture is that it occasionally—but rarely—engages one's attention.

Even assuming that Zero had lost all interest in his career and was performing solely to make money, it is difficult to understand why he chose to squander his talents in projects so undistinguished as *The Great Bank Robbery*, *Mastermind*, and *The Angel Levine*. By appearing in these films, Zero actually devalued the star power he and Kate had struggled to achieve. The top billing he received in *The Great Bank Robbery* and *The Angel Levine* was reduced to featured billing in most of his subsequent pictures. Prior to 1966, one could rely upon Zero Mostel's appearance in an entertainment as a guarantee that the evening would be (at the least) interestingly spent. But as Zero lost interest in the work he was doing, the results became progressively more ordinary, and one could no longer assume that the projects with which he was associated would be worthwhile.

Jan Kadar, the director of *The Angel Levine*, wanted Zero to appear in his next film, *The Lies My Father Told Me*. Mostel agreed to play a Canadian junk dealer in Ted Allan's screenplay, but whenever he got together with the director and writer, he made so many suggestions concerning the approach that the filmmakers should take to the material and insisted on so many changes in the script that Allan is reported to have said to him in frustration, "Zero, this picture is about my childhood, not yours."

Zero (supported by Kate) refused to sign a contract for the film, thinking that he would get better terms the longer he held out. When the day arrived to begin shooting in Canada, Zero remained in New York, still believing that he could extract a bigger salary by playing hard to get. The following day, however, he reported to the set—only to be told that another actor had been engaged in his place. The producers informed him that since he had not signed a contract and had not appeared on the first day of shooting, they could only assume that he was not committed to the project.

Zero and Kate were furious, accusing Jan Kadar and the producers of disloyalty. They blamed "the shmucks" for their plight; whereas they had, in fact, planted the seeds of their own misfortune. One suspects that the filmmakers were pleased to be rid of the actor who had, in effect, tried to wrest artistic control of the picture away from the writer and director even before shooting began.

In May 1971, Zero began filming *The Hot Rock*, in which he appeared in the relatively minor role of an unethical lawyer. The picture, a pleasant but undistinguished caper comedy, utilized Zero's talents efficiently; but the mere fact that he played a supporting role and received less than top billing (Robert Redford and George Segal were starred) indicated that the great reputation he had earned as the star of *Fiddler on the Roof* was beginning to fade.

Nothing would have restored Zero's declining popularity more quickly and effectively than the one role he wanted but did not get: Tevye in the film of *Fiddler*. Producer Walter Mirisch and director Norman Jewison gave a good deal of consideration to casting Mostel but eventually chose Topol, an Israeli performer who had often played Tevye on stage, most notably in the London production. Mirisch told Richard Altman, "We decided that in his movie appearances Mostel tended to become 'too big.' We felt that Topol was potentially a better *movie* actor than Mostel." It was a devastating blow to Zero, who believed, with some justice, that the role should have been his. Bettye Ackerman recalls his failure to win the part of Tevye as "Zero's greatest trauma and most painful experience."*

When a reporter asked Mostel if he regretted not having been cast, he responded, "Aaahh, I didn't give a shit." But his comments about the film betrayed his bitterness. "I would have made it smaller," he said, "with lots of mud." The film was too grand, too slick, and too overpowering, he maintained. "In those days [in Russia] people had very little to eat—and *they* show miles of wheat fields!"

Zero's attitude was obviously colored by his frustration, but many of those who had been moved by the stage presentation were disappointed in the film version of *Fiddler on the Roof*.

Zero's willingness to play Tevye in the Westbury Music Fair's production of *Fiddler* on Long Island in October 1971—his first stage appearance of any kind in three and a half years and only his second since he left the New York cast of *Fiddler* six years earlier—was prompted primarily by the opportunity to make a great deal of money: the Westbury performances paid Mostel at the rate of $30,000 a week, which was said to be the largest weekly salary ever paid a performer in a musical at that time. Zero may also have wanted audiences to be able to compare his performance directly with Topol's, for the film had opened earlier that year.

The performances at Westbury were given in the round, with the audience surrounding the action, and this arrangement necessitated considerable changes in the staging. Kate believed that Zero would not have reprised his role without the challenge of the new staging, for he was initially resistant to the proposal. But, she said, she and her husband "drove out to the Island. Zero began to walk around the stage, and when he said, 'You know, we could have "Sunrise, Sunset" up in the aisles,' I knew he'd do it."

Thelma Lee, Madeline Gilford's sister, played Yente in the Westbury

---

*Not long afterward, Zero's son Josh received a telephone call from Norman Jewison, who wanted to discuss the possibility of casting Josh as King Herod in the film version of *Jesus Christ Superstar*. Zero, overhearing the conversation, shouted from the next room, "Tell him to give it to Topol's son!"

production. She knew that Zero had seen the film of *Fiddler* and was curious to know how he felt about it. But Mostel was so distressed by the casting of Topol that "you could not mention the movie to him," she said. "He was very upset, and rightly so, but he would not talk about it."

The Westbury performances were gratifyingly successful. Even though Zero's interpolations were even more intrusive than they had been in the Broadway production, all records for attendance at the Music Fair were broken; the run, originally scheduled for four weeks, was extended to six; and Zero reveled in playing Tevye, never missing a performance and never failing to be rewarded with a standing ovation. Then, having earned enough money to pay his debt to the Internal Revenue Service, he returned to his studio.

On November 8, 1972, a year after the production at Westbury, a new play premiered at Yale University in New Haven. Assembled by Eric Bentley, the play, entitled *Are You Now or Have You Ever Been . . . ?*, was a compilation of the testimony of sixteen individuals before the House Committee on Un-American Activities. Actors playing actors and screenwriters confronted actors playing congressmen. Neither the names of the actual individuals nor the words they spoke were changed (although the testimony was often condensed). Zero and Ring Lardner, Jr., both represented as characters in the play, attended the opening night together, and their presence in the audience led to some wholly unexpected occurrences.

For Mostel and Lardner, watching themselves portrayed by actors using the words they had once spoken was an unusual sensation, to say the least. Both were offended by the production despite the fact that Bentley's adaptation portrayed them sympathetically. After the performance, Mostel loudly denounced the play and its author on the sidewalk in front of the theatre, causing a considerable commotion. Lardner also let his displeasure be known (although much more quietly), maintaining that the play was neither theatre nor history. Among other things, Lardner was bothered by the fact that in the production the hearing seemed to be a formal, polite affair, whereas the atmosphere in the actual committee room was intensely adversarial, with committee members employing dictatorial methods, sneering at witnesses and disregarding their constitutional rights.

Still, Lardner's objections were mild compared with Zero's. Mostel was upset by Eric Bentley's use of the public record as the basis of a play from which he profited, while none of the individuals whose testimony was quoted received any compensation. Lardner believed, however, that the primary reason for Zero's forceful objection to the play lay elsewhere. As he told me in 1987, "I thought that what was behind it was that Zero at that time had an ambivalent attitude about the blacklist and having been blacklisted. He did not advertise the fact that he had been blacklisted. As a matter of fact, he preferred when things were written about him that that *not* be mentioned."

Frances Chaney thought that Zero's anger was directed more toward the trivialization of a profound experience: "taking lives that were destroyed and making a theatrical performance out of it." But she also felt that Mostel may have been "throwing his weight around a little bit, feeling that he was so important that somebody should have asked him" before using his persona in the play.

Zero told a newspaper interviewer, "I was furious about [the play]. I think the whole theatre of fact is a lot of malarkey. I think truth can only be told by fiction."

Some attributed Zero's anger to the fact that Lionel Stander, who had angrily and articulately defied the committee when he testified before it, emerged as the real hero of the play. One observer who saw Bentley's drama offered this theory: "While Zero flirted with the Committee and was cute and coy, Stander slapped their face. And the Stander role was a longer one in the play. Mostel thought the Mostel role should always be the longest and most dashing." Another viewer, himself a victim of the blacklist, felt that the play's portrait of Abe Burrows, an informer, was too genial to suit Zero. Most people, though, were simply puzzled by his fury.

When the published version of *Are You Now or Have You Ever Been . . . ?* appeared, Mostel's scene was omitted. Ironically, Zero Mostel, who had eloquently defended the freedom to speak openly when he appeared before HUAC, had directly or indirectly exerted a censorship of his own.

Zero did not perform at all in 1972 (although *The Hot Rock* was released in January of that year). In 1973, he appeared in two hour-long musical television specials: *Old Faithful* in March and *Saga of Sonora* in May. Both were damned by the critics. Howard Thompson was especially hard on the latter, calling it "a wretchedly strained and stale Western spoof."

Later that year, Zero was lured back to Westbury (and other stops on the Guber and Gross music fair circuit), this time to reprise his role as Pseudolus in *A Funny Thing Happened on the Way to the Forum*.* Burt Shevelove saw the revival and was dismayed that Mostel's deviations from the script had become even more pronounced. In the original, Zero's ad libs had at least remained within the bounds of good taste, but he evidently felt no such obligation when he was performing in the revival. The line, "I know Gusto, the body snatcher. He owes me a favor," for example, was changed by Zero to "I know Gusto, the body snatcher. He owes me a snatch." Shevelove observed, "That's [like] a little child sitting at the table saying cocky, cocky, doodle, doodle, and that's not funny." Still, the six-week run at Westbury set another record, exceeding the box-office income from Zero's revival of *Fiddler* two years before.

While Mostel was touring in *Forum*, the ACA Galleries in New York City held an exhibition of his paintings, his first one-man show. This must have been a gratifying moment: Zero's achievements as a painter were being recognized on a significant scale after more than forty years. But, publicly, Mostel did not display much greater enthusiasm about the exhibit than he did about his performing work. He claimed that he had agreed to the exhibit only because "I couldn't get into my studio anymore; the paintings were pushing me out." About eighty paintings went on display, occupying two floors of the gallery. All the works were oils and collages, most of them drenched in yellows and reds, with titles like *Year of the Egg, What Is It? Capillary Attraction, Loser's Viewpoint*, and *Painter with No Hands*, titles arbitrarily assigned to the paintings by Zero because the gallery asked that they be named. Sidney Bergen, the owner of ACA, initiated the idea for the exhibition after having visited Zero in his studio. "I almost exploded with excitement and joy," Bergen said. "He had thousands of pastels, drawings, watercolors—everything. But we decided to limit the show to some of

---

*He toured in *Fiddler on the Roof* for the same organization in 1975.

the oil paintings and collages of the past ten years—just his recent and most important work."

Bergen reluctantly agreed to Zero's demand that the exhibition be covered only by those newspapers and magazines with established art critics. "Television wants to come, the newspapers—everybody—but Zero says he doesn't want this one and he doesn't want that one, because they don't really care about *art*," Bergen said. "He [is] afraid his work [will] be mixed up with his being an actor. He wants his paintings to stand on their own."

Mostel, perhaps still privately harboring a wish not to be judged as an artist, expressed some apprehension about the finality of having his works on exhibition. When he first saw his paintings on display, he said, "One thing about seeing them all together like this—with the light on them, they look different. I want to take them all away and change them. In the studio, I keep taking care of them like children."

Although Henry Rothman, who framed the paintings, said, "If it had been anyone else's work, it would have been received much better," the critic for *ARTnews* praised Mostel's "professional technique and sophisticated pictorial sense." Another critic commented, "The works were unusual for their constant high pitch of emotion, as though they were not large enough to contain so much intensity." The public's reception of Zero's paintings was also favorable, although, according to Sidney Bergen, the sales were not as great as either the painter or the gallery owner had hoped.

After a guest appearance on *Sesame Street* early in 1974 (which led to a children's book, *The Sesame Street Book of Opposites*, with photographs of Zero in long underwear and diapers), Zero appeared in a film version of *Rhinoceros* for the American Film Theatre. The operator of the venture intended to film a number of successful plays and to show them only twice to create a sense of occasion paralleling that of the live theatre.*

Rhinoceros, in which Gene Wilder took over the role Eli Wallach had played on Broadway, was directed by Tom O'Horgan, who had achieved considerable success with his productions of *Hair, Jesus Christ*

---

*Years later, however, the films were released for general distribution.

Superstar, and other plays that tapped the rebellious spirit of the late 1960s and early 1970s. O'Horgan turned out to be a regrettable choice.

Wilder, who confessed that he "did not really understand the play at first, but I wanted to work again with Zero," remarked that Mostel "was very concerned to capture the moments he had had before [on stage], and he had lots of ideas." But he was unable to communicate them to O'Horgan, whose philosophy of directing, according to Wilder, was "not to do or say much, because he believed it would all evolve by itself." Wilder called O'Horgan's approach "a strange concept. It might work for a musical like *Hair*, but it doesn't work in a movie. It was chaos, and you've got to have planning in a movie."

Zero was also frustrated by O'Horgan's method—or lack of one—but he kept his irritation in check, never allowing it to burst into an open conflict. After the picture was released, however, he announced that the experience was enough to make him swear off movies forever. "They had this boy direct it," he said, contemptuously. "With his long hair and his dinosaur on his lapel. It gives me a pain. He used to say, 'Groovy, baby.' I don't think he knew what he was doing. He didn't trust the material." Wilder felt that things might have been improved had a producer been present to suggest that the director take a firmer approach, but "there was never a producer there." Consequently, there was no one to act as a corrective to O'Horgan's methods.

If O'Horgan underdirected the actors, he was guilty of overdirecting *Rhinoceros* in another sense. Under his guidance, a good deal of extraneous visual material intruded on the film: Zero, for example, lurching around the set during his transformation scene, smashing bookshelves and destroying works of sculpture, lamps, and other items. "The film fractures into so many directions," lamented *Film Information*. A series of ineptly staged slapstick scenes did not help matters. The picture "sinks into a crazy-clumsy miasma of thudding jokes and overzealous visual tricks," reported David Sterritt in the *Christian Science Monitor*.

The film is "so grossly overdirected by Tom O'Horgan that you might get the idea Mr. O'Horgan thought he was making a movie for an audience made up entirely of rhinoceroses," said Vincent Canby of the New York *Times*, who praised Mostel's performance as "comparatively subdued" and "extremely funny" when he is "slipping unaware into the early stages of rhinoceritis, munching the leaves of a potted plant." But

Zero was clearly unable to duplicate the impact of his stage performance because of the directorial intrusions—and, perhaps, because his unsuitability for the film medium was again made evident. On the screen, his character already seemed oversized and intimidating even before he began to change to a rhinoceros, thus diminishing the effect of the transformation.

Eugène Ionesco, who had serious reservations about the Broadway production of his play, was even more distressed by the movie. "It was a bad film," he said, "and destroyed the meaning of my play."

Having revived all of his greatest stage successes except for *Ulysses in Nighttown*, Zero proceeded to complete the cycle by redoing *Ulysses* on Broadway in March 1974. But just as the film of *Rhinoceros* failed to live up to the stage version, so the revival of *Ulysses in Nighttown* was a severe disappointment to those who had seen the off-Broadway production in 1958. Although the main elements were substantially the same—Marjorie Barkentin's script was somewhat revised to include Molly's soliloquy, but remained largely intact, Burgess Meredith once again served as director, and Zero repeated his role as Bloom—they failed to achieve the same harmony as before.

It was Mostel's idea to revive the play, and he who urged Meredith to redirect it for Broadway. Meredith was hesitant from the beginning because he did not think the play would work well in a large theatre, but he eventually agreed. Unfortunately, the producer leased one of the largest theatres in New York, the Winter Garden, whose stage was several times larger than the acting space in the Rooftop Theatre; consequently, the production had to be enlarged, broadened, and—in the opinion of nearly everyone who saw it—vulgarized in the process. Meredith, who said he "had trouble filling that huge Winter Garden," added that the producer "brought in somebody and added a lot of doodads, and all the soul was gone." Marjorie Barkentin's intimate piece, a play that might be compared to chamber music, was turned into a symphony with every instrument blaring at once.

In contrast to the original production, which called upon the audience to use its imagination, the revival featured elements that distracted from the play itself. One of these was the extensive use of nudity. No one denied the beauty of Fionnuala Flanagan, who played Molly Bloom, but many questioned whether her soliloquy, delivered almost entirely in the nude, served to enhance the play. This was not a question of prudery but of simple theatrical effectiveness. As Edwin Wilson wrote in his *Wall Street Journal* review, "To see her nude for a time would be very much in keeping with the spirit of the play, but to see her nude for such an extended period of time tends to become self-defeating. Those who are captivated by her appearance—as well they might be —will not hear a word she is saying, while those who become immune to her appearance through over-exposure will lose sight of the sensuality that should be present. Either way the point of the scene is lost."

Meredith's production (assisted on this occasion by Swen Swenson's dance movement) seemed to be swallowed up by the huge stage and auditorium. "The elaborate, scenically striking production . . . is a vast, vulgar, and at times repulsive spectacle," John Beaufort wrote in the *Christian Science Monitor*. "The notion seems to be to make up with sensationalism and displays of nudity for the lack of authentic feeling and drama."

Even Zero's performance was perceived as less satisfactory than before; some regarded it as little better than adequate. In Burgess Meredith's view, Mostel's performance was as good as it had been in 1958, but "it was overwhelmed by the production. The pathos that he had been able to get was lost in doing it in a theatre that big and in the kind of production that was wanted by the producer." It should be noted, however, that Zero, as the star and instigator of the production, could have vetoed the choice of the Winter Garden. But rather than selecting a theatre that would have better suited the play, he and the producer chose the house with the largest seating capacity—one which, they hoped, would bring about the greatest possible profit.

After a few weeks of performances, Zero began to indulge in his habitual ad-libbing and clowning, something he had for the most part resisted when he first appeared in the play. Still, Mostel was nominated for a Tony award for his portrayal of Bloom. The distinction could not save the production, however, which closed within two months.

Zero took the experience philosophically. "My motto is 'upward and downward,'" he said. But the trajectory of his career had been edging steadily downward since 1965, and he must have yearned for the satisfaction of being in an unqualified success once again.

Nevertheless, his next several projects represented the nadir of his career. Everything he touched seemed to turn to dross. The films he made in 1974 and 1975—*Marco, Once Upon a Scoundrel*, and *Foreplay*—have rarely been seen, and deservedly so. Zero played Kublai Khan in *Marco*, a role that was supposed to provide him with an opportunity to demonstrate his comic, dramatic, and musical skills, but the listless script and score undercut any such possibility. After receiving poor reviews in its initial screening, the film was withdrawn from distribution. About all that Zero derived from the picture (other than a handsome salary) was a trip to Japan for the filming.

Once Upon a Scoundrel, shot in Mexico, with Zero playing a wealthy landowner who is obsessed with lust for a beautiful young woman, might have been a charming fable had it not been for the financial backer, who insisted upon rearranging the raw footage so often and so clumsily that the result is all but incomprehensible. Only after years of threatened litigation between the director and the financier was the film released, and then primarily for television. Still, George Schaefer, the director, recalled the shooting itself as enjoyable, primarily because of Zero, "a man full of ideas and invention," who contributed the ideas for several scenes that were not in the original script.

Foreplay was filmed at an estate on Long Island with a reputable cast that included Zero, Estelle Parsons, Pat Paulsen, Jerry Orbach, and Professor Irwin Corey, and a competent director, John G. Avildsen, but the movie's episodic script was so ludicrously tasteless and inept that at least some of those who worked on it were certain the picture was being made only as a tax write-off and would never be released. When it finally was shown in New York in 1981—seven years after it was completed and retitled *The President's Women*—it was greeted with derision. Zero and Estelle Parsons played the president of the United States and his wife, whose daughter has been kidnapped by terrorists. As ransom, the kidnappers demand that the president and the First Lady make love on network television. The antics that follow are best described as embarrassing. One review, which called the film "ugly, unfunny and misogynistic," may serve as a typical example of critical sentiment.

Zero's attitude toward his work while performing in *Foreplay* was perhaps characteristic of his feelings about show business throughout the early 1970s. Orel Odinov Protopopescu, who served as a production assistant on the film, was assigned solely to look after Zero's needs; consequently, she spent a good deal of time with him. One of her responsibilities was to see that Zero knew his lines before each day's shooting. "I tried to be conscientious about it," she said, "because I took the whole thing much more seriously than he did. He thought the film was a lot of garbage, so it wouldn't matter what he said during the scene. Every once in a while I'd say, 'We really have to learn this page or two today,' and he'd make a half-hearted attempt to work on it. But he generally improvised. He didn't take the film business seriously."

Mostel learned that Protopopescu had a master's degree in English and had recently married a man who had earned a Ph.D. in physics. She recalls that Zero "was absolutely astonished that I was working on the set of this film. He said, 'What on earth are you doing here?' I told him I was very interested in a career in the film business, and he said, 'This business, this is for bimbos.'" Zero told her about his devotion to painting and his fondness for Monhegan Island, leaving no doubt how he felt about his work in the movies. "My real life is elsewhere," she quoted him as saying.

Although he was contemptuous of the *Foreplay* script, Protopopescu said, "I don't think he had contempt for the people working on it. I think he had genuine affection for the people working on the crew. He was very friendly with the lady who did his makeup, for instance. I think in a sense he felt sorry for people who had to make their living that way—himself included, maybe."

Zero spent most of his time during the filming reading and listening to classical music, she recalled. Often, when he put on a record, he would ask if she were familiar with the piece. If not, he would tell her about the composer or about the piece's structure. She cannot recall any occasion when he expressed the slightest enthusiasm for the film he was making.

Most of Mostel's television ventures during the period were equally unsatisfactory. He appeared in a special called *Love, Life, Liberty and Lunch* and provided the voice for an animated production, *The Little Drummer Boy, Book II*. Neither project was in any way distinguished, but Zero does not seem to have cared. His interest in performing had diminished to the point where it was strictly financial.

Perhaps Zero was a trifle more enthusiastic about his participation in a BBC-CBS coproduction of Puccini's *Gianni Schicchi*, a one-act comedy in which he made his operatic debut. Simply the challenge of working in a new medium may have aroused a greater degree of interest than usual, while Mostel's love of operatic music no doubt made the venture attractive.

He took an opera coach with him to his Monhegan home for two weeks in the summer of 1975, during which time he learned the music. In England, he clowned his way through the early rehearsals with the full cast, seeming to convey the notion that he was not taking the project seriously. At last, however, he did get down to serious work and persuaded the singers that he was, in the words of one of them, "a very cultured man [who] really knows a good deal about opera."

On one occasion, Zero and a trained opera singer stumbled over one another's vocal lines. The conductor, Robin Stapleton, consulted the score and found that Mostel had been right. "Hah!" Zero shouted in triumph.

Telecast in November 1975, *Gianni Schicchi* was hailed as "delightful" by John J. O'Connor of the New York *Times*, who said, "The enormous (in more ways than one) reason for its success is Zero Mostel in the title role. . . . His Schicchi is a mountain of outrageous and hilarious mugging. His face is a mass of contortions. His voice ranges from husky shouting to hoarse bellowing. He is an unbelievable and unforgettable addition to the 'CBS Festival of Lively Arts for Young People.' "

One hopes that Zero enjoyed working on *Gianni Schicchi* and that he was pleased with the result, for his career in the performing arts, which had reached extraordinary heights during his most creative period (from 1958 to 1966), had disintegrated so thoroughly in a decade that neither he nor his once-devoted audiences were able to derive much satisfaction from his performances.

In 1975, Zero turned sixty. Although he remained jovial in his relationship with most of the world, he also presented the sad spectacle of a performing artist of great ability who was in the process of self-destructing. At least his activities from 1966 to 1975 kept his name before the public, which made possible a return to the creative vitality of his middle years during the last chapter of his life.

10

Incline and Fall

At sixty-one years of age, and with his career in decline for a decade, Zero Mostel's return to the pinnacle of show business seemed unlikely. Nevertheless, he brought it off, appearing once again in the role for which he was most famous, playing in his most satisfying film, and acting in a new play that offered him his most challenging dramatic role.

Although Mostel did not win the part of Tevye in the film version of *Fiddler on the Roof*, he remained associated with the character in the public's mind. The identification was reinforced by his summer tours in the musical produced by Bill Ross for the Guber and Gross music fairs. Ross was delighted when Zero agreed to appear in the production—"No one was ever going to play *Fiddler* like Zero when he was good," Ross said, "and when he was good, he was very good"—but he remembers the tours as "one of the most horrendous times of my life, because of Zero," who threw his ample weight around emphatically and often. On one occasion, Mostel insisted on replacing the conductor of the orchestra with a conductor of his choosing. Ross said of the person who was hired, "He was a very nice man, but he had never conducted an orchestra. Z, as usual, started screaming, 'Hey, what do you know about it, you no-good son of a bitch? I'm the one who's on the stage. I've got to follow him, you don't know anything about it.' So he got his man. Two weeks later he called me and said, 'You gotta come up here and get me another conductor.' "

Ross felt that all of the problems he had with Zero occurred because "Z had an automatic hatred for whoever was the boss." He recalled an occurrence when the company was preparing to move to Albany. "Z said, 'How am I gonna get there?' I said, 'A big Cadillac and a chauffeur will come here at nine in the morning, will pick you up, you'll be there by twelve. It'll give you a chance to rest.' He said, 'You cheap son of a bitch, I'm not going by any car, I want to fly! I want you to charter me a flight!' So I arranged to have a plane take him up there. I told him that I was going to drive, and 'By the time you get there I'll be waiting for you at the airport.' And I was. When he got out of the plane he yelled, 'I made you pay the extra money! I made you pay the extra money!' So I said, 'No, it was cheaper this way. You want to see the bill?' I think it ruined his week."

The tours Ross produced led, in turn, to Zero's participation in a year-long engagement in *Fiddler* sponsored by the Shubert Organization, the Nederlander Producing Company, and Roger Stevens (representing the John F. Kennedy Center for the Performing Arts) that culminated in a twenty-one-week run on Broadway.* The production, directed by Ruth Mitchell, who had been the production stage manager for *Fiddler* twelve years earlier, was mounted with as much care as the original. Rather than attempting to duplicate the 1964 version—often a recipe that yields only a stale imitation—the 1976 production represented a fresh, invigorating approach to the material.

The revival played ten major cities before arriving in New York: Los Angeles, Denver, St. Louis, Toronto, Philadelphia, Detroit, Chicago, Boston, Miami, and Washington, D.C. In nearly every location, the production broke the house record for box-office receipts—as it did at the Shubert Theatre in Los Angeles and the Opera House of the Kennedy Center in Washington. Throughout the run, Zero received $30,000 a week. His salary was worth every penny to the producers,

---

*Zero accepted the assignment in preference to an offer to perform in a new musical, *The Baker's Wife*. Ironically, when Mostel declined that show, producer David Merrick cast Topol instead. *The Baker's Wife* closed before reaching New York.

for the revival, bolstered primarily by Zero's presence, grossed $5.2 million.

Ruth Mitchell's relationship with Zero was a good one, based on mutual respect. She confessed, however, that the help she was able to offer him was minimal. "Basically, that part was so ingrained in him that he needed very little direction," she said. "What I wanted to do was take out the embellishments [he had inserted during the summer tours] and get back to the real performance which he gave in the beginning." To a degree, she succeeded, though not without some resistance from Mostel. "I'd give him notes after every performance and he'd give me just as many back about other people," she said.

She observed that Zero would be at his best each time the production opened in a new city. But "as the weeks went on he would get naughty again," and begin to add unrehearsed material. "The audiences absolutely adored him; and that's what encouraged him," she added.

Despite Zero's age, he was as effervescent as ever. "Mostel in rehearsal is a clown in perpetual flight—nudging ribs, tweaking noses, joking with his co-workers between and, occasionally, during scenes," wrote Mel Gussow. "During one break he turned to Ruth Mitchell . . . and said, 'Did you ever see the Japanese version?' Then he did an uproarious 30-second, eye-popping, air-chopping samurai version of *Fiddler*."

Mostel's performances also displayed the zest for which he was famous. One Washington review noted that he still brought "the zaniness of a young nightclub comic to the puzzled, reverent character whose world is collapsing around him."

Zero needed to be in peak physical condition to play the long and exhausting role. Consequently, he carried his Exercycle with him on the road and worked out daily. He also cut down on his smoking and drinking, and even made some effort to eat more moderately than usual—although Thelma Lee, who played Golde on the tour, noted, "I felt that he really didn't take as good care of himself as he should have. He was very heavy when we were working, and he worked very hard."

Zero asked Howard Rodney, who had been with him during the original production of *Fiddler*, to serve as his dresser once again. During the tour, Mostel came to depend upon Rodney for a myriad of services. "He'd call me at two in the morning," Rodney recalled, "and if he needed something I'd grab a cab and go to his hotel. Then later he said to me, 'How about staying where I'm staying?' I said, 'Zero, I can't afford that kind of a hotel.' He said, 'How about if I pay for half?' I said, 'Well, even then, I couldn't afford it.' So he paid for the whole thing. Wherever he stayed, I was next door."*

Mostel also demanded that Rodney join him every day for lunch and dinner. "He never ate alone," Rodney said. "When we got to California I said to Zero, 'I've made arrangements to have dinner with my friends,' and he said, 'Bring them along; I'll take them all to dinner.' And when Zero went to have dinner with his friends, he always wanted me there with him."

Mostel rewarded his dresser with gifts of various kinds. Kate, who was unable to accompany her husband on the tour because of her asthma attacks, called Rodney "the Mrs. Mostel of the road." She bought him an expensive ring, telling him, "You deserve it. I know that it's hard to work with Zero."

Thelma Lee, who had begun by playing Yente during the summer tours and graduated to Golde, also helped look after Mostel. Madeline Gilford, Lee's sister, said, "Zero's bad leg had to be bathed, so whenever they'd get to a town she would see that whatever hotel they'd checked into had a tub that was large enough for him to be comfortable in. She was very solicitous and involved in his physical comfort."

Lee's solicitousness was based upon her respect for Zero as well as her affection for him and for Kate. "I just admired a man who could run up and down the aisle of the theatre [during the Guber-Gross performances in the round] with a rebuilt leg in that terrible heat we used to play in and never complain. He never said anything about it."

His leg was not the only discomfort he suffered with during the tour. He was plagued by swollen vocal cords during the month prior to the New York opening. Nevertheless, he never took a night off, and even found that his condition "added another quality to the performance. I got through with grit and greed. I sang above my voice. They [the

---

*"Zero needed to have a 'nursemaid' " when he went on tour, one actress told me, "because Zero was very childish, and he needed to have someone he was comfortable with who would take care of him." Rodney added, "He was like a little baby. He needed somebody with him at all times. He rested easy knowing I was in the suite next door to him—that he could call me for anything."

audience] didn't know the difference. It came off very pathetic in a lot of places. It had the humor . . . but it had a certain difference because I couldn't project as well as I wanted to."

Zero was primarily concerned with his own performance, as one would expect, but he also functioned as an unofficial director because Ruth Mitchell left the production after it opened, returning only once every four or five weeks. Mostel "paid a lot of attention to what went on in the show," said Thelma Lee. "He would give notes: 'The energy level is too low. Get the energy up.' He always knew what was happening with the other people in the show."

Howard Rodney recalled an occasion when Mostel invited the young actor playing Motel to join him in his dressing room. Zero engaged the performer in seemingly casual conversation until any apprehensions he may have had were dissolved. Then, Rodney remembered, Zero turned to the actor and said, "Why can't you talk to me like this when we're onstage? Why are you 'acting'? The way we're talking now is the way I'd like to see you onstage." According to Rodney, "At the next performance Motel was brilliant." In similar ways, Zero helped to sharpen the performances of several of the actors on the tour.

The revival of *Fiddler* gave Zero the opportunity to demonstrate to the world his self-proclaimed superiority to all the other actors who had played Tevye. "If you read Sholem Aleichem, you know there is only one way to interpret the character," he said. "I *made* Tevye. Every moment I put in they [all the actors who succeeded him in the role] continued to use. Therefore, everyone else can only do it more poorly. The others didn't dance. They didn't sing. They didn't tear themselves apart the way I do every night. I do it my way, but it's the only way to do it."

The production followed Ruth Mitchell's direction until the company reached Boston, the last stop before New York. Then, one week before the New York opening, Jerome Robbins invoked the clause in his contract that permitted him to take over and restage the production for Broadway.

Again, as they had twelve years earlier, Robbins and Mostel engaged in an ongoing battle—sometimes verbal, often silent—over every gesture, every alteration of rhythm. When Robbins told Mostel that the pace was becoming too leisurely and asked him to sacrifice a piece of business in order to recover some time, Zero eyed the director warily and said, "We'll talk about it later." He repeated the sentence whenever he was unwilling to accept any of Robbins's suggestions.

The New York production, which opened at the Winter Garden in late December 1976, may have been the most satisfactory occasion in Zero's professional life, for it brought him the kind of adulation only show business legends achieve. The first-night audience included hundreds of his friends and acquaintances, who cheered when he first entered, laughed appreciatively in all the right places, rewarded him with a standing ovation during his curtain call, and jammed his dressing room to overflowing afterward. Then Zero and his family joined the celebration at the Tavern on the Green. The invitations to the affair called for "black tie only," but Zero had his own ideas. He arrived looking "like a Talmudic cowboy," wearing what Mel Gussow described as "a very strange outfit, a cross between a tuxedo and a prayer shawl." Referring to his get-up, Zero commented, "It's my last stab at uniformity."

Zero spent most of the night basking in the praise for his performance, accepting thanks for the Cartier bracelets he had given as opening-night gifts to everyone in the company, and complaining good-naturedly about his physical condition. "Oy vay! Am I tired, does my back hurt, is my throat sore!" he shouted. "Oy vay!"

The critical reception was even more enthusiastic than it had been in 1964. Douglas Watt said in the *Daily News* that Mostel's performance was "deeper, richer, infinitely more satisfying" than it had been in the original production. Watt suggested that Zero was also considerably more disciplined. "Now that he has grown into Tevye . . . there is none of [the direct playing to the audience that marred the earlier performance]. He is no less agile or amusing. He is, in fact, hilarious at times, his comedy endlessly inventive and beautifully shaded. But he is also wonderfully touching. The performance is a masterpiece . . . one of those rare theatregoing experiences of a lifetime, something to be treasured and ever grateful for."

Zero "owns the part of Tevye," wrote Martin Gottfried in the *Post*. "His understanding of the pragmatic dairyman's Jewish heritage; his one-to-one relationship with God; his connection of tradition with survival—these are all complete and united. His stagemanship is tremendous."

Subsequent audiences reacted with an enthusiasm nearly equal to that of opening night, and the reception for his performance renewed Mostel's claim to Broadway greatness. For a man whose career had foundered for a dozen years, who believed that he had never received sufficient recognition for his contribution to the original *Fiddler*, and that he had been underpaid to boot, the revival was, as Mel Gussow said in the New York *Times*, "an act of restoration: the king returns to his throne."

Even more than in the original, perhaps, Zero demonstrated the ability to achieve the ideal balance between Tevye's comic side and his reactions to the heartbreaks the character must face. For example, whenever Golde nagged him, Tevye would go through an intricate pantomime, flapping his arms, widening his eyes, pretending to cut his throat and to strangle his wife. But when the Russian police arrived to break up his daughter's wedding celebration, Zero adopted the artistic principle, "less is more": he simply moved downstage, looking silently and reproachfully to God. Later, when Tevye discovered that Chava had married a non-Jew—the most serious blow the character undergoes— Zero made no attempt to exaggerate Tevye's response; he stood quietly, giving God a look that combined wrath and incomprehension, affectingly showing that Tevye's spirit had come perilously close to being broken.

But it was as impossible as ever for Zero to subdue his impluse to play with the audience after the New York run was under way. "Zero's feeling was that 'Once I'm on stage it's between me and the audience,'" said Joseph Stein, "so if he felt like doing something to titillate the audience, he'd do it."

Martin Gottfried, who was so delighted with Zero's opening night performance, took him to task in a February 1977 column for "messing up *Fiddler on the Roof* with ad-libs, shtick and his various other self-indulgences." Gottfried called such behavior "unprofessional . . . disdainful of theatre; inconsiderate of the company; contemptuous of the audience." He particularly lamented that such "a magnificent performer capable of giving a magnificent performance" should "be making a fool of himself."

Gottfried's irritation was justified and understandable, but, once again, audiences did not share the critic's outrage. They savored each ad lib, then told their friends about Zero's antics; their friends then came to the theatre expecting Mostel's spontaneous comments and actions and were disappointed when they did not occur. Zero may have been mistaken in believing that the original production of *Fiddler* would not succeed after he left the show, but the revival was indeed generally thought of as "the Zero Mostel musical." In fact, when Zero was forced to miss four performances because of laryngitis, the box-office receipts dropped by a whopping $50,000.

Not all of the performers in *Fiddler* were upset by Zero's departures from the script. Thelma Lee even enjoyed them. "It didn't bother me because I was a stand-up comic," she said, "and I could deal with anything that Zero did. I actually liked it; it was interesting. In the dream sequence one night he ripped my nightgown off. But I just finished the number in a blanket. And the audience just screamed. Then afterwards they built me another nightgown underneath the nightgown, so that if he pulled one off, the other one stayed."

Interestingly, Zero would not tolerate any deviation from the script from other actors in the company. One night, according to Lee, Zero entered on cue after Golde called offstage to him. "He looked at me and he said, 'Are you talking to me?' That's not a line in the script. And I looked at the backdrop and said, 'No, I'm talking to the trees.' He walked up to the backdrop and looked at the trees and said, 'She's talking to you, so *you* answer.' Later the stage manager came to me and said, 'Thelma, there will be no ad-libbing.' So I didn't do any more of that."

Zero was behind the stage manager's message. Mostel enforced on others a rigid adherence to Robbins's direction as well as to the script—although he continued to insert his own business as the mood struck him. Lee offered this example: "He had a thing about my looking at him during 'Do You Love Me?' except when I said, 'Do I what?' Then I was allowed to look at him. But for the rest of the number I wasn't allowed to look at him until the very end when he touched my hand." One night, at the beginning of the song, Lee, who was dutifully looking away from Zero, heard him sing, "Do you love me?" as if it were coming from far away, "like an echo. I turned around to see where he was, and he had a bucket over his head. He did the entire number with a bucket."

On another occasion, Lee remembered, "I once pointed a finger at him for some reason, I don't remember why. He said, 'If you ever lift your finger and point it at me above your waist, I'll break it off!' So I never went above my waist with my hands. Zero was the boss."

But, far from resenting Mostel's attitude, Lee delighted in working with him. "Really, he was very disciplined with me, except for a couple of times," she said. "I really got a lot from that man. If you watched Zero closely, you saw he had wonderful timing. I never saw him do a move with his hands or his body that didn't mean something. There wasn't a night when I walked out on that stage that I didn't say to myself, 'How could I be so fortunate as to work with such a wonderful star?'" Lee confirmed that Mostel's performance retained its sharp edge throughout the run, saying, "Zero never 'walked through' the show; he *worked* it."

Regardless of how audiences or members of the cast responded to the actor, Jerome Robbins believed that Zero's performance did not measure up to the standards of 1964. Although the 1976 production was videotaped and the tape deposited in the archives at Lincoln Center, Robbins has not—as of the summer of 1987—permitted anyone to see it, except for members of the revival cast and prospective choreographers of *Fiddler* who wished to study Robbins's dance movements for future productions. According to one individual in whom Robbins confided, he continued to withhold permission for anyone else to view the tape because he was so extremely dissatisfied with Mostel's performance, believing that "Zero played around too much." However, a cast member insisted, "Zero did not. He was very well behaved."

Some observers felt that Zero was a less vital Tevye than he had been twelve years before. Sheldon Harnick, who did not attend rehearsals of the revival, noted that Mostel's "performance had become surprisingly mechanical by the time I saw it, I don't know why. Exhaustion, perhaps. In the past, whatever new business he invented was always added to a characterization of inner richness and emotional truth. Now, as far as I was concerned, his Tevye was hollow. One saw a performer who knew where all the laughs were and who knew how to press the right buttons and pull the right strings to manipulate the audience."

James Bronson, who stage-managed the original production, was even more emphatic. "I [saw] a single performance of his revival and was a little shocked—and angry. And I told him so." But Zero firmly denied all charges that his performance had lost any of its zest. "Do I look as if I'm stale?" he asked a New York *Times* reporter irately, his face drenched in sweat after a performance. "Do I look as if I'm not giving everything I have to the part?"

*   *   *

The revival of *Fiddler* was only the first of three chapters in Mostel's second comeback, conferring upon him the status of show business elder statesman. In September 1976, while the musical was on tour, *The Front* was released. Zero was not the leading actor—that role was taken by Woody Allen—but his part was second in importance and in billing. More significantly, the film had a special meaning for him, for its plot dealt directly with the blacklist of the early 1950s and treated those who had been blacklisted with sympathy, while portraying those who had informed as selfish and cowardly. The script was written by Zero's friend Walter Bernstein, directed by Martin Ritt, and featured actors such as Joshua Shelley, John Randolph, and Herschel Bernardi. Thus, many of the principal contributors to the film had themselves once been victims of the blacklist.* The character Zero played was modeled partly upon himself and his own experiences and partly upon his late friend Philip Loeb.

Mostel played Hecky Brown, who, at the beginning of the film, is a popular television comedian; soon, however, he finds himself on the blacklist. A mysterious figure named Hennessey who works for Hecky's network suggests that the comic's name can be cleared if he will appear as a friendly witness before HUAC. Hecky cannot bring himself to inform, however, and the network drops him. His efforts to earn a living become progressively more desperate. In one of the film's most effective scenes, taken directly from Zero's experience at the Concord Hotel in 1958, the manager of a resort hotel in the Catskills tells Hecky that he will not pay the comedian the agreed-upon fee for his routine.

---

*Several of the leading performers, however, including Woody Allen, Michael Murphy, and Andrea Marcovicci, were too young to have been affected by the blacklist.

Still, despite the humiliation he feels, Hecky goes onstage, for he desperately needs the money. Later, back in New York City, Hecky, in despair because of his inability to sustain his career, kills himself by leaping from a hotel room window—just as Philip Loeb had committed suicide in a New York hotel (by taking an overdose of sleeping pills) in 1955.

A minor character in the film is named Hubert Jackson, the owner of three supermarkets. The character, obviously based on Laurence Johnson, is shown wielding incredible influence over Hecky's network, as executives rush to fire anyone whom Jackson suspects of harboring Communist sympathies.

The film's focal character is Howard Prince (Woody Allen), a cashier who agrees to "front" for a blacklisted writer, signing his name to the writer's scripts, then taking a percentage of the sale price. The premise was based upon historical fact. In the early days of blacklisting, a writer could submit and sell scripts under an assumed name, but by the early fifties a writer was forced to hire a front, an individual who could believably pass himself or herself off as a professional writer. In the film, Howard Prince agrees to serve as a front only in order to gain money and prestige, giving no thought to the morality of blacklisting—until Hecky's suicide. The comedian's shocking death forces Howard to confront the issues he has thus far avoided, and the film ends when he refuses to cooperate with a congressional investigating committee and is led off to jail as a result. In the final analysis, he has achieved the greater stature he sought, for he has become a hero to his girl friend and to a crowd waving supportive placards.

In a sense, the most moving moment of *The Front* occurs after the final fade-out. As the credits roll, the name of each artist connected with the film who had been blacklisted appears with a notation indicating when the blacklisting occurred. For spectators who were too young or who were unaware of the phenomenon and might have thought the premise for the film was fictional, the credits made it clear that the events depicted were based on actual events.

Zero indulged in no temperamental outbursts during filming of *The Front*, no arguments with the director (except for a few conflicts of the most minor kind), no clashes with the writer. Undoubtedly, as Walter Bernstein suggested, his uncharacteristic docility can be attributed to the fact that "it was a work that had a great deal of meaning to us, and nobody wanted to be difficult."

Martin Ritt concurred. "I think it had a special significance for all of us," he said, "and I include Woody in that, though obviously he wasn't blacklisted. I had a good time working with Z. He could be difficult. He didn't always get along perfectly with Woody. But they respected each other. I thought Z was terrific in the film—incredibly himself, and unashamedly, fantastically theatrical. I did have the occasional problem of his doing too much, and I had to cut out some of the film that he was most devoted to, but that's my job."

The notion of approaching the issue of blacklisting from an essentially comic point of view, as Bernstein did, was an inspired idea. Unfortunately, *The Front* is not a wholly successful film—although it is probably the finest picture Zero ever made. The pace is so slow that it undermines the comic premise, the characters are inconsistent, the direction often heavy-handed, and despite the presence of such performers as Mostel and Allen, whose screen personalities are normally highly animated, there is a muted quality to most of the performances that deprives the movie of excitement.* Even so, the picture was important if for no other reason than that it provided a significant historical perspective for a wide audience. As Zero said, "It's part of the history of this country, and a lot of kids don't even realize that blacklisting ever existed."

*   *   *

Many actors have been identified throughout their careers with a single role—as Zero was identified with Tevye—because they were never fortunate enough to play another character with as much richness and depth. In Mostel's case, however, several other roles seemed to offer that sort of potential. Earlier in Zero's career, Toby Cole had hoped that he would play in *The Last Analysis* because she saw Bummidge as such a character. John Morley in *The Latent Heterosexual* might have been another portrayal for which Zero would always have been remembered if circumstances had not conspired to prevent all but a relative handful of people from seeing him in that play.

---

*Walter Bernstein maintained that Zero's performance suffered because he found it painful to relive the experiences portrayed in the film.

In 1977, Zero discovered another role that offered him everything he wished. The character was Shylock, in Arnold Wesker's *The Merchant*, a modern adaptation of Shakespeare's *The Merchant of Venice*. Shylock has been interpreted in a variety of ways, but most frequently as demented, or as vicious, or as a comic buffoon. Wesker redefined Shylock as an elderly scholar, a gentle, kindly man of inner nobility.

In Wesker's play, as in Shakespeare's, the plot describes a bargain between a Jewish moneylender (Shylock) and a Venetian merchant (Antonio) in the sixteenth century. When Antonio seeks to borrow money, Shylock specifies that the debt is to be repaid within three months. If Antonio is unable to pay the debt in that time, he must forfeit a pound of his flesh. In Shakespeare's version, Shylock is jubilant when Antonio cannot pay his debt, for he prefers to see the Christian dead rather than recover his money, and he is devastated when Portia, using a legal ruse, deprives him of Antonio's flesh. Wesker's play alters the situation, depicting Shylock as a peaceful and benevolent man, and a close friend of the merchant's, desperately seeking a way to avoid killing Antonio.

The genesis of Wesker's play occurred when the Jewish dramatist saw Laurence Oliver in Jonathan Miller's production of *The Merchant of Venice* at the National Theatre in England in 1971, and was offended. Wesker found the play anti-Semitic (as many others have done), believing that Shakespeare had drawn upon age-old stereotypes to create the caricature of an evil, grasping Jew.* During the scene in which Shylock is deprived of his pound of flesh and bemoans its loss, Wesker said he was struck by "a flash of inspiration": what Shylock *would* have done under the circumstances, Wesker said, was to "have stood up and said 'Thank God.' " Wesker thus used the same basic plot and many of Shakespeare's characters to write a play about friendship, trust, and understanding between Shylock and Antonio.

---

*Many readers believe otherwise, however. They agree that Shakespeare gave the character stereotypically villainous traits, but suggest that the conception of Jews in Shakespeare's England as malefactors was so strong that he had no other choice. And, they add, Shakespeare gave Shylock unexpected dimension, making it possible to interpret him as a pitiable character, one who has been wronged. Further, they maintain that it is even possible to view Shylock as a man who has lost his reason because of the vicious treatment he receives from the Christians in the play.

The complicating factor in *The Merchant* is a Venetian law requiring that all loans must be repaid in full. Wesker has Shylock and Antonio agree to the contract calling for a pound of the merchant's flesh purely as a joke—since both men are certain that the money will be repaid. When Antonio's ventures fail and he is unable to pay the debt, Shylock is horrified, and entirely unwilling to enforce the contract. What, then, motivates him to take Antonio to court and demand the merchant's life? As Wesker himself describes the incidents in the play:

> Shylock's sister Rivka persuades him that he must follow the law to the letter. If he fails to do so—if he bends the law by forgiving the loan—that will persuade the Christians of Venice that the Jews do not follow the laws; and that might lead to greater persecution than before. So, she says, Shylock's choice is between saving Antonio and saving the Jewish community.
> . . . Shylock has no alternative but to safeguard his community and sacrifice his friend.

Mostel saw in Wesker's drama an opportunity to play the most important role of his career. *The Merchant* would demonstrate that Zero was not what he had often been accused of being: an undisciplined nightclub comic who could not give a legitimate portrayal of a character in a play. Nor was he solely a comedian, unable to invest his characterizations with significance and depth. Perhaps he also saw something of his own personality in the character Wesker had created, and wished to show the public that he, too, had a humane, gentle disposition. Finally, Zero's image of himself as a scholar and philosopher probably influenced his attitude toward the character and the play.

The financial terms Zero accepted to appear in *The Merchant* represented a significant reduction from the salary and perquisites he had received for *Fiddler on the Roof* and for his performances in the movies and on television, but for once money was a minor consideration. Zero accepted the role of Shylock because of his desire to appear in a play he thought genuinely important. Still, he hardly worked for starvation wages, and his contract specified that he would have a private dresser of his choice (he selected Howard Rodney), the star's dressing room in any theatre in which the play was given, and limousine transportation between his residence and the playhouse.

Also engaged for the company were Sir John Clements, Sam Levene,

Roberta Maxwell, and Marian Seldes, all experienced and respected actors. John Dexter, the British director who had recently achieved great success with his Broadway production of *Equus*, was engaged to direct.

Dexter was the first to suggest an American production of *The Merchant*. As soon as the director read Wesker's play, he maintained, "I told him 'I want to do it, I want to do it in New York, and I want to do it with Zero Mostel.' "

In preparing to play Shylock, Zero spent the summer on Monhegan Island painting all the characters in the play, completing 105 paintings in thirty-five days. Also, so that he would not have to be concerned about memorization during rehearsals, he memorized his long and difficult role in advance—an unusual step for Zero, as it would have been for most performers.

For many years, Zero had been unable to lose weight, despite his wife's entreaties, despite the advice of friends and physicians. The lure of good food had always outweighed the benefits he might gain from a loss of excess poundage. At last, however, the character of Shylock gave him the motivation to stick to a diet, for if he did not conceive of Shylock as gaunt (that would have been asking *too* much), he did believe that the character must be as thin as Zero could possibly make him. As a result, he began to reduce from the moment *Fiddler on the Roof* closed. By August 1, 1977, when *The Merchant* went into rehearsal, he had lost sixty pounds in less than three months. During the next month, he would lose twenty-nine more, by sticking rigorously to a liquid protein diet, passing up the pastrami sandwiches and Jewish delicacies he loved. Even at an early party given by Zero for the cast at a restaurant in Greenwich Village, "our host drank seltzer," while everyone else overate, said Marian Seldes, who played Shylock's sister, Rivka.

The members of the company were concerned that Zero was overdoing his diet. "We all felt that his missing meals and constantly drinking seltzer water was not the right diet for the amount of work he did in rehearsal every day," Seldes observed. Howard Rodney thought that he looked "a little haggard" throughout rehearsals.

During the rehearsal process, Zero not only *looked* different, he *was* different: still affable, but less unruly, occasionally even subdued. Perhaps it was the seriousness of the play itself, perhaps it was Mostel's conviction that the play and its theme were of great significance not only to him as a performer, but to the world. In any case, the new, slimmer Mostel seemed almost a different person.

Still, although Zero approached his role with utmost seriousness during rehearsals, and carefully watched the scenes he was not in, offering comments about them to the director, he enjoyed telling jokes and playing games during breaks. The "old Zero" had by no means been altogether eradicated.

John Dexter was determined that the actors should pay particular attention to the language of the characters. "Shape the phrasing, like music," he kept telling them. As an exercise, he had the actors read sonnets aloud, after which he would offer criticisms. Zero was skeptical about Dexter's approach. As Marian Seldes said, he "was firm in his belief that sound and speech were secondary to true acting impulses." His own method was more visceral. "He worked on his part obsessively," Seldes said, "watchful, wary, guarding his acting moments as an animal guards his young."

Some of Zero's wary behavior was a response to the ambience John Dexter created. Julie Garfield, who played Shylock's daughter, Jessica, and who had known Zero since her childhood, said, "Dexter was so strange in his approach toward the work. The atmosphere in rehearsals was so tense that you could cut it with a knife. Everyone was trying to maintain a sense of balance. And the way Zero dealt with it was by doing these very inane things that would crack everybody up. Dexter would be very serious and very intense and very intellectual and suddenly Zero would be sucking on his nose."

The director "had this way of finding scapegoats and punishing them in front of everybody else and humiliating them," Garfield said. "In the case of *The Merchant* it was me" and a young actor. "He always seemed to be going after us. But Zero looked out for me. He was very fatherly toward me. He protected me and reassured me. But I think he himself was quite thrown by Dexter's behavior and didn't quite know how to handle it."

Zero accepted Dexter's ability to assist him in developing some aspects of his characterization, and when the director offered a useful suggestion Mostel took it and absorbed it swiftly and seamlessly into his portrayal. Often, however, he felt that Dexter's ideas were of no value to him. When those occasions occurred, he never contested the point; he simply ignored the direction.

Still, Dexter and Mostel must have established a satisfactory relationship, for they spoke of working together on future projects. Once again, Zero became interested in playing Falstaff; Galileo (in Brecht's play of the same name) was also discussed. Perhaps the conversations indicate that Mostel was at last determined to change the course of his career and do what he had wanted long ago: to play challenging roles in outstanding plays regardless of the size of his billing or the amount of his salary.

A few days before the company left New York, a special run-through was given for the producers. Perhaps because Kate was also in the audience, Zero was brilliant—a revelation to the producers and the cast alike.* "It was at this particular rehearsal that we saw what Zero was going to do with the part," Seldes said. "It had a kind of innocence and thrilling inventiveness that completely justified the risk of casting such an eccentric actor in a classically oriented play."

The production was to open at the Forrest Theatre in Philadelphia on September 6, 1977, move to the John F. Kennedy Center for the Performing Arts in Washington on September 28, and open at the Imperial Theatre on Broadway on November 15.

The first preview performance was given in Philadelphia on Friday, September 2. Merle Debuskey, who served as press representative for the production, recalled that "Zero's performance was very moving. He was magnificent." Afterward, Debuskey visited Mostel in his dressing room and was surprised by the atmosphere that prevailed. "You know," he said, "Zero was a very ebullient, even Rabelaisian character, but on this occasion, because of the nature of the play and what he felt about it, his manner was very subdued and quiet."

The following day, as Zero was applying his makeup for the matinee performance, he became ill and nearly fainted. Howard Rodney, who was in the dressing room, described what followed: "I had just put his

---

*Marian Seldes felt that many of Zero's best performances were given when Kate was in the audience; that he was particularly focused on those occasions because her approval meant so much to him.

wig on and he said he didn't feel well. I said, 'Why don't you lie down on the couch?' He said, 'I can't, because there's a show.' But I got him on the couch and he lay down. He took my hands because he was very nervous about what was wrong. So I called the management and I said, 'Zero doesn't feel well.' "

A doctor was called. The physician examined Zero and suggested that the actor should be taken to the Thomas Jefferson University Hospital, across the street. The stage manager informed the audience that the day's performance was canceled.

At the hospital, Zero was given an electrocardiogram and other tests, all of which indicated that his condition was not serious. His illness was diagnosed as an upper respiratory disorder. The producers, told that Zero would soon be released from the hospital, suspended performances until he could return. Zero called Kate in New York to reassure her that he was all right, but she traveled to Philadelphia the following day.

By the time she arrived, he had already been released from the hospital. Certain that he was in no danger, Zero persuaded Kate to return to New York. In Manhattan, she told columnist Earl Wilson that Zero would be returning to *The Merchant* in a day or so. That night, however, the symptoms recurred, and he was readmitted to the hospital. Still, the doctors could find little wrong with him. This time, they diagnosed his condition as a simple case of exhaustion and suggested that he remain in the hospital for a few days' rest.

Howard Rodney was constantly at Zero's side, running errands for him whenever he asked for anything. Sam Levene, a friend of many years, stopped by daily. The other actors and well-wishers were asked not to visit so that Zero would be able to rest. He seemed in good spirits, exchanging jokes with Rodney and Levene. His physicians encouraged him to think that he would be released on the morning of September 9 and would be able to resume performances soon afterward.

On the evening of the eighth, Zero asked Rodney to bring him some food from Shore's restaurant. Meanwhile, as Marian Seldes described it:

Sam went to see Zero . . . , gave him [some] art books and got the expected reaction: "I don't want to read anything serious." Sam offered to get him a copy of *Hustler*. Zero laughed and said it might arouse him. As they laughed together discussing the various nurses in attendance Zero said, "I feel dizzy—you better call a nurse." He reached out for the bell and pitched forward out of the bed. Sam thought he might strike his head on the night table and pulled it away. He tried to break Zero's fall but was unable to. He was lying on the floor when the nurses and doctors arrived to help him. They did everything they could as swiftly as possible. They performed surgery and inserted a pacemaker, but to no avail.

At the age of sixty-two, Zero had suffered an aortic aneurysm from which he did not recover; he died at 7:47 P.M. Many of his friends, including Dr. Norman Pleshette, believed that his death was hastened by the excessive weight loss brought about by a diet that was later shown to be nutritionally unsound. Pleshette called it "basically a starvation diet." Mostel had dropped from 304 to 215 pounds in the last four months of his life.

Howard Rodney later recalled, "The thing I remember vividly is when I used to go to the hospital I used to bring Zero's Perrier water and his newspaper in a shopping bag, an old A&P shopping bag that I have. And he used to say, 'How can you bring this to me in a shopping bag? I'm a star! What are people going to think?' And then when he passed away they gave me his clothes and his watch and the things he had in the hospital in that A&P bag. I said to myself, 'Oh God, if Zero could see this, he'd be furious. He's going out in an A&P bag.' " Tears streamed down Rodney's face as he recalled the incidents.

Before he died, Zero had told Kate he did not wish to have a funeral or memorial service. She complied with his wish to be cremated "like Einstein." He left an estate of a million dollars. Half of the money and property went to Kate directly, along with the income from the other half during her lifetime. After her death, the principal would go to Josh and Tobias.

The general manager of *The Merchant* said that no immediate decision could be made about the future of the production, for everyone connected with it felt only "a numbness." The following day, Bernard Jacobs, head of the Shubert Organization, indicated that the play would probably continue, with the management seeking an actor of the stature of Orson Welles, Laurence Olivier, or Richard Burton to play Shylock.

Less than a week later, however, Mostel's understudy, Joseph Leon, was given the role, and *The Merchant* immediately went back into rehearsal. Sam Levene, however, elected to leave the cast. Zero's death had been a devastating blow for Levene and he could not contemplate continuing in the play.

The Merchant opened in Washington and New York on schedule. But Joseph Leon faced an impossible task: taking over for a famous actor whose performance had been eagerly anticipated, and performing without sufficient rehearsal to become comfortable in the role. The play received negative reviews in New York and closed after five performances.*

* * *

In tribute to Zero, special showings of his paintings and drawings were given at the Forum Gallery and the Vincent Astor Gallery of the New York Public Library in 1978. The show at the Forum consisted mostly of self-portraits, many of them in the roles he had played on stage. The second exhibit, called "Remembering Zero: The Actor, the Artist, the Man," also included photographs of Mostel, posters and programs from the plays in which he had appeared, and his costumes and props from *Fiddler on the Roof.* A videotape of Zero being interviewed by Beverly Sills was shown on New York television shortly after he died. Another program, *Adding Up to Zero*, featured friends and

---

*Even if Zero had played Shylock, it is questionable whether *The Merchant* would have succeeded. In turning Shylock into a kindly old scholar and a close friend of Antonio, Arnold Wesker robbed the situation of conflict, and few plays can succeed without that vital element. What little action the play possesses unfolds in a series of long, undramatic discussions. The premise of the play—that Shylock will extract a pound of flesh from Antonio if the merchant cannot repay his debt—is undercut by the deep friendship of Antonio and Shylock, so that one is all but unable to accept the reality of the dramatic circumstances. Moreover, Wesker's prose dialogue is inevitably disappointing to anyone who is familiar with *The Merchant of Venice*. Still, those few people who saw Zero perform in *The Merchant* felt that his presence transformed the play, making it seem far better than it actually was. Merle Debuskey, who saw the one preview performance in Philadelphia, said, "There were moments in his performance that were unforgettable. When he talked about his love of books, when he rhapsodized about the significance and the importance and the beauty of literature it was extremely moving."

relatives reminiscing about Mostel and his twin careers. Kate, Josh, Tobias, Jack and Madeline Gilford all appeared; Eli Wallach served as host.

Herbie Kallem, who had occupied a studio in Zero's building for more than forty years, moved out a few months after Mostel's death. "I'd look up sometimes and see a shadow there, and know it was Z," he said. "Zero's passing marked the end of an era down there" on Twenty-eighth Street.

Kate went through a long period of depression. Not only had she lost her husband but her life became considerably less eventful. As her friend Mary Yohalem put it, "Mrs. Zero Mostel would not necessarily get all the invitations that Mr. and Mrs. Zero Mostel would get."

Kate must have taken solace from Josh's reconciliation with his father before Zero's death. After not speaking to one another for several months as the result of an argument, Josh called Zero a few days before he died and they had what Josh described as a "nice" and "amiable" conversation.

In the mid-1970s, Kate and Madeline Gilford had begun to collaborate on a humorous cookbook. One of the recipes, for example, came from the comic Orson Bean, who told how he used to scramble eggs on the flat side of an iron when he lived in boardinghouses where no cooking was permitted. Anecdotes of the authors' lives and the lives of their husbands were sprinkled liberally among the recipes. Eventually, they showed the manuscript to an editor friend, who advised them, "Throw out the recipes and keep the anecdotes." They did precisely that, writing a memoir of the life Kate had shared with Zero and Madeline with Jack. Zero died in the midst of the writing, which brought the project to a temporary halt and for a while threatened to end it altogether. But Kate felt that her husband would have wanted her to complete the book. He had bought her a desk—"a real writing desk," said Jack Gilford—when she began serious work on the book and, she said, every time she passed it, she could hear Zero roar, "Why aren't you using the desk?"

Eventually, Jack Gilford was persuaded to write a chapter containing some anecdotes for inclusion in the book. Although Zero did not do any of the writing, when *170 Years of Show Business* (the combined number of years the four of them had spent in the performing arts) was published in 1978, all received authorial credit: "by Kate Mostel and Madeline Gilford with Jack Gilford and Zero Mostel."

The book was therapeutic for Kate. As she indicated, "I wrote the book so I would be recognized as myself, instead of as the woman who was with Zero." Later, Madeline tried to persuade Kate to work with her on a sequel to *170 Years of Show Business*, but nothing came of it.

Kate died of an asthma attack on January 22, 1986, at the age of sixty-seven. Six months later, fifty lots of furnishings and memorabilia from the Mostels' estate were sold at auction in Manhattan.

* * *

Some performing artists achieve immense success once. A combination of talent and good fortune permits the performer to become one of the most prominent figures in show business—as Zero Mostel did in 1942. Occasionally, performers have fallen from such heights only to rise again; Frank Sinatra is one prominent example. Zero Mostel also made such a comeback when he emerged from the depths of the blacklist to win even greater fame than he had known before. But how many artists have returned to the spotlight for a *third* time after a lengthy hiatus? Only Zero Mostel comes to mind. His appearances in 1976 and 1977 returned him to a position of eminence that had steadily eroded since his triumph in the 1964 production of *Fiddler on the Roof*.

To return to the top so often and after such discouraging setbacks called for an extraordinary resiliency, an inner drive that simply would not permit his spirit to be crushed; perhaps it is this spirit of resiliency, more than any other quality, that most accurately characterized Zero Mostel. Still, it would be impossible—and inaccurate—to describe the man in a single word or phrase.

Mostel's personality always included a strong element of aggressiveness. His technique was to push to the limit, to say what no one else would dare to say, to act as no one else would dare to act, to walk the line between insult and sweetness by offering a highly disparaging remark with an endearing smile or a grimace so fierce that one felt it *must* have been meant in jest. Zero alternated between fury and kindness, expressing anger and contempt one moment and affection the next. Simply to be recognized by Mostel must have been an unsettling experience. One was likely either to be the victim of a scalding verbal attack or the recipient of a smothering embrace. Only one thing was certain: Zero did not react to any person or any event with indifference. He muscled his way through life shouting at the top of his voice, unafraid to show passion, unwilling to moderate the extremes of emotion he always seemed to feel. And yet . . .

One cannot ignore the gentle, compassionate side of his nature. It gave the man a dimension that inspired intense loyalty among his friends; and it gave to his performances the sudden, surprising qualities of sweetness and tenderness.

What made Zero Mostel's character singular was that both his virtues and his faults were so gargantuan, so extreme. Beyond uniqueness, what made his character *extraordinary* was that his virtues and faults all tended to be opposite sides of the same coin. His unswerving loyalty to his friends was one of his most admirable characteristics, for example; but on the other side must be placed his insensitivity to his immediate family and to Toby Cole. His selfishness in throwing other performers into near-panic when he tossed them lines of dialogue they had never heard before or when he altered the blocking in the middle of a performance was neatly balanced by the generosity and selflessness he demonstrated in dealing with people such as Howard Rodney, Deborah Salt, Julie Garfield, and Gene Wilder. One is awed by his ever-present sense of humor and his ability to create laughter anywhere, at any time; but each gag involved someone—an unsuspecting waiter, a family member, a casual acquaintance, a complete stranger, a colleague—as the butt of the joke, made to look and feel foolish. One cannot overlook his lack of courage in refusing to deal with conflicts, including those within his own family, but one must pay tribute to his courage in overcoming the blacklist and the handicap of a crippled leg. Each virtue in Mostel's character was offset by a flaw; each flaw by a virtue. On stage and off, Zero Mostel was a study in contrasts. Had it not been so, he would not have inspired so much love—or so much antipathy. Nor would he have been such a brilliant actor, for it was the presence of so many conflicting elements within himself and his ability to tap into them that gave his performances such dimension. He could convincingly render nobility, pettiness, delight in life, anguish, generosity, meanness, and every other set of emotions precisely because he knew them so intimately.

Acting is not a competitive undertaking, and it would be misleading to claim that the awards an actor has won are proof of his greatness. Nevertheless, it is impossible to ignore Zero's dominance of the Tony awards in the early 1960s: winning for *Rhinoceros* in 1961, for *A Funny Thing Happened on the Way to the Forum* in 1963, and for *Fiddler on the Roof* in 1965. Few other performers have achieved such a monopoly. Some of the recognition Zero won was probably given grudgingly, for he had his share of enemies in show business; but no one could deny the enormity of his gifts.

Mostel's legacy is harder to define. The degree of his influence on actors of his generation was probably minimal because his style was uniquely his own, not susceptible to emulation. Furthermore, his tendency to wreak havoc with a playwright's script and a director's production is not an example of behavior one would encourage other performers to follow. Perhaps geniuses can be granted such license (and Zero may justly be described as a comic genius), but even that proposition is open to argument.

Why is it reasonable to describe Mostel as a comic genius? Because he contained the capacity for invention in abundance, and anyone who considers the nature of genius will agree that the ability to be endlessly inventive is a characteristic of genius of *any* sort. However, in order to produce great art, the artist must combine the inventiveness of genius with *control*—and that frequently seemed to be beyond Mostel's ability. One could extend this observation to his behavior offstage as well, for Zero's shenanigans in public—at parties, in restaurants, etc.—always impressed onlookers with the powers of his invention, but often, when the inventions became vulgar or went on for too long—in short, when they were uncontrolled—those who watched tended to lose interest.

Mostel the painter may have lacked that degree of invention necessary to genius, but he did seem able to exert control over his work. Why he was unable to do so on the stage is a mystery, but it is central to any evaluation of his skill as a performer. Onstage, it may be said that he was both a beneficiary and a victim of his creative genius.

It does not take remarkable acuity to recognize that much of Mostel's invention came at the expense of others, even to the point of humiliating them. Offstage, he humiliated waiters, friends, family; onstage, he humiliated those actors who could not cope with his unpredictable flights of invention. Only his wife Kate seemed able to moderate Zero's behavior, and even she was occasionally unsuccessful; moreover, Mostel subjected her, too, to the sting of humiliation, although there is no doubt that he loved and needed her more than anyone else in his life.

Despite the punishment he inflicted upon other actors when he humiliated them, there is no question that at his best—when his invention was particularly inspired—Zero was a magnificent clown. Thus, he kept alive the tradition of great comics on the American stage. The history of our theatre during the past one hundred years would be far less vigorous had it not been for a progression of clowns, from Harrigan and Hart, through the Marx Brothers and Bert Lahr, to present-day performers such as Bill Irwin. Zero's place in the roster of American stage comedians is secure.

Zero is important in the development of the musical theatre in that he was one of the first performers to achieve stardom in that medium despite the fact that he was not a trained singer. Rex Harrison's performance in *My Fair Lady* was the first important link in that chain of development; Zero forged another, demonstrating conclusively that musicals, no less than nonmusical plays, require superior acting if they are to be totally fulfilling experiences.

One cannot but regret the roads Zero did not take. For much of his career he subordinated creative satisfaction to attaining stardom. During the last twelve years of his life—except for his appearances in *The Latent Heterosexual, Fiddler on the Roof*, and *The Merchant*—Mostel sublimated his desire for excellence to a willingness to accept financially rewarding projects that required little creative effort. Had Zero performed in the plays of Brecht, Shakespeare, Molière, Pinter, and other first-rate dramatists, as he once aspired to do, his theatrical legacy would perhaps be more significant.

Shortly after he died, a number of his friends were asked to write brief reminiscences of him for the New York *Times*. Eli Wallach's recollection described Mostel's character elegantly and concisely: "There's an old adage in theatrical circles—never share the stage with children, clowns or animals. Disregarding this advice in 1961, my wife Anne

Jackson and I appeared in [*Rhinoceros*] with one man in the guise of all three. Zero was a clown with a child's heart playing an animal."

Finally, one must return to the central event of Mostel's life: the political turmoil that was the blacklist. Some, caught in the terrible predicament of that time, succeeded professionally by destroying the careers of others, or by abasing themselves before unprincipled men and women in an attempt to "clear" themselves. To his everlasting credit, Zero Mostel refused to take either of those paths. As Martin Ritt said of him, "He was an extraordinary talent and an extraordinary man and he lived in extraordinary times. And," Ritt added, "he met his times. He behaved like a man should behave. Although he had an appetite for success and approval, he didn't capitulate to the shadier aspects of his character like the guys who behaved badly. He met his times."

This book is dedicated to Lauren and Ned;
and to my parents, John and June Brown.
John Brown was an actor who, like Zero Mostel,
was victimized by the blacklist.
Unlike Zero Mostel, he did not live to see the blacklist end.

Bibliography

I. Interviews

The following individuals provided me with valuable firsthand information about the life and the career of Zero Mostel. I am grateful to all of them. They provided me with the most important information for this biography. All of the interviews were held during 1987 and 1988.

Abbott, George
Ackerman [Jaffe], Bettye
Allen, Steve
Avery, Val
Bentley, Eric
Bergen, Sidney
Berkman, Aaron
Bernstein, Walter
Bronson, James
Brooks, Mel
Chaney, Frances
Chodorov, Jerome
Cole, Toby
Corey, Jeff
Debuskey, Merle
Faye, Joey

Fishko, Bella
Freedman, Bill
Garfield, Julie
Gelbart, Larry
Gibson, Ted
Gilford, Jack
Gilford, Madeline Lee
Harmon, Louis
Harnick, Sheldon
Hunter, Ian
Jarrico, Paul
Kaplan, Sol
Kilty, Jerome
Kobart, Ruth
Lardner, Ring, Jr.
Lee, Ngoot

Lee, Thelma
Malden, Karl
Meredith, Burgess
Mitchell, Ruth
Mostel, Aaron
Mostel, Bill
Mostel, Josh
Mostel, Raphael
Ostrow, Lucille
Peterson, Lou
Pleshette, Norman
Protopopescu, Orel Odinov
Randolph, John
Richardson, Don
Ritt, Martin
Rodney, Howard
Ross, Bill

Salt, Deborah
Schaefer, George
Schelble, Bill
Seldes, Marian
Siegler, Robert
Solomon, Wilma
Stein, Joseph
Stein, Rebecca Kramer
Stevenson, Margot
Tzerko, Aube
Tzerko, Saida
Vogel, Speed
Wallach, Eli
Warshaw, Mal
Wilder, Gene
Wilder, Joseph
Yohalem, Mary

If the views of certain individuals are not represented fully in this biography, it is because Sidney Elliot Cohn, Tobias Mostel, and Jerome Robbins declined, for whatever reasons, to be interviewed. Some others who worked with Zero Mostel responded politely to my requests for interviews, but said that they did not wish to speak about him.

II. Books

Those books that proved particularly useful in the writing of this biography are preceded by asterisks.

Abbott, George. *Mister Abbott*. New York: Random House, 1963.

Allen, Steve. *The Funny Men*. New York: Simon and Schuster, 1956.

————. *Funny People*. Briarcliff Manor, New York: Stein and Day, 1981.

*Altman, Richard, with Mervyn Kaufman. *The Making of a Musical*. New York: Crown Publishers, 1971.

Bentley, Eric. *Thinking About the Playwright*. Evanston, Illinois: Northwestern University Press, 1987.

*————. *Thirty Years of Treason*. New York: The Viking Press, 1971.

Block, Maxine, ed. *Current Biography, 1943*. New York: The H. W. Wilson Co., 1943.

Brustein, Robert. *Making Scenes*. New York: Random House, 1981.

*Caute, David. *The Great Fear: The Anti-Communist Purge Under Truman and Eisenhower*. New York: Simon and Schuster, 1978.

*Cogley, John, ed. *Report on Blacklisting*. 2 vols. The Fund for the Republic, Inc., 1956.

*Cohen, Sarah Blecher, ed. *From Hester Street to Hollywood: The Jewish-American Stage and Screen*. Bloomington: Indiana University Press, 1983 (includes "Yiddish Theatre and American Theatre," by Nahma Sandrow; "Yiddish Origins and Jewish-American Transformations," by Sarah Blecher Cohen; "The Jew in Stand-up Comedy," by Anthony Lewis).

Dick, Bernard F. *The Star-Spangled Screen: The American World War II Film*. Lexington: The University Press of Kentucky, 1985.

Donner, Frank J. *The Un-Americans*. New York: Ballantine Books, 1961.

Dunning, John. *Tune in Yesterday*. Englewood Cliffs, New Jersey: Prentice-Hall, Inc., 1976.

Ernst, Jimmy. *A Not-So-Still Life*. New York: St. Martin's/Marek, 1983.

Fabian, Monroe H. *On Stage*. New York: A Main Street Press Book, Published by Mayflower Books, Inc., 1980.

*Faulk, John Henry. *Fear on Trial*. Austin: The University of Texas Press, 1983 (revised and updated edition).

Feibleman, James. *In Praise of Comedy*. New York: Russell & Russell, 1939 (revised 1962).

Garfield, David. *A Player's Place: The Story of the Actors Studio*. New York: Macmillan Publishing Co., Inc., 1980.

Goldman, William. *The Season*. New York: Harcourt, Brace & World, Inc., 1969.

Goodman, Walter. *The Committee*. New York: Farrar, Straus and Giroux, 1968.

Heller, Joseph, and Speed Vogel. *No Laughing Matter*. New York: G. P. Putnam's Sons, 1986.

Hirsch, Foster. *Love, Sex, Death, and the Meaning of Life: Woody Allen's Comedy*. New York: McGraw-Hill Book Company, 1981.

Holtzman, William. *Seesaw: A Dual Biography of Anne Bancroft and Mel Brooks*. Garden City, New York: Doubleday & Company, Inc., 1979.

*Howe, Irving. *World of Our Fathers*. New York: Simon and Schuster, 1976.

Jacobs, Diane. *. . . But We Need the Eggs*. New York: St. Martin's Press, 1982.

Kanfer, Stefan. *A Journal of the Plague Years*. New York: Atheneum, 1973.

Kazan, Elia. *Elia Kazan: A Life*. New York: Alfred A. Knopf, 1988.

Laufe, Abe. *Broadway's Greatest Musicals*. New York: Funk & Wagnalls, 1977 (revised edition).

Leeming, Glenda. "Commentary" to Arnold Wesker's *The Merchant*. London: Methuen, 1983.

Lewis, Emory. *Stages*. Englewood Cliffs, New Jersey: Prentice-Hall, Inc., 1969.

Magill, Frank N. *Magill's Survey of Cinema*. Englewood Cliffs, New Jersey: Salem Press, 1980.

*McKinzie, Richard D. *The New Deal for Artists*. Princeton, N.J.: Princeton University Press, 1973.

Miller, Arthur. *Timebends*. New York: Grove Press, 1987.

*Miller, Merle. *The Judges and the Judged*. Garden City, N.Y.: Doubleday & Company, Inc., 1952.

Mischel, Florence D., ed. *Palimpsest: An Oral History of Seniel Lucien Ostrow*. Malibu, California: Clef Press, 1985.

Moritz, Charles, ed. *Current Biography, 1963*. New York: The H. W. Wilson Co., 1963.

Morley, Sheridan. *The Great Stage Stars*. New York: Facts on File Publications, 1986.

*Mostel, Kate, and Madeline Gilford, with Jack Gilford and Zero Mostel. *170 Years of Show Business*. New York: Random House, 1978.

Mostel, Zero, with Israel Shenker (photographed by Alex Gotfryd). *Zero Mostel's Book of Villains*. Garden City, New York: Doubleday and Company, Inc., 1976.

*Navasky, Victor S. *Naming Names*. New York: The Viking Press, 1980.

O'Connor, Francis, ed. *The New Deal Art Projects*. Washington, D.C.: Smithsonian Institution Press, 1972.

*Prince, Hal. *Contradictions*. New York: Dodd, Mead & Company, 1974.

*Raeburn, Ben, ed. *Zero by Mostel: Photographs by Max Waldman with Some Personal Notes & Drawings by Zero Mostel*. New York: Horizon Press, 1965.

Red Channels: The Report of Communist Influence in Radio and Television. New York: American Business Consultants, 1950.

Robinson, David. *Chaplin: His Life and Art*. New York: McGraw-Hill Book Company, 1985.

*Rosenblum, Ralph, and Robert Karen. *When the Shooting Stops*. New York: The Viking Press, 1979.

*Sandrow, Nahma. *Vagabond Stars: A World History of Yiddish Theatre*. New York: Harper & Row, 1977.

*Seldes, Marian. *The Bright Lights*. Boston: Houghton Mifflin Company, 1978.

*Stasio, Marilyn. *Broadway's Beautiful Losers*. New York: Delacorte Press, 1961.

Swortzell, Lowell. *Here Come the Clowns*. New York: The Viking Press, 1978.

Vaughn, Robert. *Only Victims*. New York: G. P. Putnam's Sons, 1972.

Walker, Forrest A. *The Civil Works Administration: An Experiment in Federal Work Relief, 1933–1934*. New York and London: Garland Publishing, Inc., 1979.

Wesker, Arnold. "Preface" to *The Merchant*. London: Methuen, 1983.

*Zadan, Craig. *Sondheim & Co*. New York: Macmillan Publishing Co., Inc., 1974.

Zero Mostel Reads a Book. Photographed by Robert Frank. New York: The New York *Times*, 1963.

III. Selected Articles

Those articles that proved particularly helpful in the writing of this biography are preceded by asterisks.

"Alpha Plus for Zero Mostel—A Great Character Comedian." *Times* (London), June 21, 1961.

*Aurthur, Robert Alan. "Hanging Out with Zero Mostel." *Esquire*, October 1973.

Berman, Audrey. "Now That He's a Rich Man . . ." *Village Voice*, April 18, 1974.

*Bernstein, Walter; Jack Gilford; Ian McLellan Hunter; Ring Lardner, Jr.; Neil Simon; Eli Wallach. "Mostel Remembered." New York *Times*, September 18, 1977.

Butterfield, Roger. "Zero Mostel." *Life*, January 18, 1943.

Counterattack, various issues.

*Crichton, Kyle. "Podden the Expression." *Colliers*, September 19, 1942.

*Dundy, Elaine. "Zero Is a Teddy Bear." New York *Herald Tribune*, November 8, 1964.

"Eating With Their Mouths Open." New York *Times Magazine*, November 3, 1985.

Esterow, Milton. "Play's Cast Dotes on Critics' Quotes." New York *Times*, January 13, 1961.

———. "Stormy Route." New York *Times*, February 12, 1961.

Foster, Hugh G. "The Antic Arts: The Infinite Zero." *Holiday*, March 1963.

*Gussow, Mel. "A Mostel 'Mazel Tov!' for *Fiddler*." New York *Times*, December 30, 1976.

"Hail the Conquering Zero." *Newsweek*, October 19, 1964.

*Hamblin, Dora Jane. "Big Mouth + Massive Wit + Soul of a Daffodil = Zero." *Life*, December 4, 1964.

Hammel, Faye. "A Laurel for Zero." *Cue*, December 29, 1962.

Hughes, Allen. "A Lean and Hungry Zero Mostel Starting Rehearsals for Arnold Wesker's *Merchant*." New York *Times*, August 2, 1977.

*"Infinite Zero." *Newsweek*, January 13, 1964.

Kroll, Jack. "Transition: The Conquering Zero." *Newsweek*, September 19, 1977.

Mason, Arthur. "Zero Mostel Turns Villain." New York *Times*, August 6, 1950.

McFadden, Robert D. "Zero Mostel Is Dead at 62." New York *Times*, September 7, 1977.

Meehan, Thomas. "Actor Comedian Painter Litterateur . . . They All Add Up to Zero." *Horizon*, May 1962.

*Meredith, Burgess. "Zero Mostel: A Remembrance of the Artist Behind the Greasepaint." Los Angeles *Times*, September 18, 1977.

*Millstein, Gilbert. "A Funny Man Happened." New York *Times Magazine*, June 3, 1962.

"Mostel in Opera, Gets Zero for Conduct." New York *Times*, September 10, 1975.

*Musel, Robert. "It All Adds Up to Zero." *TV Guide*, April 29, 1967.

Novick, Julius. "Can I Call You Zero, Zero?" New York *Times*, March 31, 1968.

*"The Painter." *New Yorker*, November 5, 1973.

"Radio Funnyman in the Money." *Newsweek*, August 17, 1942.

*Roman, Dun. "The Ferocious Art of Zero Mostel." Los Angeles *Times*, September 18, 1977.

*Ross, Lillian. "Profiles: The Player—II." *New Yorker*, October 28, 1961.

*Stang, Joanne. "At Home With Tevye." New York *Times*, October 4, 1964.

"The Talk of the Town." *New Yorker*, January 2, 1965.

Tallmer, Jerry. "Starting With Zero." New York *Post Magazine*, November 25, 1962.

———. "Zero Mostel: Why Explain . . . ?" New York *Post*, March 16, 1974.

Trillin, Calvin. "Eating Out." *New Yorker*, August 6, 1973.

Viorst, Milton. " 'Everyone Else Does It More Poorly,' Says the First Tevye." New York *Times*, August 1, 1976.

Weiner, Bob. "Zero Speaks—Mostely Explosively." New York *Sunday News*, December 20, 1976.

*Wilner, Norman. "Zero." *Esquire*, February 1962.

"Zero in Dallas." *Newsweek*, April 1, 1968.

"Zero Televised." *Life*, November 22, 1948.

Zolotow, Maurice. "Ulysses on Houston Street." New York *Times*, June 1, 1958.

Zolotow, Sam. "Meredith and Mostel Forming Repertory Unit for Next Year." New York *Times*, February 28, 1966.

IV. Other Sources

American Arbitration Association Administration Voluntary Labor Arbitration Tribunal in the Matter of the Arbitration Between Toby Cole and Actors Equity Association/[representing] Zero Mostel, Case No. L-48292, NY L-75665, August 8, 1967.

Brattle Theatre Company programs (housed at Harvard Theatre Collection, Harvard University).

Correspondence, clippings, photographs, etc., in the Billy Rose Theatre Collection at the Lincoln Center Library for the Performing Arts in New York City.

Federal Bureau of Investigation file on Samuel Joel Mostel (obtained through the provisions of the Freedom of Information Act and the Privacy Act).

Hatch-Billops Collection, New York (contains interview with Lou Gilbert).

Kuhlke, William. "Vakhtangov's Legacy." Unpublished Ph.D. dissertation, State University of Iowa, 1965.

Material (including correspondence, contracts, notes, clippings) from the "Toby Cole Archive," housed at the University of California at Davis.

New York *Times*, 1935–78.

Ninety-second Street YM-YWHA records.

Notes from art gallery catalogues.

"Presentation to Mr. Zero Mostel by the Alumni Association of Seward Park High School." Program, April 7, 1963.

Press releases for various plays and films.

Programs for various Broadway productions.

Reviews and commentary from all New York City newspapers and numerous periodicals.

Script for pilot of television series, *The Zero Mostel Show*.

Scripts of the plays and films in which Zero Mostel appeared.

Transcripts and records concerning Samuel Joel Mostel from P.S. 97, P.S. 188, Seward Park High School, City University of New York, and New York University.

U.S. Army record of Samuel Joel Mostel.

Zero Mostel's speech on comedy delivered at Harvard University, 1962.

Zero Mostel's testimony before the House Committee on Un-American Activities, 1955.

Index

JARED BROWN, born in New York City and raised in Los Angeles, was educated at Ithaca College, San Francisco State College, and the University of Minnesota. He is professor of theatre at Western Illinois University, where he directs the programs in theatre history, directing, and playwriting. He has contributed articles—among them a series that amounts to a comprehensive study of the theatre in America during the Revolution—to many leading theatrical and historical journals, written eight plays, directed more than fifty, and for a brief time, acted professionally. Mr. Brown is the author of the highly acclaimed biography of Alfred Lunt and Lynn Fontanne *The Fabulous Lunts* (Atheneum 1986).